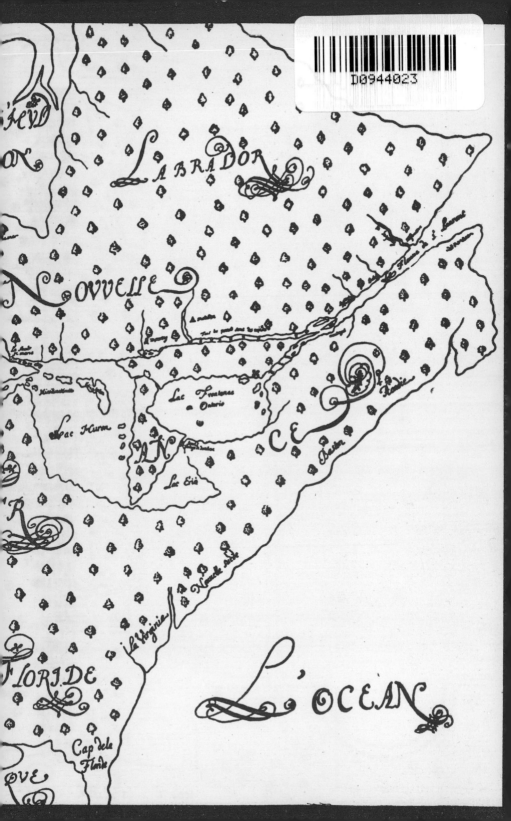

THE JESUIT RELATIONS AND ALLIED DOCUMENTS

The Jesuit Relations
And Allied Documents

TRAVELS AND EXPLORATIONS OF THE
JESUIT MISSIONARIES IN NORTH AMERICA

(1610–1791)

With an Introduction by
REUBEN GOLD THWAITES

Selected and Edited by
EDNA KENTON

Preface by Dr. George N. Shuster

NEW YORK, THE VANGUARD PRESS

PREFACE

One puts down this noble and moving book again (for reading it was one of the pleasant literary adventures of the twenties) sure that, although the theme is early American spiritual history, nothing, not even a Congressional Investigation nor a debate in the United Nations, could be more pertinent for our lives and times. For, as everyone will see at a glance, what we have here is a collection of reports sent back home by men passionately interested in what we now call cultural relations. Countless thousands of similar letters have been written since the dawn of the seventeenth century and, indeed, continue to be dispatched from all parts of the world. A French Jesuit missionary to the Hurons, like Father Paul le Jeune, had for his assignment teaching (he would have said bringing to) the Indians the Christian faith. Therefore, he was of necessity compelled, in our current jargon, to establish communication with them. He would have to learn their language, and then their customs, crafts, religious ideas, methods of warfare, weaknesses. This is what Christian missionaries of every denomination still try to do. Something of the sort Communists likewise attempt, in their disruptive way. It is also what the many servants of present-day enterprises in international relations, the Technical Assistance Program, for instance, endeavor to do. More generally we Americans have found out, sometimes to our amazement, that upon our tact in meeting cultural-relations situations abroad the character of public opinion there concerning our nation, its aspirations, and its interests will often depend. Even the tourist has, whether he likes it or not, become part of Exhibit A of our virtues, quirks, and foibles.

This book, to be sure, contains letters written by extraordinarily selfless and dedicated men. One cannot read, for example, without a mood akin to awe, the account of how Father Marquette prepared to die in the Northern forest. But life was even for him a business of shouldering obligations, of little pleasures and occasional great satisfactions, of hardships, and of minor adjustments to the here-and-now. The missionary worked hard to learn the languages of Huron and Iroquois, and after he made some headway he began to wish he had a few students, lest the precious knowledge be lost, were something to happen to him. Acquiring the art of learning table manners as practised in Indian villages, so that one could suffer the host to put juicy pieces of fat roast beef into one's mouth without blinking; learning to relish smoked-meat (it is interesting and salutary to observe that we who covet almost anything that has been suffocated in hickory fumes are the descendants of Europeans who thought such viands inedible and unsanitary); perfecting oneself in the art of bartering tobacco for food and buffalo robes, thus becoming as shrewd in commerce as befitted a man of God—these were some of the chores these men of France nonchalantly performed as they marched ahead with Gospel

i

and Cross. Contemporary with us also is their constant dedication to the cause of peace, then as now so self-evidently good and yet so difficult to serve effectively.

Two things stand out, however, most clearly in these letters, which are unvarnished chronicles of the grandeur and the tragic comedy of man. On the one hand, there is the unflagging, loving awareness of the dignity of each human being, untutored and savage though he be. In this respect there was for the Jesuit no sundering of races or creeds. Father Garnier, for example, was fated to die with the women and children of his Huron mission when that was overrun by a band of Iroquois. But with his last breath he sought to aid a poor Indian in his death travail, just as if that were the most natural thing in the world to do. To read this book is therefore to be greatly strengthened in the belief that is the essence of our civilization—the conviction that the worth of the person is beyond question, is immemoriably ordained, and that neither justice nor order can prevail unless this principle abide.

On the other hand, there was the saddening realization that the impact of European culture on the Indian was often everything the Jesuit desired it not to be. Some of the letters are filled with grimly condemnatory accounts of traders who plied the natives with brandy and seduced their women; who were motivated by zest for orgies rather than by the wish to serve their fellow men; and who were so ruthless in commerce that association with them could not help making the Redskin even less moral than he would otherwise have been. And I fancy that nearly everyone who has latterly endeavored to serve his country abroad, in any of the lands with which it is now concerned, must have felt his gorge rising at the sight of the self-same spectacles. In every great enterprise, from the Crusades to the reconstruction of Korea, men of good will have carried camp-follower and carpet-bagger with them, as prisoners do ball and chain.

And so, I am persuaded, these tales of illustrious missionary endeavor will distill a tonic for our comfort. When the nobility of man is made so evident, with no thought of literary artifice or public adulation, our minds and hearts cannot fail to be strengthened for the task which remains before us—difficult, visionary, and sometimes unrealizable though it may seem to be.

GEORGE N. SHUSTER.

FOREWORD

It rarely happens that the heroic story of a new country's colonization is written by adventurous scholars, "from the midst of a forest," or
on the trail with aborigines, day by day, from its earliest beginnings
over a period of more than one hundred and fifty years. But to
America, with the first French colonists to Canada, came the Jesuits,
men astutely trained in letters and fortitude, and even more astutely
selected for their planned and ordered work. From 1611 to 1768 their
reports—their *Relations*—of their life in North America were sent to
the superior at Quebec or to the provincial of the order in France;
and these reports—letters, journals, formal *Relations* or whatever—
are travel, exploration and adventure narrations of high dramatic
calibre, as well as rare source material for the historian, the geographer,
the philologist and the ethnologist. Three hundred years ago
America belonged to the Indian; today he has all but vanished,
as the "lost tribes" and clans of his race have already gone, leaving behind them no temples, no libraries, no buried cities for
record of their past. Yet, in the *Jesuit Relations*, the folk-lore, the
religion, the mythology, the manners and the morals, even the speech
and detailed daily living of these vanished people, what they did and
what they were, are set down minutely, keenly, zestfully by men than
whom no men of the 17th and 18th centuries were more shrewdly
trained in the subtle arts of rhetoric, diplomacy, observation, psychology,
and humanity.

The *Jesuit Relations*, as the term is generally used, comprise the reports from 1632 to 1673, published annually by Sébastien Cramoisy,
in Paris. After 1673 the *Relations*, published and unpublished, sank
into obscurity that lasted for almost two hundred years. In 1858 the
Canadian government reissued the Cramoisy series, and nine years
later, in his *The Jesuits in North America*, Francis Parkman rewrote
their heroic story. No narratives have ever called less for rewriting,
but the original stories of these men of unsurpassable courage have
never been easy to obtain.

In 1894 the Burrows Brothers Company, of Cleveland, Ohio,
decided to republish the rare Quebec edition of the *Relations*, with a
page-for-page English translation, and this work was begun. Within
a few months, however, the scope broadened, and Reuben Gold

iii

Thwaites, Secretary of the State Historical Society of Wisconsin, became editor of documents that reached from 1610 to 1791. Half a dozen volumes would have held the Cramoisy series. But, from 1896 to 1901, at the rate of over one a month, seventy-three volumes of *The Jesuit Relations and Allied Documents* appeared. Not only were all the *Relations,* published and unpublished, included, but personal letters, memoirs, journals, state and church records—whatever ecclesiastical or secular archives offered in the way of additional light on the more formal *Relations.* A page-for-page English translation was made of the original French, Latin, or Italian texts: old portraits, maps, engravings and facsimile texts were added, together with a mass of prefatory, historical, geographical, biographical and bibliographical notes, that make these seventy-three volumes a vast storehouse of related data on early American history, the American Indian, and the heroic men who wrote the story. But, since only 750 sets were published, the *Relations* of the Jesuits were, for the general reader, as inaccessible as ever.

In this volume of Selections from *The Jesuit Relations and Allied Documents* is presented for the first time in a single volume, and in their own words, the story of the Jesuit missionaries in North America from the establishment of their first Acadian mission in 1611, to their final surrender of the Jesuit estates, in gift, to Canada, in 1789. Fortunately for a representative volume, many of the *Relations* overlap, and for the editor it has often been less a matter of choice between events than between narratives of the same event. Sometimes a personal letter has told the story of a year better than that year's *Relation,* more dramatically, because more briefly; and, always, the aim in selection has been for blocks of narrative that could be used in full. With a very few exceptions that explain themselves the chronological order has been followed.

Two of what are perhaps the four most valuable sections in *The Jesuit Relations and Allied Documents* it has been possible to include here in full: the Marquette manuscripts (Marquette's *Journal* on the Mississippi, his unfinished *Journal* written on the Chicago River, and Dablon's note on his death), and Coquart's *Memoir upon the Posts of the King's Domain.* The first is "drama"—its climax the strange water procession that rounded Mackinac in 1677 with Marquette's bones. The second is economics—a Jesuit's confidential report to the Intendant of Canada on the Eastern trading posts: " . . . for purposes of economic study," says the prefatory note, "one of the most valuable documents in our series."

The other sections of unique value are the *Journal des Jésuites*—the running story of daily life at Quebec kept by the superiors there from 1645 to 1668—and the "account book" of the Jesuit mission farm near Detroit, with entries from 1733 to 1756. Of these sections, which alone would fill several volumes, it has been possible to give only a few extracts—but enough to suggest that beneath the stolid dates and figures, so invaluable to the student of economics, lie clear and intimate pictures of colonial social life at an Eastern port and at a frontier post, penciled, some of them, almost three hundred years ago.

Old, odd and variable spellings are retained here as they appear in the text of *The Jesuit Relations and Allied Documents*. The prefatory, historical, and biographical notes have been drawn on when necessary. Reuben Gold Thwaites's Historical Introduction to the volumes he edited (the reader is referred herewith to pp. xlviii-liv for his account of the *Relations*, not for history so much as story) provides additional data; and the Index will serve, though to a necessarily limited degree, as a glossary for many names and terms that would call otherwise for a host of minor footnotes. For the rest, the records of the Jesuits speak for themselves as authentic documents and for their writers as scholars, most of them; as statesmen, some of them; but for all of them, above all else, as brave men. To them we owe and we shall owe always the best we have of our early history, written on the spot and in the hour of its making. Their annals and letters, only so recently gathered together, are still an unworked treasure mine, for the student and the general reader alike; and thanks are due the Burrows Brothers Company for their cordial permission to make, from *The Jesuit Relations and Allied Documents*, this volume of Selections.

EDNA KENTON.

CONTENTS

PAGE

PART II

THE DEVELOPMENT OF THE HURON MISSIONS. (1635-1642)

PART III

THE HURON MARTYRS AND THE IROQUOIS WARFARE. (1642-1659)

CONTENTS

PART IV

THE EXPANSION WESTWARD OF NEW FRANCE, AND THE JESUIT MISSIONS. (1659-1763)

CONTENTS

PART V

THE BANISHMENT OF THE JESUITS FROM THE KING'S DOMAIN. (1763)

THE LIFE OF A MONTAGNAIX MISSIONARY, PRESENTED TO HIS SUCCESSORS IN THE MONTAGNAIX MISSION FOR THEIR INSTRUCTION AND GREATER CONSOLATION.

By father François De crepieul, Jesuit, and an unprofitable servant of the Missions of canada from 1671 to 1697,— which completes the 26th wintering in The Service of The Tadoussak Mission, and the 4th at The Mission of st. Xavier,—at chegoutimy, April 21, 1697.

The Life of a Montagnaix Missionary is a Long and slow Martyrdom:

Is an almost continual practice of patience and of Mortification:

Is a truly penitential and Humiliating life, especially in the cabins, and on journeys with the Savages.

1 The cabin is made of poles and Birch-bark; and Fir-Branches are placed around it to cover the Snow and The frozen Ground.

2 During nearly all the day, The Missionary remains in a sitting or kneeling position, exposed to an almost continual smoke during The Winter.

3 Sometimes he perspires in the day-time and most frequently is cold during The Night. He sleeps in his clothes upon The frozen Ground, and sometimes on the Snow covered with Fir-Branches, which are very hard.

4 He eats from an ouragan (dish) that is very seldom clean or washed, and in most cases is wiped with a greasy piece of skin, or is Licked by The dogs. He eats when there is any-

thing to eat, and when some is offered to him. Sometimes
The meat is only half-cooked; Sometimes it is very tough,
especially when Smoked (dried in the smoke). As a rule, they
have a good meal only once—or, when provisions are abundant
twice; but it does not last long.

5 The savage Shoes, or the dogs' hairy skins, serve him as
napkins, as the hair of the Savage men and women serves them.

6 His usual Beverage is water from the Streams or from
some pond—sometimes melted snow, in an ouragan that is
usually quite greasy.

7 He often scorches his clothes, or his blanket, or his stockings during the Night—especially when the cabin is small or
narrow. He cannot stretch himself, but he curls himself up,
and his head rests upon the Snow covered with fir-branches;
this chills his brain, and gives him toothache, etc.

8 He always sleeps with his clothes on, and takes off his cassock and his Stockings only to protect himself against vermin,
which always swarm on the Savages, especially the Children.

9 Usually when he wakes he finds himself surrounded by
dogs. I have sometimes had 6, 8, or 10 around me.

10 The smoke is sometimes so strong that it makes his eyes
weep; and when he sleeps he feels as if some one had thrown
salt into his eyes; when he Awakes, he has much difficulty in
opening them.

11 When the Snow Thaws, while he is walking upon Lakes or
long Rivers, he is so dazzled for 4 or 5 days by the water
that drops continually from his eyes that he cannot read his
Breviary. Sometimes he has to be led by the hand. This has
happened to father Silvy, to father Dalmas, and to myself;
while on the march I could not see further than the edge of
my Snowshoes.

12 He is often annoyed by little Children, by their cries, their
weeping, etc.; and sometimes he is made ill by the stench of
those who have Scrofula, with whom he even Drinks out of
the same kettle. I have spent more than 8 days in the cabin
of Kawitaskawat, the chief man among the Mystassins, and
have slept near his son, who was troubled with that disease;

and the stench from him often caused me nausea, both by day and night. I have also eaten and drunk from his ouragan.

13   He is sometimes reduced to drinking only water obtained from melted snow, which smells of smoke and is very dirty. For 3 Weeks I have drunk nothing else, while I was with Strangers in the Region of Peokwagamy. I have never seen Savages dirtier than these, as regards eating, drinking and sleeping. Among them the meat was often covered with moose-hairs or Sand. An old woman, with her long nails, gathered up handfuls of grease in the Kettle into which Snow had been thrown, and then offered it to us to eat, in a very dirty ouragan: and all drank broth out of the same Kettle.

14   In the summer-time, while Traveling, especially on The Saguenay and on the great River, he oftens drinks the very dirty water obtained from Ponds. During 3 days, while detained by contrary winds, we drank no other water. Sometimes the Wind compels him to take refuge in Places where there is none at all. This has happened to me more than once —indeed, more than 3 times. I have even been obliged to drink from Ponds in which I Saw toads, etc.

15   In most cases during the winter, while on long and difficult journeys, he does not find a drop of water wherewith to quench his thirst, although exhausted with toils and fatigues.

16   He suffers greatly from cold and from smoke, before the Cabin is finished, for 2 or 3 hours when the Weather is very severe in winter. His shirt, which is wet with perspiration, and his soaked stockings, render him Benumbed with cold; he suffers also from Hunger, because in most cases he has had nothing but a piece of dried meat, eaten before the camp was struck.

17   Suffering and hardship are the appanages of these holy but arduous Missions. Faxit Deus ut iis diu immoretur et immoriatur Servus Inutilis Missionum Franciscus, S. J. (God grant that in them may long remain and die the Useless Servant of the Missions, Francois, S. J.)

[The Jesuit Relations and Allied Documents, lxv, Doc. clxx.]

I N T R O D U C T I O N

By Reuben Gold Thwaites

[This is the Historical Introduction by Reuben Gold Thwaites to the seventy-three volume edition of *The Jesuit Relations and Allied Documents* which he edited and from which this volume of Selections has been compiled. It is given in full, although several references are made in it to Documents not included in this volume. Because of its remarkable clarification and condensation of the long and intricate period in early American history with which the *Relations* are concerned, it will be found an invaluable aid to the pages that follow it.]

Doubtless Norse vikings, venturing far southward from outlying colonies in Iceland and Greenland, first coasted New France, and beached their sturdy ships on the shores of New England. But five centuries passed without result, and we cannot properly call them pioneers of American civilization. Columbus it was, who unlocked the eastern door of the New World. Five years later, John Cabot, in behalf of England, was sighting the gloomy headlands of Cape Breton. Cortereal appeared in the neighborhood, in 1501, seeking lands for the Portuguese crown. About this time at intervals, there came to Newfoundland certain Norman, Breton, and Basque fishers, who, erecting little huts and drying-scaffolds along the rocky shore, sowed the first seed of that polyglot settlement of French, Portuguese, Spanish and English which has come down to our day almost uninterruptedly.

By 1511, these fishermen appear to have known the mainland to the west: for on the map of Sylvanus, in his edition of Ptolemy, that year, we find delineation of the "Square Gulf", which answers to the Gulf of St. Lawrence. In 1520, Fagundus visited these waters for the Portuguese, and four years later Verrazano was making for the French an exploration for the coast between North Carolina and Newfoundland. Whether or not Cartier (1535) was the first to sail up the St. Lawrence "until land could be seen on either side", no man can now tell: apparently, he was the first to leave a record of doing so. Progress up the river was checked by Lachine Rapids, and he spent the winter on Montreal Island.

France and Spain were just then engaged in one of their periodical quarrels, and adventurers were needed to fight battles at home, so that it was six years before any attempts were made to colonize the river-lands to which Cartier had led the way. In 1541, a Picard seigneur named Roberval, enjoying the friendship of Francis I., was commissioned as viceroy of the new country beyond the Atlantic, with Cartier as his chief pilot and captain-general, and a choice selection of jailbirds for colonists. Cartier started off before his chief, built a fort at Quebec, and, after a long and miserable winter, picked up a quantity of glittering stones which he took to be gold and diamonds, and gladly set sail for home. Tradition has it that Roberval met him near the mouth of the river, but was unable to induce him to return to his cheerless task of founding a state in an inhospital wilderness, with convicts for citizens. Roberval, however, proceeded to Quebec with his consignment of prison dregs, and throughout another protracted winter the flag of France floated from the little intrenched camp which Cartier had planted on the summit of the cliff. Roberval's principal occupation appears to have been the disciplining of his unruly followers, a work in which the gibbet and the lash were freely employed. He also essayed explorations up the river: but the rude task was not to his liking, and, with what remained of his battered band, he followed Cartier to France.

It is commonly said that Canada was abandoned by the French between the going of Roberval and the coming of Champlain. But, though little was done toward colonizing

on the St. Lawrence, Newfoundland was by no means neglected. Its fishing industry grew apace. The rules of the
church, prescribing a fish diet on certain holy days, led to a
large use of salted fish throughout Catholic Europe: and,
by 1578, full a hundred and fifty vessels alone, chiefly Breton,
were employed in the Newfoundland fisheries, while a good
trade with the mainland Indians, as far south as the Potomac,
had now sprung up. The island colony proved valuable as a
supply and repair station for traders and explorers, and thus
served as a nucleus of both French and English settlement
in America.

It is difficult for us of today to realize that, at any time
in the world's history, enlightened folk should have thought
good colonists could be made out of the sweepings of the jails
and gutters of the Old World. But in the sixteenth and
seventeenth centuries that delusion was quite generally entertained by would-be founders of states across the sea: It
required the lessons of more than a hundred years of disastrous
experiments to teach discerning men that only the best of the
middle class and the masses, can successfully plant a new community in the wilderness. The experiences of Cartier and
Roberval on the St. Lawrence, and of Laudonnière in Florida
(1564), were of no avail in influencing governmental policy
at Paris. In 1590, the Marquis de la Roche was sent out with
the usual dissolute crew to succeed Roberval as the king's
agent on the banks of the St. Lawrence. Leaving part of his
ill-favored gang on the desert Sable Isle, off Nova Scotia
(where early in the century Baron de Léry had vainly attempted to plant a colony), La Roche set forth to explore
the mainland for a site. A wild storm blew his vessels to
France, and the wretched skin-clad survivors of the band
which he had left behind were not rescued until thirteen years
had elapsed. Their tale of horror long rang in the ears of
Europe.

In 1600-1603, Chauvin and Pontgravé made successful trading voyages to the St. Lawrence. Samuel de Champlain was
one of the party which, in the latter year, followed in Cartier's

track to Montreal. The same season, a Calvinist, named De
Monts, was given the vice-royalty and fur-trade monopoly
of Acadia, and in 1604 he landed a strangely-assorted company of vagabonds and gentlemen on St. Croix Island, near
the present boundary between Maine and New Brunswick:
but in the spring following they settled at Port Royal, near
where is now Annapolis, Nova Scotia, thus planting the first
French agricultural settlement in America. Five years later,
Champlain reared a permanent post on the rock of Quebec,
and New France was at last, after a century of experiments,
fairly under way.

Various motives influenced the men who sought to establish
French colonization in America. The ill-fated agricultural
colony of the Huguenots in Florida (1562-68), was avowedly
an attempt of Admiral Coligny to found an enduring asylum
for French Protestants. The enterprise of New France, on
the other hand, was the outgrowth of interests more or less
conflicting. Doubtless the court had deepest at heart the
kingly passion for territorial aggrandizement: next upper-
most, was the pious wish to convert heathen nations to the
Catholic faith, explorers like Cartier being authorized to discover new lands "in order the better to do what is pleasing to
God, our Creator and Redeemer, and what may be for the increase of his holy and sacred Name, and of our holy mother,
the Church:" the desire for pelf, through the agency of the
fur trade, and the possibility of the discovery of precious
metals, gave commercial zest to the undertaking, and to
many was the *raison d'être* of the colony: and, lastly, was the
almost universal yearning for adventure, among a people who
in the seventeenth century were still imbued with that chivalric
temper which among Englishmen is assigned to the Middle
Ages. The inner life of New France, throughout its century
and a half of existence, was largely a warring between these
several interests.

Missionaries came early upon the scene. With the Calvinist De Monts were Huguenot ministers for the benefit of
the settlers, and Catholic priests to open a mission among

the savages, for the court had stipulated with him that the latter were to be instructed only in the faith of Rome. But no missionary work was done, for the colony was through several years on the verge of dissolution, and the priests became victims of scurvy. Poutrincourt, who held under De Monts the patent for Port Royal, did nothing to further the purposes of the court in this regard, until 1610, when, admonished for his neglect, he brought out with him a secular priest, Messire Jessé Fléché, of Langres, who on June 24, "apparently in some haste," baptized twenty-one Abenakis, including the district sagamore, or chief. The account of this affair, which Poutrincourt sent in triumph to France, is the initial document in the present series. [1]

On the twelfth of June, 1611, there arrived at Port Royal, at the instance of King Henry IV., two Jesuit fathers, Pierre Biard and Ennemond Massé. They were, however, not favorably received by Poutrincourt and his followers: they found great practical difficulties in acquiring the Indian languages, and made slight progress in the herculean task to which they had been set. To them came, the following year, a lay brother, Gilbert du Thet, who was soon dispatched to the head of the order, in France, with an account of the situation. In the spring of 1613, he returned, in company with Father Quentin. The little band of missionaries had no sooner established themselves at the new French colony on Mt. Desert Island, than the latter was attacked and dispersed by the Virginian Argall. Du Thet was killed in the fight, Massé was, with other colonists, set adrift in a boat, and Biard and Quentin were taken to Virginia, to be eventually shipped to England, and thence allowed to return to France.

In 1615, Champlain thought the time ripe for the institution of Indian missions upon the St. Lawrence, a spiritual field hitherto neglected, and introduced to Quebec four members of the fraternity of Récollets, the most austere of the three orders of Franciscans: these were Fathers Denis Jamay, Jean d'Olbeau, and Joseph le Caron, and a lay brother, Paci-

[1] *The Jesuit Relations and Allied Documents*, 1, *Doc.* 1.

fique du Plessis. To D'Olbeau was assigned the conversion
of the Montagnais of the Lower St. Lawrence: Le Caron went
to the Hurons, or Wyandots, in the vast stretch of forested
wilderness west of the Ottawa River, and before the coming of
autumn had established a bark chapel in their midst: Jamay
and Du Plessis remained in the neighborhood of Quebec,
ministering to the colonists and the wandering savages who
came to the settlement for purposes of trade or sociability,
or through fear of scalp-hunting Iroquois. For ten years did
these grey friars practise the rites of the church in the Canadian woods, all the way from the fishing and trading outpost
of Tadoussac to the western Lake of the Nipissings. Barefooted, save for heavy wooden sandals, coarsely clad in gown
and hood, enduring in a rigorous climate, to which they were
unused, all manner of hardships by flood and field, they were
earnestly devoted to their laborious calling in a time when
elsewhere the air of New France was noisy with the strife
of self-seeking traders and politicians. Yet somehow their
mission seemed without important result. Even less successful
was the enterprise of some fellow Récollets, who, in 1619,
began independent work among the French fishermen and
Micmacs of Nova Scotia, New Brunswick, and Gaspé, but were
forced in 1624, after many disasters, to abandon their task,
three of them joining the party at Quebec.

The little band on the St. Lawrence, although thus reinforced, felt impelled in 1625, to invite the powerful aid
of the Jesuits, who in the face of great odds were just then
holding most successful missions in Asia, Africa, and South
America. In response to the call, three fathers of the black
gown came to Quebec this year,—Massé, who had been of
the old Acadian mission, Charles Lalemant, and that giant
among them, in both stature and deeds, Jean de Brébeuf. Immediately the work began to broaden, but the records of the
dual mission do not give evidence of many converts,—a few
Huron youth taken to France, and there instructed and baptized, being the chief gains. The wandering habits of the Indians were not favorable to persistent instruction of the young,

and adults were unwilling to commit themselves to the new doctrine, even when not openly opposed to its promulgation. The
summer months were usually spent by the missionaries at
Tadoussac, Quebec and Three Rivers, where trading parties
from the tribes were wont to assemble: and, when the latter
scattered for their winter hunts, the missionaries accompanied
them, sharing the toils, dangers, and discomforts of the mov-
able camps, and often suffering much from positive abuse at
the hands of their not over-willing hosts.

The settlements of Port Royal and Quebec were at this
time wretched little hamlets of a few dozen huts each, surrounded by a palisade, and these fell an easy prey to small
English naval forces (1628-1629). With their fall, ended
the slender mission of the Récollets and Jesuits, who were
in triumph carried off to England. For a few months, France
did not hold one foot of ground in North America. But
as peace had been declared between France and England
before this conquest, the former received back all of its possessions, and the inevitable struggle for the mastery of the
continent was postponed for four generations longer.

With the release of Canada to France, in 1632, the Jesuits
were by the home authorities placed in sole charge of the
spiritual interests of both settlers and Indians, and the history
of their greatest missions begins at this time. On the fifth
day of July, there landed at Quebec, Fathers Paul le Jeune
and Anne de Nouë, and a lay brother named Gilbert. Le
Jeune was the superior, and at once devoted himself to learning the language and customs of the savages, and so studying
the enormous field before him as intelligently to dispose of
his meagre forces.

THE INDIANS

The existence of rival tribes among the Red Indians of
North America, was, perhaps, the most formidable obstacle in
the path of missionaries. It has always been impossible to
make any hard-and-fast classification: yet the Indians presented a considerable variety of types, ranging from the South-

ern Indians, some of whose tribes were in a relatively high stage of material advancement and mental calibre, down to the savage root-eaters of the Rocky Mountain region. The migrations of some of the Indian tribes were frequent, and they occupied over lapping territories, so that it is impossible to fix the tribal boundaries with any degree of exactness. Again, the tribes were so merged by intermarriage, by affiliation, by consolidation, by the fact that there were numerous polyglot villages of renegades, by similarities in manner, habits, and appearance, that it is difficult even to separate the savages into families. It is only on philological grounds that these divisions can be made at all. In a general way we may say that between the Atlantic and the Rockies, Hudson Bay and the gulf of Mexico, there were four Indian languages in vogue, with great varieties of local dialect:

I. The Algonkins were the most numerous, holding the greater portion of the country from the unoccupied "debatable land" of Kentucky northward to the Mississippi. Among their tribes were the Micmacs of Acadia, the Penobscots of Maine, the Montagnais of the St. Lawrence, the ill-defined tribes of the country round about Lake St. John, and the Ottawas, Chippewas, Mascoutens, Sacs, Foxes, Pottawattomies, and Illinois of the Upper Lakes. These savages were rude in life and manners, were intensely warlike, depended for subsistence chiefly on hunting and fishing, lived in rude wigwams covered with bark, skins, or matted reeds, practised agriculture in a crude fashion, and were less stable in their habitations than the Southern Indians. They have made a larger figure in our history than any other family, because through their lands came the heaviest and most aggressive movement of white population, French or English. Estimates of early Indian populations necessarily differ, in the absence of accurate knowledge: but it is now believed that the number was never so great as was at first estimated by the Jesuit Fathers and the earliest English colonists. A careful modern estimate is, that the Algonkins at no time numbered over 90,000 souls and possibly not over 50,000.

II. In the heart of this Algonkin land was planted the ethnic group called the Iroquois, with its several distinct branches, often at war with each other. The craftiest, most daring, and most intelligent of North American Indians, yet still in the savage hunter state, the Iroquois were the terror of every native band east of the Mississippi, before the coming of the whites, who in turn learned to dread their ferocious power. The five principal tribes of this family—Mohawks, Oneidas, Onondagas, Cayugas, and Senecas, all stationed in palisaded villages south and east of lakes Erie and Ontario,— formed a loose confederacy styled by themselves and the French "The Long House," and by the English "The Five Nations," which firmly held the waterways connecting the Hudson and Ohio rivers and the Great Lakes. The population of the entire group was not over 17,000—a remarkably small number, considering the active part they played in American history, and the control which they exercised through wide tracts of wilderness. Related to, but generally at war with them, were the Hurons of Canada, among whom the Jesuits planted their earliest missions. Champlain, in an endeavor to cultivate the friendship of his Huron and Algonkin neighbors, early made war on the Iroquois, and thus secured for New France a heritage of savage enmity which contributed more than any other one cause to cripple its energies and render it at last an easy prey to the rival power of the English colonies.

III. The Southern Indians occupied the country between the Tennessee River and the Gulf, the Appalachian Ranges and the Mississippi. Of a milder disposition than their Northern cousins, the Cherokees, Chickasaws, Choctaws, Creeks, and Seminoles were rather in a barbarous than a savage state: by the time of the Revolution, they were not far behind the white proprietors in industrial or domestic methods, and numbered not above 50,000 persons. With them, this story of the Jesuit missions has little to do: the Louisiana mission, an offshoot of that of New France did faithful work here, but the documentary result was neither as interesting nor as prolific, and necessarily occupies but small space in the present series.

IV. The Dakotah, or Sioux, family occupied for the most part the country beyond the Mississippi. They were and are a fierce, high-strung people, genuine nomads, and war appears to have been their chief occupation. The Jesuits worked among them but in slight measure, on the waters of the Upper Mississippi: they met this family chiefly in the persons of the Winnebagoes, one of their outlying bands, which at the time of the French occupation was resident on and about Green Bay of Lake Michigan, at peace and in confederacy with the Algonkins who hedged them about.

The mission of the French Jesuits to these widely-scattered hordes of savages forms one of the most thrilling chapters in human history. It is impossible, in this brief Introduction, to attempt anything more than the barest outline of the theme: Rochemonteix, Shea, and Parkman have told the story in detail, from differing points of view, and with these authorities the student of the following documents in the case is presumed to be familiar. A rapid summary of results will, however, be useful: and this we may best obtain, at the expense of occasional repetition of narrative, by following the fortunes of the pioneers of the Cross through the several district missions into which their work was naturally divided.

I. *THE ABENAKI MISSION*

This mission was chiefly in Maine and Acadia, and on Cape Breton Island. The Abenakis (or Abnakis) were a strong but mild-mannered Algonkin tribe, settled in villages or cantonments: but, like others of their race, in the habit of taking long semi-annual journeys—each winter to hunt, and each summer to fish. We have seen that the French Jesuits, Biard and Massé, were in the field as early as 1611, soon after the establishment of Port Royal; their predecessor being the secular French priest, Fléché, who had been introduced to the country by Poutrincourt, the patentee. Biard and Massé met

with many discouragements, chiefly the opposition of Poutrincourt's son, Biencourt (sometimes called Baron St. Just), who
had been left in charge of the colony.   Nevertheless the missionaries learned the native language, and made many long
journeys of exploration, one of Biard's trips extending as far
as the mouth of the Kennebec.   They were later joined by a
lay brother, Du Thet, and by Fathers Quentin and Lalemant.
Joining the new French colony on Mt. Desert Island, in the
spring of 1613, the establishment was almost immediately destroyed by the Virginian Argall.   In the skirmish Du Thet
was killed.

    In 1619, a party of Récollets from Aquitaine began a mis-
sion on St. John River, in Acadia, but five years later, as we
have seen above, abandoned the task, the survivors joining the
Quebec mission of their order.   Other Récollets were in
Acadia, however, between 1630 and 1633, and later we have
evidence of a small band of Capuchins ministering to French
settlers on the Penobscot and Kennebec: but it is probable that
they made no attempt to convert the natives.

    A Jesuit mission was founded on Cape Breton in 1634, by
Father Julian Perrault: and a few years later, Father Charles
Turgis was at Miscou.   Other missionaries soon came to minister to the Micmacs, but for many years their efforts were
without result: and sickness, resulting from the hardships of
the situation, caused most of the early black gowns to retreat
from the attempt.   Finally, an enduring mission was established among these people, and, until about 1670, was conducted with some measure of success by Fathers Andrew Richard, Martin de Lyonne, and James Fremin.   About 1673, the
Récollets took up the now abandoned work, occasionally aided
by secular priests from the Seminary of Quebec, and Jesuits,
until at last the Micmacs from Gaspé to Nova Scotia were declared to be entirely converted to the Catholic faith.

    Father Gabriel Druillettes, of the Jesuit mission at Sillery,
near Quebec, went to the Kennebec country in 1646, invited
thither by converted Abenakis who had been at Sillery, and
during visits, extending through a period of eleven years, was

more than ordinarily successful in the task of gaining Indian converts to Christianity. In 1650, he made a notable visit to the Puritans of Eastern Massachusetts, during which was discussed the proposed union between New France and New England, against the Iroquois. Upon the final departure of Druillettes in 1657, the Abenakis were but spasmodically served with missionaries: occasionally a Jesuit appeared among them, but the field could not be persistently worked, owing to the demands upon the order from other quarters. The fathers now sought to draw Abenaki converts to Sillery, and later to St. Francis de Sales, at the falls of the Chaudière, which soon became almost exclusively an Abenaki mission.

In 1688, Father Bigot, of this mission, again entered the field of the Kennebec, at the same time that Rev. Peter Thury, a priest of the Quebec Seminary, opened a mission on the Penobscot, and the Récollet F. Simon gathered a flock at Medoktek, near the mouth of the St. John. They were in time aided and succeeded by others; the Jesuits being Julian Binneteau, Joseph Aubery, Peter de la Chasse, Stephen Lauverjeat, Loyard, and Sebastian Rale; the death of Rale, the greatest of them all, at the hands of New England partisans in the border strife of 1724, is a familiar incident in American history. Jesuits succeeded to the Penobscot mission in 1703, and with great zeal, but amid continual hardships and discouragements, carried on the principal work among the Abenakis until the downfall of New France in 1763. The majority of the Kennebec converts, however, emigrated to the mission of St. Francis de Sales, and from there frequently went forth upon avenging expeditions against the New England borderers.

II. *THE MONTAGNAIS MISSION*

This was centered at Tadoussac, and ministered to the Montagnais, Bersiamites, Porcupines, Oumaniwek, Papinachois, and other tribes of the Lower St. Lawrence and the Saguenay. Tadoussac had, from the earliest historic times, been a favorite harbor and trading-station for the French: for, being at the junction of two great rivers, it was convenient as a place of assembly for the natives of the lower country. The first priests in the district had said mass there; but it was not until 1640 that a Jesuit mission was formed by Father Jean du Quen, its sphere of influence soon reaching to the upper waters of the Saguenay, Lake St. John, Hudson Bay, and the coast of Labrador. Du Quen was actively assisted by Charles Meiachkwat, a Montagnais convert, who erected the first chapel, became a catechist, and made extended tours through the neighboring tribes. In time, there were associated with Du Quen, Fathers Buteux and Druillettes. Protracted missionary tours were made by them, with results which were considered satisfactory as compared with other missions; although they had serious difficulties to contend with, in the prevalent intemperance which the fur trade introduced among the natives, the belief in dreams, the laxity of morals, and the wiles of medicine-men, or sorcerers, as they were called by the Jesuits.

For the first few years, the missionaries spent their winters in Quebec, ministering to the colonists, and each spring went down the Tadoussac to meet the summer trading parties; but greater persistency of effort was deemed desirable, and thereafter, instead of returning home in the autumn, they followed the Indians upon their winter hunts, and in the course of these wanderings endured the usual privations and hardships of traveling camps. Bailloquet, Nouvel, Beaulieu, Albanel, De Crépieul, Dalmas, Boucher, Peter Michael Laure, and Jean Baptiste Labrosse, are other names of Jesuit Fathers who at different periods were engaged upon this toilsome mission.

In 1670, Tadoussac was almost deserted, owing to Iroquois raids and the ravages of smallpox; the Montagnais and kindred tribes were in hiding, through the vast country between Lake St. John and Hudson Bay. They were still followed by their devoted shepherds, whom no hardship could discourage. The following year, Crépieul began a mission on Hudson Bay, and here in 1694 his auxiliary Dalmas was killed. Laure

(1720-37) left us a monument of his labors in a Montagnais grammar and dictionary. Labrosse, the last of his order at Tadoussac, instructed many of his flock to read and write, and left a legacy of native education, which has lasted unto the present day: he lived and taught long after his order had been suppressed in New France, and died at Tadoussac in 1782.

III.   THE QUEBEC AND MONTREAL MISSIONS

These included the several missions at Quebec, Montreal, Three Rivers, Sillery, Bécancourt, and St. Francis de Sales, which were designed for the wandering Montagnais of the district, those Algonkins of the West who could be induced to come and settle on the lower waters, and in later years such Abenakis of Acadia and Maine as sought asylum upon distinctively French soil.

We have seen that Récollets were first at Quebec, ministering both to colonists and Indians, and that, in 1625, they invited the Jesuits to aid them. In 1629, the joint mission came to a close through the surrender of Quebec to the English. When the mission was re-opened in 1632, Jesuits alone were in charge, their operations being at first confined to the neighboring Montagnais, although they soon spread throughout the entire Canadian field. In 1658, Bishop Laval founded the Seminary of Quebec, whereupon the Jesuits resigned their parishes among the colonists, and thereafter confined themselves to their college and the Indian missions. In addition to their parish work, the priests of the seminary conducted missions in Acadia, Illinois, and on the lower Mississippi.

The year following the return of the Jesuits to Canada, Father Buteux, of that order, began his labors at Three Rivers, which was a convenient gathering-place for the fur trade. The village was frequently raided by Iroquois, but remained until the fall of New France one of the prominent centers of missionary influence. The efforts of Buteux, which lasted until his death at the hands of Iroquois in 1652, met with consid-

erable success. His custom, like that of the other missionaries, was to be present at the French posts during the annual
trading "meets," and when savages returned to the wilderness,
to accompany some selected band. In thus following the nomadic tribes, he made some of the longest and most toilsome
journeys recorded in the annals of the Society of Jesus, and
shared with his flock all the horrors of famine, pestilence and
inter-tribal war.

It was soon realized by the missionaries that but meagre
results could be obtained until the Indians were induced to lead
a sedentary life. Their wandering habit nullified all attempts
at permanent instruction to the young; it engendered improvi-
dence and laziness, bred famine and disease; and the constant
struggle to kill fur-bearing animals for their pelts rapidly
depleted the game, while the fur trade wrought contamination
in many forms. Missionary efforts were at first conducive to
the interests of the fur trade, by bringing far-distant tribes
within the sphere of French influence; but so soon as the
Jesuit sought to change the habits of the natives, to cause them
to become agriculturists instead of hunters, and to oppose the
rum traffic among them, then the grasping commercial
monopoly which controlled the fortunes of New France, and
was merely "working" the colony for financial gains, saw in
the Jesuit an enemy, and often placed serious obstacles in his
path.

In pursuance of the sedentary policy, and also to protect
the wretched Montagnais from Iroquois war-parties, the Jesuits, in 1637, established for them a palisaded mission four
miles above Quebec, at first giving it the name St. Joseph,
but later that of Sillery, in honor of Commander Noël Brulart
de Sillery, of France, who had given ample funds for the
founding of this enterprise. Here were at first gathered
twenty of the Indians, who began cultivation of the soil, varied
by occasional hunting and fishing trips, which the missionaries
could not prevent. The little town slowly grew in importance,
both Algonkins and Montagnais being represented in its population. Three years later, nuns opened a hospital at Sillery,

for the reception of both French and Indian patients, and thus greatly added to the popularity of the mission. But in 1646 the nuns removed their hospital to Quebec; a few years later, the church and mission house were destroyed by fire; disease made sad havoc in the settlement; the thin soil became exhausted through careless tillage; Iroquois preyed upon the converts, until at last the Algonkins almost entirely disappeared; and although their place was taken by Abenakis from Maine and Acadia, until the attendance became almost solely Abenaki, the enterprise waned. In 1685, it was abandoned in favor of St. Francis de Sales, a new mission established at the falls of the Chaudière River, not far from the St. Lawrence. Beyond a monument of later days, to the memory of Fathers Massé and De Nouë, whose names are prominently connected with this work, nothing now remains to mark the site of the old Sillery mission.

From St. Francis, the mission work began to spread into Maine. Of its character and extent there, mention has already been made. St. Francis achieved a certain measure of prosperity, as Indian missions go. It became in time a source of serious trouble to the New England borderers, for many a French and Indian war-party was here fitted out against the latter, during the series of bloody conflicts which marked the three-quarters of a century previous to the fall of New France. Finally, in September, 1759, Maj. Robert Rogers descended upon the village with his famous rangers, and in retaliation pillaged and burned houses, and killed "at least two hundred Indians." New France soon after fell into the hands of the English, and, the Jesuits being suppressed, we hear little more of St. Francis de Sales.

In 1641, the missionary settlement of Montreal was founded by Maisonneuve. The Jesuits were the first resident clergy, and soon began mission work among the neighboring Indians and those who resorted thither from the valleys of the Lower St. Lawrence and the Ottawa. Soon, however, the Sulpitians, established in Paris by the Abbé Olier, one of the Society of Montreal, took charge of the mission on Montreal Island, which in after years was moved to the Sault au Récollet, and thence to the Lake of the Two Mountains, where there was gathered a polyglot village composed of Iroquois, Algonkins, and Nipissings. Upon the opening of the English régime, the Jesuit and Récollet missions were suppressed, but those of the Sulpitians were undisturbed, so that this mission at the lake is the oldest now extant in Canada.

Among the Algonkins of the Ottawa River (or Grande Rivière), no permanent missions were attempted by any of the orders. Long the chief highway to the West, the river was familiar to travelling missionaries, who frequently ministered to the tribesman along its banks, either at the native villages or during the annual trading councils at the French posts of Montreal, Three Rivers and Quebec.

IV. *THE HURON MISSION*

At the time of the advent of the French, the Hurons (or Wyandots), allied in origin and language to the Iroquois, numbered about 16,000 souls, and dwelt in several large villages in a narrow district on the high ground between Lake Simcoe and Georgian Bay of Lake Huron. Their dwellings were bark cabins, clustered within stoutly-palisaded walls, and near each fortified town were fields of corn, beans, pumpkins, and tobacco. Agricultural in habit, keen traders, and in the main sedentary, these semi-naked savages made short hunting and fishing expeditions, and laid up stores for the winter. They were better fighters than the Algonkins around them, yet were obliged gradually to withdraw northward and westward from Iroquois persecution, and during the period of the Jesuit missions were almost annihilated by the latter. To the southwest, across a wide stretch of unpopulated forest, were the allies and kindred of the Hurons, the Tionontates, called also Petuns, or Tobacco Nation, a term having its origin in their custom of cultivating large fields of tobacco, which commodity they used in a widespread barter with other tribes. To the southeast of the Petuns, west of Lake Ontario and on both sides of the gorge of Niagara, were the peacful Atiwandaronks, who, being friends alike of Iroquois, Algonkins, and Hurons, were known as the Neutral Nation. To the eastward of the Neutrals, strongly intrenched in the interlocking basins of the Genesee and the Mohawk, lay the dread confederacy of the Iroquois, who in time were to spread like a pestilence over the lands of all their neighbors.

The intelligence and mobility of the Hurons rendered the early prospects for missionary effort among them more promising than with the rude and nomadic Algonkins. But while at first the missionaries of New France were well received, the innate savagery of these people in time asserted itself. Their medicine-men, as bitterly fanatical as the howling dervishes of the Orient, plotted the destruction of the messengers of the new faith: the introduction of European diseases was attributed to the "black gowns"; the ravages of the Iroquois were thought to be brought on by the presence of the strangers; the rites of the church were looked upon as infernal incantations, and the lurid pictures of the Judgment, which were displayed in the little forest chapels, aroused unspeakable terror among this simple people; finally, an irresistible wave of superstitious frenzy led to the blotting out of the mission, accompanied by some of the most heartrending scenes in the history of Christian evangelization.

It will be remembered that in 1615 the Récollet friar, Joseph le Caron, made his way into the far-away country of the Hurons, but returned in the following year, having learned much of their language and customs. Five years later, another of his order, William Poulin, took up the weary task, being joined in 1623 by Fathers Le Caron and Nicholas Viel, and the historian of the Récollet missions, Brother Gabriel Sagard. All of them soon left the field, however, save Viel, who alone amid almost incredible hardships, attained some measure of success; but in 1625 when descending the Ottawa to meet and arrange for co-operation with the Jesuit Brébeuf, at Three Rivers, he was willfully drowned by his Indian guide in the last rapid of Des Prairies River, just back of Montreal.

Such is the origin of the name of the dread Sault au Récollet.

In 1626, the Jesuits Brébeuf and Anne de Nouë, having received some linguistic instruction from Récollets who had been in the Huron field, proceeded thither, with a Récollet friar, Joseph de la Roche Daillon, to resume the work which the Récollets had abandoned. Daillon attempted a mission to neighboring Neutrals, but, being roughly handled by them, rejoined his Jesuit friends among the Hurons. Two years later, he returned to Quebec, having been preceded by De Nouë, who found it impossible to master the difficult language of their dusky flock. Brébeuf, now left alone, labored gallantly among these people, and, winning the hearts of many by his easy adoption of their manners, gathered about him a little colony of those favorably inclined to his views. He was recalled to Quebec in 1629, arriving there just in time to fall into the hands of Louis Kirk, and be transported to England.

When Canada was restored to France, by the treaty of St. Germain, the Jesuits were given sole charge of the Indian missions, but it was 1634 before the Huron mission could be reopened. In September, Brébeuf, Antoine Daniel, and Davost returned to Brébeuf's old field, and commenced, in the large town of Ihonatiria, the greatest Jesuit mission in the history of New France. Others soon joined them. Additional missions were opened in the neighboring towns, some of the strongest of these being each served by four fathers, who were assisted by laymen donnés (or given men): while in the cultivation of the soil, and the fashioning of the implements and utensils both for the fathers and for the Indians, numerous hired laborers, from the French colonies on the St. Lawrence, were employed in and about the missions. Charles Garnier and Isaac Jogues, with their attendants, made a tour of the Petun villages; other Jesuits were sent among the Neutrals; and even the Algonkins as far northwestward as Saulte Ste. Marie were visited (1641) by Raymbault and Jogues, and looked and listened with awe at the celebration of the mass. In 1639, there was built, on the River Wye, the fortified mission house of St. Mary's, to serve as a center for the widespread work, as a place for ecclesiastical retreat for the fathers, and a refuge when enemies pressed too closely upon them.

The story of the hardships and sufferings of the devoted missionaries, as told by Rochemonteix, Shea and Parkman, and with rare modesty recorded in the documents to be contained in this series, is one of the most thrilling in the annals of humanity. Space forbids us to dwell upon the theme. No men have, in the zealous exercise of their faith, performed hardier deeds than these Jesuits of the Huron mission; yet, after three years of unremitting toil, they could (1640) count but a hundred converts out of a population of 16,000, and these were for the most part sick infants or aged persons, who had died soon after baptism. The rugged braves scorned the approaches of the fathers, and unmercifully tormented their converts; the medicine-men waged continual warfare on their work; smallpox and the Iroquois were decimating the people.

Jogues was (1642) sent down to the colonies for supplies for the missions, but with his Huron companions was captured by an Iroquois war-party, who led them to the Mohawk towns. There most of the Hurons were killed, and Jogues and his donné, René Goupil, were tortured and mutilated, and made to serve as slaves to their savage jailers. Finally Goupil, a promising young physician, was killed and Jogues, being rescued by the Dutch allies of the Mohawks, was sent to Europe. Supplies thus failing them, the Huron missionaries were in a sad plight until finally (1644) relieved by an expedition to the lower country undertaken at great hazards by Brébeuf, Garreau, and Noël Chabanel. The same season, Francis Joseph Bressani, attempting to reach the Huron missions, had been captured and tortured by the Mohawks; like Jogues, he was rescued through Dutch intercession and sent back to Europe, but both of these zealots were soon back again facing the cruel dangers of their chosen task.

A temporary peace followed, in 1645, and the hope of the Jesuits was rekindled, for they now had five missions in as many Huron towns, and another established for Algonkins who were resident in the Huron district. But in July, 1648, the Iroquois attacked Teanaustayé, the chief Huron village, and while encouraging the frenzied defense, Father Daniel lost his life at the hands of the enemy. He was thus the first Jesuit martyr in the Huron mission, and the second in New France—for Jogues had been tortured to death in the Iroquois towns, two years before. The spirit of the Hurons was crushed in this bloody foray; large bands, deserting their towns, fled in terror to seek protection of the Petuns, while others made their way to the Manitoulin Islands of Lake Huron, and even as far west as the islands of Green Bay and the matted pine forests of Northern Wisconsin. Here and there a town was left, and one of the largest of these, called St. Ignatius by the Jesuits, was stormed by a thousand Iroquois, March 16, 1649. The three survivors fled through the woods to neighboring St. Louis, where were Brébeuf, now grown old in his service of toil and young Gabriel Lalemant. Bravely did they aid in defending St. Louis, and administering to wounded and dying; but at last were captured, and being taken to the ruined town of St. Ignatius were most cruelly tortured until relieved by death. Early in November, Fathers Garnier and Chabanel met their death in the Petun country, the former at the hands of Iroquois, the latter being killed by a Huron who imagined that the presence of the Jesuits had brought curses upon his tribe.

The missions in the Huron country were now entirely abandoned. A few surviving Jesuits followed their flocks to the islands of Lake Huron; but in June, 1650, the enterprise was forsaken and the missionaries, with a number of their converts, retired to a village, founded for them, on the Island of Orleans, near Quebec. This settlement being in time ravaged by the Iroquois, a final stand was made at Lorette, also in the outskirts of Quebec, which mission exists to this day.

The great Huron mission, which had been conducted for thirty-five years, had employed twenty-nine missionaries, of whom seven had lost their lives in the work. This important field forsaken, many of the missionaries had returned to Europe disheartened, and apparently the future for Jesuit missions in New France looked gloomy enough. The Iroquois had now practically destroyed the Montagnais between Quebec and the Saguenay, the Algonkins of the Ottawa, and the Hurons, Petuns, and Neutrals. The French colonies of Quebec, Three Rivers, and Montreal had suffered from repeated raids of the New York confederates, and their forest trade was now almost wholly destroyed. In this hour of darkness, light suddenly broke upon New France. The politic Iroquois, attacked on either side by the Eries and the Susquehannas, and fearing that while thus engaged their northern victims might revive for combined vengeance, sent overtures of peace to Quebec, and cordially invited to their cantonments the once detested black gowns.

V. *THE IROQUOIS MISSION*

Champlain had early made enemies of the Iroquois, by attacking them as the allies of his Algonkin neighbors. This enmity extended to all New France, and lasted, with brief intervals of peace, for over half a century. We have seen that Jogues was the first of his order (1642) to enter the Iroquois country, as a prisoner of the Mohawks, the easternmost of the five tribes of the confederacy. Two years later, Bressani, while on his way to the Huron missions, was captured by the Mohawks, passed through a similar experience of torture, was sold to the Dutch, and transported back to France, and again like Jogues resumed his hazardous task of attempting to tame the American savage. During the first peace (May, 1646), Jogues, now in civilian costume, paid a brief visit to his former tormentors on the Mohawk, this time conveying only expressions of good-will from the governor of New France. His political errand accomplished, he returned to Quebec; but in August was back again, with a young French attendant named Lalande, intent on opening a mission among the Iroquois. Meanwhile, there had been a revulsion of sentiment on their part, and the two Frenchmen had no sooner reached the Mohawk than they were tortured and killed.

During an Iroquois attack upon Quebec, seven years later
(1653), Father Joseph Anthony Poncet was taken prisoner
by the marauders and carried to the Mohawk, where he suffered in the same manner as his predecessors; but his captors
being now desirous of a renewal of peace with the French,
spared his life, and sent him back to Quebec with overtures
for a renewal of negotiations. Early in July, 1654, Father
Simon le Moyne was sent forth upon a tour of inspection, and
returned to Quebec in September, with glowing reports of the
fervor of his reception by both Mohawks and Onondagas. It
was determined to rear a mission among the latter, and
thither (1655),—a four weeks' voyage,—proceeded Claude
Dablon and Peter Mary Joseph Chaumonot: while to appease
the jealous Mohawks, Le Moyne at the same time reopened a
brief but unprosperous mission among that tribe.

At first, Dablon and Chaumonot had high hopes of their
Onondaga enterprise; but mistrust soon arose in the minds of
the natives, and Dablon found it necessary to proceed to Quebec
and obtain fresh evidences of the friendship of the French.
He returned in the early summer of 1656, accompanied by
Fathers Francis Le Mercier, superior of the Canadian mission,
and René Ménard, two lay brothers, and a party of French
colonists under a militia captain, who designed founding a
settlement in the land of the Iroquois. By the close of the
year, the work was in a promising stage; a number of
Christianized Hurons, who had been adopted into the confederacy, formed a nucleus for proselyting, several Iroquois
converts had been made, and all five of the tribes had been
visited by the missionaries.

Fathers Paul Ragueneau and Joseph Imbert Dupéron, who
had been sent from Quebec in July, 1657, to assist the Onondaga mission, reached it only after many perils en route; for
meanwhile, there had been a fresh Iroquois uprising against
the Hurons and Ottawas, in which Father Leonard Garreau
lost his life near Montreal, and the entire confederacy was
soon in an uproar against the white allies of its ancient enemies.
The intrepid Le Moyne joined the party in November, and in

the following March (1658), on learning that all of the French
had been condemned to death, the entire colony stole away in
the night, and reached Montreal only after a long and
hazardous voyage. The great Iroquois mission, which had
promised so happily and cost so much in blood and treasure,
was now thought to be a thing of the past.

There was, however, still another chapter to the story. In
the summer of 1660, after two years of bloody forays against
New France, a Cayuga sachem, who had been converted at
Onondaga, came to Montreal as a peace messenger, asking for
another black gown to minister to the native converts and a
number of French captives in the Iroquois towns. Once more
Le Moyne cheerfully set out upon what seemed a path to
death; but he passed the winter without molestation, and in the
spring following was allowed to return to Canada with the
French prisoners.

It was five years later (1665), before the government of
New France felt itself sufficiently strong to threaten chastisement of the raiding Iroquois, who had long been making life
a torment in the colonies on the St. Lawrence. The Oneidas,
Onondagas, Cayugas, and Senecas sued for peace; but the
Mohawks were obstinate, and their villages were wasted by
fire until they too asked for mercy and the ministrations of the
Jesuits. Fathers James Fremin, James Bruyas, and John Pier-
ron were sent out in 1667; later, they were assisted by Julian
Garnier, Stephen de Carheil, Peter Milet, and Boniface, so
that by the close of 1668 a mission was in progress in each of
the five cantonments. A few notable converts were made,
among them Catherine Tegakouita, known as the "Iroquois
Saint"; Catherine Ganneaktena, an Erie captive who afterwards founded a native mission village on the banks of the St.
Lawrence; the head-men Assendasé, Kryn, and Soenrese. But
a great success was never possible; here as elsewhere, the
vices and superstitions of the tribesman were deep-rooted, and
they had not yet reached a stage of culture where the spiritual
doctrines of Christianity appealed strongly, save to a few
emotional natures. The converts were subjected to so many

annoyances and dangers, that isolation was thought essential, and there was established for them opposite Montreal the palisaded mission of St. Francis Xavier; this settlement, fostered by the French as a buffer against Iroquois attack on the colonists, was subsequently removed to Sault St. Louis, and is known in our day as Caughnawaga. This mission, and that of the Sulpitians on Montreal Mountain—later removed to the neighboring Lake of the Two Mountains—, and at Quinté Bay, were frequently recruited by Iroquois Christians who were carefully instructed by the missionaries in the arts of agriculture and the rites of the church.

This depletion of the Iroquois population alarmed the sachems of the confederacy. To please them, Governor Dongan of New York, himself a Catholic, introduced to the Five Nations three English Jesuits, who sought in vain to counteract the movement. The French did not abandon the Iroquois mission field until 1687, when the rising power of the English obliged them to withdraw from the country. We have, however, glimpses of occasional attempts thereafter to revive the work, Bruyas being on the ground in 1701, joined the following year by James de Lamberville, Garnier, and Le Valliant, and later by James d'Hue and Peter de Marieul. The entire party were again driven from the cantonments in 1708, De Marieul being the last of his order to remain on duty.

Thereafter, the Jesuits were chiefly devoted to their mission at Caughnawaga, whither many Iroquois retreated before the inroads of Dutch and English settlers who were now crowding upon their lands. When the black gowns were at last expelled from New France, secular priests continued their work among the remnants of those New York Indians who had sought protection by settling among the French colonists on the St. Lawrence.

VI. *THE OTTAWA MISSION*

This embraced the tribes beyond Lake Huron,—the Chippewas at Sault Ste. Marie, the Beavers, the Crees, the Ottawas and refugee Hurons on Lake Superior, the Menomonees, Pottawattomies, Sacs, Foxes, Winnebagoes, Miamis, Illinois, and those of the Sioux who lived on or near the banks of the Mississippi. The Ottawas were the first Indians from the upper lakes to trade with the French, hence that vast district became early known as the country of the Ottawas.

The Huron mission was the door to the Ottawa mission. Jogues and Raimbault were with the Chippewas at Sault Ste. Marie in 1641; but it was nineteen years after that (1660), before they were followed by another Jesuit, the veteran Father Ménard, who accompanied an Ottawa fleet up the great river of that name, through Lake Huron and the Sault, and on to Keweenaw Bay, where he said the first mass heard on the shores of the northern sea. After a wretched winter on that inhospitable coast, spent in a shanty of fir boughs, with savage neighbors who reviled his presence, he proceeded inland intent on ministering to some Hurons who had fled from Iroquois persecution to the gloomy pine forest about the upper waters of Black River, in what is now Wisconsin. In August, 1661, he lost his life at a portage, thus being the first martyr upon the Ottawa mission.

Four years later, Claude Allouez set out for Lake Superior, and reaching Chequamegon Bay in October (1665), built a little chapel of bark upon the southwest shore of that rock-bound estuary,—the famous mission of La Pointe. His flock was a medley, Hurons, and Algonkins here clustering in two villages, where they lived on fish, safe at last from the raging Iroquois, although much pestered by the wild Sioux of the west. For thirty years did Allouez travel from tribe to tribe, through the forests and over the prairies of the vast wilderness which a century later came to be organized into the Northwest Territory, and established missions at Green Bay, Sault Ste. Marie, on the Miami, and, with Marquette, among the Illinois at Kaskaskia.

Later, there arrived on the scene Fathers Louis Nicholas, James Marquette, Dablon, Louis André, Druillettes, Albanel, and others. The field of the Northwest seemed at first, as did the Huron mission, highly promising. The missionaries were everywhere greeted by large audiences, and much curiosity was displayed concerning the rites of the church; but, as usual, the nomadic habits of the Indians rendered instruction difficult. The fathers, with great toil and misery, and subject to daily danger and insult, followed their people about upon long hunting and fishing expeditions; and even when the bands had returned to the squalid villages, life there was almost as comfortless as upon the trail. Among the donnés and the Jesuit coadjutor brothers were skillful workers in metal, who repaired the guns and utensils of the natives, and taught them how best to obtain and reduce the ore from lead and copper deposits. We have evidence that the copper region of Lake Superior was at times resorted to by the lay followers and their Indian attendants, to obtain material for crucifixes and for the medals which the missionaries gave to converts; and in the lead mines centering about where are now Dubuque, Iowa, and Galena, Ill., the missionary attendants and Indians obtained lead for barter with French fur-traders, who, like the soldiers of the Cross, were by this time wandering all over the Northwest.

Marquette had succeeded Alloüez at La Pointe, in 1669; but it was not long before the Hurons and Ottawas of Chequamegon Bay foolishly incurred the fresh hostility of the Sioux, and the following year were driven eastward like autumn leaves before a blast. Marquette established them in a new mission, at Point St. Ignace, opposite Mackinaw; and it was from here that, in 1673, he joined the party of Louis Joliet, en route to the Mississippi River. The St. Ignace mission became the largest and most successful in the Northwest, there being encamped there, during Marquette's time, about 500 Hurons and 1,300 Ottawas. The interesting story of Marquette, a familiar chapter in American history, will be fully developed in the documents of this series: and we shall be able to present for the first time a facsimile of the original Ms. Journal of his final and fatal voyage (1674), which is preserved among the many treasures of the Jesuit College of St. Mary's, in Montreal.[1]

After the suspension of the publication of the *Relations*, in 1673, we obtain few glimpses of the Ottawa mission, save in the occasional references of travelers. The several local missions in the district were, in the main, probably more successful than those in any of the other fields of endeavor. La Pointe, Green Bay, St. Ignace (later Mackinac), Sault Ste. Marie, St. Joseph's, and Kaskaskia became the most important of them all; and at some of these points Catholic missions are still maintained by Franciscan friars and secular priests, for resident French Creoles and Indians. The uprising of the Foxes against French power, which lasted spasmodically from about 1700 to 1755, greatly hampered the work of the Jesuits; they did not, during this period, entirely absent themselves from the broad country of the Ottawas, but conversions were few and the records slight.

There was, for a time, governmental attempt to supplant the Western Jesuits with Récollets. Several friars were with La Salle, who had a great antipathy to the disciples of Loyola,— Father Hennepin's adventures belong to this period of Récollet effort, his colleagues at Fort Crèvecoeur being Brothers Ribourde and Membré; but their mission closed with the Iroquois repulse of the French from Crèvecoeur, and the consequent death of Ribourde. When La Salle retired from the region, Allöuez resumed the Illinois mission of the Jesuits; and soon after there arrived upon the ground Fathers Gravier, Marest, Mermet, and Pinet, who, because of the more docile character of the tribes collectively known as the Illinois,— Kaskaskias, Cahokias, Peorias, and Tamaroas,—found here a relatively fruitful field. In time, French settlements grew up around the palisaded missions, inter-marriages occurred, and the work flourished for many years. Black gowns visited the properous Illinois towns as late as 1781, when the death of Father Meurin closed the work of his order in the Northwest.

[1] *Ibid.*, lix, p. 212, ff.

VII. *THE LOUISIANA MISSION*

The Jesuit Marquette was in Louisanna in 1673, but established no mission. Nine years later, Membré, of the Récollets, accompanied La Salle into the region, and instructed natives as far down the Mississippi as the mouth; and with La Salle at his death were Anastasius Douay, of the Récollets, and the Sulpitian Cavalier. In 1698, Francis Jolliet de Montigny and Anthony Davion, priests of the Seminary of Quebec, established missions on the Yazoo, among the Natchez, and elsewhere in the neighborhood; to their aid, soon came others of their house,—St. Côme, Gaulin, Fonçault, and Erborie, who labored until 1710, when St. Côme and Fonçault being killed by roving Indians, the survivors retired to the North. The Jesuit Du Rue accompanied Iberville into the country in 1699-1700, followed by De Limoges and Dongé, of his order, their work continuing until about 1704.

In 1721, Father Charlevoix reported that but two priests were then in Louisiana, one at Yazoo and another in New Orleans; at the latter post, a chaplain of some sort was established throughout the French régime. Capuchins and Jesuits were both admitted to Louisiana, in 1722, the former to serve as priests to the French of the country, chiefly at New Orleans and Natchez, while the Jesuits were restricted to the Indian missions, although permitted to maintain a house in the outskirts of New Orleans. It was not long before the Illinois mission became attached to Louisiana, and missionaries for that field usually entered upon their work by way of the New Orleans house. Missions were maintained in the villages of the Arkansas, Yazoo, Choctaws, and Alibamons; but the uprising of the Indians in the Natchez district, in 1727, led to the fall of these several missions, together with that of the French colonies above New Orleans. Father Du Poisson was killed by savages at Natchez, where he was temporarily supplying the French settlers in the absence of their Capuchin friar; Souel fell a victim to the Yazoos, at whose hands Doutreleau narrowly escaped destruction. However, the Jesuits did not despair, but soon returned to the Lower Mississippi, where they continued their labors until about 1770, although the order had in 1762 been suppressed in France.

The Louisiana mission of the Jesuits, while producing several martyrs, and rich in striking examples of missionary zeal, has yielded but meagre documentary results; few of the papers in the present series touch upon its work, and indeed detailed knowledge thereof is not easily obtainable. Severed from Canada by a long stretch of wilderness, communication with the St. Lawrence basin was difficult and spasmodic, and in the case of the Jesuits generally unnecessary; for, having their own superior at New Orleans, his allegiance was to the general of the order in France, not to his fellow-superiors in Quebec and Montreal. The several missions of New France played a large part in American history; that of Louisiana, although interesting, is of much less importance.

THE RELATIONS

A few explorers like Champlain, Radisson, and Perrot have left valuable narratives behind them, which are of prime importance in the study of the beginnings of French settlement in America; but it is to the Jesuits that we owe the great body of our information concerning the frontiers of New France in the seventeenth century. It was their duty annually to transmit to their superior in Quebec, or Montreal, a written journal of their doings; it was also their duty to pay occasional visits to their superior, and to go into retreat at the central house of the Canadian Mission. Annually, between 1632 and 1673, the superior made up a narrative, or *Relation*, of the most important events which had occurred in the several missionary districts under his charge, sometimes using the exact words of the Missionaries, and sometimes with considerable editorial skill summarizing the individual journals in a general account, based in part upon the oral reports of the visiting fathers. This annual *Relation*, which in bibliographies occasionally bears the name of the superior, and at other times of the missionary chiefly contributing to it, was forwarded to the provincial of the order in France, and, after careful scrutiny and re-editing, published by him in a series of duodecimo volumes, known collectively as *The Jesuit Relations*.

The authors of the journals which formed the basis of the *Relations* were for the most part men of trained intellect, acute observers, and practised in the art of keeping records of their experiences. They had left the most highly civilized country of their times, to plunge at once into the heart of the American wilderness, and attempt to win to the Christian faith the fiercest savages known to history. To gain these savages, it was first necessary to know them intimately,—their speech, their habits, their manner of thought, their strong points and their weak. These first students of the North American Indian were not only amply fitted for their undertaking, but none have since had a better opportunity for its prosecution. They were explorers, as well as priests. Bancroft was inexact when he said, in the oft-quoted phrase, "Not a cape was turned, not a river entered, but a Jesuit led the way." The actual pioneers of New France were almost always coureurs de bois, in the prosecution of the fur trade; but coureurs de bois, for obvious reasons, seldom kept records, even when capable of doing so, and as a rule we learn of their previous appearance on the scene only through chance allusions in the *Relations*. The Jesuits performed a great service to mankind in publishing their annals, which are, for historian, geographer, and ethnologist, among our first and best authorities.

Many of the *Relations* were written in Indian camps, amid a chaos of distractions. Insects innumerable tormented the journalists, they were immersed in scenes of squalor and degradation, overcome by fatigue and lack of proper sustenance, often suffering from wounds and disease, maltreated in a hundred ways by hosts who, at times, might more properly be called jailers; and not seldom had savage superstition risen to such a height, that to be seen making a memorandum was certain to arouse the ferocious enmity of the band. It is not surprising that the composition of these journals of the Jesuits is sometimes crude; the wonder is, that they could be written at all. Nearly always the style is simple and direct. Never does the narrator descend to self-glorification, or dwell unnecessarily upon the details of his continual martyrdom; he never complains of his lot; but sets forth his experience in phrases the most matter-of-fact. His meaning is seldom obscure. We gain from his pages a vivid picture of life in the primeval forest, as he lived it; we seem to see him upon his long canoe journeys, squatted amidst his dusky fellows, working his passage at the paddles, and carrying cargoes upon the portage trail: we see him the butt and scorn of the savage camp, sometimes deserted in the heart of the wilderness, and obliged to wait for another flotilla, or to make his way alone as best he can. Arrived at last, at his journey's end, we often find him vainly seeking for shelter in the squalid huts of the natives, with every man's hand against him, but his own heart open to them all. We find him, even when at last domiciled in some far-away village, working against hope to save the unbaptized from eternal damnation; we seem to see the rising storm of opposition, invoked by native medicine-men,—who to his seventeeth century imagination seem devils indeed,—and at last the bursting climax of superstitious frenzy which sweeps him and his before it. Not only do these devoted missionaries, —never in any field, has been witnessed greater personal heroism than theirs,—live and breathe before us in the *Relations;* but we have in them our first competent account of the Red Indian, at a time when relatively uncontaminated by contact with Europeans. We seem, in the *Relations,* to know this crafty savage, to measure him intellectually as well as physically, his inmost thoughts as well as open speech. The fathers did not understand him from an ethnological point of view, as well as he is today understood; their minds were tinctured with the scientific fallacies of their time. But, with what is known today, the photographic reports in the *Relations* help the student to an accurate picture of the untamed aborigine, and much that mystified the fathers, is now, by aid of their careful journals, easily susceptible of explanation.

Few periods of history are so well illuminated as the French regime in North America. This we owe in large measure to the existence of the Jesuit *Relations*.

What are generally known as the *Relations* proper, addressed to the superior and published in Paris, under direction of the provincial, commence with Le Jeune's *Brieve Relation du Voyage de la Nouvelle-France* (1632); and thereafter a duodecimo volume, neatly printed and bound in vellum, was issued annually from the press of Sebastien Cramoisy, in Paris, until 1673, when the series was discontinued, probably through the influence of Frontenac, to whom the Jesuits were distasteful. The *Relations* at once became popular in the court circles of France; their regular appearance was always awaited with the keenest interest, and assisted greatly in creating and fostering the enthusiasm of pious philanthropists, who for many years substantially maintained the missions of New France. In addition to these forty volumes, which to collectors are technically known as "Cramoisys," many similar publications found their way into the hands of the public, the greater part of them bearing date after the suppression of the Cramoisy series. Some were printed in Paris and Lyons by independent publishers; others appeared in Latin and Italian texts, at Rome and other cities in Italy; while in such journals as *Mercure François* and *Annuae Litterae Societatis Jesu*, occasionally were published letters from the missionaries, of the same nature as the *Relations*, but briefer and more intimate in tone.

It does not appear, however, that popular interest in these publications materially affected the secular literature of the period; they were largely used in Jesuit histories of New France, but by others were practically ignored. General literary interest in the *Relations* was only created about a half century ago, when Dr. E. B. O'Callaghan, editor of the *Documentary History of New York*, called attention to their great value as storehouses of contemporary information. Dr. John G. Shea, author of *History of the Catholic Missions Among the Indian Tribes of the United States*, and Father Felix Martin,

S. J., of Montreal, soon came forward, with fresh studies of the *Relations*. Collectors at once commenced searching for Cramoisys, which were found to be exceedingly scarce,—most of the originals having been literally worn out in the hands of their devout seventeenth century readers; finally, the greatest collector of them all, James Lenox, of New York, out-stripped his competitors and laid the foundation, in the Lenox Library, of what is today probably the only complete collection in America. In 1858, the Canadian government reprinted the Cramoisys, with a few additions, in three stout octavo volumes, carefully edited by Abbés Làverdière, Plante, and Ferland. These, too, are now rare, copies seldom being offered for sale.

The Quebec reprint was followed by two admirable series brought out by Shea and O'Callaghan respectively. Shea's *Cramoisy Series* (1857-1866), numbers twenty-five little volumes, the edition of each of which was limited to a hundred copies, now difficult to obtain; it contains for the most part entirely new matter, chiefly *Relations* prepared for publication by the superiors, after 1672, and miscellaneously printed; among the volumes, however, are a few reprints of particularly rare issues of the original Cramoisy press. The O'Callaghan series, seven in number, (the edition limited to twenty-five copies), contains different material from Shea's, but of the same character. A further addition to the mass of material was made by Father Martin, in *Relations Inédites de la Nouvelle-France*, 1672-79 (2 vols., Paris, 1861); and by Father Carayon in *Première Mission des Jésuites au Canada* (Paris, 1864). In 1871 there was published at Quebec, under the editorship of Abbés Laverdière and Casgrain, *Le Journal des Jésuites*, from the original manuscript in the archives of the Seminary of Quebec (now Laval University). The memoranda contained in this volume,—a rarity, for the greater part of the edition was accidentally destroyed by fire,— were not intended for publication, being of the character of private records, covering the operations of the Jesuits in New France between 1645 and 1668. The *Journal* is, however, an indispensable complement of the *Relations*. It was reprinted by a Montreal publisher (J. M. Valois) in 1892, but even this later edition is already exhausted. Many interesting epistles are found in *Letters Édifiantes es Curieuses, écrites des Missions Étrangères,* which cover the Jesuit missions in many lands, between the years of 1702 and 1776; only a small portion of this publication (there are several editions, ranging from 1702-1776 to 1875-77) is devoted to the North American Missions.

American historians from Shea and Parkman down, have already made liberal use of the *Relations,* and here and there antiquarians and historical societies have published fragmentary translations. The great body of the *Relations* and their allied documents, however, has never been Englished. The text is difficult, for their French is not the French of the modern schools; hence these interesting papers have been doubly inaccessible to the majority of our historical students. The present edition,[1] while faithfully reproducing the old French text, even in most of its errors, offers to the public, for the first time, an English rendering side by side with the original.

In breadth of scope, also, this edition will, through the generous enterprise of the publishers, really be first in the field. Not only will it embrace all of the original Cramoisy series, the Shea and O'Callaghan series, those collected by Fathers Martin and Carayon, the *Journal des Jésuites,* and such of the *Lettres Édifiantes* as touch upon the North American Missions, but many other valuable documents which have not previously been reprinted. It will contain, also, considerable hitherto-unpublished material from the manuscripts in the archives of St. Mary's College, Montreal, and other depositories. The several documents will be illustrated by faithful reproductions of all the maps and other engravings appearing in the old editions, besides much new material obtained especially for this edition, a prominent feature of which will be authentic

---

[1] *The Jesuit Relations and Allied Documents,* in 73 volumes, edited by Reuben Gold Thwaites, 1896-1901.

portraits of many of the early fathers, and photographic facsimiles of pages from their manuscript letters.

In the preface to each volume will be given such Bibliographical Data concerning its contents, as seem necessary to the scholar. The appended notes consist of historical, biographical, archeological, and miscellaneous comment, which it is hoped may tend to the elucidation of the text. An exhaustive General Index to the English text will appear in the final volume of the Series.

Ibid., i., p. 1, ff.

PART I
THE BEGINNINGS OF THE JESUIT MISSIONS IN NORTH AMERICA
1611—1634

I

AN ACCOUNT OF THE CANADIAN MISSION FROM THE YEAR 1611 UNTIL THE YEAR 1613

By Joseph Jouvency, a Priest of the Society of Jesus

[Father Jouvency, one of the eighteenth-century historians of the Society of Jesus, herein gives an historical account of the Canadian missions of his order, in 1611-13; and, by way of comparison, tells of the condition of the same missions in 1703, ending with a list of the Jesuit missions in North America in the year 1710, the date of original publication.—*The Jesuit Relations and Allied Documents.* i., 47.]

BEGINNING AND FIRST FRUITS OF THE CANADIAN MISSION

The French had, since the year 1524, often visited the coasts of America opposite to France, but cursorily, and, as it were, while passing by. Finally, at the beginning of the last century, Samuel Champlain, who well deserves to be called the parent of the Canadian colony, entered the region of the interior. Already was the undertaking progressing very favorably, when Henry IV., more solicitous for religion than for commerce, resolved, in the year 1608, to introduce Christian rites into this part of the New World, and asked members of the Society to undertake this Apostolic enterprise.

Upon being informed of the plan of the King, and ordered to choose as soon as possible energetic priests who would lay solidly the foundations of so great a work, Father Coton, the confessor of the King, informed the Commander of the Society. From the whole number, not only of youths, but

3

also of old men, who sought this laborious duty, there were
chosen Father Peter Biard, of Grenoble, a professor of theology
in the college of Lyons, and Father Ennemond Massé, of
Lyons. The unforeseen death of the King delayed this auspi-
cious enterprise, and diminished the enthusiasm of the friends
of the Society, who were providing a ship and other necessaries
for the voyage. But the pious Coton, unconquered by adversity,
brought in the authority of the Queen, in order that he might
overcome the difficulties in his way. As a result, the time was
set for their departure, and the Fathers hastened to Dieppe,
in order that they might sail thence for New France.

Having entered at last the mouth of the St. Lawrence River
on the 22nd day of May, on the holy day of Pentecost, they
came upon some traces of the Christian religion, which had
been superficially impressed by those whom we have mentioned
as having journeyed from France into this region. For, since
the speech of the people was unknown to them, and they had
no certain and fixed residence in this savage land, there was no
opportunity for educating those whom they chanced to
baptize, and who, plunging again into their former habits,
scarcely retained the Christian name, while defiling it with
their native vices.

The first concern of the Fathers was to build a chapel, to
learn the language of the country, and to instruct the Frenchmen who had emigrated from old to new France. Then, going
forth, as it were, from the city walls, the heralds of the church
traversed a great part of the country. A godly act was performed whenever opportunity allowed; hands were laid upon
the sick; services were rendered to the French who were establishing new homes, nor were seamen and ships' passengers neglected. Meanwhile, so great a scarcity of provisions existed,
that for each week a ration was allotted, so scanty that it was
hardly sufficient for one day; namely, ten ounces of bread,
half a pound of salted meat, and a handful of pease or beans.
In addition to this, each man was his own mechanic, mender,
miller, cook, hewer of wood and drawer of water. There
occurred sometimes to the Fathers, in the midst of the miseries,

the words of those to whom Moses had given the task of reconnoitering Canaan: *This land . . . devoureth . . . the inhabitants . . . there we saw certain monsters of the sons of Enac of the giant-kind: in comparison of whom, we seemed like locusts.* But at the same time there came into mind the speech of Joshua and of Caleb, full of divine trust: *The land which we have gone round is very good. If the Lord be favorable, he will bring us into it. . . . Fear ye not the people of this land . . . the Lord is with us.*

SETTLEMENTS AND MISSIONS OF THE SOCIETY IN NEW FRANCE

And that the Lord is with his servants and soldiers, the outcome has proved. For, in the beginning of this year, 1703, while we are writing these things, there are numbered in this formerly *solitary and unexplored country* more than thirty very prosperous and well-equipped Missions of our Society, besides the college of Quebec. The first of these, in sight of Quebec, at the tenth mile-stone from the city, is called Lorette. Another is situated in the district of Tadoussac, on the shore of the river St. Lawrence, sixty leagues below Quebec toward the east. Three others, above Quebec itself, extend far into the North about Lake St. John; one in that place which takes its name from the seven islands; another in the district of Chigutimini, the third on the Saguenay River. There they minister to the Montagnais, the Papinachois, the Mistassins, and other wandering tribes.

Now, if you journey toward the regions of the setting sun, and the source of the St. Lawrence River, you will find upon its northern bank a district called Three rivers, because there three rivers flow together; it is distant from Quebec, seven or eight days' journey. Here, there formerly flourished the most successful mission of the Algonquins; but it has been much weakened through drunkenness induced by brandy, brought in by the European merchants who thus wickedly derive an easy profit. But these losses are compensated by the virtue and

piety of the Abenakis. Among them a mission of three stations has been established; one located among them, not far
from Quebec, on the forty-sixth parallel of latitude, distinguished by the name and patronage of St. Francis de Sales:
the other two are more remote, at a place named Nipisikouit.
Across the St. Lawrence River, to the South, extend the five
nations of the Iroquois. There are among them seven stations
of the Evangelists, scattered through a hundred and fifty
leagues. Of these, six were destroyed in the war, which arose
between the French and the Iroquois, about the year 1682.
Peace, together with the recall of the missionaries, in the year
1702, restored all things to their previous condition. Among
these Missions of the Iroquois, that one is especially flourishing which is named for St. Francis Xavier, at Montreal.[1]

Above the Iroquois, toward the west and North, between the
fortieth and the forty-fifth parallels, one may see two great
lakes joined by a narrow strait; the larger one is called the
lake of the Ilinois, the other the lake of the Hurons.[2] These
are separated by a large peninsula, at the point of which is
situated the Mission of St. Ignatius, or Missilimakinac.[3] Above
those two lakes there is a third, greater than either, called lake
superior. At the entrance of this lake has been established the
Mission of Ste. Marie at the Sault.[4] The space between this
and two smaller lakes is occupied by the Outaouki, among
whom the Society has many stations. Three such citadels of
religion (for thus it is proper to call the Missions), whence
she leads forth her soldiers and unfurls her sacred standards,

[1] The Iroquois mission of St. Francis Xavier was founded in 1669 by Iroquois
Christians,—emigrants from the "castles" of the Five Nations. The mission was
finally removed to Sault St. Louis, on the St. Lawrence.—Ibid., i., note 52. See
p. 291, ff.

[2] Lake Michigan and Lake Huron.

[3] The mission of St. Ignace was founded by Marquette in 1670, on Point
Ignace, on the mainland north and opposite the Island of Michellimackinac (now
shortened to Mackinaw or Mackinac, as fancy dictates).—Ibid., i, note 55.

[4] The mission of Sault Ste. Marie, at the outlet of Lake Superior, was founded
by Raimbault and Jogues in 1640. The place was always an important rallying
point for the natives, and naturally became the center of a wide-spreading fur
trade, which lasted, under French, English, and American dominations in turn,
until about 1840.—Ibid., i, note 56.

have been located about the lake of the Ilinois; the first, among the Puteatamis, and called the Mission of St. Joseph; another, among the Kikarous, Maskoutens, and Outagamies, and possessing the name of St. Francis Xavier [1], the third, among the Oumiamis, has the name of the Guardian Angel.

Below the lakes which have been mentioned, above Florida, the Ilinois roam throughout the most extensive territories. There, a very large station, named from the immaculate conception of the Virgin Mother, is divided into three Missions, and extends as far as the river Mississippi. Upon the banks of the same river is situated the mission of Baiogula, at the thirty-first parallel of latitude; and it extends down that stream toward the gulf of Mexico.

There remains unknown to Europeans, up to the present time, an immense portion of Canada, beyond the Mississippi River, situated beneath a milder sky, well-inhabited, and abounding in animal and vegetable life. So it is, likewise, with another region far dissimilar to that, around the frozen Hudson bay, from the fifty-fifth parallel to the sixtieth or seventieth; lying at the north, plunged in snows and frosts, it even more justly implores aid, as it is afflicted by more weighty ills. Here the Society, a few years ago, first began to plant its footsteps. Not without great exertion are the gates of Tartarus, which hold burdened souls in unmerited bondage, broken down; nor did the Canadian Mission itself, now flourishing with so many settlements, all at once attain its full development. Grievously, through sixteen years did it, so to speak, stick in a rough road; indeed, it did not take shape until 1625; when it was extricated from its perplexities by the aid of Father Peter Coten, to whom it owed its origin.

Now we return to the natal days, full of hardships and dangers, of the toilsome Mission, which, scarcely born, was almost exterminated in its cradle by the English.

---

[1] The Western mission of St. Francis Xavier was founded by Allouez in 1669, at the first rapids in the Fox river (of Green Bay), on the east side of the river, in what is now Depere, Wis. An important Indian village had from the earliest historic times been located there.—*Ibid.*, i., *note* 57. *See* p. 338, ff.

THE CANADIAN MISSION DRIVEN OUT
BY THE ENGLISH

To our comrades residing in that place there had come as a reinforcement, on the 15th day of May, 1613, Father Quentin and Brother Gilbert du Thet, provided with a royal commission, by which they were empowered to establish a new settlement in a suitable location. They found the French intent upon founding a city, and unaware of the danger which threatened.

The English, a few years before, had occupied Virginia. While the English were sailing thither in the summer months of the year, 1613, and having lost their bearings and strayed from their course, they were gradually borne to the shore where the French had settled [1], not far from the port of St. Sauveur. When they learned that a French ship was stationed there, they made ready their weapons and entered the harbor. The English attacked the French ship, wherein few were drawn up in defense—for the others had departed to work on the buildings—and with no trouble captured her.

ONE OF THE MEMBERS OF THE SOCIETY IS
KILLED; THE OTHERS ARE EXPELLED
FROM CANADA

In the first onset Gilbert du Thet, a household assistant of the society, was stricken with a mortal wound. The rest of the Fathers, who were standing on the shore, were captured by Argall, the English commander. The unhappy crowd was placed upon two small ships, one of which directed its course straight toward France; the other, with some of the English, sailed for Virginia, thence to depart for France. Fathers Biard and Quentin embarked upon the latter; Father Massé and

---

[1] On what came to be known as Frenchman's Bay, on the east side of the island of Mount Desert. Parkman says (*Pioneers*, ed. 1865, p. 276, *note*): "Probably all of Frenchman's Bay was included under the name of the Harbor of St. Sauveur. The landing place so called seems to have been near the entrance of the bay. certainly south of Bar Harbor.—*Ibid.*, i., *note* 61.

Saussaye upon the former. The fortunes of these ships were widely diverse. While that which carried Saussaye and Father Massé was coasting along the shore, destitute of provisions, of seamen, and of equipment, she fell upon two ships preparing to return to France. She gladly joined herself to these, and, with her passengers, arrived in a few days at St. Malo, a town of Brittany.

Of the English ships which were following the lead of Argall, some were driven far from Virginia by the violence of the wind; others were swamped by the waves. One, which the Englishman Turnell commanded, and in which Fathers Quentin and Biard were being conveyed, after being driven continuously for sixteen days by tempests, was quickly borne to the Azores, islands on the coast of Africa belonging to the Portuguese.

But here a new danger arose. Turnell, fearing punishment because he was carrying with him and was holding under unjust conditions priests of the Society, who had been torn from their homes and robbed with the greatest brutality, began to consider plans for making way with them. Finally it seemed better to him to take refuge in their clemency and mildness, which he had observed amid the most grievous injuries. Nevertheless, he took measures that they should not enter the port, thinking that while the ship stood at anchor he might procure the necessary provisions by sending in a small boat.

The contrary to what he had expected happened. For, impelled by an inshore breeze, he entered the harbor, although unwillingly and reluctantly. Our friends, contrary to his deserts, interposed not even a word by which he might be accused, rejoicing because they had, in this manner, saved an enemy. The English captain recognized their kindness, and afterwards spoke with great praise of the Fathers. But this he did much more unreservedly when, borne by a storm to Pembroke, a city of England, he was suspected by the officials of that town of piracy on the high seas, because he was sailing in a French ship and produced no written authority by which he might justify his voyage. When he asserted that he had been separated by a storm from his commander, Argall, no credence was given to him.   In this crisis he mentioned as witnesses the two priests of the Society whom he had in the ship, and whose uncorrupted integrity could be doubted by no one.   When the Fathers, on being questioned, had given assurance that the affair was thus, he was released from danger.   He made the requital which was due to their kindness, and took care that they should not only suffer no harm, but even that they should be shown honor by the officials.   Meantime the ambassador of the Most Christian King, upon being informed of the toilsome voyage of the Fathers, carried on negotiations with the King of England concerning their restoration to France.   With his consent, they arrived, in the tenth month after their capture, joyfully and safely among their Brethren at Amiens.

APPENDIX

MISSIONS OF THE SOCIETY OF JESUS IN NORTH AMERICA IN THE YEAR *1710*

MISSIONS among the Abinnakis.

Mission of the Holy Guardian Angel.

Baiogula mission.

Chigoutimini mission.

Mission of St. Francis de Sales.

Mission of St. Francis Xavier

Huron residence

Mission of St. Ignatius.

Mission of the Immaculate Conception.

Mission at the seven Islands.

Mission of St. Joseph.

Missions among the Ilinois.

Missions among the Iroquois.

Mission of Lorette.

Mission on the banks and at the mouth of the Mississippi River.

Residence of Montreal.

Nipisikouit mission.

Missions among the Outakouacs.

Saguenay mission

Mission of Sault de Sainte Marie.

Forest missions.

Tadoussac mission.

Mission at Three Rivers.

Number of brethren . . . 42

[*Ibid.*, i., *Doc.* vii.]

II

LETTER FROM FATHER CHARLES L'ALEMANT,[1] SUPERIOR OF THE MISSIONS OF CANADA, TO THE VERY REVEREND FATHER MUTIO VITELLESCHI, GENERAL OF THE SOCIETY OF JESUS, AT ROME

(1626)

[The Jesuit mission in Acadia had abruptly closed with the attack by Argall (1613). Meantime, the Récollet friars were conducting their missions upon and beyond the St. Lawrence; but,—as related in the Introduction,[2]—finding themselves unequal to the great task,—they invited the Jesuits to return to New France and aid them in the conversion of the savages. The first of the "black gowns" to arrive (April, 1625), were Charles Lalemant, Massé, and Brébeuf.—*Ibid.*, iv., 2.]

VERY REVEREND FATHER IN CHRIST:

The peace of Christ be with you.

Your Paternity need not be surprised to have received no letters from us during the year since our last; for we are

[1] Charles Lalemant (also written L'ALemand, L'Almand, Lallemant and Allemand) was born at Paris, Nov. 17, 1587. In March, 1625, he was appointed superior of the mission at Quebec, whither he went with his brethren Massé and Brébeuf and the Récollet missionary Joseph La Roche-Daillen. Here Lalemant remained till November, 1627, when he went to France to procure supplies. Returning in the following May, the ship was captured by Admiral Kirk, the Jesuits being sent to England, and later to France. In June, 1629, Lalemant, with several other Jesuits, made a second attempt to return to Canada; but they were shipwrecked, and Lalemant was taken back to France by a Basque fishing vessel. Quebec having meantime been captured by the English, the Canadian missions were interrupted until 1632, when the region was restored to France. In April, 1634, his superiors granted his earnest request that he might again go to Canada. He was placed in charge, with Massé and De Noüe, of the chapel, "Notre-Dame de Recouvrance" (built by Champlain on his return to New France) and was the latter's friend and spiritual director, attending him at his death. Lalemant returned to France in 1639, and there he died Nov. 18, 1674.—*Ibid.*, iv., *note* 20.

[2] *See* p. xxiv.

so remote from the seacoast that we are visited only once a year by French vessels, and then only by those to whom navigation hither is allowed, for to others it is interdicted, so that, if by any mischance these merchant ships should be wrecked, or be taken by pirates, we could look to Divine providence alone for our daily bread. For from the savages, who have scarcely the necessaries of life for themselves, nothing is to be hoped; but he who hitherto provided for the needs of the French, who have dwelt here so many years only with a view to temporal gain, will not abandon his faithful ones who seek only the glory of God and the salvation of souls. During the past year we have devoted ourselves almost entirely to learning the dialect of the savages, excepting a month or two spent in cultivating the soil, in order to obtain such slight means of subsistence as we could. Father Jean Brebeuf,[1] a pious and prudent man, and of a robust constitution, passed the sharp winter season among the savages, acquiring a very considerable knowledge of this strange tongue. We, meantime, learning from interpreters who were very unwilling to communicate their knowledge, made as much progress as we could hope, contrary to the expectation of all. But these are only the rudiments of two languages; many more remain. For the languages are multiplied with the number of the tribes; and this land, extending so far in every direction, is inhabited by at least fifty different tribes, truly an immense field for our zeal. The harvest is great, the laborers are few; but they have, by God's grace, a courage undaunted by any obstacles, although the promise of success is not yet very great, so rude and almost brutish are the natives.

Our labors this year have had no further fruit than a knowledge of the country, of the natives, and of the dialects of two tribes, if the savages alone be considered. As regards the French, whose number does not exceed forty three, we have not been negligent. We have heard their general confessions, relating to their whole past life, after first holding an exhor-

[1] See p. 98, *note* 1.

tation on the necessity of this confession. Each month we have, moreover, preached two sermons to them.

We are, God be thanked, all well. . . . Hardly one of us uses bed linen when he sleeps. All our time that is not devoted to seeking the salvation of our fellow men and of ourselves is occupied in tilling the soil. Far greater would be our growth in virtue, if another of Our Brothers were not more desirable as superior. This is easy for Your Paternity to remedy, as I feel myself far better fitted for obedience than for command. I truly hope that Your Paternity, from whom I ask it with all possible submission, will grant me this.

Some workmen have been sent to us this year from France, to construct the first dwelling of the Society here, which we considered as quite indispensable on account of our French, who settle here and nowhere else. Others will be built later among other tribes from whom we expect greater results. To those that have fixed settlements we shall in a short time send one of our number, or rather two: Father Jean de Brébeuf and Father Anne de Noue. If their mission is successful, a most promising field will be opened for the Gospel. They must be taken there by the savages, for they cannot use any other boatmen.

With the consent of his superior, Father Philibert Noyrot [1] returns to France to promote as hitherto the interests of our enterprise. He stands in need of the influence of Your Paternity in order to negotiate freely with those who have charge of our affairs. Our own Father at Paris, for some reason, put difficulties in our way, and seems rather unfriendly to our mission; so that, but for the favor of Father Cotton of blessed memory, our affairs would have fallen to the ground.

---

[1] In 1626 Noyrot went to Quebec, taking with him twenty workmen to build a residence for the Jesuit missionaries there. Lalemant immediately sent him back to France, to report to Richelieu on the affairs of Canada, and to secure the removal of the Huguenots from the direction of the mercantile company. This resulted in the formation of the Company of New France.—*Ibid.*, iv., *note* 32. *See* p. 45, *note* 1.

As Father Noyrot is to return at the beginning of spring, another of our members will be absolutely necessary at Paris, or at Rouen, to fill his place and to look after our interests, sending us yearly what supplies we need, and receiving our letters, if Your Paternity so decide.   There remain thus seven of us here: four priests, Father Enemond Massé, as admonitor and confessor, Father Jean de Brébeuf, Father Anne de Nouë, and myself; and three lay brothers, Gilbert Burel, Jean Goffestre, and François Charreton, all of us ready to undertake any labors whatsoever for the glory of God.   We all commend ourselves to the Most Holy Sacrifices of Your Paternity.

Your Paternity's most humble son,

CHARLES LALEMANT.

New France,
   August 1st. [1626.]

[*Ibid.*, iv., *Doc.* xvii.]

III

BRIEF RELATION OF THE JOURNEY TO NEW FRANCE, MADE IN THE MONTH OF APRIL LAST BY FATHER PAUL LE JEUNE,[1] OF THE SOCIETY OF JESUS

Sent to Reverend Father Barthelamy Jacquinot, Provincial of the same Society, in the Province of France

(1632)

[This document is Le Jeune's famous *Relation* of 1632, the first of the Cramoisy series, which were thereafter annually issued until 1672. In this document, Le Jeune, the new superior of the Canada mission, relates to the French provincial of his order, in Paris, the particulars of the stormy passage recently made by the two missionaries to the New World, in De Caen's ship. Le Jeune gives his impressions of the country and of the natives. . . . The circumstances are related of the landing of De Caen's party at Quebec, which is found in ruins: mass is celebrated in

---

[1] Paul Le Jeune was born in July, 1591, at Chalons-sur-Marne, France. His parents were Huguenots; but, upon attaining his majority, he became a Catholic, and entered the Jesuit novitiate, at Rouen, Sept. 22, 1613. Pursuing his studies at La Flèche and Clermont, he became an instructor at Rennes and Bourges, and, later, professor of rhetoric at Nevers and at Caen. He then spent two years as a preacher at Dieppe, and two years more as superior of the residence there. On the return of the French to Quebec, he came there with De Caen, as superior of the Canadian Mission. His first year was spent in the French settlements; in the second, he wintered among the Montagnais, in order to learn their language. When the settlement of Three Rivers was founded (1634), he went there with Buteux, returning to Quebec before the death of Champlain, whose funeral sermon he preached. La Jeune remained superior of the mission until 1639, and continued his labors in Canada during ten years more. In 1649, he returned to France, where he became procurator of foreign missions, and died there Aug. 7, 1664. Rochmonteix says of Le Jeune: "He carried a will of steel in a heart of fire." Sulte thus characterizes him: "He was a typical missionary,—fervent, devoted, asking only to be directed toward sacrifice." *Ibid.*, v., *note* 1.

15

the house of Madame Hébert, and the condition of that pioneer family is described. Quebec being surrendered to De Caen by the English garrison, the Jesuits return to their old habitation on the St. Charles, only the walls of which have withstood the shock of war. Le Jeune then reverts in his story to the condition of the savages, telling of their simplicity and their entire confidence in the missionaries. The Jesuits baptize an Iroquois lad, and a native child has been left in their charge.—*Ibid.*, v., 1.]

My Reverend Father: Having been notified by you on the last day of March that I should embark as early as possible at Havre de Grace, to sail directly for New France, I left Dieppe the next day, and, going to Rouen, Father de Noüe, our Brother Gilbert, and I united in one company. Being in Havre, we went to pay our respects to monsieur du Pont, nephew of Monseigneur the Cardinal, who gave us a passport signed by his own hand, in which he said that it was the wish of the Cardinal that we should go to New France. We are under peculiar obligations to the benevolence of monsieur the Curé of Havre and of the Ursuline Mothers; for, as we had not foreseen our departure, if Father Charles Lallemant of Rouen, and these good people in Havre, had not assisted us in the hasty preparations we were obliged to make, we should, without doubt, have been very badly off. From Havre we went to Honfleur, and on Low Sunday, April 18th, we set sail.

We had fine weather at first, and made about six hundred leagues in ten days, but we could hardly cover two hundred on the following thirty three days. I had sometimes seen the angry sea from the windows of our little house at Dieppe; but watching the fury of the Ocean from the shore is quite different from tossing upon its waves. It is one thing to reflect upon death in one's cell, before the image on the Crucifix, but it is quite another to think of it in the midst of a tempest and in the presence of death itself. We found winter in summer; that is to say, in the month of May and a part of June, the winds and the fogs chilled us; Father de Nouë's feet and hands were frozen; and besides this, I had pains in my head or heart, which scarcely left me at all during the first month; and a keen thirst, because we ate nothing but salted food, and there was no fresh water upon our vessel. The size of our cabins was such that we could not stand upright, kneel, or sit down; and, what is worse, during the rain, the water fell at times upon my face. Still it seems to me that I got along better than Father de Nouë, who for a long time, was hardly able to eat; as to our brother, he is like the Amphibious animals; he is just as much at home on the sea as on the land.

On Pentecost day, just as I was ready to preach, as I usually did on Sundays and great Fete days, one of our sailors began to cry out, "Codfish! codfish!" He had thrown in his line and had brought out a large one. We had already been on the banks several days, but had caught very little. On that day we drew in as many as we liked. These fresh supplies were very welcome to us after such continuous storms.

On the following Tuesday, the first day of June, we saw land. It was still covered with snow, for the winter, always severe in this country, was extremely so this year. Some days before, we had encountered two icebergs of enormous size, floating upon the sea. They were longer than our ship and higher than our masts, and as the Sunlight fell upon them you would have said they were Churches, or rather, mountains of crystal. I would hardly have believed it if I had not seen it.

On Thursday, June 3rd, we passed into the country through one of the most beautiful rivers in the world. The great Island of newfoundland intercepts it at its mouth, leaving two openings whereby it can empty into the sea. Upon entering, you discover a gulf 150 leagues wide; going further up, where this grand river begins to narrow, it is even there 37 leagues wide. Where we are, in Quebec, distant over 200 leagues from its mouth, it is still half a league wide. In this great river, which is called the St. Lawrence, white porpoises are found, and nowhere else. The English call them white whales, because they are very large compared with the other porpoises; they go up as far as Quebec.

On the day of Holy Trinity, we were compelled to stop at Gaspay, a large body of water extending into this country. It was here that we trod land for the first time since our departure. Never did man, after a long voyage, return to his country with more joy than we entered ours; it is thus that we call these wretched lands. After Mass we went into the woods; the snow was still very deep, and so strong that it bore our weight. Here our people killed a number of large grey partridges, as large as our chickens in France. They also killed some hares, larger-footed than ours, and still a little white: for in this country the hares are all white, while the snow lasts, and during the summer they resume their color like that of the European hares.

The next day we again set sail, and on the 18th of June we cast anchor at Tadoussac.[1] This is another bay or very small cove, near which there is a river named Sagué [Saguenay]; which empties into the great river St. Lawrence. This river is as beautiful as the Seine, about as rapid as the Rosne [Rhone], and deeper than many places in the sea, for it is said to be 80 fathoms deep in its shallowest places. As we were on our way to say Holy Mass on the Shore, one of our soldiers killed a great white eagle near its eyrie. Its head and neck were entirely white, the beak and feet yellow, the rest of the body blackish; it was as large as a Turkey-cock. We sojourned here 19 days.

It was here that I saw Savages for the first time. As soon as they saw our vessel they lighted fires, and two of them came on board in a little canoe very neatly made of bark. The next day a Sagamore, with ten or twelve Savages, came to see us. When I saw them enter our Captain's room, where I happened to be, it seemed to me that I was looking at those maskers

---

[1] Tadoussac [at the mouth of the Saguenay river], from earliest times a favorite rendezvous of the Montagnais and other Eastern tribes, became under the French an important fur-trade center and Jesuit mission; and is, today, a notable watering place.—*Ibid.*, ii., *note* 51.

who run about in France in Carnival time. There were some whose noses were painted blue, the eyes, eyebrows, and cheeks painted black, and the rest of the face red; and these colors are bright and shining like those of our masks; others had black, red and blue stripes drawn from the ears to the mouth. Still others were entirely black; except the upper part of the brow and around the ears, and the end of the chin; so that it might have been truly said of them that they were masquerading. There were some who had only one black stripe, like a wide ribbon, drawn from one ear to the other, across the eyes, and three little stripes on the cheeks. Their natural color is like that of those French beggars who are half-roasted in the Sun, and I have no doubt that the Savages would be very white if they were well covered.

To describe how they were dressed would be difficult indeed. All the men, when it is a little warm, go naked, with the exception of a piece of skin which falls from just below the navel to the thighs. When it is cold, or probably in imitation of Europeans, they cover themselves with furs, of the Beaver, Bear, Fox, and other animals of the same kind, but so awkwardly, that it does not prevent the greater part of their bodies from being seen. I have seen some of them dressed in Bear skin, just as St. John the Baptist is painted. This fur, with the hair outside, was worn under one arm, and over the other, hanging down to the knees. They were girdled around the body with a cord made of a dried intestine. Some are entirely dressed. They are like the Grecian Philosopher who would wear nothing that he had not made. It would not take many years to learn all their crafts.

All go bareheaded, men and women; their hair, which is uniformly black, is long, greasy, and shiny, and is tied behind, except when they wear mourning. The women are decently covered; they wear skins fastened together on their shoulders with cords; these hang from the neck to the knees. They girdle themselves also with a cord, the rest of the body, the head, the arms and the legs being uncovered. Now that they trade with the French for capes, blankets, cloths, and shirts, there are many who use them, but their shirts are as white and as greasy as dishcloths, for they never wash them. Furthermore, they have good figures, their bodies are well made, their limbs very well proportioned, and they are not so clumsy as I supposed them to be. They are fairly intelligent. They do not all talk at once, but one after another, listening patiently. A Sagamore or Captain, dining in our room one day, wished to say something; and, not finding an opportunity, because they were all talking at the same time, at last prayed the company to give him a little time to talk in his turn, and all alone, as he did.

Now, as in the wide stretches of territory in this country there are a great many wholly barbarous tribes, so they very often make war upon each other. When we arrived at Tadoussac the Savages were coming back from a war against the Hiroquois, and had taken nine of them; those of Quebec took six, and those of Tadoussac three. Monsieur Emery de Caen [1] went to see the captives, hoping to save the life of the youngest one. I pleaded very earnestly for all three, but was told that great presents were necessary, and I had none.

Having arrived at the cabins of the Savages, which are made of poles, clumsily covered with bark, the top left uncovered for the purpose of letting in light and of leaving an opening for the smoke to go out, we entered that of the war Captain, which was long and narrow. We sat down on the ground, which was covered with little branches of fir, for they have no other seats. This done, they brought in the prisoners, who sat down beside each other. The eldest was over 60, the second about 30, and the third was a young boy from 15 to 16 years old. They all began to sing, in order to show that they were not at all afraid of death, however cruel it might be. Their singing seemed to me very disagreeable; the cadence always ended with reiterated aspirations; "oh! oh! oh! ah! ah! ah! hem! hem! hem!" *etc.* After singing

---

[1] Emery de Caen, with his uncle, Guillaume de Caen, was placed by Montmorency in charge of commercial affairs in New France; both were Huguenots, the latter a merchant, the former a naval captain.—*Ibid.*, iv., *note* 21.

for some time, they were made to dance, one after the other. The eldest one rose first, and began to walk through the room. He stamped his feet continuously upon the ground while marching, and sang continuously. This was all the dance; and while it was going on all the other Savages in the hut clapped their hands, or beat their thighs, drawing this aspiration from the depths of their stomach, "a-ah, a-ah, a-ah," and then, when the prisoner stopped, they cried, "o-oh, o-oh, o-oh," and when the one reseated himself, the other took up the dance. Monsieur de Caen asked when they would be killed. "To-morrow," they answered. I went to see them again, and found three wooden stakes erected; but news came from Quebec that a treaty of peace was being negotiated with the Hiroquois, and it would perhaps be necessary to surrender the prisoners, and thus their death was delayed. There is no cruelty comparable to that which they practice on their enemies. . . . In short, they make them suffer all that cruelty and the Devil can suggest. At last, as a final horror, they eat and devour them almost raw. If we were captured by the Hiroquois, perhaps we would be obliged to suffer this ordeal, inasmuch as we live with the Montagnards,[1] their enemies. So enraged are they against every one who does them an injury, that they eat the lice and other vermin that they find upon themselves,— not because they like them, but only, they say, to avenge themselves and to eat those that eat them.

Let no one be astonished at these acts of barbarism. Before the faith was received in Germany, Spain, or England, those nations were not more civilized. Mind is not lacking among the Savages of Canada, but education and instruction. They are already tired of their miseries and stretch out their hands to us for help. It seems to me that the tribes which have stationary homes could be easily converted. I can say of the Hurons all that was written to us awhile ago by the Father of a young Paraguyan: to wit, that much suffering must be en-

---

[1] The Montagnards or Montagnais, a wretched tribe of nomads, were, at this time, chiefly centered upon the banks of the Saguenay river. *Ibid.*, i., *note* 70. The Montagnais mission was centered at Tadoussac.

dured among them, but that great results may be expected; and that, if the consolations of the earth are lacking there, those of Paradise may already be enjoyed. It is only necessary to know the language; and, if Father Brébeuf had not been compelled by the English to leave here, they having taken possession of the French fort, he would have already advanced the glory of God in that country.

As to the strange and wandering tribes, like those near Quebec, where we live, there will be more difficulty. The means of assisting them, in my opinion, is to build seminaries, and to take their children, who are very bright and amiable. The fathers will be taught through the children. Even now there are some among them who have begun to cultivate the soil and sow Indian corn, having become weary of their difficult and miserable way of living. In truth any one who knew their language could manage them as he pleased. Therefore I will apply myself, but I shall make very little progress this year, for reasons which I shall write in detail to your Reverence. But let us come back to the continuation of our voyage.

The 3rd of July we left Tadoussac and went to cast anchor at the Basque scaffold, a place so called because the Basques go there to catch whales. As it was very calm and we were awaiting the tide, I went ashore. I thought I would be eaten up by the mosquitoes, which are little flies, troublesome in the extreme. The great forests here engender several species of them; there are common flies, gnats, fireflies, mosquitoes, large flies, and a number of others; the large flies sting furiously, and the pain from their sting lasts a long time. The gnats are very small, hardly visible, but very perceptibly felt; the fireflies do no harm; at night they look like sparks of fire, casting a greater light than the glowworms that I have seen in France. As to the mosquitoes, they are disagreeable beyond description. Some people are compelled to go to bed after coming from the woods, they are so badly stung. If the country were cleared and inhabited, these little beasts would not be found here, for already there are but few of them at the fort of Kebec, on account of the cutting down of the neighboring woods.

At length, on the 5th of July,—two months and 18 days since the 18th of April, when we sailed,—we reached the much desired port. We cast anchor in front of the fort which the English held; we saw at the foot of this fort the poor settlement of Kebec all in ashes. The English, who came to this country to plunder and not to build up, not only burned a greater part of the detached buildings which Father Charles Lallemant had had erected, but also all of that poor settlement of which nothing now is to be seen but the ruins of its stone walls. We celebrated the holy Mass in the oldest house in the country, the home of madame Hebert,[1] who had settled near the fort during the lifetime of her husband. She has a fine family, and her daughter is married here to an honest Frenchman. God is blessing them every day; he has given them very beautiful children, their cattle are in fine condition, and their land produces good grain. This is the only French family settled in Canada. They were seeking some way of returning to France; but, having learned that the French were coming back to Quebec, they began to regain courage. When they saw our ships coming in with the white flags upon the masts, they knew not how to express their joy. But when they saw us in their home, to celebrate the holy Mass, which they had not heard for three years, good God, what joy! Tears fell from the eyes of nearly all, so great was their happiness.

The Englishman, having seen the Patents signed by the hand of his King, promised that he would go away within a week, and, in fact, he began preparations for going, although with regret; but his people were all very glad of the return of the French, for they had been given only six pounds of bread, French weight, for an entire week. They told us that the Savages had helped them to live during the greater part

[1] The widow of Louis Hébert. He was the first settler with a family, and the first at Quebec to cultivate the soil as a means of livelihood, and on this account has sometimes been called "the father of Canada,"—an appellation also given, and with more propriety, to Champlain.—*Ibid.,* ii., *note* 80.

of the time. On the following Tuesday, the 13th of July, they restored the fort to the hands of monsieur Emery de Caen and monsieur du Plessis Bochart,[1] his Lieutenant; and on the same day set sail in the two ships that they had anchored here. God knows if our French people were happy, seeing the dislodgment of these Anglicised Frenchmen, who have done so much injury to these poor countries.

The English dislodged, we again entered our little home. The only furniture we found there was two wooden tables, such as they were; the doors, windows, sashes, all broken and carried away, and everything going to ruin. It is still worse in the house of the Recolet Fathers. We found our cleared lands covered with peas: our fathers had left them to the English covered with wheat, barley, and Indian corn, and meantime this Captain Thomas Ker had sold the full crop of peas, refusing to give them to us for the harvest he had found upon our lands. It is a great deal that such a guest has left our house and the entire country.

Here is something that has consoled me: A certain Savage named La Nasse, who lived near our Fathers and cultivated the land, seeing that the English molested him, withdrew to the islands, where he continued to cultivate the land; hearing that we had returned, he came to see us and has promised that he will come back and build his cabin near us, and that he will give us his little boy. This will be our first pupil; we shall teach him to read and write. This good man told us that the Savages do not act right; that he wished to be our brother, and live as we do. Madame Hebert told us that he has wished for our return for a long time.

Several Savages ask us news of the Reverend Father Lallemant, of Father Masse, and of Father Brebeuf, whom they

---

[1] Guillaume Guillemot, sieur Duplessis-Bochart; the lieutenant of Emery de Caen, upon the latter's return in 1632, and afterwards admiral of the fleet under Champlain. In 1634, he transported Robert Gifford's colony to Beauport; and in the same year, he took active part in foundation of Three Rivers. In November, 1651, he was appointed governor of Three Rivers, in which position he remained until Aug. 19, 1652, when he was slain by the Iroquois, while endeavoring to repel an attack upon his post. *Ibid.*, v., *note* 34.

very readily call by their names, and inquire if they will not return next year. These simple creatures have confidence in us; here is an example of it.

The 6th of August, monsieur Emery de Caën coming to see us in our little house, distant a good half league from the fort, remained to dine with us. While we were at the table, two families of Savages, men, women, and little children, approached the spot. One of them approached me, and said: *Ania Kir Capitana?* "My brother, art thou Captain?" They were asking for the superior of the house. They call their Captain "Sagamore", but by associating with the Europeans, they have come to use the word *Capitana.* Our Brother answered them, *eoco;* that is to say, "yes." Thereupon he made a speech to me, saying that they were going hunting or fishing for Beavers, and that I should keep their baggage; that they would return when the leaves fell from the trees. They asked if thieves ever came into our house, and very carefully scrutinized the places where their baggage might be best concealed. I answered that everything was safe in our house, and having shown them a little room which could be locked, they seemed very happy, placing therein three or four packages covered very neatly with the bark of trees, telling me that they contained great riches. I do not know what is there; but, at the best, all their riches are only poverty. Their gold and silver, their diamonds and pearls, are little white grains of porcelain which do not seem to amount to much. Having piled up their baggage, they asked me for a knife, and I gave them one; then they asked me for some string. Having made them a present of the piece of string, they said to me: *Ania Capitana ouias amiscou:* "My brother, the Captain, we will bring thee the meat of a Beaver," and they gave me very clearly to understand that it would not be smoked. They know very well that the French people do not like their dried food; that is, their meat dried in smoke; for they have no other salt than smoke to preserve their meats.

I have become teacher in Canada: the other day I had a little Savage on one side of me, and a little Negro or Moor on the other, to whom I taught their letters. After so many years of teaching, behold me at last returned to the A., B., C., with so great content and satisfaction that I would not exchange with my two pupils for the finest audience in France. This little Savage is the one who will soon be left entirely with us. The little Negro was left by the English with this French family which is here. We have taken him to teach and baptize: but he does not yet understand the language well: therefore we shall wait some time yet.

I calculated the other day how much earlier the Sun rises on your horizon than it does on ours, and I found that you have daylight a little over six hours earlier than we do. Our Sailors usually count 17 leagues and a half for a degree of the equinoctial and all other great circles, and otherwise reach the conclusion that there are from here to you 1000 leagues and over, which will consequently make 57 degrees 12 minutes of a great circle upon which we ought to calculate a direct route from here to you. I am writing this about eight in the morning, and it is two in the afternoon where you are.

All considered, this country here is very fine. As soon as we had entered into our little home, the 13th of July, we began to work and dig the earth, to sow purslane and turnips, and to plant lentils, and everything grew very well; a very short time afterwards we gathered our salad. But the misfortune was that our seeds were spoiled, I mean a part of them. You would be astonished to see the great number of ears of rye which were found among our peas; they are longer and more grainy than the most beautiful I have ever seen in France.

Tomorrow, on the 25th of August, I am to baptize a little Hiroquois child who is to be taken to France, never to return to this country; he was given to a Frenchman, who made a present of him to monsieur de la Rade. Enough of this, we are in such a hurry that I have not observed any order in this narrative. Your Reverence will excuse me, if you please. I beseech you to give succor to these poor people who are in goodly numbers, the Canadians, Montagnards, Hurons and Algonquains, the Nation of the Bear, the Tobacco Nation, the

Nation of the Sorcerers, and many others. I saw the Hurons arrive; in their 50 canoes and more, they made a very fine sight upon the river.

I expected to end this little narrative on the 24th of August, but it will not be until after the baptism of this little child. I have just baptized him. Monsieur Emery de Caën is his Godfather; madame Coullart, daughter of madame Hebert, his Godmother. His name is Louys, and he was baptized on saint Louys's day. This poor little one, who is only about four years old, cried all the time before his baptism, and ran away from us; I could not hold him. As soon as I began the ceremony, he did not say a word; he looked at me attentively and did everything that I would have him do. I believed that he was an Hiroquois, but I have learned that he belongs to the fire Nation; his Father and his Mother and he were taken in war by the Algonquains, who burned the parents and gave the child to the French.

Louys, formerly Amantacha,[1] came to see us and promised that he would come back next year, to return with Father Brebeuf to his country; he is rather intelligent, and showed me that he had a correct conception of God. I could not tell you how cunning this Nation is. I recommend myself a thousand times to the holy sacrifices of your Reverence and to the prayers of your whole Province.

Of Your Reverence,
The very humble and obedient servant,
in God, Paul Le Jeune.

From the midst of a forest more than 800 leagues in extent, at Kebec, this 28th of August, 1632.
[*Ibid.,* v., Doc. xx.]

[1] Also known among the French as Louis de Sainte-Foi; the Huron lad who, in 1626, was sent to France by the missionaries and baptized. Having been instructed there by the Jesuits, he returned to Canada before the capture of Quebec, after which event he entered into the service of the English; but, after the return of the French, he was very useful to the missionaries in their intercourse with the natives.—*Ibid.,* v., *note* 21.

IV

LETTER FROM FATHER PAUL LE JEUNE, TO THE REVEREND FATHER PROVINCIAL OF FRANCE, AT PARIS

(*1634*)

[This is a letter from Le Jeune to his provincial, written in the year 1634 but not bearing specific date. He describes the condition of the Quebec mission; states that at last the Huron country is open to them, and that Brébeuf and others have gone thither. He, with Buteux, will go to the new settlement at Three Rivers, for which he gives his reasons at length.

Le Jeune describes the dwelling of the Jesuits at Quebec, and asks for means to fence in a tract of land for their cattle, and to repair their buildings, injured by the English. He plans how they may provide a portion of their own food, hitherto wholly brought from France. He deprecates the formation of too many missions, preferring to strengthen those already formed.—*Ibid.*, vi., 1.]

Quebec, 1634

My Reverend Father:

The peace of Christ be with you.

The tears which fell from my eyes at the sight of the letters of Your Reverence stop my pen; I am as hard as bronze, and yet your love has so greatly softened me, that joy makes me weep. But let us enter upon affairs; I shall spare neither ink nor paper, since Your Reverence endures with so much love my tediousness and simplicity. After having thanked you with all my heart for the help which you have been pleased to send us, as well as for the food and fresh supplies, I will describe to you fully the state of this mission.

Let us begin with what has occurred this year. We have lived in great peace, thank God, among ourselves, with our working people, and with all the french. I have been greatly pleased with all our Fathers. Father Brébeuf [1] is a man chosen of God for these lands; I left him in my place for six months, with the exception of nine days, while I passed the winter with the Savages. Everything went on peacefully during that time. Father Daniel [2] and Father Davost [3] are quiet men. They have studied the Huron language thoroughly, and I have taken care that they should not be diverted from this work, which I believe to be of very great importance. Father Massé, [4] whom I sometimes playfully call Father *Useful*, is well known to Your Reverence. He has had the care of the domestic affairs and of our cattle, in which he has succeeded very well. Father de Noue, who has a good heart, has had the care of our laborers, directing them in their work, which is very difficult in these beginnings.

For the year which we are about to begin at the departure of the ships, this is the way in which we shall be distributed and what we shall do:

Father Brebeuf, Father Daniel, and Father Davost, with three brave young men and two little boys, will be among the Hurons. At last our Lord has opened to them the door. M. Duplessis has aided greatly in this; let us say M. de Lauson, who has without doubt recommended this affair to him, of which he has acquitted himself very well, as Your reverence will see by the letter which Father Brebeuf has

[1] Jean de Brébeuf, of a noble family of Normandy, one of the first Jesuit missionaries, came to Canada in 1625, and was martyred in the country of the Hurons, in 1649, by the Iroquois.

[2] Antoine Daniel, a native of Dieppe, arrived the preceding year, 1633, and was martyred by the Iroquois in 1649.

[3] Ambrose Davost arrived the preceding year, at the same time as Father Daniel.

[4] Father Ennemond Massé, the same one who had evangelized the savages of Acadia in the year 1611 with Father Biard. He came to Canada in 1633, and died at the residence of Saint-Joseph de Sillery, in 1646, at the age of 72 years.

sent me on his way to the Hurons. I believe that they must now be near the place where they intend to go. This stroke is a stroke from heaven: we shall hope for a great harvest from this country. Father Brebeuf and Father Daniel exposed themselves to great suffering; for they went away without baggage, or without the money necessary to live. God has provided therefore, as M. Duplessis has taken care that all should go well. So much for the Hurons.

We shall live at Three Rivers, Father Buteux[1] and I. This place is upon the great river, 30 leagues farther up than Kebec, upon the way to the Hurons; it is called Three Rivers, because a certain river which flows through the land empties into the great river by three mouths. Our French people are this year beginning a settlement there,[2] and two of our fathers must be there. I have been doubtful for a long time as to who should go. Father Brebeuf and Father de Nouë thought that I should remain at Kebec, but I perceived that Father Lalemant was apprehensive of this new abode, believing that he would never return if he were sent there, offering himself freely, however, to do what should be desired. It is true that some persons generally die in these beginnings, but death is not always a great evil.

After having commended this affair to our Lord, I resolved to go there myself, for the following reasons:

1st. I believed that I was doing nothing contrary to the designs of your Reverence in leaving the house for seven or eight months, for I can return in the spring; however, I do not know whether I shall come back before the coming of

---

[1] Father Jacques Buteux, a native of Abbeville, in Picardie, who was killed by the Iroquois on the 10th of May, 1652.

[2] Three Rivers. This point was long a favorite fur-trade rendezvous for the Indians. The Récollet missionaries established a residence here in June, 1615, which was maintained until 1628. The fortified French settlement at Three Rivers was established by Champlain in 1634, to protect the Huron and Algonkin fur trade from the incursions of the Iroquois, and to serve as an outpost of defence for Quebec. Within two months after La Violette, Champlain's lieutenant, had erected his stockade at Three Rivers, two of the Jesuit Fathers,—Le Jeune and Buteux,—had established a residence there, which was for many years an important center of missionary work. *Ibid.*, iv., *note* 24.

the ships. Moreover, I leave it in the hands of a person who will do a hundred times better than I.

2nd. I thought that it would be more agreeable to our Lord that I should give the Father this satisfaction, that he need not leave Kebec, where we are rather comfortably situated; and that, if there be any danger, I ought to take it upon myself.

3rd. The son of God, dying on the Cross, has obligated us to bear the cross, so we should not flee from it when it presents itself; this is my strongest reason, for in truth there is suffering in a new settlement, especially in one established so hurriedly as that one. I do not know how the house will be arranged; we shall be mixed up with working men, drinking, eating, and sleeping with them; they cannot make other provision for us of any kind whatever. All this does not appall me, for the cabins of the savages, in which I lived this winter are much worse. Father Buteux pleases me greatly, for he takes this cheerfully; I see him strongly determined to bear the cross. Your Reverence is right in saying that this is the kind of spirit that we should have. We shall study the language there, although less advantageously than at Kebec, on account of the lodging in which there will be greater hubbub than in the cabins of the savages: for our french people, with whom we shall be in company, are not so calm and patient as these barbarians. Furthermore I had intended this winter to keep a savage with me at Kébec to instruct me, since I am beginning to be able to question them: this cannot be done at Three Rivers; but it is of no importance, I shall do what I can.

There will remain at Kébec, Father Lallemant, Father Massé, Father de Noüe, and our two Brothers with all our men.[1] The gentleness and virtue of Father Lallemant will

[1 All our men: a number of skilled artisans had been sent over in 1634, with Le Jeune; and they proceeded, under De Noüe's direction, to rebuild the Jesuit residence, which had suffered greatly during the capture of Quebec and the English occupation. They also built a small house for the priests in charge of Champlain's chapel, Notre Dame de Récouvrance.—*Ibid.*, vi., *note* 6.

hold all in peace, and will cause the work of our people to prosper. I did not think it feasible to send Father de Noüe and Father Brebeuf to Three Rivers,—1st, because Father de Noüe looks after our men here; 2nd, Father Buteux would have lost a year, he would have done nothing at all in the language; 3rd, *Satis calidus est. licet alioquin optimus, P. de Noüe*; so Father Lallemant or myself had to go. I have chosen this lot for myself, believing that I should leave the house in greater peace than if I remained, and I believe that Your Reverence will approve my action. So that is what we shall do this year. It is a great occupation, to suffer nobly; may God give us grace for it! Let us speak now of our household servants.

I have said that we lived peacefully on all sides. The murmurs and escapades which occasionally happen should not be placed in the list of great disorders, when one rises as soon as he has fallen, and when the fall is not great. A number of our men have occasionally shown some impatience; but we have reason to bless God, for nothing of importance has happened. Here are the causes for their discontent.

1st. It is the nature of working people to complain and grumble.

2nd. The difference in wages makes them complain; a carpenter, a brickmaker, and others will earn more than the laborers, and yet they do not work so much; I mean that it is not so hard for them as for the others, because they are following their professions, and the others are doing more laborious things; *inde querimoniae*. They do not consider that a master-mason may exert himself less than a laborer, although he earns more.

3rd. The greater part do not follow their trades, except for a short time; a tailor, a shoemaker, a gardener, and others, are amazed when required to drag some wood over the snow; besides they complain that they will forget their trades.

4th. It must be confessed that the work is great in these beginnings: the men are the horses and oxen; they carry or drag wood, trees, or stones; they till the soil, they harrow it.

The insects in summer, the snows in winter, and a thousand other inconveniences, are very troublesome. The youth who in France worked in the shade find here a great difference. I am astonished that the hardships they have to undergo, in doing things they have never done before, do not cause them to make a greater outcry than they do.

5th. They all lodge in one room; and, as they have not all learned to control their passions, and are of dispositions altogether different, they have occasions for causeless quarrels.

6th. As we are more or less dependent upon them, not being able to send them back when they fail to do right, and as they see that a stick for the purpose of chastising them is of little use in our hands, they are much more arrogant than they would be with laymen, who would urge them with severity and firmness.

Your Reverence will weigh all these reasons, if you please, and will aid us in praising God; for notwithstanding all this, we have not failed to pass the year peacefully, reprimanding some, punishing others, though rarely—very often pretending not to see; *Deus sit in aeternum benedictus!* and, as it is not enough that peace should dwell among us, but that it should be firmly established if it be possible, I deem it best to do what I am about to say.

Only good workmen are needed here; hence it would be well for us to have three capable Brothers, to perform the minor duties of the house—cooking, baking, making shoes, making clothes, looking after the garden, the sacristy, washing, tinkering, caring for the cattle, the milk, butter, etc. All these duties would be divided among these three good Brothers, and thus we would be relieved of giving wages to workmen who are occupied with these duties, and who complain when they are given other things to do. All our men should be engrossed with the heavy tasks, and consequently I beg Your Reverence to send us two good Brothers. Our Brother Liegeois, who is beginning very well, will be a third. As to brother Gilbert, perhaps he will be sent back; if not, he will work slowly at carpentry, for he is already broken down and hindered by a rupture. The following are the Brothers upon whom my choice would fall, if it please Your Reverence; our Brother Claude Frémont and our Brother the locksmith, whom you promised in your letters to send us next year. I do not know either of them, but I am told they are both peaceable and good workmen. If this be true, Your Reverence will send them to us, if you please. One of them could be easily sent to the Hurons or the Three Rivers according to the course of events.

With these good Brothers, we should have at least ten men capable of building, cultivating, and reaping,—in a word, of doing everything. Whoever could do still more, would be best.

The following ought to be the arrangement of the household for the coming year in regard to work, if it so please Your Reverence. Ten good workmen and three or four of our Brothers; namely Our Brother Liegeois, Our Brother Claude Frémont, Our Brother the locksmith, whose name I do not know, and our Brother Gilbert, if he remain. In regard to the six workmen for whom we ask, the following will be their trades; two strong carpenters, at least one of them understanding how to erect a building,—in a word, let him understand his trade; a joiner, and three workmen who can be employed in clearing the land, in using the pit saw (they need not know this trade, but must have only willingness and strength to do it), in reaping, in helping the carpenters, the mason, the brick maker, in watching the cattle, in doing everything that is required of them; for this, strong men are needed, and those who are willing. If we cannot have two carpenters, let us have one good one, at least, come over; and, instead of the other, such a workman as I have just described. It is very easy to describe a good workman, but quite difficult to find one.

Let us speak of the Fathers whom this mission needs.

Two are needed among the Hurons: if they make peace with the Hiroquois for I am told that it is being negotiated, a number more will be needed, as we must enter all the stationary tribes. If these people receive the faith, they will cry with hunger, and there will be no one to feed them, for lack of persons who know the languages. Moreover, the Brothers who should be among the Hiroquois would exert themselves to preserve the peace between them and the Hurons; nevertheless, on account of the uncertainty of this peace, we ask for only two fathers to go to the Hurons. There must be a superior at Three Rivers, and two Fathers must remain at Kebec, near our french people; so this makes five priests and two Brothers. Let us see what need there is of having so many men.

As for the two Fathers who will be sent to the Hurons, they could be sent from there to the Neutral tribe, or among the Hiroquois, or to some other tribe; or even kept among the Hurons, who number thirty thousand souls in a very small extent of country. For Kebec, I ask two Fathers; if Father Lallemant is superior, he will remain with Fathers Masse and de Noüe, and with our people, to ensure the success of the house; the two Fathers will be at the fort, where they talk of building them a little house or room; they will preach, will hear confessions, they will perform the offices of pastors, and will learn the languages of the savages, going to visit them when they encamp around the place. They will have a boy, who will every week bring them their food from our house, distant from the fort a good half league.

I ask a superior for Three Rivers, for it is not too much to keep three Fathers there, so that there may be always two free for the savages. But if Your Reverence wishes to send only two, Father Buteux, to whom I shall this year teach what I know of the language, will remain with the one at Kebec, or at Three Rivers, and I with the other; I am inclined to think that Father Brebeuf may ask more than two; so that, if Your Reverence can send five Fathers and two Brothers, it will not be too many. I am restricting myself as much as I can; because, for the good of this mission, it would be well to have more people than we are asking.

Just here I have two humble requests to make of Your

Reverence. I make them in the name of Jesus Christ from the very depths of my heart. My Reverend Father, I beg Your Reverence to discharge me. I sometimes say to the little crosses which come to me, "And this also and as many as you wish, O my God." But to those which Father Lallemant has brought me in Your Reverence's letters, which continue me in my charge, I have said this more than three times, but with a shrinking of the heart which could not drink this cup. In truth, my Reverend Father, I have not the talents, nor the qualities, nor the mildness, necessary to be superior; besides, I say it, and it is true, it is a great disturbance in the study of the language; I say a very great disturbance,—I will even say that this, during the present year, is preventing the salvation, perhaps, of some savages. I learn that the Savages who are at Three Rivers are all sick, and are dying in great numbers. Also Father Brebeuf, who passed through there, writes me that it would be fitting that I should go there; I am busy with the letters, I have nothing or very little ready; the ships will soon be ready to sail away; I shall not have my letters and reports prepared to send Your Reverence in regard to our needs, but I am hurrying as much as possible.

If I were not Superior, I would be free from all this and would have been up there a long time ago. I am preparing to go there and remain until spring; or until the coming of the ships. I have not a mind capable of so many things; the care of our people, little difficulties of so many kinds, in short, all are brought to the Superior; and that distracts him greatly, especially at Kebec, where we are quite numerous. Add to this sermons, confessions, and visits. I am willing to think that all these things would not greatly interfere with Father Lallemant's study of the language; as for me, I say it before God, it distracts me greatly therefrom.

Since the month of April, when I returned from my stay with the savages, I have not looked at a word of their language. Father Lallemant, who is not so studious, wished, when he first came, to pay a little attention to the work of our men. Finally he got rid of this duty, confessing to me frankly, what he had been unwilling to believe, that it was impossible to study with this care. Time altogether free is given to those who study in our classes, they have good teachers, they have good books, they are comfortably lodged; and I, who am without books, without masters, badly lodged, shall I be able to study engrossed with cares which very often occupy me almost entirely? Your Reverence will consider this before God, if you please; I wish only his greater glory. It is true that I start at my own shadow; but time speaks for me,—it is more than three years (or will be at the coming of the ships) since I have been in charge. Father Lallemant, being what he is, and dwelling at Kebec, will give great satisfaction. I thank Your Reverence in advance for granting me this request. Here is a second.

Father Benier writes me that he would be inconsolable at not coming to Canada, if he were not confronted with his sins, which prevent him from it; he begs me to write to Rome for him. I tell Your Reverence frankly that he hopes they will open to him, from there, the door which the Provincials have closed to him in France. I have written them, as he requested me; but it is not from there that I expect my greatest consolation, my Reverend Father. Permit me to ask him for God, in the name of God, for the salvation of many souls: I renounce entirely anything immoderate in my affection; no, my Reverend Father, it is not the affection of the creature which speaks. If Your Reverence, to whom God communicates himself more fully than to a poor sinner, should deem, in the presence of Jesus Christ, uninfluenced by any motive whatsoever, that he is more necessary in France and near a woman [1] than in the midst of these barbarous people, I ask for him no more. If he renders more service to Our Lord where he is, however little it may be, than he would in New France, let him remain there, in the name of God; it is there where I wish him to be. But if Your Reverence thinks that God wishes him here, I ask for him with all my heart. My fear that some changes may occur makes me conjure Your

---

[1] Father Benier was confessor of the princess X***. *Ibid.*, vi., 65.

Reverence to give to us according to your affection for us. If I knew that he who may succeed you would inherit your love, I would not be so importunate; for truly I am ashamed to be so urgent.

Yet this one favor, my Reverend Father, which will be in harmony with your affection; give us, if you please, Father Benier and Father Vimont. If Father Benier does not come over while you are in charge, I shall never expect him; I shall ask fervently from God, and I am confident that he will give him to us.

It is at this point that my tediousness will become wearisome, for it is not yet finished. Let us speak of the condition of our house [1] at the present time. We have a house which contains four rooms below; the first serves as chapel, the second as refectory, and in this refectory are our rooms. There are two little square rooms of moderate size, for they are proportioned to a man's height; there are two others, each of which has a dimension of eight feet; but there are two beds in each room. These are rather narrow quarters for six persons; the others, when we are all together, sleep in the garret. The third large room serves as kitchen, and the fourth is the room for our working people; this is our entire lodging. Above is a garret, so low that no one can dwell there; to this we mount with a ladder.

There was another building of the same size, opposite this one. The English burned half of it, and the other half is covered only with mud; it serves us as a barn, a stable, and a carpenter's room. Our workingmen this year have made boards, have gone to the woods to get the trees, have placed doors and windows throughout, have made little rooms in the refectory, some furniture, tables, stools, credence-tables for the chapel, and other similar things; they have enclosed our

[1] *Notre-Dame des Anges:* this name was given first by the Récollets to their convent at Quebec; the Jesuits adopted the appellation for their own church and residence not far distant, on the site once occupied by Cartier's fort, at the confluence of the St. Charles and Lairet rivers. The Jesuits were granted, in 1626, a seigniory on the St. Charles, which was named Notre-Dame des Anges.— *Ibid.,* vi., *note* 7.

house with large poles of the fir tree, making for us a fine court about a hundred feet square, being superintended in this work by Father de Noüe. These poles are fourteen feet high, and there are about twelve hundred of them. It looks well, and is quite useful. We have placed some gates therein, which Louys has bound with iron. In addition to all this, we have cultivated, tilled, and seeded our cleared lands. So these are the more important works of our people, and the condition of the house.

The following is what must be done in the future:

We must erect a small house upon a point of land which is opposite. We need only cross the river to reach it; the water almost surrounds this point, forming a peninsula. We have begun to enclose it with stakes on the land side, and we shall keep there our cattle; that is, our cows and pigs; for this purpose we must build a little house, for those who will care for them, and also soon good stables sheltered from the cold.

Last year they sent us a carpenter who was not one; and for this reason there has been no building this year, which has done us great harm. We must also repair the damages in the building burned by the English. They have been doing this since the coming of the ship, which brought us a carpenter; we must have planks with which to cover it, and make doors and windows, etc. We must make a barn in which to put our crops. We must have a well, we have to go for water two hundred steps from the house, which causes us great trouble, especially in the winter, when we have to break the ice of the river in order to get it. We must repair and enlarge our cellar, which until now we have kept in good order. We must rebuild more than half of the building where we are now, and put a new roof on it, for the rain and snow penetrate everywhere; at first, our Fathers made only a miserable hut in which to live; the English neglecting it, it would have fallen to the ground if we had not returned to preserve it; it is made only of planks and small laths, upon which some mud has been plastered. We must have people to look after the cattle; the little ground that we have must be tilled and sown; the harvest must be cut and gathered in. We must prepare firewood, which we have to get at some distance away without a cart. We must have some lime made.

There are a thousand things which I cannot mention, but Your Reverence may see whether ten persons are too many for all of this. We would ask for twenty or thirty, if there were anything with which to feed and maintain them; but we restrict ourselves to ten, with three of our Brothers; and even then I do not know if they will be able to furnish, in France, what will be necessary for these for us, so great are the expenses.

WHAT MAY BE EXPECTED OF THIS HOUSE FOR THE ASSISTANCE OF THE MISSION, AND THE EXPENSES NECESSARY FOR OUR SUPPORT

There are four staples which make up the greatest expense of this mission; the pork, butter, drinks, and flour, which are sent; in time, the country may furnish these things. As to pork, if from the beginning of this year we had had a building, no more of it, or not much, would have had to be sent next year; we have two fat sows which are each suckling four little pigs, and these we have been obliged to feed all summer in our open court. Father Masse has raised these animals for us. If that point of which I have spoken were enclosed, they could be put there and during the summer nothing need be given them to eat; I mean that in a short time we shall be provided with pork, an article which would save us 400 livres. As to butter, we have two cows, two little heifers, and a little bull. M. de Caen having left his cattle here when he saw he was ruined, we took of them three cows, and, for the family which is here, three others. They and we gave each to M. Giffard [1] a cow, so

---

[1] Robert Giffard, sieur of Beauport, was born in 1507, at Mortagne, France. He was a physician. He left Canada upon its seizure by the English; but having obtained the concession of Beauport, below Quebec, he, in the following May, conducted thither a colony, under the escort of Duplessis-Bochart. He was (after Hébert) the first real colonist in Canada, the first who obtained from the soil support for his establishment. *Ibid.*, vi., *note* 8.

we have remaining the number that I have just stated. For lack of a building, they cost us more than they are worth, for our working people are obliged to neglect more necessary things for them; they spoil what we have sown; and they cannot be tended in the woods, for the insects torment them. They have come three years too soon, but they would have died if we had not taken them in; we took them when they were running wild. In time they will provide butter, and the oxen can be used for plowing, and will occasionally furnish meat.

As to drinks, we shall have to make some beer; but we shall wait until we have built, and until a brewery is erected; these three articles are assured with time. As to grains, some people are inclined to think that the land where we are is too cold. Let us proceed systematically, and consider the nature of the soil; these last two years all the vegetables, which came up only too fast, have been eaten by insects, which come either from the neighborhood of the woods, or from the land which has not yet been worked and purified, nor exposed to the air. In midsummer these insects die, and we have very fine vegetables.

As to the fruit trees, I do not know how they will turn out. We have two double rows of them, one of a hundred feet or more, the other larger, planted on either side with wild trees which are well rooted. We have eight or ten rows of apple and pear trees, which are also well rooted; we shall see how they will succeed. I have an idea that cold is very injurious to the fruit, but in a few years we shall know from experience. Formerly, some fine apples have been seen here.

As to the indian corn, it ripened very nicely the past year, but this year it is not so fine.

As to peas, I have seen no good ones here; their growth is too rapid. They succeed very well with this family, who live in a higher and more airy location.

The rye has succeeded very well for two years. We planted some as an experiment, and it is very fine.

Barley succeeds also. There remains the wheat; we sowed some in the autumn at different times; in some places it was lost under the snow, in others it was so preserved that no finer wheat can be seen in France. We do not yet know very well which time it is best to take before winter to put in the seed; the family living here has always sown spring wheat, which ripens nicely in their soil. We sowed a little of it this year, and will see whether it ripens. So these are the qualities of our soil.

I report all this because M. de Lauson[1] wrote to us that we should transport our people to Three Rivers, where we are going to make a new settlement, saying that everything would ripen better in that quarter. There was much hesitation as to whether it should be done; at least they wanted us to send three or four men there. I have always thought that our forces should not be divided, and that one house should be made successful, which might afterwards be the support of the others; for it is necessary to see some result before undertaking anything else. In fact, those who went there first send word that the soil is very sandy, and that all would mature better for a time; but that this soil will soon be exhausted. I am going to live there, as I have said, with Father Buteux; we shall see what there is in it. Even if the soil is very good, I do not think that the care of this house, where we are should be given up; it is the landing place of the ships, it ought to be the store-house, or place of refuge; the advantages for raising cattle here, on account of the meadows, are great. As to the cereals, if the worst comes to the worst, we have oats, but I hope that we shall also have good wheat, and that time will show us when it ought to be sown; if the spring grains ripen, wheat, oats, and

[1] Jean de Lauson (or Lauzon), one of the most influential men in the affairs of Canada during more than thirty years, was born in 1582. In 1627, he was member of both state and privy councils. . . . In the same year he was appointed intendant of Richelieu's Company in New France, holding this Post for about ten years. In January, 1651, he was appointed governor of Canada, where he arrived in October following. Nine days later he married (as his second wife) Anne Despres, sister-in-law of Sieur Duplessis-Bochart. He cared less, apparently, for the needs or welfare of the country than for his own aggrandizement; and he was unfitted, by age and by lack of resolution, for the position he held,—especially at this time, when the Iroquois were a constant menace to the entire St. Lawrence region. He was, however, friendly to the Jesuits, and conferred many favors upon them. He died in February, 1666.—*Ibid.*, vi., *note* 2.

barley will be produced here very well. From this let us draw some conclusions as to what should be done.

First, we must build some place where we ourselves can stay, and can keep our animals and crops.

Second, we must now sow what is necessary for the cattle, and try as soon as possible, in a few years, to have some pork and butter.

Third, being lodged, all our working people will apply themselves to clearing and cultivating the land in order to have grains. The following is the order which seems to me we ought to follow, in regard to the temporal: when we shall have built, we shall no longer keep any carpenters or artisans, but only woodchoppers and laborers, for the maintenance of the house. Occasionally we shall borrow an artisan from the fort, giving a man in his place for the time during which we shall keep him.

Or rather, what seems to me better, we shall keep domestic servants, and shall maintain men who will clear and cultivate the land by shares, and thus, being interested in their work, we shall not have to take any trouble for them. There is still time to think of that.

Here is another matter:

They are talking about beginning new settlements in different places, and of having there some of our Fathers. I have an idea that we could not undertake to settle and build everywhere; it will be all we can do if we make the place where we are prosper. We are going, Father Buteux and I, as I have said, to live at Three Rivers expressly to assist our countrymen, for we would not go, were it not for that; however, we are going to take furniture for the sacristy, and clothes for ourselves, and what seems stranger to me still, our own food, which we shall give to them; for we shall eat with them, for lack of a dwelling where we might be by ourselves.

Let us come to the spiritual.

First, we shall hope to have in time a great harvest among the Hurons. These people are sedentary and very populous: I hope that Father Buteux will know in one year as much of the montagnais language as I know of it, in order to teach it to the others, and thus I shall go wherever I shall be wanted. These people, where we are, are wandering, and very few in number; it will be difficult to convert them, if we cannot make them stationary.

As to the Seminary, alas! if we could only have a fund for this purpose! In the structure of which I have spoken, we marked out a little space for the beginning of one, waiting until some special houses be erected expressly for this purpose. If we had any built, I would hope that in two years Father Brébeuf would send us some Huron children. They could be instructed here with all freedom, being separated from their parents.

Your Reverence sees, through all that has been said, the benefits to be expected for the glory of God from all of these countries, and how important it is, not only to divert to some other places what is given for the mission at Kebec, but still more to find something which may serve as a retreat for Our Association, as a seminary for the children, and for Our Brothers who will one day learn the language, for there are a great many tribes differing altogether in their language.

Still further . . .

(The rest of this manuscript is lacking.)

[*Ibid.*, vi., Doc. xxii.]

V

RELATIO𝒩 OF WHAT OCCURRED I𝒩 𝒩EW FRA𝒩CE O𝒩 THE GREAT RIVER ST. LAWRE𝒩CE, I𝒩 THE YEAR O𝒩E THOUSA𝒩D SIX HU𝒩DRED THIRTY-FOUR

By Father Paul Le Jeune

MY REVEREND FATHER:

The Letters of your Reverence, the coming of our Fathers whom you have been pleased to send this year for our reinforcement, the desires of so many of our society to come to these countries and sacrifice their lives and their labors for the glory of Our Lord: All this, added to the successful return of our ships last year, and the fortunate arrival of those which have come this year, with the zeal which the Honorable associates of the Company of new France[1] show for the conversion of these barbarous people,—all these blessings together,

---

[1] This association was personally controlled and managed by Richelieu; and had members in official positions about the court; and in Paris, Rouen, and other cities of France. Among these were Marquis Deffiat, superintendent of finance; Champlain; Claude de Roquemont; the Commander de Razilly; Sebastian Cramoisy, the Parisian publisher; Jean de Lauson, long the president of the company, and intendant of Canada; Louis Houel, secretary of the King, and controller of the salt works at Brouage; and several leading merchants of Paris, Rouen, Dieppe, and Bordeaux. . . . The company was granted jurisdiction over the territory extending from Florida to the Arctic Circle, and from Newfoundland to the "great fresh lake" (Huron). Only Catholics were permitted to join this association, or to settle in its colonies; and no Huguenot or foreigner might enter Canada. The capture of Quebec by the English (1629) temporarily broke up this monopoly; but it resumed operations when that region was retroceded to France. The charter of the company obliged it to send 4,000 colonists thither before 1643; to lodge and support them during three years; and then to give them cleared lands for their maintenance. The vast expense attending this undertaking was beyond the ability of the Associates; therefore, in 1645, they transferred to the inhabitants of Quebec their monopoly of the fur trade, with their debts and other obligations,—retaining, however, their seigniorial rights. Finally (Feb. 24, 1663), the Hundred Associates abandoned their charter, and New France again became the property of the crown.—*Ibid.*, iv., *note* 21.

pouring down at once into our great forests through the arrival of Monsieur du Plessis, General of the fleet, who makes possible for us the enjoyment of some, and brings us good news of the others, overwhelm us with a satisfaction so great that it would be exceedingly difficult to express it well.

I shall divide the Relation of this year into chapters, at the end of which I shall add a journal of things which have no other connection than the order of time in which they happened. All that I shall say regarding the Savages, I have either seen with my own eyes or have received from the lips of natives, especially from an old man very well versed in their beliefs, and from a number of others with whom I have passed six months with the exception of a few days, following them into the woods to learn their language. It is, indeed, true that these people have not all the same idea in regard to their belief, which will some day make it appear that those who treat of their customs are contradicting each other.

OF THE GOOD CONDUCT OF THE FRENCH

We have passed this year in great peace and on very good terms with our French. The wise conduct and prudence of Monsieur de Champlain,[1] Governor of Kebec and of the river St. Lawrence, who honors us with his good will, has caused our words and preaching to be well received; and the Chapel which he has had erected near the fort, in honor of our Lady, has furnished excellent facilities to the French to receive the Sacraments of the Church frequently. The fort has seemed

---

[1] Samuel de Champlain was born probably between 1567 and 1570 (the exact date is unknown); his parents lived at Brouage, where was a large manufacture of salt and the finest harbor on the French coast. Champlain became a navigator early in life, and was a quartermaster in the royal army in Brittany, from 1592 to 1598.

His first voyage to America was in the service of the King of Spain; he spent from January, 1599, to March, 1601, in the West Indies and Mexico, and on the northern coast of South America. His valuable MS. report of this voyage, illustrated by his own sketches, was first printed in 1859 (but in an English translation), by the Hakluyt Society, at London; in it he suggests a ship canal across the isthmus of Panama. In 1603, he sailed with Pontgravé to Canada, exploring

like a well-ordered Academy; Monsieur de Champlain has some one read at his table, in the morning from some good historian, and in the evening from the lives of the Saints. He has the Angelus sounded at the beginning, in the middle and at the end of the day, according to the custom of the Church.

OF THE CONVERSION, BAPTISM, AND HAPPY DEATH OF CERTAIN SAVAGES

Some Savages have become Christians this year; three have been baptized this Winter during my absence. The first was a young man named Sasousmat. Father Brébeuf gave me this account of him.

"Having learned of the illness of this young man, I went to visit him, and, having sounded him, we found him filled with a great desire to receive Holy Baptism; we deferred this for a few days, in order to instruct him more fully. At last he sent word to me, through our Savage named Manitougatche, and surnamed by our French 'la Nasse,' that I should come and baptize him, saying that the night before he had seen me in his sleep, coming to his Cabin to administer to him this Sacrament; and that, as soon as I sat down near him, all his sickness went away; he confirmed this to me when I saw him. Nevertheless I refused his request, in order the more to stimulate his desire, so that another Savage who was present, not being able to bear this delay, asked me why I did not baptize him, since it was only necessary to throw a little water upon him. But, when I answered that I myself

the St. Lawrence as far as the Falls of St. Louis; and again, with De Monts, early in 1604, when they founded the St. Croix colony. Champlain remained in Canada three years, carefully exploring the Atlantic coast from Canso to Wood's Holl, and returned to France in October, 1607. The next summer he explored the valley of the St. Lawrence, with the Saguenay and other tributaries, and founded the settlement of Quebec. October 15, 1612, he was formally appointed commandant in New France. Quebec was captured by the English, July 20, 1629; but was restored to the French by the treaty of St. Germain-en-Laye, March 29, 1632. Champlain, being again appointed Governor to New France, returned to Quebec in May, 1633, where he died December 25, 1635.—*Ibid.*, ii., *note* 42.

would be lost, if I baptized an infidel and a poorly taught unbeliever, the sick man said, 'Matchounon has no sense'—it was thus they called the other Savage—'he does not believe what the Father says; as for me, I believe it entirely.' The next day, as he had fallen into a deep stupor, we baptized him, believing that he was going to die. He regained consciousness, and, having learned what had taken place, expressed his joy at having been made a child of God. He passed his time constantly until his death, which was two days later, in different acts that I caused him to practice, sometimes of Faith and Hope, sometimes of the Love of God, and of remorse for having offended him."

The second Savage to be baptized was our Manitougatche, otherwise La Nasse, of whom I have spoken in my former Relations. He had begun to get accustomed to our ways before the capture of the country by the English, having commenced to clear and cultivate the land; the bad treatment he received from these new guests drove him away from Kebec; he sometimes expressed to Madame Hebert, who remained here with her whole family, his strong desire for our return. As soon as he heard of our arrival, he came to see us, and settled near our house, saying that he wished to become a Christian, and assuring us that he would not leave us unless we chased him away.

The sojourn made in our house by Pierre Antoine,[1] a Savage and a relative of his, has been of use to him, inasmuch as we have declared to him through his lips the principal articles of our faith. This wretched young man, who was so well instructed in France, has become an apostate, renegade, excommunicate, atheist, and servant to a Sorcerer[2] who is his brother. These are the qualities I shall assign to him hereafter, when speaking of him.

---

[1] Pierre Antoine, surnamed Pastedechouan: a young Montagnais or Canadian, who was taken to France (1620) by the Récollet missionaries, and there baptized and educated. A brother of Carigonan, the Sorcerer.—*Ibid.*, v., *note* 33.

[2] The Sorcerer: Carigonan, a noted medicine man among the Montagnais, and a brother of Pierre Antoine. A third brother, with whom Le Jeune lived while wintering with the tribe, was named Mestigoit.—*Ibid.*, vi., *note* 14.

I shall finish this Chapter with an account of the very remarkable punishment of a Canadian Woman, who, having closed her ear to God during her sickness, seems to have been rejected at her death. When Father Brébeuf went to see her, she laughed at him and scorned his words. Having been prostrated by sickness, and the Savages wishing to break camp, they carried her to this worthy family who have lived here for quite a long time; but, as they had no place to keep her, these Barbarians dragged her to the fort. Monsieur de Champlain, as it was already late, gave her shelter for one night. Those who were in the room where she was placed, had to leave, as they could not bear the odor from this woman.

In the morning, Monsieur de Champlain caused a number of the savages to be called; and, reproached by him for abandoning this creature, who was of their tribe, they took her and dragged her toward their Cabins, repulsing her as they would a dog, and giving her no covering. This wretched woman, finding herself abandoned by her own people, asked that we should be called. But the Savages did not care to take the trouble to come all the way to our house, a good league from their Cabins; so that hunger, cold, disease, and the children of the Savages, as it is reported, killed her.

If we had a Hospital here, all the sick people of the country, and all the old people, would be there. As to the men, we will take care of them according to our means; but, in regard to the women, it is not becoming for us to receive them into our houses.

ON THE MEANS OF CONVERTING THE SAVAGES

The great show of power made at first by the Portuguese in the East and West Indies inspired profound admiration in the minds of the Indians, so that these people embraced, without any contradiction, the belief of those whom they admired. Now the following is, it seems to me, the way in which to acquire an ascendency over our Savages.

First, to check the progress of those who overthrow Religion, and to make ourselves feared by the Iroquois, who have killed some of our men, as every one knows, and who recently massacred two hundred Hurons, and took more than one hundred prisoners. This is, in my opinion, the only door through which we can escape the contempt into which the negligence of those who have hitherto held the trade of this country has thrown us, through their avarice.

The second means of commending ourselves to the Savages would be to send a number of capable men to clear and cultivate the land, who, joining themselves with others who know the language, would work for the Savages, on condition that they would settle down, and put their hands to the work, living in houses that would be built for their use; by this means becoming located, and seeing this miracle of charity in their behalf, they could be more easily instructed and won. While conversing this Winter with my Savages, I communicated to them this plan, assuring them that when I knew their language perfectly, I would help them cultivate their land if I could have some men, and if they wished to stop roving,—representing to them the wretchedness of their present way of living, and influencing them very perceptibly, for the time being. The Sorcerer, having heard me, turned toward his people and said, "See how boldly this black robe lies in our presence." I asked him why he thought I was lying. "Because," said he, "we never see in this world men so good as thou sayest, who would take the trouble to help us without hope of reward, and to employ so many men to aid us without taking anything from us; if thou shouldst do that," he added, "thou wouldst secure the greater part of the Savages, and they would all believe thy words."

I may be mistaken but if I can draw any conclusion from the things I see, it seems to me that not much ought to be hoped for from the Savages as long as they are wanderers; you will instruct them today, tomorrow hunger snatches your hearers away, forcing them to go and seek their food in the rivers and woods. Last year I stammered out the Catechism to a goodly number of children; as soon as the ships departed, my birds flew away. This year, I hoped to see them again, as I speak a little better; but, as they have settled on the other side of the great river St. Lawrence, my hopes have been frustrated. To try to follow them, as many Religious would be needed as there are cabins, and still we would not attain our object; for they are so occupied in seeking their livelihood in these woods, that they have not the time, so to speak, to save themselves.

These reasons, and many others that I might give, were I not afraid of being tedious, make me think that we shall work a great deal and advance very little, if we do not make these Barbarians stationary. As for persuading them to till the soil of their own accord, without being helped, I very much doubt whether we shall be able to attain this for a long time, for they know nothing whatever about it. Besides, where will they store their harvests? As their cabins are made of bark, the first frost will spoil all the roots and pumpkins they will have gathered. If they plant peas and Indian corn, they will have no place in their huts to store them. But who will feed them while they are beginning to clear the land? For they live only from one day to another, having ordinarily no provisions to sustain them during the time that they must be clearing. Finally, when they had killed themselves with hard work, they could not get from the land half their living, until they understood how to make the best use of it.

Now, with the assistance of a few good, industrious men, it would be easy to locate a few families, especially as some of them have already spoken to me about it, thus of themselves becoming accustomed, little by little, to extract something from the earth.

The third means of making ourselves welcome to these people, would be to erect here [at Quebec] a seminary for little boys, and in time one for girls, under the direction of some brave mistress, whom zeal for the glory of God and a desire for the salvation of these people, will bring over here, with a few Companions animated by the same courage. May it please his divine Majesty to inspire some to so noble an enterprise, and to divest them of any fear that the weakness of their sex might induce in them at the thought of crossing so many seas and of living among Barbarians.

I would like to keep here, where we are, the children of the Hurons. Father Brébeuf leads us to hope that we shall have some, if he goes with our Fathers into those well-peopled countries, and if there is anything with which to found a seminary. If the little Hurons, or the children of more distant tribes, are kept here, a great many advantages will result, for we would not be annoyed and distracted by the fathers while instructing the children; it will also compel these people to show good treatment to the French who are in their country, or at least not to do them any injury.

ON THE BELIEFS, SUPERSTITIONS, AND ERRORS OF THE MONTAGNAIS SAVAGES

I have already reported that the Savages believe that a certain one named Atachocam had created the world, and that one named Messou had restored it. I have questioned upon this subject the famous Sorcerer and the old man with whom I passed the Winter; they answered that they did not know who was the first Author of the world,—that it was perhaps Atachocam, but that was not certain; that they only spoke of Atachocam as one speaks of a thing so far distant that nothing can be known about it; and, in fact, the word "Nitatahokan" in their language means, "I relate a fable, I am telling an old story invented for amusement."

As to the Messou, they hold that he restored the world, which was destroyed in the flood; whence it appears that they have some tradition of the great universal deluge which happened in the time of Noë, but they have burdened this truth with a great many irrelevant fables. This Messou went to the chase, and his Lynxes, which he used instead of dogs, having gone into a great lake, were held there. The Messou, seeking them everywhere, was told by a bird that it had seen them in the midst of this lake. He went in, to get them out; but the lake overflowed, covering the earth and swallowing up the world. The Messou, very much astonished, sent a raven in search of a little piece of ground, with which to rebuild this element (the earth), but he could not find any; he made an Otter descend into the abyss of waters, but it could not bring back any; at last he sent a muskrat, which brought back a little morsel, and the Messou used this to rebuild the earth which we inhabit. He shot arrows into the trunks of trees, which made themselves into branches; he performed a thousand other wonders, avenged himself upon those who had detained his Lynxes, and married a muskrat, by whom he had children who have repeopled this world. Our Savage related to Father Brébeuf that his people believe that a certain Savage had received from Messou the gift of immortality in a little package, with a strict injunction not to open it; while he kept it closed he was immortal, but his wife, being curious and incredulous, wished to see what was inside this present; and having opened it, it all flew away, and since then the Savages have been subject to death.

They also say that all animals, of every species, have an elder brother, who is, as it were, the source and origin of all individuals, and this elder brother is wonderfully great and powerful. The elder of the Beaver, they tell me, is perhaps as large as our Cabin, although his Junior (I mean the ordinary Beaver) is not quite as large as our sheep. Now these elders of all the animals are the juniors of the Messou. Behold him well related, this worthy restorer of the Universe, he is elder brother to all beasts. If any one, when asleep, sees the elder or progenitor of some animals, he will have a fortunate chase; if he sees the elder of the Beavers, he will take Beavers; if he sees the elder of the Elks, he will take Elks, possessing the juniors through the favor of their senior whom he has seen in the dream. I asked them where these elder brothers were. "We are not sure," they answered me, "but we think the elders of the birds are in the sky, and that the elders of the other animals are in the water."

They recognise two progenitors of the seasons; one is called Nipinoukhe; it is this one that brings the Spring and Summer. The other is called Pipounoukhe, which means Winter. I asked them if this Nipinoukhe and Pipounoukhe were men, or if they were animals of some other species, and in what place they usually dwelt; they replied they did not know exactly what form they had, but they were quite sure they were living, fcr they heard them, they said, talking or rustling, especially at their coming, but they could not tell what they were saying. For their dwelling place they share the world between them, the one keeping on one side, the other upon the other; and when the period of their stay at one end of the world has expired, each goes over to the locality of the other, reciprocally succeeding each other. Here we have, in part, the fable of Castor and Pollux. When Nipinoukhe returns, he brings back with him the heat, the birds, the verdure, and restores life and beauty to the world; but Pipounoukhe lays waste everything. They call this succession of one to the other *Achitescatoueth;* meaning that they pass reciprocally to each other's places.

Furthermore, they believe that there are certain Genii of light, or Genii of the air, which they call *Khichikouai,* from the word *Khichikou,* which means "light" or "air." The *Khichikouai* are acquainted with future events, they see very far ahead; this is why the Savages consult them, not all [the savages] but certain jugglers, who know better than the others how to impose upon and amuse these people.

Now I had a great desire to know the nature of these Genii; the Apostate knew nothing about them. The Sorcerer did not wish to explain anything to me, so that I was compelled to make use of my wits. I allowed a few weeks to pass; then, springing this subject upon him, I spoke as if I admired his doctrine, saying to him that it was wrong to refuse me, since to all the questions which he asked me with regard to our belief, I answered him frankly and without showing any reluctance. At last he allowed himself to be won over by this flattery, and revealed to me the secrets of the school. Here is the fable which he recounted to me touching the nature and the character of these Genii.

Two Savages having consulted these Genii at the same time, but in two different tents, one of them, a very wicked man who had treacherously killed three men with his hatchet, was put to death by the Genii, who, crossing over into the tent of the other Savage to take his life, as well as that of his companion, were themselves surprised; for this juggler defended himself so well that he killed one of these *Khichikouai* or Genii; and thus it was found out how they were made, for this One remained in the place where he was killed. Then I asked what was his form. "He was as large as the fist," he replied; "his body was of stone, and rather long." I judged that he was cone-shaped, large at one end, and gradually becoming smaller toward the other. They believe that in this stone body there is flesh and blood, for the hatchet with which this Spirit was killed was bloody. I inquired if it had feet and wings, and was told that it had not. "Then how," I asked, "can they enter or fly into these tents, if they have neither feet nor wings?" The Sorcerer began to laugh, saying in explanation, "In truth, this black robe has no sense." This is the way they pay me back when I offer some objections to something which they cannot answer.

So that is their belief touching the foundations of things good. What astonishes me is their ingratitude, for although they believe that Messou has restored the world, that Nipinoukhe and Pipounoukhe bring the seasons, that their Khichikouai teach them where to find Elks or Moose, and render them a thousand other good offices—yet up to the present I have not been able to learn that they render them the slightest honor. I have only observed that, in their feasts, they occasionally throw a few spoonsful of grease into the fire, pronouncing these words: *Papeouekou, Papeouekou;* "Make us find something to eat, make us find something to eat." I believe this prayer is addressed to these Genii, to whom they present this grease as the best thing they have in the world.

Besides these foundations of things good, they recognise a Manitou, whom we may call the devil. They regard him as the origin of evil; it is true that they do not attribute great malice to the Manitou, but to his wife, who is a real she-devil. The husband does not hate men. He is only present in wars and combats, and those whom he looks upon are protected, the others are killed. So, for this reason, my host told me, that he prayed this Manitou every day not to cast his eyes upon the Hiroquois, their enemies, and to always give them some of them in their wars.

As to the wife of the Manitou, she is the cause of all the diseases which are in the world. It is she who kills men; otherwise they would not die; she feeds upon their flesh, gnawing them upon the inside, which causes them to become emaciated in their illnesses. She has a robe made of the most beautiful hair of the men and women whom she has killed; she sometimes appears like a fire; she can be heard roaring like a flame, but her language cannot be understood.

Furthermore, the Savages persuade themselves that not only men and other animals, but also all other things, are endowed with souls, and that all the souls are immortal: they imagine the souls as shadows of the animate objects: never having heard of anything purely spiritual, they represent the soul of man as a dark and sombre image, or as the shadow of the man himself, attributing to it feet, hands, a mouth, a head, and all other parts of the human body. Hence this is the reason that they say the souls drink and eat, and therefore they give them food when any one dies: and they have often told me that the next morning they find meat which has been gnawed during the night by the souls.

Now, having declared to me this fine article of their faith, I propounded to them several questions. "First, where do these souls go, after the death of man and other creatures?" "They go," they say, "very far away, to a large village situated where the Sun sets." "All your country," I say to them (meaning America), "is an immense Island, as you seem to know; how is it that the souls of men, of animals, of hatchets, of knives, of kettles,—in short, the souls of all things that die or that are used, can cross the water to go to this great village that you place where the sun sets?" "They go on foot," they answer me, "fording the water in some places." "And how," I respond, "can they ford the great Ocean which you know is so deep, for it is this great sea which surrounds your country?" "Thou art mistaken," they answer; "either the lands are united in some places, or there is some passage which is fordable over which our souls pass."

Secondly, I ask them, "What do those poor souls eat, making so long a journey?" "They eat bark," they said, "and old wood which they find in the forests." "I am not astonished," I replied, "that you are so afraid of death, that you shun it so greatly, there is hardly any pleasure in going and eating old wood and bark in another life."

Thirdly: "What do these souls do when they arrive at their dwelling place?" "During the day time they are seated with their two elbows upon their two knees, and their heads between their two hands, the usual position of sick Savages: during the night they go and come, they work, they go to the chase." "Oh, but they cannot see at all during the night," I rejoined. "Thou art an ignoramus, thou hast no sense," they answered: "souls are not like us, they do not see at all during the day, and see very clearly at night; their day is in the darkness of the night, and their night in the light of day."

"In the fourth place, what are these poor souls hunting during the night?" "They hunt for the souls of Beavers, Porcupines, Moose, and other animals, using the soul of the snowshoes to walk upon the soul of the snow, which is in yonder country; in short they make use of the souls of all things, as we here use the things themselves." "Now, when they have killed the soul of a Beaver, or of another animal, does that soul die entirely, or has it another soul which goes to some other village?" My Sorcerer was nonplussed by this question, and, as he is quick-witted, he said to me, "Be silent, thou hast no sense: thou askest things which thou dost not know thyself: if I had ever been in yonder country, I would answer thee."

At last I told them that the Europeans navigated the whole world. I explained to them and made them see by a round figure what country it was where the sun sets according to their idea, assuring them that no one had ever found this great village: that the souls of men alone were immortal; and, that if they were good, they would go to heaven, and if they were bad they would descend into hell, there to burn forever; and that each would receive according to his works. "In that," he said, "you lie, you people, in assigning different places for souls,—they go to the same country, at least, ours do; for the souls of two of our countrymen once returned from this great village, and explained to us all that I have told thee, then they returned to their dwelling place." They call the milky way *Tchipaï meskenau,* the path of souls, because they think that the souls raise themselves through this way in going to that great village.

The Savages are great singers; they sing, as do most of the nations of the earth, for recreation and for devotion, which, with them, means superstition. The tunes which they sing for pleasure are usually grave and heavy. It seems to me that occasionally they sing something gay, especially the girls, but for the most part, their songs are heavy, so to speak, sombre and unpleasant; they do not know what it is to combine chords to compose a sweet harmony. They use few words in singing; varying the tones, and not the words. I have often heard my Savage make a long song with these three words: *Kaie, nir, khigatoutaouim,* "And thou wilt also do something for me." They say that we imitate the warbling of birds in our tunes, which they do not disapprove, as they nearly all take pleasure both in singing and in hearing others sing; and although I told them that I did not understand anything about it, they often invited me to sing some song or prayer.

As for their superstitious songs, they use them for a thousand purposes, for which the Sorcerer and that old man, of whom I have spoken, have given me the reason. Two Savages, being once in great distress, seeing themselves within two finger lengths of death for want of food, were advised to sing; and when they had sung, they found something to eat; since that time all their religion consists mainly in singing, using the most barbarous words that come into their minds. The following are some of the words that they sang in a long superstitious rite which lasted more than four hours: *Aiasé manitou, aiasé manitou, aiasé manitou, ahiham, hehinham, hanhan, heninakhé hosé heninahkhe, enigouano bahano anihé auibini naninaouai nanahouai nanahouai aouihé ahahé aouihé:* concluding with *ho! ho! ho!* I asked what these words meant, but not one could interpret them to me, for it is true that not one of them understands what he is singing, except in the tunes they sing for recreation.

These poor wretches sing also in their sufferings, in their difficulties, in their perils and dangers. During the time of our famine, I heard nothing throughout these cabins, especially at night, except songs, cries, beating of drums and other noises. Their songs and their drums also play a part in the witchcraft of the Sorcerers.

Their Religion, or rather their superstition, consists besides in praying; but O, my God, what prayers they make! In the morning, when the little children come out from their cabins, they shout, *Cacouakhi, Pakhais Amiscouakhi, Pakhais Mousouakhi, Pakhais,* "Come, Porcupines; come, Beavers; Come, Elk," and this is all of their prayers.

When the Savages sneeze, and sometimes even at other times during the Winter, they cry out in a loud voice, *Etouctaian miraouinam an Mirouscamikhi,* "I shall be very glad to see the Spring."

At other times I have heard them pray for the Spring, or for deliverance from evils and other similar things; and they express all these things in the form of desires, crying out as loudly as they can, "I would be very glad if this day would continue, if the wind would change," etc. I could not say to whom these wishes are addressed, for they themselves do not know, at least those whom I have asked have not been able to enlighten me.

They recognise only ten Moons in the year,—I mean the greater part of the Savages, for I made the Sorcerer admit that there are twelve.

They believe that the February Moon is longer by several days than the others, and therefore they call it the great Moon. I asked them whence came the Eclipse of the Moon and of the Sun. They answered that the Moon was eclipsed, or appeared to be dark, because she held her son in her arms, which prevented her brightness from being seen. "If the Moon has a son, she is married, or has been," I told them. "Oh yes," they replied, "the Sun is her husband, who walks all day, and she all night; and if he be eclipsed, or darkened, it is because he also sometimes takes the son which he has had by the Moon, into his arms." "Yes, but neither the Moon nor the Sun has any arms," I answered them. "Thou hast no sense: they always hold their drawn bows before them, and that is why their arms do not appear." "And whom do they wish to shoot?" "Ah, how do we know?"

I asked them what those spots meant that appear on the Moon. "Thou knowest nothing at all," they said: "it is a cap which covers her head, and not spots." I inquired why the son of the Sun and of the Moon was not bright like his parents, but black and gloomy. "We do not know," said they; "if we had been in the sky, we might answer thee." I asked them if they had never seen Comets, those Stars with long tails, and what they were. "We have seen them," they answered: "it is an animal that has a long tail, 4 feet, and a head; we can see all that," they said.

I asked them about the thunder; they said that they did not know what animal it was; that it ate snakes and sometimes trees; that the Hurons believed it to be a very large bird. They were led to this belief by a hollow sound made by a kind of swallow which appears here in the Summer. I have not seen any of these birds in France, but have examined some of them here. They have a beak, a head, and a form like the swallow, except that they are a little larger; they fly about in the evening, repeatedly making a dull noise. The Hurons say that they make this noise from behind, as does also the bird which they think is the thunder; and that there is only one man who has seen this bird, and he only once in his lifetime. This is what my old man told me.

These are some of their superstitions. How much dust there is in their eyes, and how much trouble there will be to remove it that they may see the beautiful light of truth! I believe, nevertheless, that any one who knew their language perfectly, in order to give them good reasons promptly, would soon make them laugh at their own stupidity; for sometimes I have made them ashamed and confused, although I speak almost entirely by my hands, I mean by signs.

OF THE MEATS AND OTHER DISHES WHICH THE SAVAGES EAT, THEIR SEASONING, AND THEIR DRINKS

Among their terrestrial animals they have the Elk, which is here generally called the Moose; Castors, which the English call Beavers; Caribou, by some called the Wild ass; they also have Bears, Badgers, Porcupines, Foxes, Hares, Whistler or Nightingale,[1]—this is an animal larger than a Hare; they also eat Martens, and three kinds of squirrels.

As to birds, they have Bustards, white and gray Geese, several species of Ducks, Teals, Ospreys and several kinds of Divers. These are all river birds. They also catch Partridges or gray Hazel-hens, Woodcocks and Snipe of many kinds, Turtle doves, etc.

As to Fish, they catch, in the season, different kinds of Salmon, Seals, Pike, Carp, and Sturgeon of various sorts; Whitefish, Goldfish, Barbels, Eels, Lampreys, Smelt, Turtles, and others.

---

[1] So named from the shrill whistle which it utters on the approach of the enemy. The hoary marmot, or whistler. A hibernant rodent, of the squirrel family; its flesh is esteemed a delicacy by the Indians, who also sew the skins into robes or blankets.—*Ibid.,* vi., *note 22.*

They eat, besides some small ground fruits, such as rasp-berries, blueberries,[1] strawberries, nuts which have very little meat, hazelnuts, wild apples sweeter than those of France, but much smaller; cherries, of which the flesh and pit together are not larger than the pit of the Bigarreau cherry in France. They have also other small wild fruits of different kinds, in some places Wild Grapes; in short, all the fruits they have (except strawberries and raspberries, which they have in abundance), are not worth one single species of the most ordinary fruits of Europe.

They eat, besides, roots, such as bulbs of the red lily; a root which has a taste of liquorice; another that our French People call "rosary," because it is distinguished by tubers in the form of beads, and some others, not very numerous.

When they are pressed by famine, they eat the shavings or bark of a certain tree, which they call *Michtan*,[2] which they split in the Spring to get from it a juice, sweet as honey or as sugar; I have been told of this by several, but they do not enjoy much of it, so scanty is the flow.

These, then, are the meats and other articles of food upon which the Savages, of these countries where we are, subsist.

Besides these foods, which this people find in their own country without cultivating the soil, they have also cereals and Indian corn, which they trade for Moose skins with the Hurons, who come down as far as Kebec or the Three Rivers. They also buy Tobacco from that nation, who bring large quantities of it with them every year.

Besides, they get from our French People galette, or sea biscuit, bread, prunes, peas, roots, figs, and the like. You have here the food of these poor people.

As to their drinks, they make none, either from roots or

---

[1] "Some of them [the Indians] imagine a Paradise abounding in blueberries; these are little blue fruits, the berries of which are as large as the largest grapes. I have not seen any of them in France. They have a tolerably good flavor, and for this reason the souls like them very much."—*Le Jeune's Relation, 1639, Ibid.*, xvi., 191.

[2] *Michtan:* the sugar-maple. This tree was found, by early explorers, growing abundantly throughout Canada and the Atlantic regions.—*Ibid.*, vi., *note* 24.

fruits, being satisfied with pure water. It is true that the broth in which they have cooked the meat, and another broth which they make of the ground and broken bones of the Elk, serve as beverages. A certain peasant said in France that, if he were King, he would drink nothing but grease; the Savages do drink it very often, and even eat and bite into it, when it is hard, as we would bite into an apple. When they have cooked a very fat Bear, or two or three Beavers, in a kettle,[1] you will see them skim off the grease from the broth with a large wooden spoon, and taste this liquor as if what they had were the sweetest Parochimel. Sometimes they fill with it a large bark dish, and it goes the rounds of the guests at the feast, each one drinking with pleasure. At other times, having gathered their clear grease, they throw into it a quantity of snow; this they do also in their greasy soup, when they wish to drink it somewhat cool. There was a time when they had a horror of our European drinks; but they have now become so fond of these, that they would sell themselves to get them. I almost have forgotten to say that they generally drink everything warm or tepid, and sometimes blame me when they see me drink cold water, telling me that I will become thin, and that it will chill me to the bone.

Also they do not mix their eating and drinking as we do; but they first distribute the meat or other dishes; then having eaten what they want, they divide the broth, or it is put in a certain place, and each one goes and drinks as he likes.

Let us say, in concluding this subject, that with all their animals, birds and fish, the Savages are almost always hungry; the reason for this is, that the birds and fish are migratory,

---

[1] I have been told that, before kettles were brought to them from France, they cooked their meat in bark dishes which they called *ouragana*. I wondered how they could do that, for there is nothing easier to burn than this bark. I was answered that they put their meat and water into these dishes, then they place five or six stones in the fire; and when one is burning hot, they throw it into this fine soup, and, withdrawing it to place it in the fire again, they put another one which is red-hot in its place, and this continues until their meat is cooked. Pierre, the Savage, assured me that some of them, having lost or broken their kettles, still resorted to this old custom, and that it did not take so long to cook the meat as one would imagine.—*Le Jeune's Relation,* 1633, *Ibid.,* v., 97.

going and returning at certain times. Besides, they are not very great hunters and are still poorer managers; for what they kill in one day is not seen the next, except the Elk and eels, which they dry when they have them in great abundance. So that during the months of September and October, they live for the most part upon fresh eels; in November and December and often in January, they eat smoked eels, some Porcupines, which they take during the lighter snowfalls, as also a few Beavers, if they find them. When the heavy snows come, they eat Moose meat; they dry it, to live upon the rest of the time until September; and with this they have a few birds, Bears, Beavers, which they take in the Spring and during the Summer. Now if the hunt for all these animals does not succeed, they suffer greatly.

ON THEIR HUNTING AND FISHING

Let us begin with the Elk. When there is very little snow, they kill it with arrows, the first that we ate being taken this way. But it is a great stroke of luck when they can approach these animals within range of their bows, as they scent the Savages at a great distance, and run as fast as the deer. When the snow is deep they pursue the Elk on foot, and kill it with thrusts from javelins which are fastened on long poles for the purpose, and which they hurl when they dare not or cannot approach the beast. Sometimes they chase one of these animals for two or three days, the snow being neither hard nor deep enough; while at other times a child could almost kill them, for, the snow being frozen after a slight thaw or rain, these poor Moose are hurt by it, and cannot go far without being slaughtered.

I had been told that the Elk was as large as the Auvergne mule. True, its head is as long as that of a mule, but I find it as large as an ox. I have only seen one of them alive; it was young, and the branches or horns were just emerging from its head; I never saw in France either a heifer or young bullock that was as big or as high as it was. It is tall and erect, like a

Deer; its horns are lofty, branching, and somewhat flat, not round like those of a Deer. I speak of the horns that I have seen, there may be other kinds. I have been told that the female always bears two little ones, always male and female. On the contrary, my Savages tell me that she sometimes bears one, and sometimes two; and that once they found three in a female, which astonished them as if it were a prodigy.

I have sometimes thought that, in time, these animals might be domesticated, and could be used to till the soil and draw sledges over the snow, which would be a great comfort.

When the Savages have killed a number of Elks, and passed several days in feasting, they begin to think about drying them and laying them away. They will stretch upon poles the two sides of a large Moose, the bones thereof having been removed. If the flesh is too thick, they raise it in strips and slash it besides, so that the smoke may penetrate and dry all parts. When they begin to dry or smoke this meat they pound it with stones and tramp it under foot so that no juice may remain to spoil it. At last, when it is smoked, they fold and arrange it in packages, and this forms their future store. Dried meat is poor food, but the fresh meat of the Elk is very easy to digest. It does not remain long in the stomach, therefore the Savages do not cook it much. In regard to taste, it seems to me that beef is not inferior to good Elk meat.

The Castor or Beaver is taken in several ways. The Savages say that it is the animal well-beloved by the French, English and Basques,—in a word, by the Europeans. I heard my host say one day, jokingly, *Missi picoutau amiscou,* "The Beaver does everything perfectly well, it makes Kettles, hatchets, swords, knives, bread; and in short, it makes everything." He was making sport of us Europeans, who have such a fondness for the skin of this animal and who fight to see who will give the most to these Barbarians, to get it; they carry this to such an extent that my host said to me one day, showing me a very beautiful knife, "The English have no sense; they give us twenty knives like this for one Beaver skin."

In the Spring, the Beaver is taken in a trap baited with the wood it eats. The Savages understand perfectly how to handle these traps, which are made to open, when a heavy piece of wood falls upon the animal and kills it. Sometimes when the dogs encounter the Beaver outside its House, they pursue and take it easily; I have never seen this chase, but have been told of it; and the Savages highly value a dog which scents and runs down this animal.

During the Winter they capture them in nets and under the ice, in this way: They make a slit in the ice near the Beaver's house, and put into the hole a net, and some wood which serves as bait. This poor animal, searching for something to eat, gets caught in a net made of good, strong, double cord; and, emerging from the water to the opening made in the ice, they kill it with a big club.

The other way of taking them under the ice is more noble. Not all the Savages use this method, only the most skilful; they break with blows from the hatchet the Cabin or House of the Beaver, which is indeed, wonderfully made. In my opinion no musket ball can pierce it. During the winter it is built upon the shore of some little river or pond, is two stories high, and round. The materials of which it is composed are wood and mud, so well joined and bound together that I have seen our Savages in Midwinter sweat in trying to make an opening into it with their hatchets. The lower story is in or upon the edge of the water, the upper is above the river. When the cold has frozen the rivers and ponds, the Beaver secludes himself with wood to eat during the Winter. He sometimes, however, descends from this story to the lower one, and thence he glides out under the ice, through the holes which are in this lower story and which open under the ice. He goes out to drink and to search for the wood that he eats, which grows upon the banks of the pond and in the pond itself. This wood at the bottom is fastened in the ice and the Beaver goes below to cut it and carry it to his house.

Now the Savages having broken into this house, these poor animals, which are sometimes in great numbers under one roof, disappear under the ice, where they can breathe. Their enemies, knowing this, go walking over the pond or frozen river, carrying a long club in their hands, armed on one side with an iron blade made like a Carpenter's chisel, and on the other with a Whale's bone, I believe. They sound the ice with this bone, striking upon it and examining it to see if it is hollow; and if there is any indication of this, then they cut the ice with their iron blade, looking to see if the water is stirred up by the movement or breathing of the Beaver. If the water moves, they have a curved stick which they thrust into the hole that they have just made; if they feel the beaver, they kill it with their big club, which they call *ca ouikachit;* and, drawing it out of the water, go and make a feast of it at once, unless they have great hopes of taking others. I asked them why the Beaver waited there until it was killed. "Where will it go?" they said to me; "Its house is broken to pieces and the other places where it could breathe between the water and ice are broken; it remains there in the water, seeking air, and meanwhile it is killed." Sometimes there are two families of Beavers in the same house, that is, two males and two females, with their little ones.

The Female bears as many as seven, but usually four, five or six. They have four teeth, two below and two above, which are wonderfully drawn out; the other two are small, but these are large and sharp. They are used to cut their wood for their food, and the wood with which they build their house; they sharpen these teeth when they are dull, by rubbing and pressing them against each other, making a little noise which I myself have heard.

The Beaver has very soft fur, the hats made of it being an evidence of this. It has very short feet which are well adapted to swimming, for the nails are united by skin, in the same way as those of river-birds or seals; its tail is entirely flat, quite long and oval-shaped. But if the pelt of the Beaver excels the pelt of the sheep, the flesh of the sheep is superior, in my opinion, to that of the Beaver,—not only because it tastes better, but also because the sheep is larger than the Beaver.

The Porcupine is taken in a trap, or by coursing. The dog

having discovered it, it is sure to be killed if it is not very near its abode, which it makes under large rocks; having reached this, it is in a place of safety, for neither men nor dogs can crawl into it. It cannot run upon the snow, and is therefore very soon put to death. It is hardly larger than a good-sized sucking-pig. Its points or quills are white, long, and rather thin, interlaced and mixed with black or greyish hair. In France I have seen specimens of the Porcupine with quills three times longer and ten times thicker, and much stiffer than those of the Porcupines of this country. The Savages have told me that near the Saguenay river, toward the North, these animals are much larger. They singe them as we do pigs in France; and, after they are scraped, they are boiled or roasted, and are quite edible, although rather tough, especially the old ones, but the younger ones are tender and delicate.

Bears are taken in a trap, in the Spring. In the Winter they are found in hollow trees, to which they withdraw, passing several months without eating, and yet they continue to be very fat. They fell a tree, to make their prey emerge, which they kill upon the snow, or as it is coming from its abode.

Hares are caught in nets, or are killed with arrows or darts. I have already stated elsewhere that these animals are white during the snow, and grey at other times. They kill Martens and Squirrels in the same way.

As to birds, some are killed with bows, arrows and Darts being used; but this is done rarely. Since they have come into possession of firearms, through their traffic with the English, they have become fair Huntsmen, some of them shooting very well.

As to their fishing, they use nets as we do, which they get in trade from the French and Hurons.

In regard to Eels, they fish for them two ways, with a weir and with a harpoon. They make the weirs very ingeniously, long and broad, capable of holding five or six hundred eels. When the water is low, they place these upon the sand, securing them so they will not be carried away by the tides. At the two sides they collect stones, which they extend out like a chain or little wall on both sides; so that this fish, which always swims toward the bottom, encountering this obstacle, will readily swim toward the mouth of the nets, to which these stones guide it; sometimes they find one or two hundred eels in a single tide.

This harpoon fishing is usually done only at night. Two Savages enter a canoe,—one at the stern, who handles the oars, and the other at the bow, who by the light of a bark torch fastened to the prow of his boat, looks searchingly for his prey, floating gently along the shores of this great river. When he sees an Eel, he thrusts his harpoon down, without loosening his hold of it, pierces it, then throws it into his canoe. There are certain ones who take three hundred in one night, and even more. The Savages dry these long fish in smoke. After they are brought to their Cabins, they let them drain a little while; then, cutting off their heads and tails, they open them up the back and after they are cleaned, they are cut with slits, so that the smoke may thoroughly penetrate them. The poles of their Cabins are all loaded with these eels. Here you have their food up to the season of snow, which brings them the Moose.

They kill the Seal with blows from a club, surprising it when it comes out of the water. It goes to Sun itself upon the rocks, and, not being able to run, if it is ever so little distant from its element it is lost.

But before I pass on, I must say a few words about four animals that I have never seen in France. I do not know where to place them, except at the end of this chapter.

One of them is called by the Savages *Ouinascou;* our French call it the whistler or Nightingale. They have given it this name, because although it belongs to terrestrial animals, yet it sings like a bird; I might say that it whistles like a well taught linnet, were it not that I think it only knows one song; that is to say, it has not a great variety of tones, but it says very well the lesson that nature has taught it. It is about the size of a Hare and has a reddish skin. Some have assured me that it rolls itself into a ball, and like the Dormouse, it sleeps all winter, it being impossible to awaken it. I have only seen this

animal in the summer.   It is excellent eating and excels the
Hare.

The other is a low animal, about the size of a little dog or
cat.   I mention it here, not on account of its excellence, but
to make of it a symbol of sin.   I have seen three or four of
them.   It has black fur, quite beautiful and shining; and has
upon its back two perfectly white stripes, which join near the
neck and tail making an oval which adds greatly to their grace.
The tail is bushy and well furnished with hair, like the tail
of a fox; it carries it curled back like that of a Squirrel.   It is
more white than black; and at first glance, you would say,
especially when it walks that it ought to be called Jupiter's
little dog.   But it is so stinking and casts so foul an odor, that
it is unworthy of being called the dog of Pluto.   No sewer
ever smelled so bad.   I would not have believed it if I had
not smelled it myself.   Your heart almost fails you when you
approach the animal; two have been killed in our court, and
several days afterward there was such a dreadful odor throughout our house that we could not endure it.   I believe the sin
smelled by sainte Catherine de Sienne must have had the same
vile odor.

The third is a flying Squirrel.   There are three kinds of
squirrels, which are not so beautiful as those in France.   The
others, which our French call Swiss, because they are spotted
upon the back, are very beautiful and quite small.   The flying
Squirrels are rather pretty, but their chief merit lies in their
flying.   Not that they have wings, but they have a certain
piece of skin on both sides, which they fold up very neatly
against their stomachs when they walk, and spread out when
they fly.   I do not think they take long flights; I saw one of
them flying, and it sustained itself very well in the air.

The fourth is called by our French the fly-bird, because it
is scarcely larger than a bee; others call it the flower-bird,
because it lives upon flowers.   It is in my opinion one of the
great rarities of this country, and a little prodigy of nature.
God seems to me more wonderful in this little bird than in a
large animal.   It hums in flying, like a bee; I have sometimes

seen it hold itself in the air and stick its bill into a flower. Its bill is rather long, and its plumage seems to be a mottled green. Those who call it the flower-bird would, in my opinion, speak more correctly if they would call it the flower of birds.

ON THE LANGUAGE OF THE MONTAGNAIS SAVAGES

I wrote last year that their language was very rich and very poor, full of abundance and full of scarcity, the latter appearing in a thousand different ways. All words for piety, devotion, virtue; all terms that are used to express the things of the other life; the language of Theologians, Philosophers, Mathematicians, and Physicians, in a word, of all learned men; all words which refer to the regulation and government of a city, Province, or Empire; all that concerns justice, reward and punishment; the names of an infinite number of arts which are in our Europe; of thousands and thousands of contrivances, of a thousand beauties and riches, all these things are never found either in the thoughts or upon the lips of the Savages. As they have no true religion nor knowledge of the virtues, neither public authority nor government, neither Kingdom nor Republic, nor sciences, nor any of those things of which I have just spoken, consequently all the terms which refer to that world of wealth and grandeur must be absent from their vocabulary. Let us now turn the tables and show that this language is fairly gorged with richness.

First, I find an infinite number of proper nouns among them, which I cannot explain in our french, except by circumlocutions.

Second, they have some Verbs which I call absolute, to which neither the Greeks, nor Latins, nor we ourselves, nor any language of Europe with which I am familiar, have anything similar. For example, the verb *Nimitison* means absolutely, "I eat," without saying what; for if you determine the thing you eat, you have to use another Verb.

Third, they have different Verbs to signify an action toward an animate or toward an inanimate object. "I see a man,"

Niouapaman iriniou; "I see a stone, *niouabatê;* but in Greek, in Latin, and in French the same Verb is used to express "I see a man, a stone, or anything else."

In the fourth place, they have Verbs suitable to express an action which terminates on the person reciprocal, and others still which terminate on the things that belong to him: and we cannot use these Verbs, referring to other persons not reciprocal, without speaking improperly. I will explain myself. The Verb *nitaouin* means, "I make use of something"; *nitaouin agouniscouehon,* "I am using a hat"; but when I come to say, "I am using his hat," that is, the hat of the man of whom I speak, we must say, *Nitaouiouan outagoumiscouhon;* but if it be an animate thing, "I am using his dog," *nitaouiouan otaimai.* Also observe that all these verbs have their moods, tenses and persons: and that they are conjugated differently, if they have different terminations.

In the fifth place they use some words upon the land and others upon the water, to signify the same thing. As, for instance, I want to say, "I arrived yesterday"; if by land, I must say, *nitagochinin outagouchi,*—if by water, *nimichagan outagouchi.* "I am going to look for something," if upon land, I must say *ninaten,*—if by water, *ninahen;* if it is an animate thing and upon land, *ninatau;* if it be animate and in the water, *ninahouau.* What a variety! We have in French only a single expression for all these things.

They have so tiresome an abundance that I am almost led to believe that I shall remain poor all my life in their language. When you know all the parts of speech of the languages of our Europe, and know how to combine them, you know the languages; but it is not so concerning the tongue of our Savages. Stock your memory with all the words that stand for each particular thing, learn the knot or Syntax that joins them, and you are still only an ignoramus; with that, you can indeed make yourself understood by the Savages, although not always, but you will not be able to understand them. The reason for this is, that, besides the names of each particular thing, they have an infinite number of words which signify several things together. The verb, *nisiicatchin*, means, "I am cold"; the noun, *nissitai*, means "my feet"; if I say *nisicat chin nissitai* to say "my feet are cold," they will indeed understand me, but I shall not understand them when they say *Nitatagouasisin*, which is the proper word to say, "my feet are cold." And what ruins the memory is that such a word has neither relation, nor alliance, nor any affinity, in its sound, with the other two; whence it often happens that I make them laugh in talking, when I try to follow the construction of the Latin or French language, not knowing these words which mean several things at once.

I forgot to say that the Montagnais have not so many letters in their Alphabet as we have in ours; they confound B and P, and also C, G, and K. They do not have the letters F, L, consonant V, X, and Z. They use R instead of L, saying Monsieur du Pressi for Monsieur du Plessi; they utter the sound of P instead of consonant V, Monsieur Olipier instead of Monsieur Olivier. But, as their tongues are quite flexible, they will soon acquire our pronunciation if they are instructed, especially the children.

Father Brébeuf tells me that the Hurons have no M, at which I am astonished, for this letter seems to me almost natural, so extensively is it used.

Now if, as conclusion of this Chapter, Your Reverence asks me if I made much progress in the knowledge of this language during the winter I spent with these Barbarians, I answer frankly, "no"; and here are the reasons.

First, my defective memory, which was never very good, and which continues to wither every day. Oh, what an excellent man for these countries is Father Brébeuf! His most fortunate memory, and his amiability and gentleness, will be productive of much good among the Hurons.

Second, the malice of the Sorcerer, who sometimes prevented them from teaching me.

Third, the perfidy of the Apostate, who, contrary to his promise, and notwithstanding the offers I made him, was never willing to teach me,—his disloyalty even going so far as to purposely give me a word of one signification for another.

In the fourth place, famine was for a long time our guest: and I scarcely ventured in her presence to question our Savages, their stomachs not being like barrels which sound all the louder for being empty; they resemble the drum,—the tighter it is drawn, the better it talks.

In the fifth place, my attacks of illness made me give up the care for the languages of earth, to think about the language of the other life whither I was expecting to go.

In the sixth place and finally, the difficulty of this language, which is not slight, has been no small obstacle to prevent a poor memory like mine from advancing far. Still I talk a jargon, and, by dint of shouting, can make myself understood.

One thing would touch me keenly, were it not that we are not expected to walk before God, but to follow him, and to be content with our own littleness; it is that I almost fear that I shall never be able to speak the Savage tongues with the fluency necessary to preach to them, and to answer at once, without stumbling, their demands and objections, being so greatly occupied as I have been up to the present. It is true that God can make from a rock a child of Abraham.

WHAT ONE MUST SUFFER IN WINTERING WITH THE SAVAGES

Epictetus says that he who intends to visit the public baths must previously consider all the improprieties that will be committed there; so that, when he finds himself surrounded by the derision of a mob of scoundrels who would rather wash his head than his feet, he may lose none of the gravity and modesty of a wise man. I might say the same to those in whom God inspires the thought and desire to cross over the seas, in order to seek and to instruct the Savages. It is for their sake that I shall pen this chapter, so that they may not forget to fortify themselves with the weapons necessary for the combat, especially with patience of iron or bronze, or rather with a patience entirely of gold, in order to bear bravely and lovingly the great trials that must be endured among these people. Let us begin by speaking of the house they will have to live in, if they wish to follow them.

In order to have some conception of the beauty of this edifice, its construction must be described. I shall speak from knowledge, for I have often helped to build it. Now, when we arrived at the place where we were to camp, the women, armed with axes, went here and there in the great forests, cutting the framework of the hostelry where we were to lodge; meantime the men, having drawn the plan thereof, cleared away the snow with their snowshoes.

Imagine now a great ring or square in the snow, two, three, or four feet deep, according to the weather or the place where they encamp. This depth of snow makes a white wall for us, which surrounds us on all sides, except the end where it is broken through to form the door. The framework having been brought, which consists of twenty or thirty poles, according to the size of the cabin, it is planted, not upon the ground, but upon the snow; then they throw upon these poles, which converge a little at the top, two or three rolls of bark sewed together, beginning at the bottom, and behold, the house is made. The ground inside, as well as the wall of snow which extends all around the cabin, is covered with little branches of fir; and, as a finishing touch, a wretched skin is fastened to two poles to serve as a door, the door posts being the snow itself. Now let us examine in detail all the comforts of this elegant Mansion.

You cannot stand upright in this house, as much on account of its low roof as the suffocating smoke; and consequently you must always lie down, or sit flat upon the ground, the usual posture of the Savages. When you go out, the cold, the snow, and the danger of getting lost in these great woods drive you in again more quickly than the wind, and keep you a prisoner in a dungeon which has neither lock nor key.

This prison, in addition to the uncomfortable position that one must occupy upon a bed of earth, has four other great discomforts,—cold, heat, smoke, and dogs. As to the cold, you have the snow at your head with only a pine branch between, often nothing but your hat, and the winds are free to enter at a thousand places. For do not imagine that these pieces of bark are joined as paper is glued and fitted to a window frame; even if there were only the opening at the top, which serves at once as window and chimney, the coldest winter in France could come in there every day without any trouble. When I lay down at night I could study through this opening both the Stars and the Moon as easily as if I had been in the open fields.

Nevertheless the cold did not annoy me as much as the heat from the fire. A little place like their cabins is easily heated by a good fire, which sometimes roasted and broiled me on all sides, for the cabin was so narrow that I could not protect myself against the heat. You cannot move to right or left, for the Savages, your neighbors, are at your elbows; you cannot withdraw to the rear, for you encounter the wall of snow, or the bark of the cabin which shuts you in. I did not know what position to take. Had I stretched myself out, the place was so narrow that my legs would have been half way in the fire; to roll myself up in a ball, and crouch down that way, was a position I could not retain as long as they could; my clothes were all scorched and burned. You will ask me perhaps if the snow at our backs did not melt under so much heat. I answer, "no"; that if sometimes the heat softened it in the least, the cold immediately turned it into ice. I will say, however, that both the cold and the heat are endurable, and that some remedy may be found for these two evils.

But as to the smoke, I confess to you that it is martyrdom. It almost killed me, and made me weep continually, though I had neither grief nor sadness in my heart. It sometimes grounded all of us who were in the cabin; that is, it caused us to place our mouths against the earth in order to breathe; as it were to eat the earth, so as not to eat the smoke. I have sometimes remained several hours in that position, especially during the most severe cold and when it snowed; for it was then the smoke assailed us with the greatest fury. How bitter is this drink! How strong its odor! How hurtful to the eyes are its fumes! I sometimes thought I was going blind; my eyes burned like fire; they wept or distilled drops like an alembic; I no longer saw anything distinctly. I repeated the Psalms of my Breviary as best I could, and waited until the pain might relax a little to recite the lessons; and when I came to read them, they seemed written in letters of fire, or of scarlet; I have often closed my book, seeing things so confusedly that it injured my sight.

Some one will tell me that I ought to have gone out from this smoky hole to get some fresh air; and I answer him that the air was usually so cold at those times that the trees, which have a harder skin than man, and a more solid body, could not stand it, splitting even to the core. Nevertheless I occasionally emerged from this den, fleeing the rage of the smoke to place myself at the mercy of the cold, against which I tried to arm myself by wrapping up in my blanket like an Irishman; the trouble was, the snow had no more pity upon my eyes than the smoke.

As to the dogs, which I have mentioned as one of the discomforts of the Savages' houses, I do not know that I ought to blame them, for they have sometimes rendered me good service. These poor beasts, not being able to live outdoors, came and lay down upon my shoulders, sometimes upon my feet, and as I only had one blanket to serve both as covering and mattress, I was not sorry for this protection, willingly restoring to them a part of the heat I drew from them. These animals, being famished, as they have nothing to eat any more than we do, do nothing but run to and fro gnawing at everything in the cabin. They have often upset for me my bark dish, and all it contained, in my gown; there was not one of us who did not hold his plate down with both hands on the ground, which serves as table, seat, and bed both to men and dogs. I have said enough about the inconveniences of the Savages' houses, let us speak of their food.

When I first went away with them, as they salt neither their

soup nor their meat, and as filth itself presides over their cooking, I could not eat their mixtures, and contented myself with
a few sea biscuit and smoked eel; until at last my host took
me to task because I ate so little, saying that I would starve
myself before the famine overtook us. Meanwhile our Savages had feasts every day, so that in a very short time we found
ourselves without bread, without flour, without eels, and without any means of helping ourselves. For besides being very
far in the woods, where we would have died a thousand times
before reaching the French settlement, we were wintering on
the other side of the great river, which cannot be crossed in
this season on account of the great masses of ice which are continually floating about, and which would crush not only a small
boat but even a great ship. As to the chase, the snows not
being deep in comparison with those of other years, they could
not take the Elk, and so brought back only some Beavers and
Porcupines, but in so small a number and so seldom that they
kept us from dying rather than helped us to live.

My host said to me during this time of scarcity, "*Chibiné*,
harden thy soul, resist hunger; thou wilt be sometimes two,
sometimes three or four, days without food; do not let thyself
be cast down, take courage; when the snow comes we shall eat."
It was not our Lord's will that they should be so long without
capturing anything, but we usually had something to eat once
in two days,—indeed, we very often had a Beaver in the morning, and in the evening of the next day a Porcupine as big as
a sucking Pig. This was not much for nineteen of us, but this
little sufficed to keep us alive. When I could have, toward
the end of our supply of food, the skin of an Eel for my day's
fare, I considered that I had breakfasted, dined, and supped
well.

At first I had used one of those skins to patch the cloth gown
that I wore, as I forgot to bring some pieces with me; but,
when I was so sorely pressed with hunger, I ate my pieces; and,
if my gown had been made of the same stuff, I assure you I
would have brought it back home much shorter than it was.
Indeed, I ate old Moose skins, which are much tougher than

those of the Eel; I went about through the woods biting the ends of the branches, and gnawing the more tender bark.

Our neighboring Savages suffered still more than we did, some of them coming to see us, and telling us that their comrades had died of hunger. I saw some who had eaten' only once in five days, and who considered themselves very well off if they found something to dine upon at the end of two days. We occasionally had some good meals; but for every good dinner we went three times without supper. They often asked me if I was not afraid, if I had no fear of death; and, seeing me quite firm, they were astonished, on one occasion in particular, when I saw them almost falling into a state of despair. When they reach this point, they play, so to speak, at "save himself who can": throwing away their bark and baggage, deserting each other, and abandoning all interest in the common welfare, each one strives to find something for himself. Then the children, women, and for that matter all those who cannot hunt, die of cold and hunger. If they had reached this extremity, I would have been among the first to die.

After this famine, we had some good days. The snow, which had been only too deep to be cold, but too shallow to take Moose, having greatly increased toward the end of January, our Hunters captured some Moose, which they dried. Now either on account of my lack of moderation, or because this meat, dried as hard as wood and as dirty as the street, did not agree with my stomach, I fell sick. So behold me obliged to remain all the time lying upon the cold ground; this did not tend to cure me of the severe cramps that tormented me and compelled me to go out at all hours of the day and night, plunging me every time in snow up to my knees and sometimes almost up to my waist, especially when we had first begun our encampment in any one place.

Being very thirsty one day, I asked for a little water; they said there was none, and that they would give me some melted snow. As this drink was bad for my disease, I made my host understand that I had seen a lake not far from there, and that I would like very much to have some of that water. He pretended not to hear, because the road was somewhat bad, and it happened thus not only this time, but at any place where the river or brook was a little distance from our cabin. We had to drink this snow melted in a kettle whose copper was less thick than the dirt; if any one wishes to know how bitter this drink is, let him take some from a kettle just out of the smoke and taste it.

As to the food, they divide with a sick man just as with the others; if they have fresh meat they give him his share, if he wants it, but if he does not eat it then, no one will take the trouble to keep a little piece for him to eat when he wants it; they will give him some of what they happen to have at the time in the cabin, namely, smoked meat, and nothing better, for they keep the best for their feasts. So a poor invalid is often obliged to eat among them what would horrify him even in good health if he were with our Frenchmen. A soul very thirsty for the Son of God, I mean for suffering, would find enough here to satisfy it.

It remains for me yet to speak of their conversation, in order to make it clearly understood what there is to suffer among these people. I had gone in company with my host and the Renegade, on condition that we should not pass the winter with the Sorcerer, whom I knew as a very wicked man. They had granted my conditions, but they were faithless, and kept not one of them, involving me in trouble with this pretended Magician, as I shall relate hereafter. Now this wretched man and the smoke were the two greatest trials that I endured among these Barbarians. The cold, heat, annoyance of the dogs, sleeping in the open air and upon the bare ground; the position I had to assume in their cabins, rolling myself up in a ball or crouching down or sitting without a seat or a cushion; hunger, thirst, the poverty and filth of their smoked meats, sickness,—all these things were merely play to me in comparison to the smoke and the malice of the Sorcerer, with whom I have always been on a very bad footing, for the following reasons:

First, because, when he invited me to winter with him I

refused; and he resented this greatly, because he saw that I cared more for my host, his younger brother, than I did for him.

Second, because I could not gratify his covetousness. I had nothing that he did not ask me for, often taking my mantle off my shoulders to put it on his own. Now as I could not satisfy all his demands, he looked upon me with an evil eye; indeed, even if I had given him all the little I had, I could not have gained his friendship, because we were at variance on other subjects.

In the third place, seeing that he acted the Prophet, amusing these people by a thousand absurdities, which he invented, in my opinion, every day, I did not lose any opportunity of convincing him of their nonsense and childishness, exposing the senselessness of his superstitions. Now this was like tearing his soul out of his body; for, as he could no longer hunt, he acted the Prophet and Magician more than ever before, in order to preserve his credit, and to get the dainty pieces. So that in shaking his authority, which was diminishing daily, I was touching the apple of his eye and wresting from him the delights of his Paradise, which are the pleasures of his jaws.

In the fourth place, wishing to have sport at my expense, he sometimes made me write vulgar things in his language, assuring me there was nothing bad in them, then made me pronounce these shameful words, which I did not understand, in the presence of the Savages. Some women having warned me of this trick, I told him I would no longer soil my paper nor my lips with these vile words. He insisted, however, that I should read before all those of the cabin, and some Savages who had come thither, something he had dictated to me. I answered him that, if the Apostate would interpret them to me, I would read them. That Renegade refusing to do this, I refused to read. The Sorcerer commanded me imperiously, that is, with high words, and I at first begged him gently to excuse me; but as he did not wish to be thwarted before the Savages, he persisted in urging me, and had my host, who pretended to be vexed, urge me also. At last, aware that my excuses were of no avail, I spoke to him preemptorily, and, after reproaching him for his lewdness, I addressed him in these words; "Thou hast me in thy power, thou canst murder me, but thou canst not force me to repeat indecent words." "They are not such," he said. "Why then," said I, "will they not interpret them to me?" He emerged from this conflict very much exasperated.

In the fifth place, seeing that my host was greatly attached to me, he was afraid that this friendliness might deprive him of some choice morsel. I tried to relieve him of this apprehension by stating publicly that I did not live to eat, but that I ate to live; and that it mattered little what they gave me, provided it was enough to keep me alive. He retorted sharply that he was not of my opinion, but that he made a profession of being dainty; that he was fond of the good pieces, and was very much obliged when people gave them to him. Now although my host gave him no cause for fear in this direction, yet he attacked me at almost every meal as if he were afraid of losing his precedence. This apprehension increased his hatred.

In the sixth place, when he saw that the savages of the other cabins showed me some respect, knowing besides that I was a great enemy of his impostures, and that, if I gained influence among his flock, I would ruin him completely, he did all he could to destroy me and make me appear ridiculous in the eyes of his people.

In the seventh place, add to all these things the aversion which he and all the Savages of Tadoussac had, up to the present time, against the French, since their intercourse with the English; and judge what treatment I might have received from these Barbarians, who adore this miserable Sorcerer, against whom I was generally in a state of open warfare. I thought a hundred times that I should only emerge from this conflict through the gates of death. He treated me shamefully, it is true; but I am astonished that he did not act worse, seeing that he is an idolater of those superstitions which I was fighting with all my might. To relate in detail all his attacks, gibes, sneers, and contempt, I would write a Book instead of a Chapter. Suffice it to say, that he sometimes even attacked God to displease me; and that he tried to make me the laughing stock of small and great, abusing me in the other cabins as well as in ours. He never had, however, the satisfaction of inciting our neighboring Savages against me; they merely hung their heads when they heard the blessings he showered upon me.

As to the servants, instigated by his example, and supported by his authority, they continually heaped upon me a thousand taunts and a thousand insults; and I was reduced to such a state, that, in order not to irritate them or give them any occasion to get angry, I passed whole days without opening my mouth. Believe me, if I have brought back no other fruits from the Savages, I have at least learned many of the insulting words of their language. They were saying to me at every turn, *eca titou, eca titou nama khitirinisin,* "Shut up, shut up, thou hast no sense." *Achineou,* "He is proud"; *Moucach-techiou,* "He plays the parasite"; *Sasegau,* "He is haughty"; *cou attimou,* "He looks like a Dog"; *cou mascoua,* "He looks like a Bear"; *cou ouabouchou ouichtoui,* "He is bearded like a Hare"; *attimonai oukhimau,* "He is the Captain of the Dogs"; *cou oucousimas ouchtigonan,* "He has a head like a pumpkin"; *matchiriniou,* "He is deformed, he is ugly"; *khich-couebeon,* "He is drunk." So these are the colors in which they paint me, and a multitude of others, which I omit. The best part of it was that they did not think sometimes that I understood them; and, seeing me smile, they became embarrassed,— at least, those who sang these songs only to please the Sorcerer. The children were very troublesome, playing numberless tricks upon me, and imposing silence when I wanted to talk. When my host was at home, I had some rest; and, when the Sorcerer was absent, I was in smooth water, managing both great and small just as I wished.

So these are some of the things that have to be endured among these people. This must not frighten anyone; good soldiers are animated with courage at the sight of their blood and their wounds, and God is greater than our hearts. One does not always encounter a famine; one does not always meet Sorcerers or jugglers with so bad a temper as that one had; in a word, if we could understand the language, and reduce it to rules, there would be no more need of following these Barbarians. As to the stationary tribes, from which we expect the greatest fruit, we can have our cabins apart, and consequently be freed from many of these great inconveniences. But let us finish this Chapter; otherwise I see myself in danger of becoming as troublesome as that imposter, whom I commend to the prayers of all those who will read this.

CONTAINING A JOURNAL OF THINGS WHICH COULD NOT BE SET FORTH IN THE PRECEDING CHAPTERS

One day, when my host had a feast, the guests made me a sign that I should make them a speech in their language, as they wanted to laugh; for I pronounce the Savage as a German pronounces French. Wishing to please them, I began to talk, and they burst out laughing, well pleased to make sport of me, while I was very glad to learn to talk. I said to them in conclusion that I was a child, and that children made their fathers laugh with their stammering; but in a few years I would become large, and then, when I knew their language, I would make them see that they themselves were children in many things, ignorant of the great truths of which I would speak to them.

Suddenly I asked them if the Moon was located as high as the Stars, if it was in the same Sky; where the Sun went when it left us; what was the form of the earth. (If I knew their language perfectly I would always propose some natural truth, before speaking to them of the truths of our belief; for I have observed that these curious things make them more attentive.) One of them, after having frankly confessed that they could not answer these questions, said to me, "But how canst thou thyself know these things, since we do not know them?" I immediately drew out a little compass that I had in my pocket, opened it, and placing it in his hand, said to him, "We are now in the darkness of night, the Sun no longer shines for us; tell me now, while you look at what I have given you, in what part of the world it is; show me the place where it must rise tomorrow, where it will set, where it will be at noon; point out the places in the Sky where it will never be." My man answered with his eyes, staring at me without saying a word. I took the compass and explained it to him, adding, "Well, how is it that I can know these things, and you do not know them? I have still other greater truths to tell you when I can talk." "Thou art intelligent," they responded, "thou wilt soon know our language." But they were mistaken.

On the first of July, Father Brébeuf and Father Daniel left in a bark to go to Three Rivers, there to wait for the Hurons. This bark was destined to begin a new settlement in that quarter. Father Davost, who had come down from Tadoussac, followed our Fathers three days later in company with Monsieur the General, who wanted to meet these people at the trading post. They waited there some time for the Hurons, who did not come down in so great numbers this year as usual; because the Hiroquois, having been informed that five hundred men of this nation were moving toward their country to make war upon them, themselves went on ahead to the number of fifteen hundred, and, having surprised those who were to surprise them, they killed about two hundred of them, and took more than one hundred prisoners.

This loss caused the Hurons to come down in small bands, only seven Canoes coming down at once. When Father Brébeuf heard of their arrival, he went to them, and did all he could to make them promise to receive him and his companions, and take them to their country.

"Never [wrote Father Brébeuf] did I see an embarcation about which there was so much quibbling and opposition. . . . We are going on by short stages, quite well as far as we are concerned; but our Savages are all sick. We paddle all the time, and do this the more because our people are sick. All our Savages are very much pleased with us. Your Reverence will excuse this writing, order and all; we start so early in the morning, and lie down so late, and paddle so continuously, that we hardly have time enough to devote to our prayers; indeed, I have been obliged to finish this by the light of the fire." These are the exact words of the Father. So that three of our Fathers and six of our Frenchmen have gone up to the Hurons.

They have three hundred leagues to make over a route full of horrors, as it is described by the Hurons; on their way down, they hide meal every two days, to eat on their return, and these hiding places are the only hotels they have. If they fail to find them, or if some one robs them, for they are the worst kind of thieves, they must get along without eating. If they do find their provisions, they cannot feast very sumptuously upon them. In the morning they mix a little of this meal with water, and each one eats about a bowlful of it; upon this they ply their paddles all day, and at nightfall they eat as they did at break of day. This is the kind of life that our fathers must lead until they reach the country of these barbarians. When they arrive, they will build themselves a bark house, and there they will live on wheat, cornmeal, and, in certain seasons, on fish.

The money with which they will buy their food, wood, bark house, and other necessaries, is little beads or tubes of glass, knives, awls, blankets, kettles, hatchets, and similar things; this is the money they must carry with them.

On the third of August, Monsieur de Champlain, having returned from three Rivers, where he had gone after the departure of our Fathers, told us that a French interpreter for the Algonquin nation had come from the Hurons, and brought the tidings that Father Brébeuf was suffering greatly; that his savages were sick; that Father Daniel had died of starvation, or was in great danger of dying, because the savages who had taken him on board had left the usual route, where they had hidden their food, and had turned off into the woods, hoping to find a certain tribe who would give them something to eat; but, not having found these wandering people, they supposed that they all, Savages and French, were in danger of death. As to Father Davost, he is getting along very well, but the Savages who have taken him have stolen part of his luggage. The Fathers will write to us next year, please God, all the particulars of their journey; but we cannot have news from them before that time. If their little outfit is lost or stolen, they will have to endure a great deal in those countries, so far from all help.

On the fourth, Monsieur du Plessis came down from three Rivers. He told me he had brought us a little orphan Savage, making a present of him to us. As soon as we shall have the means for gathering in these poor children, we shall have a number of them who will afterwards serve in the conversion of their Compatriots. He also told us that they were working with might and main in the place called the three Rivers; so, indeed, our French now have three settlements upon the great river saint Lawrence,—one at Kebec, newly fortified; another fifteen leagues farther up the river, on the Island of sainte Croix, where Monsieur de Champlain has had fort Richelieu built; the third colony is being established at three Rivers, fifteen leagues still higher up the river, that is to say thirty leagues from Kebec. Immediately after the departure of the vessels, Father Jacques Buteux and I will go there to live, to assist our French [and] to study the language.

Your Reverence will now see that the fear some people had that the foreigner would again come to ravage the country is not well founded; since households have been established here, since forts and dwellings are being built in several places, and as Monseigneur the Cardinal [1] favors this enterprise, honorable in the eyes of God and of man. That mind, —capable of animating four bodies, according to what I have heard,—sees far indeed, I confess; but I am of the opinion that he does not expect from our Savages, from this vine, which he waters with his care, the fruits which it will bear for him on earth, and which he will enjoy one day in heaven. God grant that he may see five or six hundred Hurons,—large,

[1] Cardinal Richelieu.

strong, well-made men,—ready to listen to the news of the Gospel which is being carried to them this year. I imagine that he would honor occasionally new France by a look, and that this glance would give him as much satisfaction as those great deeds with which he is filling Europe; but to cause the blood of Jesus Christ to be applied to the souls for whom it was shed, is a glory little known among men, but longed for by the great powers of Heaven and earth.

It is time to sound the retreat. The vessels are ready to depart, and still I have not read over and repunctuated this long Relation. Your Reverence will understand that I have not all the leisure that I could desire.

One word more: Give us, my Reverend Father, if you please, persons capable of learning these languages. We intended to apply ourselves to this work this year; Father Lallemant, Father Buteux, and I; but this new settlement separates us. Who knows whether Father Daniel is still living, whether Father Davost will reach the Hurons? For, as his Savages have begun to rob him, they may truly play a still worse game upon him. All this convinces us that we must retain here as many of our Fathers as we can; because if, for example, Father Brébeuf and I should happen to die, all the little we know of the Huron and Montagnais languages would be lost; and thus they would always be beginning over again, and retarding the fruits that they wish to gather from this mission.

My Reverend Father,
Your very humble and very obedient
servant in Our Lord Jesus Christ,
Paul Le Jeune.

From the little house of N. Dame des Anges,
in New France, this 7th of August, 1634.

[*Ibid.*, vi., vii., *Doc.* xxiii.]

PART II

THE DEVELOPMENT OF THE HURON MISSIONS
1635—1642

I

OF THE HURONS

[This is a brief outline, by Étienne de Villeneuve, written in 1762, of the history of the Huron nation and the missions established among them. *Ibid.*, lxx., 13.]

1st. In 1626, Fathers Brebeuf and de Nouë, Jesuits, and Father Joseph De la Roche, Récollet, went to the Huron country in the autumn of that year, to learn their language, and thereby to place themselves in a position to instruct them and teach them Christianity.

2nd. The Hurons were then settled on the shores of the lake that still bears their name,—that is to say, on the shores of lake Huron.

3rd. According to the Relations of the first Jesuits who were sent at that time among the Hurons, to labor in instructing them, the Hurons were divided into twenty villages—which, united together, formed a nation of thirty thousand souls.

4th. In 1649, on the 16th of March, the Iroquois—with whom the Hurons had been at war since the year 1638—suddenly, to the number of fifteen hundred, swooped down on one of their largest villages, and burned it. They seized some villages, alarmed others, and thereby compelled the Hurons to flee precipitately, and to disperse.

5th. The Hurons then retired: some to a distance of a hundred leagues from Lake Huron—and their descendants now constitute the Huron village at Detroit; other are said to have settled among the Illinois: others went down to Three Rivers, and others still to Quebec. Most of those who were at Three Rivers joined those of Quebec, on the 26th of April, 1654.

6th. There was at that time a considerable number of Hurons who had been settled at Sillery for about ten years.

These were Hurons who loved a peaceful life, and who—ever since a house had been built, in 1637, at Sillery for them, and for the savages of other nations who wished to dwell there—had gradually settled there among the Algonquins and formed a considerable village.

7th.   The Sillery Hurons joined those of Quebec in 1651, on the 26th of March, the day on which they were taken to the Island of Orleans to reside there.

8th.   The Hurons dwelt on the Island of Orleans from the 29th of March, 1651, to the 4th of June, 1656—that is to say, five years and some days.

9th.   On leaving the Island of Orleans, the Hurons came to live in Quebec.   They remained there until the month of April of the year 1668, when they left to go to Beauport, where they remained about a year.   Afterward, about the spring of 1669, they went to settle at côte St. Michael, where they remained from the spring of 1669 to the 28th of December of the year 1673.   From that place they went to live at Vieille Lorette, where they remained from the 28th of December, 1673, to the autumn of 1697.   Finally, from the autumn of 1697 to this present year 1762, they have lived at Jeune Lorette.

10th.   Jeune Lorette has no dependencies.   It is not a seigniory.   It is only a small piece of land of the côte petit St. Antoine, seigniory of St. Michel, on which the Jesuit Fathers, to whom the seigniory belongs, consented to allow the Hurons to settle, about the end of 1697.

11th.   The Jesuits have been seigniors of the Seigniory of St. Gabriel from the 2nd of November, 1667—on which day Monsieur Robert Giffard, the first seignior of the said seigniory, in concert with Madame Renouard, his wife, gave it to the Reverend Jesuit Fathers.

[*Ibid.*, lxx., *Doc.* ccxxvii.]

II

RELATION OF WHAT OCCURRED IN NEW FRANCE, IN THE YEAR 1635

By Father Paul Le Jeune and Father Jean de Brébeuf

[This document is known as Le Jeune's *Relation* of 1635. Heretofore the superior of Quebec has been the sole author of the annual report of the Jesuit mission in New France. But with the arrival of new missionaries, the work was greatly broadened, and hereafter we shall find the *Relation* a composite, arranged by the superior from the several individual reports forwarded to him by his assistants in the field, often with a general review from his own pen. Of such a character is the present *Relation*, which, like its successors, is, for convenience, designated by the name of the superior who forwarded it to the provincial at Paris, for publication.—*Ibid.*, vii., 2.]

My Reverend Father:

Now, at last, New France is about to experience the blessing of the mother country. We begin to see some open country, through the clearings that have been made in different places. The families who come over every year are beginning to change the barbarism of the Savages into the courtesy natural to the French. The exclusion of those who, having drained off the wealth that can be gathered in this country, left it without settlers and without cultivation,—not having, in all the years they enjoyed it, cleared a single arpent[1] of land; the great sums that the Gentlemen of the Company of New France[2]

---

[1] An old French land measure, containing 100 square perches, but varying in different provinces. The linear *arpent* of Paris was 180 French feet, the common *arpent* 200 and the standard *arpent* 220. *Ibid.*, iv., note 38.

[2] Le Jeune's expectations were somewhat too sanguine. The Company of

are expending either upon the country or upon their establishments, [all these considerations] lead us to conclude that God
is conducting this enterprise.

I shall say nothing of those whose ardent zeal warms and
at the same time confounds us. Neither shall I say anything
more about the burning desire of a great number of our Fathers,
who find the air of New France the air of Heaven. But what
surprises me is that many young Nuns, consecrated to our
Lord, wish to join us,—overcoming the fear natural to their
sex, in order to come and help the poor girls and poor women
among these Savages. There are so many of these who write
to us, and from so many Convents, and from various Orders
of the strictest discipline, that you would say that each one is
first to laugh at the hardships of the Sea and the barbarism
of these countries. They have written me that the Superior
of a very well ordered House, asked to send some Sisters
to establish a Convent of her Order in some town of France,
answered that she had no Sisters except for New France, and
for England, in case God restored the Catholic faith there.
Another one, no less zealous, said that the Relation of last year,
capable of appalling the stoutest heart, not only has not disheartened these Sisters, but on the contrary has so inspired
them, that thirteen have with their own hands signed a vow
to God, to cross over into New France, there to exercise the
functions of their Order, if their Superiors are pleased to
allow them.

But I must give this advice, in passing, to all these good
Sisters,—that they be very careful not to urge their departure
until they have here a good House, well built and well endowed; otherwise, they would be a burden to our French,
and could accomplish little for these peoples. Men can ex-
tricate themselves much more easily from difficulties; but,
as for the Nuns, they must have a good House, some cleared
land, and a good income upon which to live, and relieve the

New France was expending vast sums on its Canadian enterprise; but these
were directed more to the extension of its own commerce than to the development
of the country. *Ibid.,* vii., *note* 18.

poverty of the wives and daughters of the Savages. Behold these tender and delicate Virgins all ready to hazard their lives upon the waves of the Ocean, to come seeking little souls in the rigors of an air much colder than that of France, to endure hardships at which even men would be appalled; and will not some brave Lady be found who will give a Passport to these Amazons of the great God, endowing them with a house in which to praise and serve his divine Majesty in this other world?

OF THE CONDITION AND EMPLOYMENT OF OUR SOCIETY IN NEW FRANCE

We have six residences in New France. The first, beginning with the first land encountered in coming into these countries, is called the Residence of Sainte Anne; it is at Cape Breton. The second is the Residence of Saint Charles, at Miscou. The third, which we are going to occupy this Autumn, the Residence of Nostredame de Recouvrance, at Kebec, near the Fort. The fourth, the Residence of Nostredame des Anges, half a league from Kebec. The fifth, the Residence of the Conception, at the three Rivers. The sixth, the Residence of Saint Joseph, at Ihonatiria, among the Hurons. I hope that we shall soon have a seventh, in the same country, but in a Village other than Ihonatiria. Now, as the vessels which go to Cape Breton and to Miscou do not go up as far as Kebec, it thus happens that we have no communication with our Fathers who are in the Residences of Sainte Anne and of Saint Charles, except by way of France; hence neither letters nor other things should be sent to us to hold for them, but they should be given to those Vessels which go to these French settlements. It follows also that I can say nothing of the things which take place in these Residences, on account of their remoteness and the little commerce we have with them.

All these Residences are maintained by the Gentlemen of the Company of New France, who have had Fortresses and dwellings for our French people built in different parts of the country,—except the Residence of Nostredame des Anges.

This Residence has three great plans for the glory of our Lord; the first, to erect a College for the education of the children of the families, which are every day becoming more numerous. The second, to establish a Seminary for the little Savages, to rear them in the Christian faith. The third, to give powerful aid to the Mission of our Fathers among the Hurons and other stationary tribes. As to the College, although it is not yet built, we shall begin this year to teach a few children. Everything has its beginning; the most learned once knew only the first elements of the Alphabet.

In regard to the Seminary, we are now having one built. For a while it will be in the Residence of Nostredame des Anges; but if some pious person be found who wishes to endow it, and to support the poor little barbarians, it will have to be moved farther up the river, to a place where the Savages will not object to bring their children. I send a little boy to Your Reverence, and, if you please, you will return him to us in a couple of years; he will help to retain and teach his little compatriots; the one I did send you, and who has been returned to us, pleases us greatly. The Savages are beginning to open their eyes, and to recognise that children who are with us are well taught.

Finally, as to the Mission among the Hurons and other stationary Tribes, it is of the greatest importance. If some fund cannot be found to maintain it, I would almost willingly give up the care both of a College and of a Seminary, to make it succeed.

HOW IT IS A BENEFIT TO BOTH OLD AND NEW FRANCE, TO SEND COLONIES HERE

Geographers, Historians, and experience show us that every year a great many people leave France who go to enroll themselves elsewhere. For, although the Soil of our country is very fertile, the French women have this blessing, that they are still more so; and thence it happens that our ancient Gauls, in want of land, went to seek it in different parts of Europe. At present, our French people are no less numerous than our old Gauls; but they do not go forth in bands, but separately. Would it not be better to empty Old France into New, by means of Colonies, than to people Foreign countries?

Add to this, if you please, that there is a multitude of workmen in France, who, for lack of employment or of owning a little land, pass their lives in wretched want. Many of them beg their bread from door to door; some of them resort to stealing; others to larceny and secret frauds, each one trying to obtain for himself what many cannot possess. Now, as New France is so immense, so many inhabitants can be sent here that those who remain in the Mother Country will have enough honest work left them to do, without launching into those vices which ruin Republics; this does not mean that ruined people, or those of evil lives, should be sent here, for that would be to build Babylons.

Now there is no doubt that there can be found here employment for all sorts of artisans. Why cannot the great forests of New France largely furnish the Ships for the Old? Who doubts that there are here mines of iron, copper, and other metals? Some have been already discovered, which will soon be worked; and hence all those who work in wood and iron will find employment here. I do not pretend to recite all the advantages of the country; I will content myself by saying that it would be an honor and a great benefit to both old and new France to send over Emigrants and establish strong colonies in these lands, which have lain fallow since the birth of the world.

Your very humble and greatly obliged servant in our Lord,

PAUL LE JEUNE

AND

Father Charles l'Allemant
Father Jean Brebeuf
Father Jean Daniel
Father Ambroise d'Avost
Father Anne de Noüe
Father Enemond Masse
Father Antoine Richard

Father François Mercier
Father Charles Turgis
Father Charles du Marché
Father Claude Quantin
Father Jacques Buteux
Father Jean de Quen
Father Pierre Pijart

And our brothers Gilbert Burel, Jean Liegeois, Pierre le
Tellier, Pierre Feauté.

RELATION OF WHAT OCCURRED AMONG THE HURONS IN THE YEAR *1635*

Sent to Kebec to Father Le Jeune, by Father Brébeuf,[1] *and incorporated with the Relation of 1635*

MY REVEREND FATHER:

I send you an account of our journey into this Huron country. It has been filled with more fatigues, losses and expenses
than the other, but also has been followed, and will be, God
aiding, by more of Heaven's blessings.

When, last year, one thousand six hundred and thirty-four,

---

[1] Jean de Brébeuf was born March 25, 1593, at Condé-sur-Vire, Normandy.
He belonged to a noble family, from which, according to the *Biographie Uni-
verselle* (Paris, 1843-66), the English family of Arundel had its descent. Entering the Society of Jesus Nov. 8, 1617, at Rouen, he was ordained five years
later; and in 1625 was sent to Canada as one of the first Jesuit missionaries.
The first year he spent among the Montagnais; but in 1626 went, with De Noüe,
to the Huron country, where they settled at Toanché (known to the Récollets
as Carhagouha) in the bark cabin which Le Caron had erected eleven years before.
Here Brébeuf remained (alone, after the first year) until the capture of Quebec.
Returning to Canada with Champlain (1633) he at once resumed work in the
Huron country, where he labored until his death (excepting 1641-44, when at
Quebec). During the winter of 1640-41, he endeavored (but without success)
to establish a mission in the Neutral Nation. He lived successively at Ihonatiria,
a new village built not far from the deserted Toanché; Teanaustayé, called by
the missionaries St. Joseph, in the present township of Medonté, Simcoe county,
Ontario; and St. Ignace and St. Louis, about half way between the former
towns. In March, 1649, a thousand Iroquois attacked and destroyed the last
two-named villages, capturing there Brébeuf and Gabriel Lalemant, both of
whom were put to death with cruel tortures,—the former dying March 16, the
latter on the day following. Their bodies were rescued by their brethren, and
their bones afterwards taken to Quebec,—where, in the Hotel Dieu, Brébeuf's
head is still preserved, inclosed in a silver bust sent from France by his family.
A minute account of this martyrdom is given by one of the lay brothers of the
Huron mission, Christophe Regnaut (Regnault), in a MS. written at Caen in
1678. A copy of this document, with an English translation, is given by Brymner
in *Canadian Archives*, 1884.

Harris (*Miss. West. Canada.*; p. 212, *note*) states that he has seen in St. Martin's church (Ritualist), Brighton, England, a figured window in memory of
Father Brébeuf. A memorial church, in honor of all the Jesuit martyrs in the
Huron country, is now (January, 1897) approaching completion at Penetan-
guishene, Ontario. *Ibid., iv., note* 30.

we arrived at the three Rivers, where the trading post was, we found ourselves in several difficulties and perplexities. For, on the one hand, there were only eleven Huron canoes to embark our ten additional persons who were intending to go into their Country. On the other; we were greatly in doubt whether any others would descend this year, considering the great loss they had experienced in war with the Hiroquois, named *Sonontrerrhonons* last Spring, and the fear they had of a new invasion. This placed us in much doubt whether we ought to take advantage of the opportunity which was presented, or wait for a better one.

At last, after full consideration, we resolved to try our fortune, judging that it was of vital importance to have a footing in the country in order to open the door which seemed firmly closed to the Faith. This resolution was far easier than the execution of it, which perchance would have been impossible without the care, the favor, and the liberality of Monsieur du Plessis Bochard, General of the fleet. For immediately after his arrival, which was on the fifth of July, 1634, he held a council with the Bissiriniens,[1] to whom he proposed the plan he had of sending some men with them, and of joining us to the Hurons. They made several objections, and one of the Chiefs of the Island, named "the Partridge" (la Perdrix), more than all the rest; nevertheless arguments and presents won them over.

The next morning, the Assembly met again, by the command of Monsieur du Plessis Bochard, and both the Bissiriniens and the Hurons were present. The same plan was again presented to them; but out of respect for one another they all agreed not to embark any Frenchmen; and no arguments could, for the time being, move them. Thereupon our enterprise seemed again cut off, by this action. But, at the close of the Assembly, one of the *Attiguenongha*,[2] drawing me aside,

---

[1] *Bissiriniens:* an Algonquin tribe.

[2] This and the *Attignaouantan,* or Bear Nation, were not only the most important, but the oldest of the Huron tribes, "having received into their country, and adopted, the others" (*Relation* for 1639, chap. i), and being able to trace their tribal history for two centuries back. This tribe was the southernmost

asked me to visit him in his cabin. There he gave me to understand that he and his companion would embark three of us. I replied that we could not go unless five went; we three and two of our men.

Thereupon the *Arendarhonons*[1] became eager to embark us; we found place for six, and so we resolved to set out, and leave until some other time the two little boys we were to take. We began to distribute our baggage, and made presents to each one, to encourage them; and on the morrow, the seventh of the month, Monsieur du Plessis Bochard gave them still others, on the single consideration that they would embark us, and feasted all of them at a great feast of three large kettles.

But the contagion which spread among these Tribes last year, with great destruction, having suddenly seized several of our Savages, and filled the rest with fear, again threw us into confusion, and put us to great trouble, seeing that we had to set out immediately. Our six canoes being reduced to three, and our two Fathers and I being disembarked, I had to find new men, to unload our slender baggage, to decide who should embark and who remain, to choose among our packages those we were to carry, and to give orders as to the rest,—and all this in less than half an hour, when we would have needed entire days. Monsieur du Plessis interposed his authority, Monsieur Oliver and Monsieur Coullart their ingenuity, and all the Frenchmen their affection. Yet several times I was completely baffled and desperate, until I had special recourse to our Lord JESUS, for whose glory alone we were undertaking this painful journey, and until I had made a vow to glorious saint Joseph, the new Patriarch of the Hurons. Immediately I saw everything become quiet, and our Savages so satisfied that those who embarked Father Daniel had already placed him in their canoe, and it seemed

of the Huron clans; one of its most important towns was Teanaustayé, located in what is now Medonté township. Here was situated the Jesuit mission of St. Joseph, destroyed by the Iroquois in 1649.—*Ibid.,* viii., *note* 23.

[1] The easternmost tribe of the Hurons . . . the first of the Hurons to engage in trade with the French. It was with this tribe that Champlain spent the winter of 1615-16, at their village of Cahiagué, where, later, was established the Jesuit mission of St. Jean Baptiste.—*Ibid.,* viii., *note* 24.

as if they were going to take him without even receiving the ordinary pay. But the Father, seeing that they had not cloaks like the others, stepped out of the canoe, told me about it, and I had some given to them.

At last, then, after having briefly thanked Monsieur du Plessis, having entrusted to him the embarkation of the rest of our people, and having bid him and all our Frenchmen adieu, I embarked with Father Antoine Daniel and one of our men; the two others were coming with the Algonquains. Monsieur du Plessis honored our departure with several volleys, to recommend us still more to our Savages. It was the seventh of July. Father Ambroise Davost embarked eight days later, with two others of our people. The rest followed eight days after, to take their part in the fatigues of a journey extremely wearisome, not only on account of its length and of the wretched fare to be had, but also on account of the circuits that have to be made in coming from Kebec to this place by way of the Bissiriniens and the petite Nation; I believe that they amount to more than three hundred leagues. It is true that the way is shorter by the Saut de St. Louys and the Lake of the Hiroquois; but the fear of enemies, and the few conveniences to be met with, cause that route to be unfrequented.

Of two ordinary difficulties, the chief is that of the rapids and portages. Your Reverence has already seen enough of the rapids near Kebec to know what they are. All the rivers of this Country are full of them, and notably the St. Lawrence, after that of the Prairies[1] is passed. From there onward it has no longer a smooth bed, but is broken up in several places, rolling and leaping in a frightful way, like an impetuous torrent; and even, in some places, it falls from a height of several brasses. I remembered, in passing, the Cataracts of the Nile, as they are described by our Historians.

Now, when these rapids or torrents are reached, it is necessary to land, and carry on the shoulder, through woods, or

[1] The name "Rivière des Prairies" was at first applied to the Ottawa river, but it is now restricted to the channel that separates Isle Jésus from the island of Montreal.—*Ibid.*, viii., *note* 25.

over high and troublesome rocks, all the baggage and the canoes themselves. This is not done without much work; for there are portages of one, two and three leagues, and for each several trips must be made, no matter how few packages one has. In some places, where the current is not less strong than in these rapids, although easier at first, the Savages get into the water, and haul and guide by hand their canoes with extreme difficulty and danger: for they sometimes get in up to the neck, and are compelled to let go their hold, saving themselves as best they can from the rapidity of the water, which snatches from them and bears off their canoe. I kept count of the number of portages, and found that we carried our canoes thirty five times, and dragged them at least fifty. I sometimes took a hand in helping my Savages, but the bottom of the river is full of stones, so sharp that I could not walk long, being barefooted.

The second ordinary difficulty is in regard to provisions. Frequently one has to fast, if he misses the caches that were made when descending; and even, if they are found, one does not fail to have a good appetite after indulging in them, for the ordinary food is only a little Indian corn coarsely broken between two stones, and sometimes taken whole in pure water; it is no great treat. Occasionally one has fish, but it is only a chance, unless one is passing some Tribe where they can be bought. Add to these difficulties that one must sleep on the bare earth, or on a hard rock, for lack of a space ten or twelve square on which to place a wretched hut; that one must endure continually the stench of tired-out Savages; and must walk in water, in mud, in the obscurity and entanglement of the forest, where the stings of an infinite number of mosquitoes and gnats are a serious annoyance.

I say nothing of the long and wearisome silence to which one is reduced, I mean in the case of newcomers, who have, for the time, no person in their company who speaks their own tongue, and who do not understand that of the Savages. Now these difficulties, since they are the usual ones, were common to us as to all who come into this Country. But on our journey we all had to encounter difficulties which were unusual. The first was that we were compelled to paddle continually, just as much as the Savages; so that I had not the leisure to recite my Breviary except when I lay down to sleep, when I had more need of rest than of work. The other was that we had to carry our packages at the portages, which was as laborious for us as it was new, and still more for others than it was for me, who already knew a little what it is to be fatigued. At every portage I had to make at least four trips, the others had scarcely fewer. I had once before made the journey to the Hurons,[1] but I did not then ply the paddles, nor carry burdens; nor did the other Religious who made the same journey. But, in this journey, we all had to begin by these experiences to bear the Cross that our Lord presents to us for his honor, and for the salvation of these poor Barbarians. In truth, I was sometimes so weary that the body could do no more, but at the same time my soul experienced very deep peace, considering that I was suffering for God; no one knows it if he has not experienced it. All did not get off so cheaply.

Father Devost, among others, was very badly treated. They stole from him much of his little outfit. They compelled him to throw away a little steel mill, and almost all our books, some linen, and a good part of the paper that we were taking, and of which we have great need. They deserted him at the Island, among the Algonquains, where he suffered in good earnest. When he reached the Hurons, he was so worn out and dejected that for a long time he could not get over it.

Father Daniel was abandoned, and compelled to seek another canoe, as also was Pierre, one of our men. Little Martin was very roughly treated, and at last was left behind with the Bissiriniens, where he remained so long that he was about two months on the road, and only arrived among the Hurons on the nineteenth of September. Baron was robbed by his savages on the very day he arrived in these regions; and he would have lost much more if he had not compelled them, through

[1] *See* p. 98, *note.*

fear of his arms, to give him back a part of what they had taken. In short, all the Frenchmen suffered great hardships, incurred great expense, considering the few goods they had, and ran remarkable risks. And whosoever will come up here must make up his mind to all this, and to something more, even to death itself, whose Image we see every moment before our eyes. Sometimes a word, or a dream, or a fancy, or even the smallest sense of inconvenience, is enough to cause them to ill-treat, or set ashore, and I dare say to murder one,—as happened last year to a poor Algonquain, who was abandoned in a rapid by his own nephew.

I attribute, nevertheless, all these extraordinary difficulties to the sickness among our Savages. I know not at what price our French and the Montagnais will have become rid of it. All these poor people have been much inconvenienced by it, particularly during the Autumn, as much in their fishing as in their harvesting. Many crops are lying beneath the snow; a large number of persons are dead; there are still some who have not recovered. This sickness began with violent fever, which was followed by a sort of measles or smallpox, different, however, from that common in France, accompanied in several cases by blindness for some days, or by dimness of sight, and terminated at length by diarrhoea which has carried off many and is still bringing some to the grave.

I arrived among the Hurons on the fifth of August, after being thirty days on the road in continual work, except one day of rest, which we took in the country of the Bissiriniens. I landed at the port of the village of Toanché or of *Teandeouiata*, where we had formerly lived; but it was with a little misfortune. My Savages,—forgetting the kindness I had lavished upon them and the help I had afforded them in their sickness, and notwithstanding all the fair words and promises they had given me,—after having landed me with some Church ornaments and some other little outfit, left me there quite alone, and resumed their route toward their villages, some seven leagues distant. My trouble was that the village of Toanché[1] had changed since my departure, and that I did not know precisely in what place it was situated. The shore being no longer frequented, I could not easily ascertain my way; and, if I had known it, I could not from weakness have carried all my little baggage at once; nor could I risk, in that place, doing this in two trips. That is why I entreated my Savages to accompany me as far as the village, or at least to sleep on the shore for the night, to watch my clothes while I went to make inquiries. But their ears were deaf to my remonstrances. The only consolation they gave me was to tell me that some one would find me there. Having considered that this shore was deserted, and that I might remain there a long time before any one in the village would come to find me, I hid my packages in the woods; and, taking what was most precious, I set out to find the village, which fortunately I came upon at about three-quarters of a league—having seen with tenderness and emotion, as I passed along, the place where we had lived, and had celebrated the Holy sacrifice of the Mass during three years, now turned into a fine field; and also the sight of the old village, where, except one cabin, nothing remained but the ruins of the others.

As soon as I was perceived in the village, some one cried out, "Why, there is Echom come again" (that is the name they give me); and at once every one came out to salute and welcome me, each calling me by name and saying: "What, Echom, my nephew, my brother, my cousin, hast thou then come again?" But without stopping, for night was approaching, I found a place to lodge; and quickly set out with a volunteer band of young people to bring my slender baggage. I lodged with a man name *Aouandoié*, who is, or at least was, one of the richest of the Hurons. I did this on purpose, because another with smaller means might have been incon-

---

[1] A. F. Hunter writes, concerning the locality of these towns (Toanché and Ihonatiria): "The exact positions of these villages have not yet been established beyond question. The evidence in favor of Thunder Bay as the landing place of Brébeuf, although scanty, is superior to that produced by any other locality. Martin and Taché apparently agree in placing Ihonatiria west of Pentanguishene Bay, but no site has yet been found there which will entirely correspond with the statements made by early writers.—*Ibid.*, vii., *note* 61.

venienced with the large number of Frenchmen whom I was expecting, and who had to be provided with food and shelter until we had all gathered together, and our cabin was ready. You can lodge where you please; for this Nation above all others is exceedingly hospitable towards all sorts of persons, even toward Strangers; and you may remain as long as you please, being always well treated, according to the fashion of the country. It is quite true that not all are equally hospitable. My host is one of the first in this virtue, and perhaps it is on this account that God has crowned him until now with temporal blessings, and has preserved him among all his Fellow Countrymen; for their village, named *Teandeouihata,* having been burned twice, each time his house alone escaped the conflagration.

I lodged therefore with this man, and lived there with our two Fathers and one of our people, for the space of more than a month and a half, until we took possession of our new cabin.

That evening and the next day passed in the exchange of affection, visits, salutations, and encouraging words from the whole village. On the following days, several from other villages, who were of my acquaintance, came to see me; and all took away with them, in exchange for their visit, some trifling presents. This is a small thing in detail, but on the whole it exerts a great influence and is of great importance in these regions.

I was occupied some two weeks in visiting the villages, and bringing together, at much expense and trouble, all our party, who landed here and there, and who, not knowing the language, could only have found us out after much toil. It is true that one of our men was able to come without any other address than these two words, *Echom, Ihonatiria,* which are my name and that of our village. Among all the French I do not find anyone who has had more trouble than Father Davost and Baron; the Father from the wicked treatment of his Savages, Baron from the length of the journey. He occupied forty days on the road; often he was alone with a Savage, paddling in a canoe very large and very heavily laden. He had to carry all his packages himself; he had narrow escapes three or four times in the torrents; and, to crown his difficulty, much of his property was stolen. Truly, to come here, much strength and patience are needed; and he who thinks of coming here for any other than God, will have made a sad mistake.

Jean Nicolet,[1] in the voyage he made with us as far as the Island, suffered all the hardships of one of the most robust Savages. Being at last all gathered together, we decided to dwell here at *Ihonatiria*, and to build here our cabin, for the following reasons: First, after having earnestly recommended the matter to God, we judged that such was his will, because the harvest of souls is more ripe here than in any other place,— as much because of the acquaintance I have with the inhabitants of the place, and of the affection they showed for me formerly, as because they are already partly instructed in the Faith.

Secondly, except this village there was only la Rochelle at which we might have had any inclination to stop, and that had been our intention from last year. All the inhabitants desired it very much, and invited us there, saying that we would be, as it were, in the centre of the Nation, and adding other motives and reasons which pleased us well. Even on the road I entertained this thought, and only laid it aside a long time after my arrival here,—so long indeed, that we left for a considerable space of time the baggage of Father Daniel at the village of la Rochelle, with the Captain who had received him into his canoe,—intending to carry the rest thither, and to abide there. But, having taken into account that they were intending this Spring to change the location of the place, as they have already done, we did not wish to build a cabin for one winter. Besides, although it is a desirable thing to gather more fruit, and to have more listeners in our assemblies, which would make us choose the larger villages rather than the small, nevertheless, for a beginning, we have thought it more suitable to keep in the shadow, as it were, near a little village where the inhabitants are already disposed to associate with the

---

[1] *Jean Nicolet,* interpreter and explorer. *See* p. 176, ff.

French, than to put ourselves suddenly in a great one, where the people are not accustomed to our mode of doing things. To do otherwise would have been to expose new men, ignorant of the language, to a numerous youth, who by their annoyances and mockery, would have brought about some disturbance.

Having, therefore, determined to stay where we are, the question of building a cabin arose. The cabins of this country are neither Louvres nor Palaces, nor anything like the buildings of our France, not even like the smallest cottages. They are, however, somewhat better and more commodious than the hovels of the Montagnais. I cannot better express the fashion of the Huron dwellings than to compare them to bowers or garden arbors,—some of which, in place of branches and vegetation, are covered with cedar bark, some others with large pieces of ash, elm, fir, or spruce bark; and, although the cedar bark is best, according to common opinion and usage, there is, nevertheless, this inconvenience, that they are almost as susceptible to fire as matches. Hence arise many of the conflagrations of entire villages. There are cabins or arbors of various sizes, some two brasses[1] in length, others of twenty, of thirty, of forty; the usual width is about four brasses, their height is about the same. There are no different stories; there is no cellar, no chamber, no garret. It has neither window nor chimney, only a miserable hole in the top of the cabin, left to permit the smoke to escape. This is the way they built our cabin for us.

The people of Oënrio and of our village were employed at this by means of presents given them. It has cost us much exertion to secure its completion, we were almost into October before we were under cover. As to the interior, we have suited ourselves; so that, even if it does not amount to much, the Savages never weary of coming to see it, and seeing it, to admire it. We have divided it into three parts. The first compartment, nearest the door, serves as an ante-chamber,

---

[1] *Brasse:* a linear measure, of five old-French feet, or 1.82 metres, equivalent to 5.318 English feet.—*Ibid.,* v., *note* 16.

as a storm door, and as a storeroom for our provisions, in the fashion of the Savages. The second is that in which we live, and is our kitchen, our carpenter shop, our mill, or place for grinding wheat, our Refectory, our parlor and our bedroom. On both sides, in the fashion of the Hurons, are two benches which they call *Endicha,* on which are boxes to hold our clothes and other little conveniences; but below, in the place where the Hurons keep their wood, we have contrived some little bunks to sleep in, and to store away some of our clothing from the thieving hands of the Hurons. They sleep beside the fire, but still they and we have only the earth for bedstead; for mattress and pillows, some bark or boughs covered with a rush mat; for sheets and coverings, our clothes and some skins do duty.

The third part of our cabin is also divided into two parts by means of a bit of carpentry which gives it a fairly good appearance, and which is admired here for its novelty. In the one is our little Chapel, in which we celebrate every day holy Mass, and we retire there daily to pray to God. It is true that the almost continual noise they make usually hinders us, and compels us to go outside to say our prayers. In the other part we put our utensils. The whole cabin is only six brasses long, and about three and a half wide. That is how we are lodged, doubtless not so well that we may not have in this abode a good share of rain, snow and cold. However, they never cease coming to visit us from admiration, especially since we have put on two doors, made by a carpenter, and since our mill and our clock have been set to work. It would be impossible to describe the astonishment of these good people, and how much they admire the intelligence of the French. No one has come who has not wished to turn the mill; nevertheless we have not used it much, inasmuch as we have learned that our Sagamités[1] are better pounded in a

---

[1] *Sagamité:* a word derived by Maurault (*Hist. Abenakis,* p. 13) from sôgmôipi, "the repast of chiefs." The most common form in which Indians prepared maize as food; termed "samp" or "hominy" by the English. The corn, usually pounded into meal, was boiled in water, with the addition of meat, fish, or oil, when they had such, to enrich and flavor it. Various kinds of vegetables,

wooden mortar, in the fashion of the Savages, than ground within the mill. I believe it is because the mill makes the flour too fine. As to the clock, a thousand things are said of it. They all think it is some living thing, for they cannot imagine how it sounds of itself; and when it is going to strike, they look to see if we are all there, and if some one has not hidden, in order to shake it.

They think it hears, especially when, for a joke, one of our Frenchmen calls out at the last stroke of the hammer, "That's enough," and then it immediately becomes silent. They call it the Captain of the day. When it strikes they say it is speaking; and they ask when they come to see us how many times the Captain has already spoken. They ask us about its food; they remain a whole hour, and sometimes several, in order to be able to hear it speak. They used to ask at first what it said. We told them two things that they have remembered very well; one, that when it sounded four o'clock of the afternoon, during winter, it was saying, "Go out, go away that we may close the door," for immediately they arose, and went out. The other, that at midday it said, *yo eiouahaoua,* that is, "Come, put on the kettle;" and this speech is better remembered than the other, for some of these spongers never fail to come at that hour, to get a share of our Sagamité. They eat at all hours, when they have the wherewithal, but usually they have only two meals a day, in the morning and in the evening; consequently they are very glad during the day to take a share with us.

Speaking of their expressions of admiration, I might here set down several on the subject of the loadstone, into which they looked to see if there was some paste; and of a glass with eleven facets, which represented a single object many times, of a little phial in which a flea appears as large as a beetle; of the prism, of the joiner's tools; but above all, of the writing; for they could not conceive how, what one of us, being

in their season,—beans, peas, pumpkins,—were boiled with the corn, especially when the latter was still green; a survival of this usage remains in our modern "succotash," of corn and beans. Sagard describes, in *Grand Voyage* (Tross ed., 1865), pp. 94-98, this and various other ways of cooking maize.—*Ibid.,* v., *note* 28.

in the village, had said to them, and put down at the same
time in writing, another, who meantime was in a house far
away, could say readily on seeing the writing. I believe they
have made a hundred trials of it. All this serves to gain their
affections, and to render them more docile when we introduce
the admirable and incomprehensible mysteries of our Faith;
for the belief they have in our intelligence and capacity causes
them to accept without reply what we say to them.

It remains now to say something of the country, of the
manners and customs of the Hurons, of the inclination they
have to the Faith, and of our insignificant labors.

As to the first, the little paper and leisure we have compels
me to say in a few words what might justly fill a volume.
The Huron country is not large, its greatest extent can be
traversed in three or four days. Its situation is fine, the greater
part of it consisting of plains. It is surrounded and inter-
sected by a number of very beautiful lakes or rather seas,
whence it comes that the one to the North and to the Northwest is called "fresh-water sea" (mer douce).[1] We pass
through it in coming from the Bissiriniens. There are twenty
Towns, which indicate about 30,000 souls speaking the same
tongue, which is not difficult to one who has a master. It has
distinctions of genders, number, tense, person, moods; and, in
short, it is very complete and very regular, contrary to the
opinion of many. I am rejoiced to find that this language is
common to some Twelve other Nations, all settled and numerous. The Hurons are friends of all these people, except the
*Sonontoerrhonons, Onontaerrhonons, Oüioenrhonons, Onoio-
chrhonons,* and *Agnierrhonons,* all of whom we comprise under
the name Hiroquois. But they have already made peace with
the *Sonontoerrhonons,* since they were defeated by them a year
past in the Spring.

It is so evident that there is a Divinity who has made Heaven
and earth that our Hurons cannot entirely ignore it. But they

---

[1] Lake Huron, which has figured under many titles in the old maps and chronicles. The name has reference to the Indian family upon its eastern shores.
Champlain first named it Mer Douce ("The Fresh Sea").—*Ibid.,* i., *note* 54.

misapprehend him grossly. For they have neither Temples, nor Priests, nor Feasts, nor any ceremonies.

They say that a certain woman named *Eataensic* is the one who made earth and man. They give her an assistant, one named *Jouskeha,* whom they declare to be her little son, with whom she governs the world. This *Jouskeha* has care of the living, and of the things that concern life, and consequently they say that he is good. *Eataensic* has care of souls; and, because they believe that she makes men die, they say that she is wicked. And there are among them mysteries so hidden that only the old men, who can speak with authority about them, are believed.

This God and Goddess live like themselves, but without famine; make feasts as they do, are lustful as they are; in short, they imagine them exactly like themselves. And still, though they make them human and corporeal, they seem nevertheless to attribute to them a certain immensity in all places.

They say that this *Eataentsic* fell from the Sky, where there are inhabitants as on earth, and when she fell, she was with child. If you ask them who made the sky and its inhabitants, they have no other reply than that they know nothing about it. And when we preach to them of one God, Creator of Heaven and earth, and of all things, and even when we talk to them of Hell and Paradise and of our other mysteries, the headstrong reply that this is good for our Country and not for theirs; that every Country has its own fashions. But having pointed out to them, by means of a little globe that we had brought, that there is only one world, they remain without reply.

I find in their marriage customs two things that greatly please me; the first, that they have only one wife; the second, that they do not marry their relatives in a direct or collateral line, however distant they may be. There is, on the other hand, sufficient to censure, were it only the frequent changes the men make of their wives, and the women of their husbands.

They believe in the immortality of the soul, which they

believe to be corporeal. The greatest part of their Religion consists of this point. We have seen several stripped, or almost so, of all their goods, because several of their friends were dead, to whose souls they had made presents. Moreover, dogs, fish, deer, and other animals have, in their opinion, immortal and reasonable souls. In proof of this, the old men relate certain fables, which they represent as true; they make no mention either of punishment or reward, in the place to which souls go after death. And so they do not make any distinction between the good and the bad, the virtuous and the vicious; and they honor equally the interment of both, even as we have seen in the case of a young man who poisoned himself from the grief he felt because his wife had been taken away from him. Their superstitions are infinite, their feast, their medicines, their fishing, their hunting, their wars,—in short almost their whole life turns upon this pivot; dreams, above all have here great credit.

As regards morals, the Hurons are lascivious, although in two leading points less so than many Christians, who will blush some day in their presence. You will see no kissing nor immodest caressing; and in marriage a man will remain two or three years apart from his wife, while she is nursing. They are gluttons, even to disgorging; it is true, that does not happen often, but only in some superstitious feasts,—these, however, they do not attend willingly. Besides they endure hunger much better than we,—so well that after having fasted two or three entire days you will see them still paddling, carrying loads, singing, laughing, bantering, as if they had dined well. They are very lazy, are liars, thieves, pertinacious beggars. Some consider them vindictive; but, in my opinion, this vice is more noticeable elsewhere than here.

We see shining among them some rather noble moral virtues. You note, in the first place, a great love and union, which they are careful to cultivate by means of their marriages, of their presents, of their feasts, and of their frequent visits. On returning from their fishing, their hunting, and their trading, they exchange many gifts; if they have thus obtained something unusually good, even if they have bought it, or if it has been given to them, they make a feast to the whole village with it. Their hospitality towards all sorts of strangers is remarkable; they present to them, in their feasts, the best of what they have prepared, and, as I have already said, I do not know if anything similar, in this regard, is to be found anywhere. They never close the door upon a Stranger, and, once having received him into their houses, they share with him the best they have; they never send him away, and when he goes away of his own accord, he repays them by a simple "thank you."

What shall I say of their strange patience in poverty, famine, and sickness? We have seen this year whole villages prostrated, their food a little insipid sagamité; and yet not a word of complaint, not a movement of impatience. They receive indeed the news of death with more constancy than those Christian Gentlemen and Ladies to whom one would not dare to mention it. Our Savages hear of it not only without despair, but without troubling themselves, without the slightest pallor or change of countenance. We have especially admired the constancy of our new Christians. The next to the last one who died, named Joseph *Oatij*, lay on the bare ground during four or five months, not only before but after his Baptism,— so thin that he was nothing but bones; in a lodge so wretched that the winds blew in on all sides; covered during the cold of winter with a very light skin of some black animals, perhaps black squirrels, and very poorly nourished. He was never heard to make a complaint.

We have been employed in the study of the language, which, on account of the diversity of its compounds, is almost infinite. One can, nevertheless, do nothing without this study. All the French who are here have eagerly applied themselves to it, reviving the ancient usage of writing on birchbark, for want of paper. Fathers Davost and Daniel have worked at it, beyond all; they know as many words as I, and perhaps more; but they have not yet had practice in forming and joining them together promptly, although Father Daniel already explains himself passably well. As for me, who give lessons therein to our French, if God does not assist me extraordinarily, I shall yet have to go a long time to the school of the Savages, so prolific is their language. That does not prevent me from understanding almost all they say, and from making them fairly understand my meaning, even in the explanation of our most ineffable mysteries.

About the month of December, the snow began to lie on the ground, and the savages settled down into the village. For, during the whole Summer and Autumn, they are for the most part either in their rural cabins, taking care of their crops, or on the lake fishing, or trading; which makes it not a little inconvenient to instruct them. Seeing them, therefore, thus gathered together at the beginning of this year, we resolved to preach publicly to all, and to acquaint them with the reason of our coming into their Country, which is not for their furs, but to declare to them the true God and his son, Jesus Christ, the universal Saviour of our souls.

The usual method that we follow is this: We call together the people by the help of the Captain of the village, who assembles them all in our house as in Council, or perhaps by the sound of the bell. I use the surplice and the square cap, to give more majesty to my appearance. At the beginning we chant on our knees the *Pater noster*, translated into Huron verse. Father Daniel, as its author, chants a couplet alone, and then we all together chant it again; and those among the Hurons, principally the little ones, who already know it, take pleasure in chanting it with us. That done, when every one is seated, I rise and make the sign of the Cross for all; then, having recapitulated what I said last time, I explain something new. After that we question the young children and the girls, giving a little bead of glass or porcelain to those who deserve it. The parents are very glad to see their children answer well and carry off some little prize, of which they render themselves worthy by the care they take to come privately to get instruction. On our part, to arouse their emu-

lation, we have each lesson retraced by our two little French
boys, who question each other,—which transports the Savages
with admiration. Finally the whole is concluded by the talk
of the Old Men, who propound their difficulties, and sometimes make me listen in my turn to the statement of their
belief.

Two things among others have aided us very much in the
little we have been able to do here, by the grace of our Lord;
the first is, as I have already said, the good health that God
has granted us in the midst of sickness so general and so widespread. The second is the temporal assistance we have rendered to the sick. Having brought for ourselves some few
delicacies, we shared them with them, giving to one a few
prunes, and to another a few raisins, to others something
else. The poor people came from great distances to get their
share.

Our French servants having succeeded very well in hunting, during the Autumn, we carried portions of game to all
the sick. That chiefly won their hearts, as they were dying,
having neither flesh nor fish to season their sagamité.

Before drawing to a close, I shall say only this one word
about Louys de saincte Foy, which I would prefer not to say
were it not that it may help to make this Nation more correctly
known; it is this,—he is not such as he ought to be, and as we
had wished. Nevertheless, we still have good hope. He was
taken prisoner last year by the Hiroquois, in the common
defeat, and carried away a captive. It cost him a finger. This
severe stroke ought to suffice to bring him back to duty.

We hope one day to see here a flourishing Christianity.
Indeed, their minds are docile and flexible; I see only the
liberty with which they change their wives at pleasure, and
some superstitions, difficult to abolish, for in other respects
they have no aversion to the Faith. They turn willingly to
God in their necessities; they come to get their crops blessed
before sowing them; and ask us what we desire of them.
A thousand entreaties for the holy sacrifices of your Reverence
and of all our Fathers and Brothers.

Your Reverence's:

From our little House of St. Joseph, in the village of Ihonatiria in the Huron country, this 27th of May, 1635, the day on which the Holy Spirit descended visibly upon the Apostles.

Very humble and obedient
servant in our Lord,
Jean De Brebeuf.

[*Ibid.*, vii., viii., *Doc.* xxv.]

III

INSTRUCTIONS FOR THE FATHERS OF OUR SOCIETY WHO SHALL BE SENT TO THE HURONS

By Father Jean de Brébeuf

(From the Relation for 1637)

The Fathers and Brethren whom God shall call to the holy Mission of the Hurons ought to exercise careful foresight in regard to all the hardships, annoyances, and perils that must be encountered in making this journey, in order to be prepared betimes for all emergencies that may arise.

You must have sincere affection for the Savages,—looking upon them as ransomed by the blood of the son of God, and as our Brethren with whom we are to pass the rest of our lives.

To conciliate the Savages, you must be careful never to make them wait for you in embarking.

You must provide yourself with a tinder box or with a burning mirror, or with both, to furnish them fire in the daytime to light their pipes, and in the evening when they have to encamp; these little services win their hearts.

You should try to eat their sagamité or salmagundi in the way they prepare it, although it may be dirty, half-cooked, and very tasteless. As to the other numerous things which may be unpleasant, they must be endured for the love of God, without saying anything or appearing to notice them.

It is well at first to take everything they offer, although you may not be able to eat it all; for, when one becomes somewhat accustomed to it, there is not too much.

You must try and eat at daybreak unless you can take your meal with you in the canoe; for the day is very long, if you have to pass it without eating. The Barbarians eat only at Sunrise and Sunset, when they are on their journeys.

You must be prompt in embarking and disembarking; and tuck up your gowns so that they will not get wet, and so that you will not carry either water or sand into the canoe. To be properly dressed, you must have your feet and legs bare; while crossing the rapids, you can wear your shoes, and, in the long portages, even your leggings.

You must so conduct yourself as not to be at all troublesome to even one of these Barbarians.

It is not well to ask many questions, nor should you yield to your desire to learn the language and to make observations on the way; this may be carried too far. You must relieve those in your canoe of this annoyance, especially as you cannot profit much by it during the work. Silence is a good equipment at such a time.

You must bear with their imperfections without saying a word, yes, even without seeming to notice them. Even if it be necessary to criticise anything, it must be done modestly, and with words and signs which evince love and not aversion. In short, you must try to be, and to appear, always cheerful.

Each one should be provided with half a gross of awls, two or three dozen little knives called jambettes (pocket-knives), a hundred fish-hooks, with some beads of plain and colored glass, with which to buy fish or other articles when the tribes meet each other, so as to feast the Savages; and it would be well to say to them in the beginning, "Here is something with which to buy fish." Each one will try, at the portages, to carry some little thing, according to his strength; however little one carries, it greatly pleases the savages, if it be only a kettle.

You must not be ceremonious with the Savages, but accept the comforts they offer you, such as a good place in the cabin. The greatest conveniences are attended with very great inconvenience, and these ceremonies offend them.

Be careful not to annoy anyone in the canoe with your hat; it would be better to take your nightcap. There is no impropriety among the Savages.

Do not undertake anything unless you desire to continue it; for example, do not begin to paddle unless you are inclined to continue paddling. Take from the start the place in the canoe that you wish to keep; do not lend them your garments, unless you are willing to surrender them during the whole journey. It is easier to refuse at first than to ask them back, to change, or to desist afterwards.

Finally, understand that the Savages will retain the same opinion of you in their own country that they will have formed on the way; and one who has passed for an irritable and troublesome person will have considerable difficulty afterwards in removing this opinion. You have to do not only with those of your own canoe, but also (if it must be so stated) with all those of the country; you meet some today and others tomorrow, who do not fail to inquire, from those who brought you, what sort of man you are. It is almost incredible, how they observe and remember even the slightest fault. When you meet Savages on the way, as you cannot yet greet them with kind words, at least show them a cheerful face, and thus prove that you endure gayly the fatigues of the voyage. You will thus have put to good use the hardships on the way, and have already advanced considerably in gaining the affection of the Savages.

This is a lesson which is easy enough to learn, but very difficult to put into practice; for, leaving a highly civilized community, you fall into the hands of barbarous people who care but little for your Philosophy or your Theology. All the fine qualities which might make you loved and respected in France are like pearls trampled under the feet of swine, or rather mules, which utterly despise you when they see that you are not as good pack animals as they are. If you could go naked, and carry the load of a horse upon your back, as they do, then you would be wise according to their doctrine, and would be recognized as a great man, otherwise not. Jesus Christ is our true greatness; it is He alone and His cross that should be sought in running after these people, for, if you strive for anything else, you will find naught but bodily and spiritual affliction. But having found Jesus Christ in His cross, you have found the roses in the thorns, sweetness in bitterness, all in nothing.

[*Ibid.*, xii., *Doc.* xxix.]

IV

RELATION OF WHAT OCCURRED IN THE MISSION OF THE SOCIETY OF JESUS, IN THE LAND OF THE HURONS, IN THE YEAR 1637

Sent to Kebec to the Reverend Father Paul Le Jeune, Superior of the Missions of the Society of Jesus, in New France.

By Father François Le Mercier [1]

A RECITAL OF THE MORE MEMORABLE EVENTS WHICH OCCURRED FROM THE MONTH OF JULY TO THE MONTH OF SEPTEMBER, ARRANGED IN THE FORM OF A JOURNAL

Some one may perhaps find that I am recording here many things of less importance than this title indicates. But I am writing to Your Reverence, and, on that account, I call "memorable events" all those which can afford you some consolation, and give you a knowledge of the customs of our Savages.

[1] François Joseph Le Mercier was born at Paris, Oct. 4, 1604, and at the age of eighteen, entered the Jesuit novitiate. In 1635, he came to Canada, and labored in the Huron mission until its destruction: he was at Ossossané in 1641-42, and at Ste. Marie-on-the-Wye in 1644. In June, 1656, he went, with other Jesuits, on the mission to the Onondagas, returning to Quebec the following year. He remained on the St. Lawrence during the rest of his labors in Canada, being superior of the missions in that province from August, 1653, until 1658, and again from 1665 to 1670. In November, 1659, he was assigned to a mission at Côte de Beaupré, where he labored nearly a year, being declared Vicar of Quebec in October, 1660. Sommervogel says that Le Mercier returned to France in 1673, and was then sent to Martinique as superior of that mission, where he remained until his death, June 12, 1690.

Le Mercier, as superior, wrote various *Relations* of the Canadian missions. The Hurons named him Chaüosé; the Iroquois, Teharonhiagannra.—*Ibid.*, viii., *note* 11.

I will begin with the date of the embarkation for the trading at Kebec, which was the 22nd of July, 1636. We had been waiting a long time for this day. This so notable delay, and the rumors of war which had caused many to change the paddle for bow and arrows, gave us some reason to fear that they might content themselves with their old kettles for this year—which could not be done without seriously affecting the affairs of Christianity, as both spiritual and temporal help come to us here only through the medium and the hands of the Savages.

Accordingly Father Antoine Daniel and two of our domestics embarked, in a fleet of eight or ten canoes. The day was beautiful, the lake very calm, but I cannot deny that this separation was somewhat painful; for we judged that henceforth, to work more efficiently, we should need a new settlement in the heart of the country, and the Father seemed to us to be altogether necessary for this purpose, as he was the only one we had who could, after the Reverend Father Jean de Brébeuf, our Superior, readily find his way out of the intricacies of the language. But we decided that to begin a Seminary for Huron Youth was a thing so advantageous, that we passed over that consideration, hoping that God would soon unfold to us the language, and that he would not fail to send us persons who would effectively apply themselves to the study of it. We have not been disappointed in our hope.

On the 27th Father Ambroise Davost embarked. It seemed necessary, in these beginnings, that, in case God should dispose of Father Daniel, some one should be upon the spot to take his place; and, as your Reverence often has to deal with our Savages at Three Rivers, he, being acquainted with the language, will be able to render you good service.

Father Pierre Pijart and I succeeded to the benefice of Father Antoine Daniel in the instruction of the little children of our Village. The Father Superior assigned to each of us a certain number of cabins, which we began to visit every day until the epidemic (the smallpox) was at its height—when we deemed it proper to desist therefrom, for reasons which I shall mention hereafter in their place. We derived considerable advantage from this little exercise, by improving ourselves in the language. Besides teaching the children, we took occasion to explain some of our mysteries to the fathers and mothers; these talks, however, were not very long: one must learn to put one foot before the other, before he can walk.

On the 8th, we received a package of letters from your Reverence through the medium of a Savage, uncle of Louys de Saincte Foy. We were greatly rejoiced to hear news of the fleet,—that it was composed of eight fine ships under the command of Monsieur du Plessis Bochart. Our Fathers who have come to see us this year, and above all Father Pierre Chastellain [1] and Father Charles Garnier[2] who had the honor to come over in his ship, have enjoyed a favor which cannot be highly enough appreciated, in celebrating Holy Mass almost the whole length of the passage. But our joy was dimmed by the assurances your Reverence gave us of the death of the late Monsieur de Champellain.—Rumors of it had been current for a long time, and had even reached us; but there were so many different versions, even as regarded the person, that we had some reason to persuade ourselves that what we feared had not happened. Our Society will be under eternal obligations to him for the kindness he has always shown it, both during his life time and at his death, as he bequeathed a part of what remained to him for the support of the Mission of our Fathers in these lands.

Toward the evening of the 12th (of August) father Pierre Chastellain arrived. The Father Superior and Father Pijart went to meet him; as for me, I was still in the retreat. I prepared what we had, to receive him; but what a feast it was! —a handful of small dried fish, with a little flour: I sent for

---

[1] Pierre Chastellain and Charles Garnier arrived at Quebec with Montmagny, June 11, 1636; and on July 21 they left for Three Rivers with the Indian trading canoes to join the mission in the Huron country. Both were attacked by the smallpox in the following September, but in due time recovered their health. Chastellain labored at Ihonatiria about two years; was at Ossossané in 1638-39; then at St. Joseph (Jeanaustoyé). In November, 1640, he was left in sole charge of the residence of Ste. Marie-on-the-Wye, and was there in 1644.— *Ibid.*, viii., *note* 51.

[2] *See* p. 229, ff.

some fresh ears of corn that we had roasted for him after the manner of the country. But it is true that in his heart, according to his story, he never partook of better fare. The joy which is experienced in these reunions seems to be some image of the happiness of the blessed upon their arrival in Heaven, so full is it of sweetness.

Also God so arranged it for us that we did not have it all in one day, for Father Charles Garnier did not arrive until a day later, although, up to the last two or three days' journey, he and Father Chastellain had always travelled together. They had had the good fortune to encamp together during the whole length of the journey. From the time of their departure from the three Rivers, they were in the hands of good Savages, who treated them kindly. All this, added to the happy meeting they had with Father Antoine Daniel, and four or five days later with Father Ambroise Davost in the country of the Bissiriniens, went far toward mitigating a great part of the fatigues of this voyage. We, also, received them in very good health, and as strong and vigorous as if we had not budged from Paris. We learned from them that Monsieur the Chevalier de Montmagny [1] had taken the place of the late Monsieur de Champellain.

On the 24th a Savage who was passing our house informed us that Soranhes, father of Louys de Saincte Foy, was sick. He did this so coldly that we did not concern ourselves further about it; but, as the Father Superior had a journey to make in that direction, he departed the next day, intending to go and visit him at the same time; but he learned on the way that he was dead. This Savage had often meditated upon his con-

---

[1] The death of Champlain, who had long been governor of New France, occurred Dec. 25, 1635. His successor was Charles Huault de Montmagny, a chevalier of the military order of St. John of Jerusalem, more commonly known as Knights of Malta.

The praises lavished by the missionaries upon Montmagny seem to have been justified by his conduct as governor, and by the opinions of other historians. He was a man of great personal courage, executive ability, good judgment, and profound piety. He was a warm friend and supporter of the Jesuit missions, as also of the new religious colony at Montreal, which he escorted thither in May, 1642.—*Ibid.*, viii., *note* 50.

version.   From time to time he came to visit us, and remained
with us several days.   The Father Superior continued to instruct him, and we taught him a few little prayers.   He urged
us strongly to baptize him, but we noticed so little stability
in his resolutions, and found him so deeply attached to worldly
interests, that we did not deem it wise to go any further.

Toward Spring he importuned us again, not so much for
Baptism, as to secure some letters of recommendation from
us,—intending, as he said, to go down to Kebec, as soon as
possible, to pass a few weeks with our Fathers, and afterwards
to be solemnly baptized at the arrival of the ships.   The
Father Superior, seeing that there was nothing but vanity in
his conduct, said that the place of his baptism was of very little
importance, that we would decide upon that later; only that,
before embarking, he should pass a few days with us, in order
to take into more mature consideration the final resolutions
upon a subject of such importance.   He promised to do this,
but he did not keep his word.   He embarked immediately
afterwards, and instead of going to Kebec, he stopped at the
Island, where he sojourned nearly two months, gambling, and
leading the usual life.   On his return he had the good fortune to have one of our Fathers in his canoe.   But, when he
reached the Bissiriniens, he changed his canoe and went directly to Teanausteaiae, his own village.   We did not see anything of him; and the first news we heard of him was that he
was sick, and almost at the same time we learned of his death.

THE EXCESSIVE CRUELTY OF MEN, AND THE GREAT MERCY OF GOD, UPON THE PERSON OF A PRISONER OF WAR FROM THE IROQUOIS NATION

On the 2nd of September, we learned that an Iroquois prisoner had been brought to the village of Onnentisati, and that
they were preparing to put him to death.   This Savage was
one of eight captured by them at the lake of the Iroquois;
the rest had saved themselves by flight.   At first we were hor-

rified at the thought of being present at this spectacle, but, having well considered all, we judged it wise to be there, not despairing of being able to win this soul for God.

Accordingly we departed, the Father Superior, Father Garnier, and I together. We reached Arontaen a little while before the prisoner, and saw this poor wretch coming in the distance, singing in the midst of 30 or 40 Savages who were escorting him. He was dressed in a beautiful beaver robe and wore a string of porcelain beads around his neck, and another in the form of a crown around his head. I will say here that, up to the hour of his torment, we saw only acts of humanity exercised toward him; but he had already been quite roughly handled since his capture.

We approached to look at him more closely; he raised his eyes and regarded us very attentively. The Father Superior was invited to make him sing; but he explained that it was not that which had brought him there. He approached him and told him that we all felt a great deal of compassion for him. Meanwhile, they brought him food from all sides,—some bringing sagamité, some squashes and fruits,—and treated him only as a brother and a friend. From time to time he was commanded to sing, which he did with so much vigor and strength of voice that we wondered how he could be equal to it,—especially as he had done hardly anything else day and night since his capture. A Captain, raising his voice, addressed to him these words: "My nephew, thou hast good reason to sing, for no one is doing thee any harm; behold thyself now among thy kindred and friends." Good God, what a compliment! All those who surrounded him, with their affected kindness and their fine words, were so many butchers who showed him a smiling face only to treat him afterwards with more cruelty.

In all the places through which he had passed he had been given something with which to make a feast; they did not fail here in this act of courtesy, for a dog was immediately put into the kettle, and he was brought into the cabin where the people were to gather for the banquet. He had some one tell the Father Superior to follow him. So we entered and placed ourselves near him; the Father Superior took occasion to tell him to be of good cheer; that he would in truth be miserable during the little of life that remained to him, but that, if he would listen to him, and would believe what he had to tell him, he would assure him of an eternal happiness in Heaven after his death.

Seeing that the hour of the feast was drawing near, we withdrew into the cabin where we had taken lodgings, not expecting to find an opportunity to speak further with him until the next day. But we were greatly astonished and much rejoiced when we were told that he was coming to lodge with us. And still more so afterwards, when the Father Superior had all the leisure necessary to instruct him in our mysteries,—in a word, to prepare him for Holy Baptism. A goodly band of Savages who were present, not only did not interrupt him, but even listened to him with close attention. What a great advantage it is to have mastered their language, to be loved by these people, and to have influence among them! I do not think the Christian truths have ever been preached in this country on an occasion so favorable, for there were present some from nearly all the nations who speak the Huron tongue. The Father Superior found him so well-disposed that he did not consider it advisable to postpone any longer his baptism. This being accomplished, we withdrew from his presence to take a little rest. For my part it was almost impossible for me to close my eyes.

The next morning, the prisoner again confirmed his wish to die a Christian, and he even promised the Father that he would remember to say, in his torments, "Jesus taïtenr," "Jesus, have pity on me." About noon he made his Astataion, that is, his farewell feast, according to the custom of those who are about to die.

The Sun, fast declining, admonished us to withdraw to the place where this cruel Tragedy was to be enacted. It was in the cabin of one Atsan, who is the great war Captain; therefore it is called "Otinontsiskiaj ondaon," meaning "the house of cut-off heads." We took a place where we could be near the victim and say an encouraging word to him when the opportunity offered. Toward 8 o'clock in the evening eleven fires were lighted along the cabin, about one brass distant from each other. The people gathered immediately, the old men taking places above, upon a sort of platform, the young men below. Before he (the victim) was brought in, Captain Aenons encouraged all to do their duty, representing to them the importance of this act, which was viewed, he said, by the Sun and by the God of war. He had hardly finished when the victim entered. . . .

For me to describe in detail all he endured during the rest of the night would be almost impossible; we suffered enough in forcing ourselves to see a part of it. Of the rest we judged from their talk. One thing, in my opinion, greatly increased his consciousness of suffering—that anger and rage did not appear upon the faces of those who were tormenting him, but rather gentleness and humanity, their words expressing only raillery, or tokens of friendship and goodwill. . . .

We would indeed have desired to prevent this act of lawlessness, but it is not yet in our power; we are not yet the Masters here; it is not a trifling matter to have a whole country opposed to one,—a barbarous country too, such as this is. Superstitions and customs grown old, and authorized by the lapse of so many centuries, are not so easy to abolish. Yet we are full of hope, and these new residences that we are about to establish in the principal villages of the country, will be, as we trust, so many forts whence we shall completely overthrow the Kingdom of Satan.

The country of the Iroquois is still an inaccessible land to us; we cannot preach the Holy Gospel there, and God brings them here into our hands. While our Hurons were on the watch for opportunities to capture this poor Savage, Heaven was meditating his freedom. Doubtless his relatives and friends will have considered this a very unfortunate fishing party, which caused him to fall into the hands of his enemies,

—not knowing that in throwing out his nets, he himself fortunately fell into the toils of St. Peter.

Before going any farther in that month of September, the season and the beauty of the grain, which was then beginning to ripen, invite me to tell your Reverence that the prophecy of that Sorcerer turned out to be false; he had threatened the country with famine, and had predicted that a white frost would ruin all the harvests. If the native grapes were as good as they are beautiful, they would have been useful to us; we gathered enough of them, nevertheless, to use in saying the Mass until Christmas. This will help to fill the little kegs that are sent us, which seldom arrive here without considerable leakage.

On the 11th Father Isaac Jogues [1] arrived. On the 17th he fell sick; at the end of some days the fever appeared each day, and in a somewhat violent form. Truly of all countries of the world it is here, perhaps, most desirable for a sick person to be able to say, with truth, "Thank God, in the place and in the condition in which I am, I have no other physician than his paternal providence; and of all the comforts an invalid may desire, I have, properly speaking, none except those which come to me directly from Heaven."

[1] Isaac Jogues was born at Orleans, France, Jan. 10, 1607. At the age of ten he became a student in the Jesuit College just established at Orleans. His studies were pursued at Rouen. La Flèche and Clermont; and he was ordained as a priest early in 1636. In April of that year he departed for Canada, in company with Chastellain, Garnier, Adam, Du Marché, Ragueneau and the lay brother Ambroise Cauvet; they came with the fleet that escorted Montmagny, Champlain's successor. Jogues went immediately to the Huron mission, and there labored six years. During this time, he, with Garnier, made an unsuccessful attempt to found a mission among the Tobacco tribe. In September, 1641, Jogues, with Charles Raymbault, made an expedition to Sault Ste. Marie, to visit the Chippewas there, and obtain information concerning that region. In June, 1642, they descended to Quebec, with a company of Hurons, to obtain supplies for their mission. On the return journey, an ambushed band of Iroquois attacked the party, 31 miles above Three Rivers, and captured Jogues, the donnés René Goupil and Guillaume Couture, and several Huron converts. The captives were taken to the Mohawk villages, where they were cruelly tortured, and some burned alive; Goupil was murdered; while Jogues and Couture were given to Indian families as slaves. In August, 1643, Jogues contrived to escape by aid of the Dutch commandant at Rensselaerswyck (also called Fort Orange; now Albany), and of Jan Megapolensis, a Protestant "dominie"; and on Nov. 5 he

The Father Superior did me the favor to give me the care of Father Jogues. Yet, before long I was not alone in this charge; for our cabin was soon afterwards changed into an infirmary, or rather into a hospital, there being as many nurses as there were well persons, and these were few for the number of patients. Your Reverence will hear only sickness mentioned from now on. During the first days, when we had as yet no game, we had almost nothing to give our invalids but some broth of wild purslane stewed in water, with a dash of native verjuice. Such were our first soups. We had, indeed, one hen; but she did not every day give us an egg,—and, besides, what is one egg for so many sick people? It was very amusing to us to see us who were well, waiting for that egg; and then afterwards we had to consider to whom we should give it, and to see who most needed it. As for our patients, the question among them was who should not eat it

On the 24th Father Jogues was in such a condition that we considered it absolutely necessary to bleed him. The great question was to find a Surgeon. We all were so skillful in this trade, that the patient did not know who should open the vein for him; and every one of us was only waiting for the benediction of the Father Superior to take the lancet in hand

left New Amsterdam (New York) on a Dutch vessel, arriving, after many dangers, at the Jesuit college in Rennes, Jan. 5, 1644.

In the following spring he returned to the Canadian mission, and was stationed at Montreal. For three years past the Iroquois had been especially hostile and dangerous, and their incursions constantly harassed the French, so that they no longer dared come down the St. Lawrence for trade. July 5, 1644, a Mohawk embassy came to Three Rivers, to negotiate a treaty of peace; they brought Couture, and restored him to the French. The treaty was concluded, after many delays, but it was not ratified until May, 1646, when Jogues and Jean Bourdon were sent to the Mohawks by Montmagny, for this purpose. Their commission was safely executed, and they returned to Quebec. In the following September Jogues was again sent to the Mohawk country, by his superiors, to spend the winter there, but the savages had renewed their hostility to the French, and, capturing Jogues not far from Fort Richelieu (on the Sorel), they took him as a prisoner, with his companion, Jean de la Lande, to the Mohawk town of Ossernenon (now Auriesville, N. Y.). A council of the tribe decided to set the prisoners at liberty, but they were treacherously assassinated (Oct. 18, 1646), by some fanatical members of the Bear clan of Mohawks.

Jogues wrote an account of the life and death of René Goupil, and a description of the Dutch colonies on the Hudson under the title *Novum Belgium.—Ibid.*, ix., *note* 41.

and do the work. However, he resolved to do it himself. We saw good results from it the same day; the next day his fever had abated considerably. The same day Father Pierre Chastellain was taken sick. Father Charles Garnier had to give up on the 27th. Now we were reduced to three persons, the Father Superior, Father Pijart, and myself.

If a bed of feathers often seems hard to a sick person, I leave your Reverence to imagine if they could rest easily upon a bed which was nothing but a mat of rushes spread over some bark, and at most a blanket or a piece of skin thrown over it. In addition to this, one of the most annoying things was the continual noise, both within and without the cabin. For you could not have prevented the visits and the importunities of the Savages, who do not know what it is to speak low. As I said one day to a Savage, "My friend, I pray thee, speak a little lower." "Thou hast no sense," he said to me: "there is a bird," speaking of our cock, "that talks louder than I do, and thou sayest nothing to him."

I have not told your Reverence that Tonneraouanont, one of the famous Sorcerers of the country, having heard that we were sick, came to see us. To hear him talk, he was a person of merit and influence, although in appearance he was a very insignificant object. He was a little hunchback, extremely misshapen. This is one of the Oracles of the whole country. "I am not" (said he) "of the common run of men: I am, as it were, a Demon; therefore I have never been sick. In the three or four times that the country has been afflicted with a contagion, I never feared the disease, for I have remedies to preserve me. Hence, if thou wilt give me something, I undertake in a few days to set all thy invalids upon their feet." The Father Superior, in order to get all the amusement he could out of it, asked him what he wanted. "Thou wilt give me," he said, "ten glass beads and one extra for each patient."

Your Reverence should, at this point, be thoroughly acquainted with the genealogy of this person, according to the version of it that he himself has given.

"I am a Demon; I formerly lived under the ground in the

house of the Demons, when the fancy seized me to become a man; and this is how it happened. Having heard one day, from this subterranean abode, the voices and cries of some children who were guarding the crops, and chasing the animals and birds away, I resolved to go out. I was no sooner upon the earth than I encountered a woman: I craftily entered her womb, and there assumed a little body. I had with me a she-devil, who did the same thing. As soon as we were about the size of an ear of corn, this woman wished to be delivered of her fruit, knowing that she had not conceived by human means, and fearing that this ocki [1] might bring her some misfortune. So she found means of hastening her time. Now it seems to me that in the meantime, being ashamed to see myself followed by a girl, and fearing that she might afterwards be taken for my wife, I beat her so hard that I left her for dead; in fact she came dead into the world.

"This woman, being delivered, took us both, wrapped in a beaver skin, carried us into the woods, placed us in the hollow of a tree, and abandoned us. We remained there until, a Savage passing by, I began to weep and cry out, that he might hear me. He did, indeed, perceive me; he carried the news to the village; my mother came, she took me again, bore me to her cabin, and brought me up such as thou seest me."

Your Reverence will hear still more extravagant stories about him in the course of time. At all events, behold in him one of the great Physicians of the country; nor did he lack practice. As for us, we could well dispense, thank God, with his remedies.

---

[1] *Oki:* a Huron appellation of various imaginary supernatural beings . . . sometimes benignant, sometimes malevolent; they were localized in streams, rocks, mountains, or the sky; *Oki* apparently signified "that which is above," and was applied to any existence or phenomenon that proved unintelligible to the savage mind. To the missionaries this word seemed oftenest synonymous with "demon" or "devil," but Brébeuf admits (vol. x., p. 161) that, with the Hurons, the *oki* they imagine in the sky is really their idea of God as the creator and ruler of the universe. . . . *Ibid.*, xiii., *note* 8.

THE HELP WE HAVE GIVEN TO THE SICK OF OUR VILLAGE

This is the order we maintained. We visited them twice a day, morning and evening, and carried them soup and meat. We ate during our own sickness a few of the raisins and prunes and some little remedies that your Reverence had sent us,— using them only in cases of necessity, so that we still had a good part of them, which we have made last up to the present. Everything was given by count, two or three prunes, or 5 or 6 raisins to one patient; this was restoring life to him. Our medicines produced effects which dazzled the whole country, and yet I leave you to imagine what sort of medicines they were. A little bag of senna served over 50 persons; they asked us for it on every side.

We had hoped that the first frosts would arrest the progress of this contagious malady. But just the opposite happened. At that time very injurious rumors about us had been scattered through the country; this little Sorcerer had already boasted loudly that he had seen the malady come from the direction of the great Lake. They talked of nothing but an imaginary cloak, poisoned, it was said, by the French; and Captain *Aënons* had already brought a report from an Island Savage, that the late Monsieur de *Champlain* had died with the determination to ruin the whole country. Besides, after having so diligently aided the sick of our Village for a month, and having taken the morsels from our own mouths to give them, there yet were found some who said that what we carried to them made them die; and others, who saw us daily skimming the grease from the soup that we were preparing for them, added that there was no cause for them to be under great obligations to us; that if we did give something to the sick, it was only what we would have thrown away, and that this pot, which was at our fire day and night, was only to accumulate a great deal of grease. Thus they talked.

On the 29th (of November) the chief men of our village assembled in our cabin, resolved to do all that we considered proper to incline God to mercy in this public calamity. The Father Superior told them that God took great pleasure in the vows that we addressed to him in these necessities; and thus, that if they would promise him, in case it might please him to make this contagion disappear altogether, to build in the Spring, a cabin, or a little Chapel in his honor, they would all have reason to hope for his approval of their request. . . .

OF THE RESIDENCE OF THE CONCEPTION OF NOSTRE DAME, AT THE HAMLET OF OSSOSANE

At last, behold our desires accomplished. I shall now express no longer mere hopes to Your Reverence, for they are working in earnest to erect for us our cabin at Ossosané; and we expect that you will send us, if you please, some workmen to build there a chapel in honor of the Immaculate Conception of our Lady.

On the 17th of May the Father Superior broached the subject of our decision to the Captain, in order to have the work begun as soon as possible. The Captain summoned the Council to assemble, where the proposition was received with much satisfaction. They bound themselves to make us a Cabin of about twelve brasses,—begging us, if they did not make it larger, to consider that the malady had carried off a part of the young men, and that the rest were nearly all gone trading or fishing; and giving us their word to make it as long and as wide as we should wish, the following year. The council over, each one took his hatchet, and they all went away in a crowd to prepare the site.

On the 21st, Father Pierre Pijart departed with two domestics, to set the laborers to work. He wrote me thus about it, on the 4th of June:

"I find myself here in the midst of extraordinary confusion, —on the one hand, I have to keep them at work upon our cabin; and, on the other, I have the sick to visit: the former do only a part of what they attempt, and I encounter near the latter more Sorcerers than occasions to speak to them of God and of the matter of their salvation. I console myself with the thought that we are not building here a simple cabin, but a house for our Lady,—or rather, many beautiful chapels in the principal villages of the country."

On the 7th (of June) I received a second letter from Father Pierre Pijart who wrote me in these terms: "I will send you further information of the state of our new Residence since my last letter. On the fifth of this month I said the first Mass in our house of la Conception de nostre Dame. . . . At the time I am writing this there remain only ten pieces of bark to finish the cabin; they have gone to get them, and this evening it will be completed. From the Residence of la Conception de Nostre Dame, this seventh of June."

[*Ibid.*, xiii., xiv., *Doc.* xxix.]

V

LETTER OF FATHER FRANCOIS DU PERON OF THE SOCIETY OF JESUS, TO FATHER JOSEPH IMBERT DU PERON, HIS BROTHER, RELIGIOUS OF THE SAME SOCIETY

(Copied from the autograph preserved in MSS. Soc. Jesu)

At the village of la Conception de Nostre Dame, this 27th of April, 1639.

MY REVEREND FATHER:

Pax Christi

I wrote last year to Your Reverence concerning the events of my journey from the time of my departure from France until my arrival in Canada. I beg you to inform me whether you have received the four letters that I wrote you; I shall not have answers to those of last year until after I have sent this one. I told you of my employment; God gave me a different one: he sent me to the Huron country. Accordingly, I shall henceforth only send you news of the Hurons, for, as for the Montagnais and the Algonquins, we receive news of them only through the printed Relations sent to us from France from year to year. You can answer my letters; as for myself, I must leave one year between two letters, because the Hurons go down from here to Three Rivers at the same time that the ships arrive there from France.

I left Three Rivers on the 4th of September, and reached the Huron country on the day of saint Michel. I fortunately embarked with a Huron captain, who showed me every courtesy along the way. Reverend Father Lallemant,[1] our su-

[1] Jerome Lalemant, brother of Charles, former superior of the mission at Quebec, and uncle of Gabriel Lalemant, one of the Huron martyrs.

137

perior, and Father Lemoyne, who departed before I did, did not fare so well. The former was almost strangled by one of the island savages (this is an Algonquin nation that is encountered upon the way), who tried several times to put a bowstring about his neck—"to avenge," he said, "the death of one of his little children," who had been bled by one of our men who had gone up a day or two before the Father. I encountered this same savage near the island, who, when he first saw me, said he must do the same thing to me, and for a long time tried to persuade our Hurons that they ought not to bring Frenchmen into their country, that it was we who made them all die.

As for Father Lemoyne,[1] he was obliged to part from his savages, as he had no longer any provisions. Accordingly, they left him on the bank of the river with one of our men, whose hunting furnished him with food for two weeks. Then he embarked in one of the canoes of our band. The master of this canoe, two days later, wished to leave him upon a rock, and I had to give him my blanket to satisfy him.

Along the way we passed three wandering Algonquin tribes: for the rest, forests and bare rocks, rapids and precipices: I am surprised that the savages dare undertake such a

[1] Simon le Moyne, at the age of eighteen, entered the Jesuit novitiate at Rouen, Dec. 10, 1622; his studies were pursued here, and at Clermont and La Flèche, and he was an instructor at the Rouen college during 1627-32 and 1636-37. While a student at Clermont, he was an active member of the "league of prayer for the Canadian mission," to which belonged Le Jeune, the Lalemants, and many others. Assigned to the mission in Canada, he went thither in the spring of 1638, and at once departed to the Huron country; by that people he was surnamed *Wane*. In the following year he began (with Daniel) a mission among the Arendarhonons, that of St. Jean Baptiste; and for several years was in charge of this mission and of that at Teanaustayé (St. Joseph). After the dispersion of the Hurons, he probably served at Quebec and other posts on the St. Lawrence, until 1653, when he was sent as an ambassador to the Iroquois, and likewise opened a mission among the Onondagas. Much of his time during the next five years was spent among the Iroquois tribes, by whom he was known as *Ondossonk*—the appellation they had formerly bestowed upon Jogues, and, after the martyrdom of the latter had conferred upon Le Moyne, in accordance with their custom. While in the Iroquois country, Le Moyne visited New Amsterdam (New York), and formed a strong friendship with the Dutch minister there, Jan Megapolensis, who had formerly aided Jogues in his captivity. Le Moyne made a fifth journey to the Iroquois country in 1661. He died Nov. 24, 1665, from a fever, at Cap de Magdeleine.—*Ibid.*, xiv., *note* 16.

journey. As for the Huron country, it is tolerably level, with many prairies, many lakes, many villages; of the two where we are, one contains 80 cabins, the other 40. In each cabin there are five fireplaces, and two families at each. Their cabins are made of large sheets of bark in the shape of an arbor, long, wide, and high in proportion; some of them are 70 feet long. Their land produces nothing but Indian corn, beans, and squashes. These are the delicacies of the country, which has nothing in common with our France, as to things to be enjoyed, except the four elements. One sees here, nevertheless, birds, fish, and forest animals, almost the same kinds as in France. The land, as they do not cultivate it, produces for only ten or twelve years at most; and when the ten years have expired, they are obliged to move their village to another place.

The nature of the Savage is patient, liberal, hospitable; but importunate, visionary, childish, thieving, lying, deceitful, licentious, proud, lazy; they have among them many fools, or rather lunatics and insane people. Their language is a regular one, as much as it can be, full of constructions like the Greek; differing from the latter in that the changes of mode and person come at the beginning, the terminations being nearly always the same; an accent changes the meaning of the word. It is not as barbarous as is imagined; the nouns are conjugated as well as the verbs: as to syntax, I cannot see that it is very different from that of the French language, especially as they do not know what case is; they have little particles of elegance; they do not use the following letters, b, f, l, m, p, q, x, y; they make much use of the letters h and k.

They nearly all show more intelligence in their business, speeches, courtesies, intercourse, tricks, and subtleties, than do the shrewdest citizens and merchants in France. They regulate the seasons of the year by the wild beasts, the fish, the birds, and the vegetation; they count the years, days, and months by the moon.

There are ten of Ours here in two Residences, one at la Conception de Notre Dame, the other at Saint Joseph; these are distant from each other five or six leagues. We expect soon to establish a third Residence in the tobacco nation, without detriment to the itinerant missions. We have with us twelve Frenchmen, who are hired by us. We are lodged and fed in the manner of the savages; we have no land of our own, except a little borrowed field, where French grain is raised just to make the host for the holy mass; we leave the rest to divine Providence, which sends us more corn than if we had broad lands; one person will bring us three ears of corn, another six, some else a squash; one will give us some fish, another some bread baked under the ashes. As their presents, we give them little glass beads, rings, awls, small pocket knives, and colored beads; this is all our money. As for the delicacies of France, we have none of them here; the usual sauce with the food is pure water, juice of corn or of squashes. The fresh food that comes from France does not go farther up than Three Rivers; all they can send is some church ornaments, some wine for the mass (only four or five drops of it is put into the chalice), and some clothes, some prunes, and raisins for the sick of the village; it all runs great risks on the way. We lost this year two of our packages. Our plates, although of wood, cost us more than yours; for they are valued at one beaver robe, which is a hundred francs.

Having safely landed on Huron soil, I started so as to arrive at one of our Residences in time to celebrate holy mass that day. But the rain, and my exhaustion, as well as the distance of five or six leagues, and my ignorance of the way, constrained me to stop at the first village and take a little nourishment. Accordingly, I entered the cabin of a captain of the village: the salutation they offered me was a *chay* in their language,—this is the usual greeting and means "good day." Then they immediately spread a mat upon the ground for me to rest upon, and afterwards brought four ears of corn which they roasted and presented to me, as well as two squashes cooked under the ashes, and a dish of sagamité; I assure Your Reverence that this food was delicious to me. My ignorance of the language rendered me mute; and their custom, which is to say not a word except *chay,* to one who arrives, made them silent also; they merely surveyed me from head to foot, and all wished to try on my shoes and my hat, each one putting the hat on his head and the shoes on his feet.

After having expressed my thanks by giving a knife, an awl, and a needle to my host, I begged him to give me a savage to carry my bag and guide me to one of our Residences; and I reached the house of our Fathers at six o'clock in the evening. They received me with every evidence of kindness, although their entertainment was no better than that of the Savages,— that is, a porridge made of the meal of Indian corn and water, morning and evening, and for drink a flagon of water.

The importunity of the savages,—who are continually about us in our cabin,—does not prevent our observance of our hours, as well regulated as one of our colleges in France. At four o'clock the rising bell rings; then follows the orison, at the end of which the masses begin and continue until eight o'clock. At eight o'clock the door is left open to the savages, until four in the evening; it is permitted to talk with the savages at this time, as much to instruct them as to learn their language. In this time, also, the Fathers visit the cabins of the town. Then follows dinner. We dine around the fire, seated on a log, with our plates on the ground.

On the 13th of November, the Reverend Father superior left here with one of our Fathers, to begin the itinerant missions. The devil seemed to try to oppose their plan; the snow fell so abundantly as to cover all the paths.

On the 2nd of March, and other days following the carnival, the devil was unchained here as well as in France. There was only deviltry and masquerading at that time throughout the Huron country; I will content myself with touching incidentally upon the deviltries of these peoples.

1. All their actions are dictated to them directly by the devil, who speaks to them, now in the form of a crow or some similar bird, now in the form of a flame or a ghost, and all this in dreams, to which they show great deference. They consider the dream as the master of their lives, it is the God of

the country. It is this which dictates to them their feasts, their hunting, their fishing, their war, their trade with the French, their remedies, their dances, their games, their songs.

2. To cure a sick person, they summon the sorcerer, who without acquainting himself with the disease of the patient, sings, and shakes his tortoise shell; he gazes into the water and sometimes into the fire, to discover the nature of the disease.[1] Having learned it, he says that the soul of the patient desires, for his recovery, to be given a present of such or such a thing,—of a canoe, for example, of a new robe, a porcelain collar, a fire-feast, a dance, etc., and the whole village straightway sets to work to carry out to the letter all the sorcerer may have ordered. As I was writing this, a Savage, greatly excited, came from a neighboring village, and begged us to give him a piece of red stuff, because the sorcerer had said that one of his sons, who was sick, desired for his recovery this bit of stuff. It was not given to him; but one of our fathers immediately repaired to the place, and baptized the little patient.

3. Nearly all the Savages have charms, to which they speak and make feasts, in order to obtain from them what they desire.

4. The devil has his religious; those who serve him must be deprived of all their possessions, they must abstain from women, they must obey perfectly all that the devil suggests to them. The sorcerer of this village came to see us, and told us all these things.

The number of those baptized this year reaches fully 300 souls; in this village of la Conception, there have been baptized in sickness, both children and others, one hundred and twenty-two persons. Besides the sick, fifty persons in health were solemnly baptized. In the village of St. Joseph, one

---

[1] They believe that there are two main sources of disease; one of these is in the mind of the patient himself, which desires something, and will vex the body of the sick man until it possesses the thing required. For they think that there are in every man certain inborn desires, often unknown to themselves, upon which the happiness of individuals depends. For the purpose of ascertaining desires and innate appetites of this character, they summon soothsayers, who, as they think, have a divinely imparted power to look into the inmost recesses of the mind. . . . *Jouvency's Account of the Canadian Mission. Ibid.,* i., 259.

hundred and twenty-six; in the itinerant mission of St. Michel, twenty-six or seven. I speak only of this country of the Hurons; as concerns Kebec and Three Rivers, you have the Relation of those before we do.

I am with all my heart,

My Reverend Father,

your very humble and very affectionate brother in our Lord,

FRANÇOIS DU PERON,

surnamed in Huron ANONCHIARA, S.J.

[*Ibid.,* xv., *Doc.* xxxi.]

VI

RELATION OF WHAT OCCURRED IN NEW FRANCE IN THE YEAR 1639

By Father Paul Le Jeune

MY REVEREND FATHER:

The birth of a Dauphin; the affection and gifts of our great King for our Savages; the solicitude of Monseigneur the Cardinal for these countries, and his donations for the Huron Mission; the offerings of the Gentlemen of New France for our Neophytes or new Christians; the continuation of Monsieur the Chevalier de Montagny in his government; the coming of the Nuns; the aid Your Reverence has been pleased to send us; the assistance of many persons of merit and condition; the wishes and prayers of pious souls—all these were the subjects of our conversations on board the ship. All these pleasures have affected me the more sensibly, since I have tasted them with the sweet liberty that I enjoyed long ago; and since at last Your Reverence has granted me that the Reverend Father Vimont should be sent to us, whose virtues will make amends for any errors that I may have committed in the discharge of the office I have handed over to him. He has given me to understand that Your Reverence desired that I should write the Relation again this year. Let us commence.

OF THE JOY FELT IN NEW FRANCE AT THE BIRTH OF MONSEIGNEUR THE DAUPHIN AND OF A COUNCIL HELD BY THE SAVAGES

The most extraordinary delay in the arrival of the fleet this year had made us very uneasy, when a ship, appearing forty leagues below Kebec, sent a short letter to Monseigneur our Governor. Every one hastened to learn the news; but, as the paper contained not a word about the birth of Monseigneur the Dauphin, it checked the course of our joy. We had heard the year before that the Queen was *enceinte* and we hoped for a child whose birth would be at once a blessing and a miracle; we all thought that God's gifts would be perfected, and that we would have a Prince. This ship, which should have brought us the first news, said not a word of it. It merely informed us that other vessels were coming, from which it had been separated at sea in a heavy fog. Finally, the winds becoming favorable to our wishes, we learned that Heaven had given us a Dauphin.

Hardly had this word "Dauphin" escaped the lips of the Messengers, than joy entered into our hearts and thanksgiving into our souls. The news soon spread everywhere; the *Te Deum Laudamus* was chanted, and bonfires and fireworks were prepared with every device possible in these countries. The Gentlemen of New France recommended these manifestations of joy, but all their recommendations served only to prove their love for this new Prince; for, even before their letters appeared, joy had taken possession of our hearts, and all the necessary orders had been given by Monsieur our Governor to manifest it before God and before men. Fireworks were shot up towards Heaven, falling in golden showers, and glittering with stars; fiery serpents ran everywhere; a fine night was illuminated by lighted torches; while the heavy thunder of the Cannon resounded in the Echoes of our great forests. The Hurons who were present placed their hands on their mouths, in token of admiration and astonishment. These poor Savages, having never seen any thing of the kind, thought that the dominion of the French extended even over the Realms of fire, and that we could do what we liked with that Element.

The fireworks were not sufficient for the expression of our joy; sometime afterwards, we formed a procession which would have delighted all France if it had appeared in Paris. Before I speak of it, I must say a few words with reference to his

Majesty's presents, which made their appearance in this very holy act of devotion which we offered to God in Thanksgiving for his Dauphin. Last year, a Canadian Savage, the son of one *Iwanchou*, a Savage captain well known to the French, went to France and was very well received by his Majesty, at whose feet he laid his Crown of Porcelain beads,[1] as a sign that he recognized that great Prince, in the name of these nations, as their true and lawful Monarch. The King and Queen showed him their Dauphin; and, after many tokens of kindness, they made him a present of six suits of clothing truly royal. They were entirely of cloth of gold, velvet, satin, silk plush, scarlet and everything else in keeping.

When this young Savage returned to his own country, he came up to Kebec with a party of his Countrymen, and went to see monsieur the Chevalier de Montmagny, our Governor to whom these gifts were brought. There happened to be present, at the time, Huron, Algonquin, and Montagnais Savages, who

---

[1] *Porcelain, which is the diamonds and pearls of this country:* According to Littre, *porcelain* (a word of Italian origin; adopted, with slight variations, into nearly all European languages) was a name given, from very early times, to an univalvular, gastropodous mollusk, *Cypraea,* especially used for the species *C. meneta,* the money cowry of Africa and the East Indies, and for its shell. The same term was applied to the nacre obtained from the shells of this and many other mollusks.

The early explorers on this continent found shells, or beads made therefrom, everywhere in use among the natives as currency. Champlain and other French writers applied the term already familiar to them, "porcelain"; the English colonists adopted the name in use among the natives of New England, "wampum" (from *wompi,* "white").

An interesting account of this Indian money is given by Roger Williams in his *Key into the Languages of America.* "Concerning their Coyne: . . . Before ever they had *Awle blades* from Europe, they made shift to bore this their shell money with stone set in a wooden staff. They hang these strings of money about their necks and wrists, as also upon the necks and wrists of their wives and children." . . . From these shells were cut beads of cylindrical shape, through which holes were drilled; these beads were then strung upon cords, or the sinews of animals, and, when woven into plaits about as broad as the hand, made wampum "belts." Wampum was used not only as money, and for purposes of ornament; it was sent with a messenger as his credentials, and was the mark of a chief's authority; it was used for "presents" or gifts, both within and without one's tribe; it was paid as a ransom for a prisoner, or as atonement for a crime; and it was used in negotiating and in recording treaties. The wampum "means nothing at all to white man, all to Indian," said recently a prominent Onondaga (Cf. Hale's "Indian Wampum Records," in Popular Science Monthly, February, 1897).—*Ibid.,* viii., note 70.

all admired the goodness of our Prince, whom they called their King. Now, when these packages were opened, it was deemed advisable in order to extend the King's honor among these nations, and to avoid any jealousy that might arise among these barbarians, if one nation were the sole recipient of these favors —to distribute them to several, especially as this Savage had gone to do homage to the King, not only in the name of his father and of his nation, but likewise in the name of the other nations of this country. Therefore, three splendid suits were given to this young Savage—one for himself, another for his son, and a third for his Father.

While they were considering to whom the three other suits should be given, Monsieur our Governor said that three Christian Savages should be chosen from three nations; that his Majesty would approve this plan, since he himself had asked this Savage if he were not baptized and if he were not sedentary. When I announced to three of our Christians the presents which the King had sent them, and exhorted them to pray for his Majesty and for his Dauphin, they were quite astonished; then, addressing me, they made an answer I did not expect from the mouth of a Savage.

"Nikanis, tell our Captain to write to our King" (thus they spoke), "that we thank him and admire him. Even if he had sent us nothing, we would still love him. However, keep these clothes thyself, for we do not wish to wear them except when we shall walk, praying to God for him, and for his son, and for his wife." (He meant that they would wear them only when there should be a Procession for the King, for the Queen, and for Monseigneur the Dauphin.) "And when we are dead, if thou or thy brothers have prayers said to God for the King, make our children wear these clothes, so that those who shall come after us may know the love our King had for us."

We now come to the first procession in which these magnificent garments were worn. The day dedicated to the glorious and triumphant Assumption of the blessed Virgin was chosen. At early morn, our Christian Neophytes came to hear holy

Mass, to confess, and to receive communion. All the other Savages who were then in the neighborhood of Kebec assembled, and we placed them in the order they were to observe. When the procession commenced its march, the Cross and the banner were carried in front. Monsieur Gand came next, walking at the head of the Savage men, the first six of whom were clad in these royal garments. They went two by two most sedately, with becoming modesty. After the men walked the foundress [1] of the Ursulines, having beside her three or four Savage girls, clothed in French fashion; then followed all the daughters and wives of the Savages in their own costume, keeping their ranks perfectly. The Clergy came next; and after them walked monsieur our Governor, and our Frenchmen, then our French women, without any other order than that suggested by humility.

As soon as the Procession commenced its march, the Cannons thundered forth, inspiring these poor Savages with a holy awe. We walked to the Hospital, and, when we had reached it, all the Savages knelt down on one side, the French on the other, and the Clergy in the middle. Then the Savages prayed all together for the King, thanking God for having given him a Dauphin. They likewise prayed for the Queen, for all the French, and afterwards for the whole of their own nation; then they chanted the principal articles of our creed. This done, the Clergy, Monsieur the Governor, and the chief among our French and the Savages, entered the Chapel dedicated to the Blood of Jesus Christ, where they prayed for the same objects. On leaving the Hospital, we went straightway to the Ursulines. Passing before the Fort, the Musketeers fired a noble salvo, and the Cannon again poured forth its thunder and flame. We observed the same ceremonies; the Nuns sang the *Exaudiat*, to the delight of our Savages; and it gave our French great joy to hear two Choirs of Virgins praising the greatness of God in this new world.

On leaving the Ursulines, we went directly to the Church, with the same modest demeanor and in the same order as when

---

[1] Madame de la Peltrie. *See* p. 153, ff.

we started. We repeated the prayers in the savage tongue, at the door of the Chapel; then re-entering the Church, the Procession ended. When it was over, monsieur the Governor gave a feast to about one hundred Savages. We took with us the six who were clad in the royal robes, and gave them to eat in our house. After dinner, they attended Vespers, wearing the same liberal gifts from the King. Some had nothing savage about them but their tanned color; their demeanor and gait were full of dignity and real grace.

After Vespers, we thought of sending them away; but one of them told me that the chief men of the Savages were assembled in our Hall, and were waiting for me to hold a council. I went there to listen to them, and seeing that they were beginning to make speeches I sent word to Reverend Father Vimont of what was happening. He brought with him monsieur the Governor and Madame de la Pelterie, who could not sufficiently admire the devotion of these good people. All being seated, a Captain addressed me as follows: "Be wise, Father Le Jeune, keep quiet; let not thy mind wander, that thou mayest not lose a word of what I am about to say." "Ho, Ho," I replied, following their custom. "It is not I who speak," said he. "It is all those whom thou seest sitting there, who have charged me to tell thee that we all desire to believe in God, and that we all wish to be helped to till the soil, so as to dwell near you. Thou didst lead us to hope that many people would come out to thee, and now thou hast but very few. Well, then, tell our Captain to write to our King and tell him this; 'All Savages thank you; they wonder that you should think of them; they say to you; "Take courage; help us, since we love you. We wish to settle down but we cannot build houses like yours unless you help us." ' Tell thy brother who has come in thy place to write also; write thyself, so that it may be known that we speak the truth." Such is the style of these Savages.

This one having finished his harangue, another addressed me as follows; "Father le Jeune, I am not of this country. There is my home, in those mountains to the South. I had not come to Kebec for a very long time. These men whom thou seest came to visit me in my country, and told me that thou wert causing houses to be built for the Savages, and that thou didst help them to till the soil. They asked me if I would come to see thee, to dwell near thee with the others. I have come; I have seen that thou hast commenced but that thou hast not done much for so many people as we are. Well, then, take courage, thou sayest good things; do not lie. I am going away again to the coldness of our Mountains, for this Winter. In the Spring, while there will still be snow on the ground, I shall come and see if thou dost tell the truth, and if thou hast men to help us to till the soil; so that we may no longer be like the beasts who seek their living in the woods."

At these words all were touched with compassion. Monsieur the Governor promised to do what he could, on his part. Reverend Father Vimont was almost impatient, seeing that, through lack of temporal assistance, Satan ever keeps these poor souls under his Dominion. Madame de la Pelterie exclaimed; "Alas! how many souls could be saved in this country with what is spent for a single repast in Paris, or for a single ballet that lasts but two or three hours! I have brought only a few laborers with me but I will do what I can to help these good people. My Father," she said to me, "assure them that if I could help them with my own arms, I would cheerfully do so. I will try to plant something for them." These good Savages, hearing what she said, began to laugh, saying that the corn planted by arms so weak would be too late. The conclusion reached was that an effort would be made to help them in the Spring.

I consoled them wonderfully when I told them that the Captain [1] who had commenced the Residence of Saint Joseph, had provided the means wherewith always to keep six work-

[1] Noël Brulard (or Brulart), chevalier de Sillery, descended from an old and noble Burgundian family, was born at Paris, Dec. 25, 1577. He was sent as ambassador to Madrid (1614) and to Rome (1622), and held important state offices; his rank, wealth, and military renown rendered him for many years a personage of distinction at the French court. In the midst of a brilliant career (1625), he renounced the world and embraced the religious life,—probably led thereto by the influence of his friend Vincent de Paul,—and was ordained a priest

men for them; and that, even after his death the workmen would not cease to work. They could not understand how this could be done, nor why these workmen could not at once take the money he left for them, nor how a dead man could make living men work; for they know not what it is to have rents and revenues. Would to God that several persons of abundant wealth would imitate the devoutness of that great man! There is no loss in exchanging earth for Heaven.

At the same time Ioanchou, and his son who had been in France, were asked if they would not join the others. They replied that they would go and consult their people, and, if they wished to come up here, they would bring them.

Now, I was glad to speak of the great things to be seen in France in the presence of a Savage just returned from there. "Reproach me now with falsehood," I said to them; "ask your Countryman if what I told you of the greatness of our King and of the beauty of our country be not true? And do not any more call in question what I shall hereafter tell you."

This good Savage related marvels, but according to his own range of understanding. Although he had greatly admired many things,—among others, the great multitude in Paris; the great number of cookshops; the collossal Saint Christophle of Nostre Dame, which at first sight, caused him much terror; the Coaches, which he called "rolling cabins drawn by Moose," —he admitted that nothing had so interested him as the King, when he saw him on the first day of the year, walking with his guards. He attentively observed all the soldiers marching in good order; the Swiss produced a great impression on his eyes, and the sound of their drum on his head. When he went away thence, he did not speak for the remainder of the day—so the Father who accompanied him told me—doing nothing but reflect upon what he had seen.

at the age of 57 (1634). By special dispensation from Rome he was, however, allowed to retain possession of his still great fortune, that he might personally expend it in pious and charitable works. He was especially interested in Le Jeune's project for rendering sedentary the wandering Indian tribes; and in 1637 he gave to the Jesuit missions in Canada the funds for establishing at Sillery (named for its benefactor) their colony of Indian neophytes. *Ibid.*, xiv., *note* 12.

He related all this to his people, who listened to him with avidity. The King's piety was of powerful assistance to us in doing honor to our faith; for this good Canadian admitted that the first time he saw the King was in the house of Prayer, where he prayed to JESUS as he is prayed to here. He also stated publicly that the King had asked him if he had been baptized. This has helped us and will again help us to make these poor peoples understand the esteem in which that great Prince holds the doctrine that we teach them. In fact, as soon as this Savage had seen the King, he said to the Father who conducted him; "Let us go away. I have seen all, since I have seen the King."

To conclude this chapter; our Savages, seeing that his Majesty had sent them clothes in the French fashion, determined to send a little dress, such as is worn by Savages, to Monseigneur the Dauphin. When they handed it to me, they had the wit to say: "It is not a present that we make him, for his riches are far greater than ours; but it is a metawagan—a small toy to amuse his little Son, who may perhaps take pleasure in seeing how our children are dressed."

We send this little dress to Your Reverence. However, as smallpox greatly prevails among our Savages, I do not know whether it is advisable to present it, for fear that it may carry even the slightest contagion with it. It is true that I had it in my possession before the disease broke out among those that gave it to me; but, when so sacred a personage is concerned, a danger even a thousand leagues distant is to be dreaded.

OF THE NUNS RECENTLY ARRIVED IN NEW FRANCE, AND OF THEIR OCCUPATION

It was in this year (1639) that Madame the Duchess d'Aiguillon [1] erected and endowed a house in honor of God

---

[1] Marie Madeleine de Wignerod (Vignerot) was the daughter of René de Wignerod and of Françoise Duplessis, sister of Cardinal Richelieu. About 1620 Marie became the wife of Antoine de Beauvoir de Roure, marquis de Combalet; two years later, an officer in the Huguenot war, he fell in battle at Montpelier. His widow refused to marry again, and devoted her time and fortune to works

in this new world. And there was found an Amazon, who has led the Ursulines, and established them on the outer confines of this world. It is indeed a remarkable fact that,—at the very moment when God touched the heart of Madame the Duchesse d'Aiguillon in Paris, and inspired her with the idea of building a Hostel-Dieu for our Savages who were dying in the forests, abandoned and without any assistance, and while she was thinking of the Hospital Nuns of Dieppe for carrying out her project,—he raised up, in another part of France, a modest and virtuous Lady, and inspired her to undertake the Seminary for the little daughters of the Savages, and to confide its management to the Ursulines. And he so arranged affairs that all was accomplished at the same time, so that these good Nuns might have the consolation of crossing the Ocean together, and that the Savages might benefit, at the same moment, by this double and equally necessary service. I would offend the reasonable desires of many, if I did not say here a word respecting the conduct of that virtuous Lady throughout her undertaking.

She is a native of Alencon; her name is Magdelaine de Chauvigny; she is the daughter of the late Monsieur de Chauvigny, seigneur of Vaubegon, and President of the Elected in the Election of Alençon. From her infancy, she did all in her power to enter the Religious life. But her father obliged her to marry an honorable Gentleman, named Monsieur de la Pelterie, who, five and a half years after their marriage, left her a childless widow. As soon as she became a widow, she began, through the perusal of the Relations that we send over every year, earnestly to consider means of contributing to the education of the little Savage girls. With that intention, she caused many prayers to be said: for, having resolved to sac-

of piety and charity. Le Jeune's *Relation* for 1635 directed her attention to the Canadian missions, and his suggestion as to the foundation of a hospital at Quebec at once appealed to her heart. She offered to send thither, at her own expense, some Hospital nuns from Dieppe; the Company of New France granted them lands; and the undertaking was aided not only by Madame de Combalet, but by Richelieu himself, who also gave his niece the estate of Aiguillon, and conferred upon her the title of Duchess. After various delays the Hotel-Dieu of Quebec was established in 1639.—*Ibid.*, viii., *note* 62.

rifice herself entirely, with all of her fortune that she could legally surrender, to the divine Majesty, she desired to learn from God whether it would be agreeable to him that she should do so in New France.

While she was in doubt, God's Providence employed a violent illness which, in a short time, brought her so low that the Physician despaired of her recovery. Seeing herself in this condition, she felt strongly inspired to vow that she would devote her wealth and her person to New France. Shortly after, the Physician came, and found her condition greatly improved; and—without knowing what she had done—he said to her: "Madame, your disease has gone to Canada." He spoke better than he knew, and made his patient laugh. When her health was fully restored, she thought of nothing but the execution of her plan. But Monsieur, her Father, urged her to marry again, and went so far as to threaten to disinherit her if she would not obey him. As she saw that her Father spoke in earnest, and that, if she did not show some compliance, she ran the risk of completely ruining her pious plan, she resolved to feign that she was willing to remarry; and by this means she regained the good graces of her Father, who in the meantime passed from this life to the other.

Then, without delay, having divided her property with her sister, she went to Tours. It is difficult to imagine the welcome she received from Monseigneur the Most Illustrious and Most Reverend Archbishop of Tours, to whom she paid her respects, and artlessly revealed all her plans. That venerable Prelate—admiring this Lady's courage and virtue—promised her all the assistance in his power to give. On their part the Ursulines [at Tours] received her with open arms, and granted her the Nun whom she asked for, and gave her for companion another Nun, full of courage and virtue.

Madame de le Pelterie, well pleased, returned to Paris, taking with her the two Ursulines. Mother Cecile of the Cross, an Ursuline, was chosen in the Dieppe Convent to join the two others.

When we were informed that a bark was about to arrive

at Kebec, bearing a College of Jesuits, an establishment of Hospital Nuns, and a Convent of Ursulines, the news seemed at first almost a dream; but at last, descending toward the great river, we found that it was a reality. As this holy band left the ship, they fell on their knees and kissed the soil of their beloved country—for thus they called these regions. From a floating prison were seen issuing those virgins consecrated to God, as fresh and rosy as when they had left their homes. All Ocean, with its waves and tempests, had not injured their health in the slightest degree.

Monsieur the Governor received them with all possible honor. We led them to the Chapel; the *Te Deum laudamus* was chanted; the Cannon thundered on all sides. Then we conducted them to the houses set apart for them until such time as they should have others more suitable for their duties. On the following day they were taken to the Residence of Sillery, where the Savages dwell. When they saw these poor people assembled in the Chapel, offering their prayers and singing the articles of our creed, the tears fell from their eyes. On going thence, they visited the settled families and the neighboring Cabins. Madame de la Pelterie, who led the party, could not meet a little Savage girl without embracing and kissing her, with marks of affection so sweet and emphatic that these poor barbarians stood astonished and edified,—all the more that they themselves are cold in their greetings.

The newly arrived Fathers were set to work; they were called upon to baptize some Savages. Madame de la Pelterie is already the godmother of several. She could not contain herself; she wished to be everywhere, whenever the Savages were in question.

These visits being soon over, these good women retired into their seclusion. Into the Hospital went the three Nuns sent by Monseigneur the Most Reverend Archbishop of Rouen. The three Ursulines withdrew to a private house. Soon afterwards, we had six savage girls given to Madame de la Pelterie or to the Ursulines; and some French girls began going to them for instruction; so that they already perform the duties of their order. But if ever they have a house with sufficient accommodation, and the means to feed the savage children, they will perhaps have so many of these as to weary them.

As for the Hospital, the Nuns were not yet lodged, and their baggage had not yet arrived, when sick people were brought to them. We had to lend our straw beds and mattresses that they might perform the first act of charity. They had sick persons to nurse and had nothing to give them; but the charity of Monsieur our Governor is delightful. Even if it is necessary to refuse some poor afflicted Savage, one cannot do everything at the first stroke. If the Savages are capable of astonishment, they will experience it here; for among them no heed is paid to the sick, especially if they are considered sick unto death; they are looked upon as beings of another world, with whom is held no intercourse, no conversation.

I must state, in passing, that here are four great works bound together by a single tie—the settlement of the Savages, the Hospital, the Seminary for little Savage boys, and the seminary for little Savage girls. These last three depend upon the first. Let these barbarians remain always nomads— then their sick will die in the woods, and their children will never enter the seminary. Render them sedentary, and you will fill these three institutions, which all need to be vigorously aided.

The Gentlemen of the Company of New France, in order to induce the Savages to settle, have granted the same favor in their store to the sedentary Christians as to the French. They have also ordered that some cleared land be given to the young girls who marry; they have, moreover, set apart every year a sum of money to make presents to the Christian Hurons who come to supply themselves with goods at their stores.

A worthy and pious person has given a hundred ecus for the wedding of a young Savage girl sought in marriage by a young Frenchman of very good character.

[*Ibid.*, xv., xvi., *Doc.* xxxiv.]

OF THE HOSPITAL

(*From the Relation of 1640*)

The Hospital Nuns arrived at Kebec on the first day of August of last year. Scarcely had they disembarked before they found themselves overwhelmed with patients. The hall of the Hospital being too small, it was necessary to erect some cabins, fashioned like those of the savages, in their garden. Not having furniture for so many people, they had to cut in two or three pieces part of the blankets and sheets they had brought for these poor sick people. In a word, instead of taking a little rest and refreshing themselves after the great discomforts they had suffered upon the sea, they found themselves so burdened and occupied that we had fear of losing them and their hospital at its very birth. The sick came from all directions in such numbers, their stench was so insupportable, the heat so great, the fresh food so scarce and so poor, in a country so new and so strange, that I do not know how these good sisters, who almost had not even leisure in which to take a little sleep, endured all these hardships.

In brief, from the first of August until the month of May, more than one hundred patients entered the hospital, and more than two hundred poor Savages found relief there, either in temporary treatment or in sleeping there one or two nights, or more. There have been as many as ten, twelve, twenty, or thirty of them at a time.

What I am about to relate is taken from the letters that the Mother Superior has written me:

"The patience of our sick astonishes me. I have seen many whose bodies are entirely covered with smallpox, and in a burning fever, complaining no more than if they were not sick, strictly obeying the physician, and showing gratitude for the slightest service rendered them.

"The remedies that we brought from Europe are very good for the Savages, who have no difficulty in taking our medicines, nor in having themselves bled. The love of the mothers toward their children is very great, for they take in their own mouths the medicine intended for their children, and then pass it into the mouths of their little ones."

On holy Thursday, as it is the custom of well regulated hospitals to wash the feet of the poor, Monsieur our Governor wished to be present at this holy ceremony. In the morning Mass was said in the hall of the sick, where the Nuns and the sick Savages received communion. Then all the men were ranged on one side, and the women and girls on the other. Monsieur the Governor began first to wash the feet of the men, Monsieur the Chevalier de l'Isle and the principal men of our French people followed. The Nuns, with Madame de la Pelleterie, Mademoiselle de Repentigny, and several other women, washed the feet of the Savage women, very lovingly and modestly. God knows whether these poor barbarians were touched, at seeing persons of such merit at their feet.

The conclusion was very agreeable to them, for a fine collation was afterward offered them. A worthy man, a resident of the country, not being able to be present at this holy act, assembled his domestics in the evening, and did the same thing to them.

[*Ibid.*, xix., *Doc.* xli.]

OF THE URSULINE SEMINARY

(From the Relation of 1642-1643)

Since the Ursuline Mothers are established at Quebec, I will here set forth what pertains to them. This Seminary is one of the fairest ornaments of the Colony, and a marked help for the detention and conversion of the Savages. The sisters went into their new dwelling, quitting the one which they held by lease, on the 21st of November of last year (1642). Their building is large and substantial, and thoroughly and carefully constructed. They have discovered an excellent spring of water in the foundations of the dwelling, to their very great convenience.

They are in a place of safety, so far as is possible in Canada, being located from 80 to 100 paces from the fort of Kebec. They have always had a fairly good number of Savage girls, both permanent and temporary boarders, besides the little French girls; and many Savages, men and women, often come to visit them and to receive some help and instruction.

The parlor of these good ladies often serves as a class room,—the Savages from without coming thither purposely to see them, and to ask to be instructed. The expenses attending these holy visits and necessary instructions are great and unavoidable, and perhaps hardly yield to those incurred for the seminary pupils ordinarily detained after the lesson; it is necessary to relieve the hunger of these poor people. I say nothing here of Madame Pelterie;[1] for a year ago from Spring she went to Montreal, to be present at the beginning of that new and holy settlement. The Nuns have this year enlarged their buildings, in order to have a Chapel, and to accommodate more Nuns and Seminary pupils. It is true that this Extension is only just begun,—there is more left to do than there has been done; patience will conquer everything. This virtue is the miracle of Canada.

OF THE RESIDENCE AT SILLERY, AND HOW THE SAVAGES THERE SPEND THE YEAR

The little village of St. Joseph, called Sillery, two scant leagues distant from Quebec, is composed of about 35 or 40 families of Christian Savages who have settled there, and live there all year, except the times for their hunting; these are often joined by many of those who are still roving,— partly to receive some assistance, partly to be instructed in the mysteries of our holy faith. This number will seem

---

[1] Madame de la Peltrie remained at the Ursuline convent until 1642, when she joined the Montreal colony established in that year. Four years later she was again in Quebec; the *Journal des Jesuites* informs us that on Nov. 21, 1642, she became a novice in the Ursuline order there. In their convent she died, Nov. 18, 1671; and her biography has been written by a nun of the order.— *Ibid.*, xi., *note* 4.

small to those who are not acquainted with the state of a roving Savage; but sufficiently large to those who are thus acquainted, and know the life which the poor wretches formerly led.

The good reputation of the Savages who have betaken themselves thither, and who there publicly exercise their Christian duties, has spread abroad on all sides; from Tadoussac and Miskou, even to the Hurons, nearly all speak of imitating them. These resident families are composed of two sorts of persons,—one Montagnais, the other Algonquins. The Montagnais are those who reside nearer Kebec, and are thus called on account of our high mountains. The Algonquins are further back,—some are of the Island and from various places, extending toward the Hurons; the others are neighbors of the Montagnais, and as if mingled with them. The knowledge of God, and intercourse with the French of Kebec, has rendered the latter more supple and docile; the others, though nearly all ruined and reduced to nothing, have remained in a strange pride, and have hitherto occasioned us great hindrances to the conversion of the other Algonquins, and of the Hurons themselves, who are obliged to pass through their country, in order to come down hither.

We have, as yet, for all these resident families only four little houses, on the French plan; to these we are going to add, this Autumn, two others, begun last Winter, by means of some alms which have been given us for this purpose. We are planning for still another, next Spring. The houses are built, half on our side, and half on the side of the Hospital, which is separated from us by a hill or mound about sixty paces wide. The Montagnais have chosen our side, the Algonquins have taken that of the Hospital; the principal Savages are lodged in these houses on the French plan; the others dwell, in their fashion, under cabins of bark,—each on the side chosen by his own tribe, waiting until we can procure for them also some small buildings, as for their companions.

The principal advantages of these houses are the little lofts in which they bestow their provisions, and their little belongings, which formerly became scattered and lost for want of a place in which to keep them. It has not been feasible to do more; for, in proportion to the houses, it is necessary to aid in clearing lands for those who are lodged. At the start, we had means of supporting eight workmen at Sillery; they are at present reduced to four; and still we hear from France that the amount of the donation of the late Monsieur de Sillery, intended for their maintenance, is detained in France. I am very certain of one thing,—that it is still more difficult to continue and maintain it than it was to begin it.

Now let us observe how the Savages have spent their years at Sillery. The ships weighed anchor from before Kebec the 7th of October of last year. Their departure produces a wonderful silence here, and directs each man's attention to his own family, in deep tranquillity.

Our Savages of Sillery, and some others who had united with them, continued their fishing for Eels which they had begun some time before; this is a very fertile harvest for the gathering at Kebec and in the surrounding regions, every year, from the beginning of September to the end of October, in the great river of St. Lawrence. At that time, they found this fish in prodigious abundance; the French salt it, the Savages smoke it, both make provision thereof for the Winter. The Savages leave their little houses to carry on this fishing, and encamp a musket range away, so that the refuse of the fish which they prepare may not infect them. Their fishing done, which was toward the beginning of November, they returned to their houses, and filled their little stores with smoked fish.

They were no sooner assembled than thirteen canoes of the nation of the Atikamegues came to see them, in order to winter with them, and to receive instruction. Father Buteux, who had come down from the three Rivers to winter at Sillery, had charge of the instruction of both parties,—that is to say, of the Montagnais and of the Atikamegues. They lived together, speaking the same language. Father Dequen had for his share the instruction of the Algonquins.

This is the plan we followed all the winter: Father Dequen went every morning to the hospital, in the Algonquin quarter, to say Mass: men, women, and children all were there. The Chapel and the ward of the sick were often filled. Before Mass, the Father pronounced aloud in their language the prayers, which each one also repeated aloud. After noon, I assumed charge of teaching the catechism to the Algonquin children. They assembled in the ward of the sick, with as much diligence and fervor as those of our France. If their stability were equally firm, they would yield to them in nothing. The reward for catechism was a knife, or a piece of bread, at other times a chaplet,—sometimes a cap, or an axe, for the tallest and most intelligent; it is an excellent opportunity for relieving the misery of these poor peoples. The parents were charmed with the fervor of their children, who went through the cabins to show their prizes.

The Hospital Nuns often intoned, at prayers and at catechism, some hymns in Algonquin speech. The Savages take much pleasure in singing, and succeed in it very well, too. When they were in need, the catechism was followed by a little feast, or sagamité, to relieve their hunger. The Nuns contributed, in their turn, to the necessary expenses; and, generally speaking, in addition to the care and succor of the sick, they have often had two or three of the cabins of the poorest on their hands; it is incredible what expenses one is obliged to incur on such occasions; the misery and necessity is such that conscience is compelled thereto. So much for the Algonquins.

Father Buteux has observed the same plan for the Montagnais and Atikamegues, except that when the latter had betaken themselves a little way into the woods on a small eminence near Sillery, he was obliged to go hither every day after Mass, and toward evening, when he assembled the men and the women apart. The snows were from three to four feet deep. I have repeatedly seen him return at evening— night having already set in—with a lantern in his hand, which the impetuous wind snatched from him or extinguished, and then overturned him in the snows from top to bottom of the hill. That may astonish those who have known him in France, —infirm to the last degree, and nearly always on the sick list.

In this manner the Savages spent the first part of the winter. Toward the middle of January, the snows being already deep and abundant, they all withdrew from the cabins at Sillery, and went to about a quarter of a league from Kebec, to make their sledges there, and to begin their first hunt; they remained there about three weeks. Father Buteux followed the Atikamegues, and went to lodge in their cabins. They went a quarter of a league every day, so as to come to Quebec and hear Mass, notwithstanding the rigor of the cold and the snows. Usually they went into the Chapel of the Ursulines, where Father Buteux taught them. They also went very often to the Nuns' parlor, and asked to repeat their prayers, in order to learn them better. The Ursulines showed them every sort of charity,—gave them to eat, and spared nothing of what they had to assist them. They do no less than this, throughout the year, for the Algonquins and Montagnais, when they come to Quebec. These are inevitable expenses, for those who have undertaken to aid the Savages.

They all left their cabins toward the beginning of February, and went into the great woods for the chase of the Moose. The day after their departure, as I was going from Kebec to Sillery, I found a single cabin of twelve or thirteen invalids, old men and children, whom the Savages had commended to me the evening before, and had asked me to send them to the Hospital. When they saw me pass, they took their coverings of bark, followed me as best they could, and came away to the Hospital to spend their winter, partly in the ward of the sick, partly in a cabin near the Hospital.

The Savages remained hardly two months in their great hunt; several returned for the Easter holidays. Each cabin usually contains a paper which marks the feast days. Jean Baptiste with his band returned on Wednesday in Passion Week, and was present in good time next day, for the washing of feet, which occurred at the Hospital; then we prepared for all a feast that was magnificent for this country. Five Hurons who wintered at Sillery and formed a little seminary there, marvelled at this festival, which Father de Brébeuf explained to them (they do not fail to relate these tidings in their own country).

Toward the end of April, all the Savages again rally together; each returns to his own quarter and sets up his cabin, prepares his little store, dresses his skins, and comes to instruction, where the same order is observed as in the autumn. When the earth is altogether free from snow, each one visits his field, and begins to till it. It was a pleasure to see them going to work. But this pleasure hardly lasted; for scarcely had they finished planting their Indian corn, when the rumors of incursions and ravages by the Iroquois obliged them to form a small body of warriors, and go to the fort of Richelieu and to the 3 rivers, in order to confront their enemies. But the disastrous news of the death of the King and of Monseigneur the Cardinal, and then the want of the succor of arms and soldiers which we were expecting from France, made them return to Sillery, quite sad; and, as the ships were very late, and as provisions failed them, they broke up into little bands, and went hunting toward Tadoussac, continually removing from their enemies, and awaiting the ships.

OF THE HOSPITAL

[Lately removed from Kebec to Sillery.]

All Canada melted in grief at the news of the death of the King and of Monseigneur the Cardinal; but this house of Mercy has more cause for it than any other,—considering the sadness which in consequence befalls Madame the Duchess d'Aguillon, who is its founder. Her sorrow has keenly pierced the heart of these good Nuns, whom she has cherished as a mother her children. But let us come to what has occurred in this house of Mercy.

Besides the adornment and consolation which it gives to the whole Colony, it serves as a strong support to the settlement of the Savages, and bears a good part of the expenses and burden thereof. The Village of Sillery is still small, but I doubt very much if, without this house which has been established there, it could have reached the state in which it is; and I know not yet if it could subsist without this help. It has indeed cost inconveniences to these good sisters; the day's time of a man has often been employed for going to Quebec in quest of a few herbs or a half dozen of eggs for the sick; but the desire that they have had to exercise their offices toward the Savages, and to contribute to their settlement, in accordance with the scope of their vocation, has caused them to abandon their building at Quebec, with all its conveniences, as that desire had caused them to abandon France,—seeing, especially, that the French, when sick, have no difficulty in going to Sillery; but the sick Savages are unable to go to Quebec, and thus it would have been a hospital for Savages, without Savages.

The fear of the Hiroquois not having hindered so many worthy persons of both sexes from going to Montreal and other places on the great River—though the Hiroquois are near by, and prowl all about,—it was not likely to have effect a league or two from Quebec, so as to impede a Religious community in its offices, and in a benevolence for which alone it came into the world, and which the Savages were ardently desiring. Moreover, their building at Quebec is being finished, little by little,—so that, if any accident occurs, they can prudently and advisedly retreat thither; and, if the French multiply further, they can establish a little separate Hospital for their succor, which would not injure that of the Savages, and would advance the colony.

The Nuns have received and assisted in the Hospital, this year, about one hundred Savages of various nations: Montagnais, Algonquins, Atticamegues, Abnaquiois, Hurons, those of Tadoussac and the Saguéné, and of some other nations, more distant. At the time I write this report, there is a woman afflicted with a slow disease, whom Father Buteux lately brought hither, on returning from Tadoussac. She is from a region above thirteen or fourteen days distant, far within the lands of the Saguéné. Five or six French workmen have also been relieved in this house of charity; they had been stricken with the land disease, at the fort of Richelieu, and were in danger of dying from it, if they had not found kind help.

A good widow called Louyse had a daughter named Ursule, who was married to a Captain of Tadoussac. This young woman fell sick, and, after two or three years of debility, finally took to bed at Sillery and retreated to the Hospital, staying now in the common ward, again in the neighboring cabin. It was necessary to give her the viaticum; she was then in her cabin near the door of the Hospital. The good Louyse adorned this little house with bark, like an oratory; but, quite in the savage fashion, she hung all round it robes of Beaver or Moose, wholly new and finely embroidered. She put the most beautiful one on the bed of the sick woman; she covered the whole floor with leaves, and also the top of the cabin; she went to the Nuns to borrow a Crucifix and two candlesticks, with the tapers, and put them near her daughter's bed. The whole neighborhood accompanied the Blessed Sacrament with great respect and devotion. Her mother had her buried with all the solemnity possible to a Savage, and put in her grave all that she had most precious in the way of Beaver, Porcelain, and other articles of which they make account. When the Nuns pointed out to her her poverty, and that that availed nothing for the dead, she said, "But you people certainly buried your sister Religious" (it was mother de sainte Marie, deceased two years ago) "with her beautiful robe, and with all the honor that you could."

I will relate how the Socoquiois made prisoner by the Algonquins arrived at this house last year. As soon as he had landed opposite the Hospital, the Savages of Sillery went forward to receive him with Charity. They led him into all their houses and cabins, one after the other, and made him dance in all,—

but with gentleness and friendship. He obeyed throughout, although he had his body all covered with wounds and sores. After that, two of the principal Savages led him to the Hospital, where he was received by the Nuns with great joy. They called the Surgeon; the whole ward was full of Savages, in order to see what state his wounds were in. . . . I was present at this sight; the first view made us chill with horror. He had endured the dressing of his wounds without ever saying a word or showing any sign of pain; he made known by signs the manner in which they had treated him, without betokening any displeasure against those who had put him in this pitiful condition. By good luck there was at the Hospital a sick Abnaquiois, baptized, and called Claude, who well understood Socoquiois. This poor wretch was extremely comforted to meet him; and, as he was astonished, at first, to see the Nuns show him so much charity, this good Christian explained to him how their whole occupation was only to assist and succor the poor and sick, and that they observed virginity all their life. That greatly impressed his mind. He was restored in a fairly short time, and sent back to his own country, in order to show the affection of the French and Savages toward him. These are so many precursors of the Gospel.

[*Ibid.*, xxiii., xxiv., *Doc.* li.]

LETTER FROM THE REVEREND MOTHER SUPERIOR OF THE HOSPITAL NUNS OF KEBEC IN NEW FRANCE

To Monsieur ******, Citizen of Paris

(From the Relation of 1664-1665)

MONSIEUR:

The Divine Providence having suffered me to continue in the charge of this Hospital, I am obliged to thank you in the name of our little Community for your continued attentions to our poor patients. We have had twice as many of the latter this year as in former years, and almost all at the same time; so that, our Hall being too small to contain half of so great a number, we have obeyed the Commandment which our Lord gives us to spare no pains to relieve his mystic members who are in need, and have chosen the least disabled to place in our Chapel.

We need more Nuns, and indeed there are some girls here who would like to become such; but as we are much burdened with patients, we would not dare receive any of them unless they brought some dowry, for fear that we would be forced to use for maintenance of the Nuns the resources entrusted to us for the support of the poor. If some virtuous persons were inclined to make a contribution for that purpose, they would perform an act very agreeable to God and of great merit. I beg you, Monsieur, to pardon the liberty I take in opening my modest thoughts to you; the above is a blessing for which I wish, but hardly dare hope. Finally, Monsieur, we have received all your bales, well stocked, and in good condition. They could not have arrived at a more fitting time; for, although we had borrowed largely, both for drugs and for equipment, we were beginning to suffer a scarcity in every department. You know that our revenue is very moderate, and the love of our Lord has so long given you an attraction for acts of piety that you must know what expenses are necessarily incurred in a Hospital, however careful one may be. Thus you will easily understand that, as Canada increases in population, our Hospital will be overwhelmed with burdens, unless God takes care to give it benefactors like yourself.

I send you a memorandum of our petty needs; it seems rather long, it is true, although I have included in it as little as I could. I doubt not that you will, with the same goodness you have displayed hitherto, work to secure us what we ask. I hope that God will shower his favors upon you in abundance. Such is the wish cherished for you daily by our poor patients and my dear Sisters; while for myself, although the most unworthy, I profess to be the first in remembering

you before our Lord, and in declaring myself on all occasions,
MONSIEUR,
>Your very humble and obedient servant
in Our Lord, Sister Marie de Saint Bon-
naventure de JESUS, Unworthy Superior.

*At the Hospital of Quebec in
New France, October 22, 1665.*

LIST AND MEMORANDUM OF THE NECESSARIES AND
NEEDFUL ARTICLES OF WHICH THE POOR NUNS OF
THE HOSPITAL OF KEBEC IN NEW FRANCE SUFFER A
GREAT LACK, FOR THE RELIEF OF THE POOR PATIENTS
NOW THERE IN LARGE NUMBERS.

Six livres of Senna.
Three livres of Rhubard.
Three livres of Jalap.
Four livres of Myrhh.
Four livres of Aloes.
Ten livres of common incense.
Four livres of male Incense.
One livre of Scammony.
One livre of Opium.
Two livres each of the six Gums.
Four livres of golden Litharge.
Four livres of silver Litharge.
Eight ounces of oil of Camomile.
Eight ounces of oil of Laurel.
Eight ounces of oil of almonds, sweet
and bitter.
Two livres of Cinnamon.
Two livres of Cloves.
Two livres of Nutmegs.
Six livres of Pepper.
Six livres of Ginger.
Eight ounces of white Vitriol.
Four livres of corrosive Sublimate.
Eight livres of white Wax.
Eight livres of yellow Wax for making
ointments.
Ten livres of Candles, or white or yel-
low tapers, for saying Mass at the
Hospital.
Sugar, fine and coarse, in as large quan-
tities as possible, for syrups and mix-
tures—our entire supply being ex-
hausted.

One dozen Lancets.
A small brazen mortar for compound-
ing Medicines.
Linen of various sorts and kinds.
Sheets.
Shirts for men and women.
Napkins, or linen for making some.
Linings for caps.
Mob-caps.
Linen for shrouding the dead.
Cotton twine; and coarse wicking for
putting in the lamps, and for mak-
ing candles.
Blankets, blue and green.
Woolen caps for men and women.
Thick cloth for making dressing gowns
for the sick.
Boxwood combs.
Eight chamber-vessels.
Two padded chamber-vessels of tin for
slipping under the patients.
Two other common vessels.
Thirty-six bowls.
Thirty-six sauce-dishes for portions.
Twenty-four cups.
Four large dishes.
A deep tin basin.
Forty-eight spoons.
Two large chafing-dishes.
Four medium chafing-dishes.
Two medium holy-water Stoups of
copper.
Pins.

Ten livres of Diapalma.
Three livres of Diachylon.
Three livres of Divinum.
Four livres of Betonica.
Four livres of Extra-Fracturas.
Four livres of Extra-Contusionem.
Two livres of Minium.
Two livres of Balm.
Four livres of white Ointment.
Two livres of Rose ointment.
Six livres of Mundificative.
Two livres of Althea.
Six livres of Burgundy pitch.
Material for making ink.
Six livres of suppurative.
Senna of Montpellier.
Four livres of Almonds.

Needles.
Thimbles.
Five livres of coarse sewing thread.
Six pairs of scissors.
Four reams of writing paper.
Two reams of paper, large and medium.
One ream of gray blotting paper.
Some *Heures de la Vierge.*
Father Chiffletius's Book.
The *Journée Chrestienne,* by Monsieur Olier, of St. Sulpice.
The *Conduite* of Monsieur de Sales.
The *Exercice de la presence de Dieu.*
Other Books of devotion, of various kinds.
Rosaries.
Holy Pictures.

Ladies and Gentlemen kindly disposed to contribute, in the cause of charity, such Drugs and other articles as are specified in the above List, are requested to send them to the house of Monsieur Cramoisy, Printer in ordinary to the King, rue St. Jacques, or to notify him, and he will not fail to send for them.
[*Ibid.,* xlix., *Doc.* cxvii.]

PART III

THE HURON MARTYRS AND THE IROQUOIS
WARFARE
1642—1659

I

RELATION OF OCCURRENCES IN NEW FRANCE, IN THE YEAR 1642 AND 1643

By Father Barthelemy Vimont

[Owing to the fact that the Iroquois had captured the year's report of the Huron missions (although it had been given to Jogues), the *Relation* for 1642-43 is written wholly by the Superior, Vimont; it is without date, but doubtless was written in the early autumn of 1643, in time for the vessel returning to France.— *Ibid.*, xxiii, 15.]

Pax Christi

YOUR REVERENCE

Will not this year find your unusual satisfaction in the Relation; for the best part of it, which is that concerning the Hurons, was taken by the Hiroquois, together with our Father's correspondence, in a defeat of 40 Hurons, which occurred on the 9th of last June, near Montreal. Father Isaac Jogues, now captive among the Barbarians, writes to us on the last day of June, that it has fallen into his hands, along with sundry letters of our Fathers among the Hurons; I know not whether he can at all convey it to Your Reverence by some way unknown to us.

I send your Reverence the Relation for this region, which will furnish examples of virtue, and show notable increase of Christianity; but it must, as usual, be tempered with the bitterness of manifold evil tidings, arising from the side of the Hiroquois, who, had we not some help from France, would undoubtedly ruin here both the faith and commerce. There is hardly an open passage left for us to reach the Hurons; our baggage last year was taken going up,—this year, coming

down. At this writing, I learn that it is now captured for the
third time on the way upward; and therefore we are obliged to
send to your Reverence Father le Jeune, as one of long experience in the affairs of these regions, that he may more effectually
represent them to those whose thoughts are favorable to this
poor land. Such has been the advice and desire of Monsieur de
Montmagny, our Governor, and of all the inhabitants, who
have urgently besought me to the same end.

OF THE RESIDENCE AT QUEBEC, AND THE STATE OF THE COLONY

The French Colony is the chief means and only foundation
for the conversion of all these tribes; there is no better or more
efficacious way of procuring their salvation than by succoring
this settlement, which, thanks be to God, increases little by
little, and overcomes the great impediments it encounters,—
as the remoteness of help from Europe, the scarcity of laborers,
difficulties of trade, and the long Winter which covers the earth,
five and even six months, with snow. Notwithstanding all
these hinderances, nearly every French household now provides
its little store of wheat, rye, peas, barley, and other grains
necessary to the life of man,—some more, some less,—some
making provision for haply six months; others, for only a part
of that time. Now they begin to understand the nature of the
place, and the right seasons for tilling the soil. The work is
well started; it still has need of help, but it makes notable
progress. After all, it would be a difficult task to set forth the
care and pains continually taken by Monsieur de Montmagny,
our Governor, both hitherto and now, in relieving the Colony's
hardships,—wherein all others would have lost courage, times
without number. Father Bressany [1] has had charge this year of
the religious instruction of the French at Quebec; which office

---

[1] Francesco Gioseppe Bressani was born at Rome, May 6, 1612, and became
a Jesuit novice Aug. 15, 1626. His studies were pursued at Rome and Clermont; the customary service as instructor being rendered at Sezza, Tivoli, and
Paris. Arriving in Canada in 1642, he ministered for a time to the French at
Quebec; in the following year, to the Algonkins at Three Rivers. In April, 1644,

he has worthily fulfilled, and has produced remarkable effects by his preaching. He has been assisted by Father Enemond Masse, who has nobly labored, though broken with age,—supplying by courage his want of strength, unto the great edification of all the residents. Father de Brébeuf and I went every Feast day and Sunday from Sillery to Quebec, to help them in hearing confessions, to speak a word of exhortation to the French, and to minister to the consolation of all.

Our Lord has called to himself, this year, Father Charles Raymbault, the first Religious of our Society to die in these quarters. He was very zealous for the establishment of the French Colony, and for the conversion of these tribes; he had managed the affairs of our Missions with much prudence and fervor, during several years in France, and the same zeal prompted him to ask urgently that he be numbered with the laborers of this new Church. His request being granted, he was sent four years ago to the Hurons, at the Request of our Fathers there, who, knowing his prudence and courage, hoped to employ him for the discovery of some remoter nations. And, as the Algonquin speech was necessary for this, they sent him, in company with Father Charles Pijart, to the Nipissiriniens, an Algonquin people,—in which mission, journeys and

he set out with an escort of Christian Indians, for the Huron Mission; but on the way they were captured by the Iroquois, and carried to one of the villages of the latter, where he was cruelly tortured, at intervals, for over two months. Finally he was ransomed by the Dutch at Fort Orange, and sent to France, where he arrived in the following November. The next year, he returned to Canada, and, after a short stay at Three Rivers, joined the Huron mission, where he labored until its destruction by the Iroquois, four years later. In the summer of 1648, he came down to Quebec for additional missionaries, returning to his field of labor with a reinforcement of five brethren. In the following year, he went with the fugitive Hurons to St. Joseph (Christian) Island, but their situation there was so perilous that Bressani was sent by his Superior to Quebec to ask for succor,—a vain quest, however, since the authorities there could spare none of their slender force of soldiers. The dangers of the road preventing his return to his flock, he was obliged to remain at Quebec, where, at various times, he officiated in the church. Nov. 2, 1650, Bressani was obliged to return to Europe —on account partly of the limited resources of the mission, partly of his own precarious health. Having regained sufficient strength in his own country, he spent many years as a missionary and preacher in the principal Italian cities, and died at Florence Sept. 9, 1672. Soon after his return to Italy, Bressani published his *Breve Relatione d'alcune Missioni* . . . nella Nuoua Francia. *Ibid.*, xxiii., note 10.

labors are past belief. There he was seized with a slow sickness, which wasted him little by little, insomuch that our Fathers had to send him down here, for greater convenience of food
and medicine. But our good God found him ripe for Heaven;
and, on October 22nd of last year, he died, after languishing
during the space of three months. Monsieur the Governor,
esteeming his virtue, desired that he be buried near the body of
the late Monsieur de Champlain; which is in a separate tomb,
erected expressly to honor the remembrance of that illustrious
personage, to whom New France has owed so much.

I will now speak of the life and death of Monsieur Nicollet,[1]
Interpreter and Agent for the Gentlemen of the Company of
New France. He died ten days after the Father (Raymbault),
and had lived in this region twenty-five years. What I shall
say of him will aid to a better understanding of the country.
He came to New France in the year sixteen hundred and

---

[1] Jean Nicolet, a native of Cherbourg, France, came to Quebec in 1618, probably at the age of about 20 years. Like Marsolet, Brulé, and others, he was
sent by Champlain to live among the Indians, that he might acquire a knowledge
of the country, of the natives, and of their language. For this purpose, Nicolet
went (1620) to the Algonkins of Allumettes Island, where he remained two years;
while among this tribe, he accompanied a large body of their warriors to the
Iroquois country, in order to arrange a treaty of peace—an enterprise successfully accomplished. He then spent some nine years among the Nipissings, during
which time he wrote an account of these savages, their customs, etc., as Le Jeune
informs us in the *Relation* for 1636.

In June, 1634, Champlain sent him on an exploring expedition westward—
partly in the hope of finding the "sea of China" which was at that time supposed
to lie not far west of the regions of America then known, and thereby discovering the long-looked-for short passage to Asia; partly to become acquainted with
the savage tribes lying beyond the "Mer deuce" (Lake Huron), and to extend
the French trade for peltries. Upon this trip (accompanying Brébeuf as far
as Allumettes Island), Nicolet went to his old abode, Lake Nipissing. Thence,
with a bark canoe and an escort of seven Hurons, he voyaged by French River
into Lake Huron, and Northward to St. Mary's Straits and Mackinac; and
thence by Lake Michigan, Green Bay, and the Fox River, as far as a village of
the Mascoutins, probably in what is now Green Lake county, Wisconsin. He
was thus the first white man who, so far as it is recorded, had entered this region.
From the Mascoutin village he journeyed southward to what is now northern
Illinois,—afterward returning to Canada by the same route on which he had
set out; he reached Quebec early in the autumn of 1635.

Nicolet, after his return to Canada, resumed his employment (begun in 1633)
as clerk and interpreter at Three Rivers. Oct. 7, 1637, he married Marguerite
(then aged eleven years), second daughter of Guillaume Couillard. . . . Nicolet
died Oct. 29, 1642, being drowned at Sillery.—*Ibid.*, viii., *note* 29.

eighteen and forasmuch as his nature and excellent memory inspired good hopes of him he was sent to winter with the Island Algonkins, in order to learn their language. He tarried with them two years, alone of the French, and always joined the Barbarians in their excursions and journeys,—undergoing such fatigues as none but eye witnesses can conceive; he often passed seven or eight days without food, and once, full seven weeks with no other nourishment than a little bark from the trees.

He accompanied four hundred Algonkins, who went during that time to make peace with the Hyroquois, which he successfully accomplished; and would to God that it had never been broken, for then we would not now be suffering the calamities which move us to groans, and which must be an extraordinary impediment in the way of converting these tribes.

After this treaty of peace, he went to live eight or nine years with the Algonquin Nipissiriniens, where he passed for one of that nation, taking part in the very frequent councils of those tribes, having his own separate cabin and household, and fishing and trading for himself. He was finally recalled and appointed Agent and Interpreter.

While in the exercise of this office, he was delegated to make a journey to the nation called People of the sea, and arrange peace between them and the Hurons, from whom they are distant about three hundred leagues Westward. He embarked in the Huron country, with seven Savages; and they passed by many small nations, both going and returning. When they arrived at their destination, they fastened two sticks in the earth, and hung gifts thereon, so as to relieve these tribes from the notion of mistaking them for enemies to be massacred.

When he was two days' journey from that nation, he sent one of those Savages to bear tidings of the peace, which word was especially well received when they heard that it was a European who carried the message; they despatched several young men to meet the Manitouririnou,—that is to say, "the wonderful man." They meet him; they escort him, and carry all his baggage. He wore a grand robe of China damask, all strewn with flowers and birds of many colors. No sooner did they preceive him than the women and children fled, at the sight of a man who carried thunder in both hands,—for thus they called the two pistols that he held.

The news of his coming quickly spread to the places round about, and there assembled four or five thousand men. Each of the chief men made a feast for him, and at one of these banquets they served six scores beavers. The peace was concluded; he returned to the Hurons, and some time later to the three Rivers, where he continued his employment as Agent and Interpreter, to the great satisfaction of both the French and the Savages, by whom he was equally and singularly loved. In so far as his office allowed, he vigorously cooperated with our Fathers for the conversion of those peoples, whom he could shape and bend howsoever he would, with a skill that can hardly be matched.

Monsieur Olivier, Chief Agent of the Gentlemen of the Company, having gone to France last year, sieur Nicollet came down to Quebec in his place with joy and lively consolation at the sight of the peace and devotion at Quebec; but his joy was not long. A month or two after his arrival, he made a journey to the three Rivers for the deliverence of a Savage prisoner; which zeal cost him his life, in a shipwreck. He sailed from Quebec, toward seven o'clock in the evening, in the shallop of Monsieur de Savigny, bound for three Rivers. Before they reached Sillery, a gust of wind from the Northwest, which had raised a horrible storm upon the great river, filled the shallop with water and caused it to sink, after two or three turns in the waves. The passengers did not immediately sink, but clung for some time to the shallop. Monsieur Nicollet had leisure to say to Monsieur de Savigny, "Sir, save yourself, you can swim. I cannot; as for me, I depart to God. I commend to you my wife and my daughter."

One by one, the waves tore them all from the shallop, which was floating overturned against a rock. Monsieur de Savigny alone plunged into the water, and swam amid the billows and waves, which were like small mountains. The shallop was not

very far from shore, but it was now black night, and there prevailed a severe frost which had already frozen the borders of
the stream; so that the sieur de Savigny, perceiving his heart
and strength fail, made a vow to God, and, soon afterward
striking with his foot, he felt ground. Drawing himself out
of the water, he came to our house at Sillery, half dead, and
remained a long time without strength to speak; then at last
he told us of the woeful mischance, which, besides the death
of Monsieur Nicollet, so grievous for all the country, had lost
him three of his best men, and great part of his furniture and
stores. He and Madamoiselle his wife endured this notable
affliction in a barbarous country with great patience and without abating a jot of their courage. The Savages of Sillery, at
the noise of Monsieur Nicollet's shipwreck, ran to the spot,
and manifested unspeakable grief to see him appear no more.

This sad news was augmented by other tidings, which renewed our affliction; this was the death of Monsieur the Cardinal Duke, who, besides the care that he had for old France,
was not forgetful of the new, which amid its great difficulties,
and its dangers, breathed afresh at the remembrance and the
promises of the great heart, and was with joy and hope awaiting
a necessary aid, when we learned of his death.

We received all these sad tidings on saint John's day, by
the Miscou vessel, which came as far as Tadoussac; the other
ships of the fleet were later than ever this year, which was a
notable increase of affliction to us, and also to the Savages. We
were beginning to fear some new mistfortune. Finally, God
sent them to us, on the holy day of our Lady's Assumption.
As we were about to begin Mass, two sails appeared a league
distant from our port; joy and consolation seized the hearts of
all the inhabitants, but it very greatly redoubled when a shallop
came and brought us the news of the persons who were there;
Father Quentin, with three worthy workers, Religious of our
Society, and very apt for the language—to wit, Fathers
Leonard Garreau, Gabriel Druillet, and Noël Chabanel.[1]

---

[1] Noel Chabanel was born Feb. 2, 1613, in the diocese of Mende. At seventeen, he entered upon his novitiate in the Jesuit college at Toulouse, where his

There were also three well-chosen Nuns, whose courage exceeds their sex—to wit, Mother Marie de Ste. Geneviefve, and Mother Anne de St. Joachim, Hospital nuns from the house of Diepe; and Mother Anne des Seraphins, Ursuline, from the Convent of Plermel in Brittany. It required great strength for these good women to overcome the dangers of the Ocean, the fear of the Barbarous country, and the importunate words of those who wished to turn them aside in France from so holy an enterprise.

OF INCURSIONS BY THE IROQUOIS AND THE CAPTIVITY OF FATHER JOGUES

There are two divisions of Iroquois,—the one, neighbors of the Hurons and equal to them in number, or even greater, are called Santweronons. Formerly the Hurons had the upper hand; at present these prevail, both in number and in strength. The others live between the three Rivers and the upper Hiroquois, and are called Agneronons. The settlement of the Dutch is near them;[1] they go thither to carry on their trades, especially in arquebuses; they have at present three hundred of these, and use them with skill and boldness. These are the ones who make incursions upon our Algonquins and Montagnais, and watch the Hurons at all places along the River,—slaughtering them, burning them, and carrying off their Peltry, which they sell to the Dutch, in order to have powder and Arquebuses, and then to ravage everything and become masters everywhere, which is fairly easy for them unless France gives

priestly studies were carried on; his term of instruction was also served there (1634-39), and at Rodez (1641-42). His course completed, he at once joined the Canadian mission (1643), at the same time with Garreau and together they went to the Huron mission. Chabanel remained there until the overthrow of the Huron nation; and, on his way to Ste. Marie, was slain by a Huron apostate, Dec. 8 or 9, 1649. *Ibid.*, xxiii., *note* 14.

[1] This settlement of the Dutch was close to the site of the present city of Albany. It was first begun as a fortified trading post, in 1614, on Castle Island. In 1623, a new fort, named Orange, was built on the west side of the Hudson; and seven years later, a colony was brought over from Holland by the patroon Kiliaen Van Rensselaer, Johannes de Late, and others. . . . Its first minister, who came in 1642, was Johannes Megapolensis; he exercised much kindness and charity to the captive Jesuit Jogues.—*Ibid.*, xxiv., *note* 22.

us help. For, sundry contagious diseases having consumed the greater part of the Montagnais and the Algonquins, who are neighbors to us, they have nothing to fear on that side; and, moreover, the Hurons who come down,—coming for trade and not for war, and having not one Arquebus,—if they are met, have no other defense than flight; and, if they are captured, they allow themselves to be bound and massacred like sheep.

In former years, the Iroquois came in rather large bands at certain times in the Summer, and afterwards left the River free; but this present year, they have changed their plan, and have separated themselves into small bands of twenty, thirty, fifty, or a hundred at the most, along all the passages and places of the River, and when one band goes away, another succeeds it. They are merely small troops well armed, which set out incessantly, one after the other, from the country of the Iroquois, in order to occupy the whole great River, and to lay ambushes along it everywhere; from these they issue unexpectedly, and fall indifferently upon the Montagnais, Algonquins, Hurons, and French.

We have had letters from France that the design of the Dutch is to have the French harassed by the Iroquois, to such an extent that they may constrain them to give up and abandon everything. I cannot believe that those Gentlemen of Holland, being so united to France, have this wretched idea; but the practice of the Iroquois being so consistent with it, they ought to apply to it a remedy in their settlement, as Monsieur the Governor has done here—often preventing our Savages from going to kill the Dutch. Now here is the miserable result of the incursions of the Iroquois this year.

The 9th of last May, as soon as the ice was gone from the great River, eight Algonquins, coming down from toward the Hurons, in two canoes, all laden with peltry, landed one morning four leagues from the three Rivers, to make a little fire; it had frozen quite hard all night, and they had paddled during the darkness, fearing surprise from their enemies. Hardly had they been half an hour refreshing themselves, when nineteen Iroquois issue from the wood, and fall upon them, kill two men, and take the others captive, with all their peltry. Father Buteux had passed by there only two days before, accompanied by three Hurons. It is a miracle that he was not perceived and taken, with his companions.

A month later, the 9th of June, another band of forty made its attack at Mont-Real. They perceived sixty Hurons coming down in thirteen canoes—without Arquebuses and without arms but all freighted with peltries,—who were coming to Mont-Real, and from there to the three Rivers, for their trade. They carried the letters of our Fathers with the Hurons, and a copy of their Relation. The Iroquois fall upon them, take twenty-three of them prisoners, and fall upon five Frenchmen, who were working at some carpentry, two hundred paces from the settlement. Three of these they beat to death, and take the two others captive. The Hiroquois passed the night rejoicing over their prize and, morning having come, they rush upon the Huron prisoners and beat thirteen of them to death, almost without selection. They reserve ten of them alive, along with our two Frenchmen, and then go away to the canoes to get robes of Beaver without number, and thus cross the River, triumphant with joy, and laden with rich spoils. Our French of the settlement see them cross, without being able to offer any remedy.

Eight or ten days later one of the two French prisoners escaped by flight. He reported that the Iroquois had not done them any harm since their capture, and had kept them bound only two days. For the rest, one must not speak of making a sally upon the enemy, for as neither their coming nor their number is known, and as they are concealed in the woods, where they are trained for running, very differently from our French, the sallies would avail only to undergo new massacres; for usually a small party attacks, and the others remain in ambush in the thick of the woods.

While this band of forty were at Mont-Real, another of like number was on lake Saint Pierre, before the fort of Richelieu. They had with them three or four Hurons, taken the year before with Father Jogues, among whom were two brothers of that great Joseph,[1] known through the Relation of the Hurons, and by his own virtue. Both escaped from the band of the Iroquois, and came toward evening to the three Rivers, where they found Father de Brébeuf, to whom they related plenty of news; that Father Jogues was still alive; that last year after his capture, though able to escape, he would not do it, in order not to separate himself from the captive Hurons until after the combat. They said that immediately the Father and the two Frenchmen, Cousture and René Goupil,[2] received many blows with fists and clubs, but that the worst treatment which was dealt them was at their encounter with two hundred and fifty Iroquois, who were returning from their attack on Richelieu, where they lost five of their people, and several were wounded. Yet they were not bound while on the road, except at their entrance into the village, when they were all stripped to their shirts, and received many affronts and outrages. Father Jogues had his left thumb cut off, and they crushed with their teeth the index finger of his right hand, which nevertheless he uses a little at present. . . . These Hurons said that two Hollanders, one of whom was mounted on horseback, had come to the village where Father Jogues was, and had tried to ransome him, but that the Iroquois would not listen to it; that an Iroquois of that band had been charged with a long letter by Father Jogues, to give to us, that the Iroquois spoke of conducting them back, but that he and the others put no faith in it.

Some other Hurons, captives of former years, escaped and came to the three rivers, and confirmed all that their companions had said. Monsieur the Governor, however, who desired the Father's deliverance, and peace if it were reason-

---

[1] Joseph Chihwatenhwa, a Huron convert, made famous by the *Relations* of the Fathers.

[2] René Goupil, a young French surgeon, born in Anjou, was for several months a Jesuit novice at Paris. He came to Canada, apparently in 1640, as a donné in that mission. In August, 1642, he set out with Jogues for the Huron mission; but, on the way, they were captured by the Iroquois, and taken to the country of that tribe. Goupil was Jogues's companion in captivity for a short time, but was slain (Sept. 29, 1642) by an Iroquois. *Ibid.*, xxiv., *note* 23.

able, equipped four shallops and went, prepared for war or peace, to the Fort of Richelieu, in order to see if the Iroquois would present themselves. But nothing appeared; as soon as they perceived the shallops, they entered further within the woods; and, the shallops having passed, they returned to the edge of the water and kept watch on the Alonquins and the Hurons.

The 15th of August, twenty Algonquins left the three rivers to go to the chase toward Richelieu. When in the lake of St. Pierre, seven or eight leagues from the settlement, they separated into two bands. The one straightway encounters twenty Iroquois. Some on both sides were killed; the Algonquins, seeing themselves weaker, took flight; three were made prisoners.

At the same time when that was occurring in the lake of St. Pierre, there were 2 other bands of Iroquois, who were prowling about the Fort of Richelieu; they had with them a captive Huron, but an Iroquois by affection. The latter took his place alone in a canoe, and advanced toward the Fort, and requested to speak; they receive him,—they have him enter, they ask him who he is, and what brings him. He answers that he is an Iroquois, and that he wishes to treat of peace for himself and for his companions; he presents some beavers with this object. They ask him if he has news of Father Jogues; he draws forth a letter from him and presents it, then asks to return. They tell him that the letter is addressed to Monsieur the Governor, who is at Kebec or at the three Rivers, and that he must wait for an answer; he requests that they fire a cannon shot, which is done, and straightway his comrades appear in 3 or 4 canoes. They paddle steadily, in order to come toward the Fort; they are hailed to stop, three or four times,—which not obeying, they are fired upon; that constrained them to go ashore, and flee into the woods, abandoning their canoes and baggage, it is not known whether they were wounded or killed.

Here follows a copy of the letter from Father Jogues, written from the Iroquois, which that Huron of whom I have spoken, brought and gave to Monsieur de Champ-flour; it is addressed to Monsieur the Governor. It is a great pity that three others, which he wrote to us previously, have been lost.

"Monsieur, here is the 4th that I have written since I am with the Iroquois. Time and paper fail me to repeat here what I have already conveyed to you at great length. Cousture and I are sitll living. Henry (one of those young men who were taken at Mont-real) was brought here the eve of saint John's day. He was not loaded with blows from clubs at the entrance to the village, like us, nor has he had his fingers cut, like us. He lives, and all the Hurons brought with him into the country. Be on your guard everywhere; new bands are always leaving, and we persuade ourselves that, until the Autumn, the river is not without enemies. There are here nearly three hundred arquebuses, and seven hundred Iroquois; they are skilled in handling them. They can arrive at the three rivers by various streams; the Fort of Richelieu gives them a little more trouble, but does not hinder them altogether. The Iroquois say that if those who took and killed the French at Mont-real had known what you have done,—in redeeming the Sokokiois whom you delivered from the hands of the Algonquins,—they would not have done that; they had started in the midst of the winter, and before the news of it came. Nevertheless, quite recently there has departed a band, and the man of Mathurin (Father Brébeuf knows him well) is in it, and leads the band, as at our capture last year. This troop desires and purposes to take some French, as well as Algonquins. Let not regard for us prevent from doing that which is to the glory of God. The design of the Iroquois as far as I can see, is to take, if they can, all the Hurons; and, having put to death the most considerable ones and a good part of the others, to make of them both but one people and only one land. I have a great compassion for these poor people, several of whom are Christians,—the others Catecheumens, and ready for baptism; when shall a remedy be applied to these misfortunes? When they shall all be taken? I have received several letters from the Hurons, with the Relation taken near Mont-real. The Dutch have tried to ransom us, but in vain; they are still endeavoring to do so at present, but it will again be, as I believe, with the same result. I become more and more resolved to dwell here as long as it shall please Our Lord, and not to go away, even though an opportunity should present itself. My presence consoles the French, the Hurons, and the Algonquins. I have baptized more than sixty persons, several of whom have arrived in Heaven. That is my single consolation, and the will of God, to which very gladly I unite my own. I beg you to recommend that prayers be said, and that masses be offered for us, and above all for the one who desires to be forever, MONSIEUR,

> *Your very humble servant, Isaac Jogues, of the Society of JESUS.*

"From the village of the Iroquois, the 30th of June, 1643."

This letter contains more substance than words; its construction is excellent, although the hand which formed its characters is all torn; it is composed in a style more sublime than that which proceeds from the most pompous schools of Rhetoric. Let us meditate, I beg you, upon these words:

Let not regard for us (he says) *prevent from doing that which is to the glory of God.* That is to say, "Have not regard for my life; regard me as a man already dead. I know well that if you illtreat the Iroquois, I am murdered,—I no longer account myself among the living. My life is God's; do all that you shall judge most suitable for his glory." How powerful is Jesus Christ in a pious heart! His goodness does not allow itself to be vanquished, it makes a glory of triumphing in the greatest desolation.

I become more and more resolved (he adds) *to dwell here as long as it shall please our Lord, and not to go away, even though the opportunity should present itself.* How agreeable is such generosity to God! This man, all whose senses have nothing but objects of pain, says that he would not escape though he could do so.

My presence (he continues) *consoles the French, the Hurons, and the Algonquins.* There are two captive Frenchmen with this good Father, many Hurons, and many Algonquins, some of whom are Christians, and other desire to be; would you, indeed, that this heart full of fire, that this Pastor full of love, should abandon his sheep? Surely he is not a thief or hireling, to commit so great a treachery. Although these words have drawn the tears from our eyes, they have not failed to augment the joy of our hearts, there is one of us who feels toward him more envy than compassion; to give up creatures for God, is not a bad exchange.

I have Baptized more than sixty persons. We suppose that these are Hurons and Algonquins, his fellow captives; and perhaps further, some little Iroquois children, dying, who pray to God in the heavens for their parents,—*that is my single consolation, and the will of God, to which very gladly I write my own.* These are glorious words! But moreover, who could console this poor Father, if not the one who alone is left for him, and whom the whole Universe cannot ravish from him! The two Frenchmen who are with the Father give us astonishment,—that one, especially, who is named Guillaume Cousture. This young man was able to escape; but the thought of it having come to him—"no," he says, "I wish to die with the Father; I cannot forsake him; I will gladly suffer the fire and the rage of these tigers, for the love of Jesus Christ, in the company of my good Father." That is speaking like a truly faithful man, as, indeed, he had not thrown himself into these dangers for any temporal consideration.

The letter states that there had started from the Iroquois a band led by the man of Mathurin,—that is to say, by a Huron taken by the Iroquois, who has lost affection for his country and his fellow countrymen, on whom he now makes war. As he knows the places where they are to pass, he goes to await and surprise them at the passage; it was this miserable renegade who defeated the Hurons with whom the Father happened to be. They call him "the man of Mathurin," because he brought back from the Hurons, before he was taken by the Iroquois, a worthy young man who bore that name; who, having well conducted himself with our Fathers in this end of the world, crossed back to France, in order to give himself to God in the holy Order of the Reverend Capuchin Fathers, wherein he has made profession.

Furthermore this letter was written partly in French, partly in Latin, partly in the Savage tongue, so that if it fell into the hands of some one else than the one to whom it was addressed, he could not easily discover the good counsel which the Father gives us.

Monsieur the Governor, who was at the three Rivers, made answer to the letter of Father Jogues. I wrote him also, quite at length, and sent Father Brébeuf to Richelieu in order to confer with that Huron about his return to the Iroquois. But the poor man placed us in a new difficulty, and a very great one,—for, fearing lest the Iroquois in the country should take him for a spy, and for having some intelligence with us, he declared very plainly that he would return no more to the Iroquois, but to the Hurons; and there was no way of persuading him of anything else. Consequently we remained deprived

of that consolation, and Father Jogues still more than we,—
having no answer or news from our country, and perhaps in
danger of being put to death upon the suspicion which the
Barbarians will have, that some harm may have been done to
the captive Huron who was of that band.

[*Ibid.*, xxiii., xxiv., *Doc.* li.]

II

HOW FATHER JOGUES WAS TAKEN BY THE IROQUOIS, AND WHAT HE SUFFERED ON HIS FIRST ENTRANCE INTO THEIR COUNTRY

(From the Relation of 1647, by Father Jerome Lalemant)

Father Isaac Jogues had sprung from a worthy family of the City of Orleans. After having given some evidence of his virtue in our Society, he was sent to New France, in the year 1638. In the same year he went up to the Hurons, where he sojourned until the thirteenth of June in the year 1642, when he was sent to Kebec upon the affairs of that important and arduous Mission.

From that time until his death, there occurred many very remarkable things,—of which one cannot, without guilt, deprive the public. What has been said of his labors in the preceding Relations, come, for the most part, from some Savages, companions in his sufferings. But what I am about to set down has issued from his own pen and his own lips.

The Reverend Father Hiersome L'alemant, at that time Superior of the Mission among the Hurons, sent for him, and proposed to him the journey to Kebec,—a frightful one, on account of the difficulty of the roads, and very dangerous because of the ambuscades of the Hiroquois, who massacred, every year, a considerable number of the Savages allied to the French. Let us hear him speak upon his subject and upon the result of his journey:

"Authority having made me a simple proposition, and not a command, to go down to Kebec, I offered myself with all my heart. So there we were, on the way and in the dangers all at once. We were obliged to disembark forty times, and

189

forty times to carry our boats and all our baggage amid the currents and waterfalls that one encounters on this journey of about three hundred leagues. At last, thirty-five days after our departure from the Hurons, we arrived, much fatigued, at Three Rivers; thence we went down to Kebec. Our affairs being finished in fifteen days, we solemnly observed the feast of St. Ignace; and the next day, we left Three Rivers, in order to go up again to the country whence we came. The first day was favorable to us; the second caused us to fall into the hands of the Iroquois.

"We were forty persons, distributed in several canoes; the one which kept the vanguard, having discovered on the banks of the great river some tracks of men, recently imprinted on the sand and clay, gave us warning. A landing was made: some say that these are footprints of the enemy, others are sure that they are those of Algonquins, our allies. In this dispute, Eustache Ahatsistari exclaimed: 'Be they friends or enemies, it matters not; they are not in greater number than we; let us advance and fear nothing.'

"We had not yet made a half-league, when the enemy, concealed among the grass and brushwood, rises with a great outcry, discharging at our canoes a volley of balls. The noise so greatly frightened a part of our Hurons that they abandoned their canoes and weapons in order to escape by flight into the depth of the woods. We were four French,—one of whom, being in the rear, escaped with the Hurons, who abandoned him before approaching the enemy. Eight or ten, both Christians and Catechumens, joined us; they oppose a courageous front to the enemy. But, having perceived that another band—of forty Hiroquois, who were in ambush on the other side of the river—was coming to attack them, they lost courage; insomuch that those who were least entangled fled.

"A Frenchman named René Goupil, whose death is precious before God, was surrounded and captured, along with some of the most courageous Hurons. I was watching this disaster," says the Father, "from a place very favorable for concealing me from the sight of the enemy, but this thought could never enter my mind. 'Could I indeed,' I said to myself, 'abandon our French and leave those good Neophytes and those poor Catechumens, without giving them the help which the Church of my God has entrusted to me?' Flight seemed horrible to me. 'It must be,' I said in my heart, 'that my body suffer the fire of earth, in order to deliver these poor souls from the flames of Hell; it must die a transient death, in order to procure for them an eternal life.' My conclusion being reached without great opposition from my feelings, I call the one of the Hiroquois who had remained to guard the prisoners. He advances and, having seized me, puts me in the number of those whom the world calls miserable. Finally they brought that worthy Christian Captain named Eustache, who, having perceived me, exclaimed, 'Ah, my Father, I had sworn to you that I would live or die with you.' The sight of him piercing my heart, I do not remember the words that I said to him.

"Another Frenchman, named Guillaume Couture, seeing that the Hurons were giving way, escaped like them into those great forests; and, as he was agile, he was soon out of the enemy's grasp. But, remorse having seized him because he had forsaken his Father and his comrade, he stops quite short. The dread of being regarded as perfidious makes him face about; he encounters five stout Hiroquois. One of these aims at him, but, his arquebus having missed fire, the Frenchman did not miss him,—he laid him, stone-dead, on the spot; the other four Hiroquois fell upon him with a rage of Lions, or rather of Demons. Having stripped him bare as the hand, they bruised him with heavy blows of clubs. . . . In short, they pierced one of his hands with a javelin, and led him, tied and bound in this sad plight, to the place where we were. Having recognized him, I escape from my guards and fall upon his neck. The Hiroquois at first remained quite bewildered; then, all at once,—imagining perhaps that I was applauding that young man because he had killed one of their captains,—they fell upon me with a mad fury, they belabored me with thrusts and with blows from sticks and war-clubs, flinging me to the ground, half dead. When I began to breathe again, those who had not struck me, approaching, violently tore out my finger nails; and then biting, one after another, the ends of my two fore-fingers, destitute of their nails, caused me the sharpest pain,—grinding and crushing them as if between two stones, even to the extent of causing splinters or little bones to protrude. They treated the good René Goupil in the same way, without doing, at that time, any harm to the Hurons.

"As I saw them engrossed in examining and distributing our spoils, I sought also for my share. I visit all the captives; I baptize those who were not yet baptized; I encourage those poor wretches to suffer with constancy, assuring them that their reward would far exceed the severity of their torments. I ascertained on this round of visits, that we were twenty-two captives, without counting three Hurons killed on the spot.

"So there we were, on the way to be led into a country truly foreign. It is true that, during the thirteen days that we spent on that journey, I suffered in the body torments almost unendurable, and, in the soul, mortal anguish; hunger, the fiercely burning heat, the threats and hatred of those Leopards, the pain of our wounds,—which, for not being dressed, became putrid even to the extent of breeding worms,—caused us, in truth, much distress. But all these things seemed light to me in comparison with an inward sadness which I felt at the sight of our earliest and most ardent Christians of the Hurons. I had thought that they were to be the pillars of the rising church, and I saw them become the victims of death. The ways closed for a long time to the salvation of so many peoples made me die every hour in the depth of my soul.

"Eight days after our departure from the shores of the great river of saint Lawrence, we met two hundred Hiroquois, who were coming in pursuit of the French and of the Savages, our allies. At this encounter we were obliged to sustain a new shock. It is a belief among these Barbarians that those who go to war are the more fortunate in proportion as they are cruel toward their enemies; I assure you that they made us thoroughly feel the force of that wretched belief.

"Accordingly, having perceived us, they first thanked the Sun for having caused us to fall into the hands of their Fellow-countrymen. That done, they set up a stage on a hill; then they seek sticks or thorns according to their fancy. Being thus armed, they form in line,—a hundred on one side, and a hundred on the other,—and make us pass, all naked, along that way of fury and anguish. I had not accomplished the half of this course when I fell to the earth under the weight of that hail and of those redoubled blows. Seeing that I had not fallen by accident, and that I did not rise again for being too near death, they entered upon a cruel compassion; their rage was not yet glutted, and they wished to conduct me alive into their own country. I would be too tedious if I were to set down in writing all the rigor of my sufferings. . . .

"I had always thought, indeed, that the day on which the whole Church rejoices in the glory of the Blessed Virgin—her glorious and triumphant Assumption—would be for us a day of pain. We arrived on the eve of that sacred day at a little river, distant from the first village of the Hiroquois about a quarter of a league. We found on its banks many men and youths. They led us in triumph into that first village; all the youth were outside the gates, arranged in line,—armed with sticks, and some with iron rods, which they easily secure, on account of their vicinity to the Dutch. Here follows the order which was observed at that funereal and pompous entry. They made one Frenchman march at the end, and another in the middle of the Hurons, and me the very last. We were following one another at an equal distance; and, that our executioners might have more leisure to beat us at their ease, some Hiroquois thrust themselves into our ranks in order to prevent us from running and from avoiding any blows. . . . Such was our entrance into that Babylon. Hardly could we arrive as far as the scaffold which was prepared for us, so exhausted were we; our bodies were all livid, and our faces all stained with blood. But more disfigured than all was René Goupil, so that nothing white appeared in his face except his eyes. . . .

"Evening having come, they made us descend, in order to be taken into the cabins as the sport of the children. They gave us for food a very little Indian corn simply boiled in water; then they made us lie down on pieces of bark, binding us by the hands and feet to four stakes fastened in the ground. Oh, my God, what nights! To remain always in an extremely constrained position; to be unable to stir or to turn, under the attack of countless vermin which assailed us on all sides; to be burdened with wounds, some recent and others all putrid; not to have sustenance for the half of one's life, in truth, these torments are great, but God is infinite. At Sunrise they led us back to our scaffold, where we spent three days and three nights in the sufferings I have just described.

"The three days having expired, they parade us into two other villages, where we make our entrance as into the first; these villages are several leagues distant from one another. The sentence decreed in the Council is intimated to me; the following night is to be (as they say) the end of my torments and of my life. My soul is well pleased with these words, but not yet was my God,—he willed to prolong my martyrdom. Those Barbarians reconsidered the matter, exclaiming that life ought to be spared to the Frenchmen, or, rather, their death postponed. They thought to find more moderation at our forts, on account of us. They accordingly sent Guillaume Cousture into the largest village, and René Goupil and I were lodged together in another. Life being granted us, they did us no more harm. But, alas, it was then that we felt at leisure the torments which had been inflicted on us. They gave us for beds the bark of trees, and for refreshment a little Indian meal, and sometimes a bit of squash, half raw. Our hands and fingers being all in pieces, they had to feed us like children. Patience was our Physician. Some women, more merciful, regarded us with much charity, and were unable to look at our sores without compassion."

GOD PRESERVES FATHER ISAAC JOGUES AFTER THE MURDER OF HIS COMPANION. HE INSTRUCTS HIM IN A VERY REMARKABLE MANNER

When these poor captives had recovered a little of their strength, the principal men of the country talked of conducting them back to Three Rivers, in order to restore them to the French. But, as their captors could not agree, the Father and his companions endured, more than ever, the pangs of death. These Barbarians are accustomed to give prisoners, whom they do not choose to put to death, to the families who have lost some of their relatives in war. These prisoners take the place of the deceased, and are incorporated into that family, which alone has the right to kill them or let them live. But when they retain some public prisoner, like the Father, without giving him to any individual, this poor man is every day within two finger-lengths of death.

The young Frenchman who was the Father's companion was accustomed to caress the little children, and to teach them to make the sign of the Cross. An old man, having seen him make this sacred sign on the forehead of his grandson, said to a nephew of his: "Go and kill that dog; that act will cause some harm to my grandson." Father Jogues leads him to a grove near the village, and explains to him the dangers in which they stood. While they were returning, the nephew of that old man, and another Savage, armed with hatchets and watching for an opportunity, go to meet them. One of the men says to the Father, "March forward," and at the same time he breaks the head of poor René Goupil, who, on falling and expiring, pronounced the Holy name of Jesus. "Give me a moment's time," the Father said to them, supposing that they would accord him the same favor as to his companion. "Get up," they reply; "thou wilt not die this time."

That young man, or that blessed martyr, being thus slain, the Father returns to his cabin; his people apply their hands to his breast, in order to feel whether fear did not agitate his heart. Having found it steady, they said to him: "Do not again leave the village, unless thou art accompanied by some one of us; they intend to beat thee to death; look out for thyself." He knew very well that they were seeking his life; a Huron, who had given him some shoes out of compassion, came to ask them of him again,—"Because," he said to him, "soon thou wilt have no more use for them, and another would use them." The Father gave them back to him, understanding very well what he meant to tell him. In brief, this good Father was every day like a bird on the branch; his life held only by a thread; and it seemed to him that at every moment some one was about to cut it; but he who held the end of it was not willing to let it go so soon.

THE FATHER IS GIVEN AS A SERVANT TO SOME HUNTERS. HE SUFFERS, HE IS CONSOLED, HE EXERCISES HIS ZEAL IN HIS JOURNEYS

They gave this poor Father to some families, to serve them as a menial in their hunts; he follows them at the approach of Winter and makes thirty leagues with them, serving them through two months, as a slave. All his clothes sheltered him no more than would a shirt and a sorry pair of drawers; his stockings and his shoes made like tennis slippers, and of a leather just as thin, without any soles,—in a word, he was all in rags. As they did not account him fit for hunting, they gave him a woman's occupation,—that is to cut and bring the wood to keep up the cabin fire. The chase beginning to furnish supplies, he could to some extent repair his strength,—meat not being stinted to him; but when he saw that they were offering to the Demon of the chase all that they took, he told them plainly that he would never eat of flesh sacrificed to the devil. He therefore contented himself with a very little sagamité, and even then he had it but seldom, because, gorged with meat, they despised their dry cornmeal. He secretly confessed to one of our Fathers that God tried him exceedingly in that journey, and that he saw himself a long time without any other support than Faith alone; his desolation was so great, and the sight of his miseries appeared to him so frightful that he knew not in what direction to turn. He had recourse to prayer; he would go to the woods as soon as it was morning, bringing back even more wood than was needed to keep up the fire which burns day and night in their cabins. His task done, he withdrew alone upon a hill covered with spruce trees, and there he spent eight or ten hours in prayer. He continued these exercises during forty days, without house, without fire, without other shelter than the sky and the woods, and a miserable scrap of I know not what, almost as transparent as the air. Those of his cabin, having perceived his retreat, and supposing that he was there preparing some spells in order to make men die, they tormented him from time to time, playing upon him a thousand tricks. In fine, they regarded him as an abomination,—even to the degree that whatever he touched was polluted and contaminated among them, so that he might not use any of the articles in the cabin. He had his thighs and legs cracked and split by the rigor of the cold, not having wherewith to cover himself.

From the month of August till the end of March, the Father was every day in the pains and terrors of death. A lesser courage had died a hundred times from apprehension. It is easier to die all at once than to die a hundred times. Toward the end of April, a Savage Captain from the country of the Sokoquiois appeared in the land of the Hiroquois, laden with presents, which he came to offer for the ransome and deliverance of a Frenchman named Ondesson,—thus the Hurons and the Hiroquois named Father Jogues. This embassy gave some credit to the Father, and caused him to be regarded for a short time with more compassionate eyes; but these Barbarians, having accepted the gifts, nevertheless did not set him at liberty,—violating the law of nations, and the law accepted among these tribes.

In the months of May and June, the Father wrote several letters, by warriors who were coming to hunt men upon the great stream of the Saint Lawrence; he told them that they should fasten these letters to some poles on the banks of that river. Be this as it may, one of them was delivered to Monsieur the Governor, on the occasion which we have described in Chapter 12 of the Relation for the year 1642, where a copy of that letter is written at full length.[1]

About that time, some Hiroquois Captains going to visit some small nations tributary to them, in order to get some presents,—that man who had the Father in custody, being of the party, led him in his train; his design was to display the triumphs of the Hiroquois over even the nations which are in Europe. There was never Anchorite more abstemious than this poor captive on that journey; his living was only a little wild purslane which he went to gather in the fields, with which he made a soup without other seasoning than clear water. They gave him, indeed, certain seeds to eat,—but so insipid and so dangerous that they served as a very quick poison to those who knew not how to prepare them; and he would not touch them.

THE FATHER ESCAPES FROM THE HIROQUOIS AND PROCEEDS TO FRANCE, THROUGH THE INTERVENTION OF THE DUTCH. HE RETURNS TO CANADA. HAVING ARRIVED THERE, HE MAKES A JOURNEY TO THE COUNTRY OF THE IROQUOIS

Upon the return from this journey, they command the Father to accompany some fishermen, who conducted him seven or eight leagues below a Dutch settlement. While he was engaged in that exercise, he learned from some Iroquois who

[1] *See* p. 185, ff.

came to that quarter that they were awaiting him in the village to burn him. This news was the occasion of his deliverance. The Dutch having given him the opportunity to enter a ship, the Iroquois complained of it,—he was withdrawn and conducted to the house of the Captain, who gave him in custody to an old man, until they should have appeased these Barbarians. In a word, if they had persevered in their demand, and rejected some presents that were made to them, the Father would have been given up into their hands, to be the object of their fury and food for their fires. Now, while they were awaiting the opportunity to send him back to Europe, he remained six weeks under the guard of that old man, who lodged him in an old garret. The Minister [1] visited him sometimes, and bethinking himself one day to ask how they treated him; he answered that they brought him very few things. "I suspect as much," the Minister answers, "for that old man is a great miser, who no doubt retains most of the provisions that are sent you."

In this garret where the Father was, there was a recess to which his Guard continually led Hiroquois Savages, in order to sell some produce which he locked up there: this recess was made of planks so slightly joined that one might easily have passed his fingers into the openings. "I am astonished," says the Father, "that those Barbarians did not hundreds of times discover me; I saw them without difficulty. I concealed myself behind casks, bending myself into a constrained posture which gave me gehenna and torture two, three, or four hours in succession, and that very often. To go down to the court of the dwelling was casting myself headlong; for every place was filled with those who were seeking to put me to death."

Finally, the Governor of the country, sending a bark of one hundred tons to Holland, sent the Father back at the beginning of the month of November.

They anchored in a port of England, toward the end of December. On Christmas eve he embarked in I know not what boat or little bark laden with mineral coal, which landed him

[1] *See* p. 130, *note;* p. 138, *note.*

the next day on the coast of lower Brittany. Finally, on the fifth of January, 1644, he was knocking at the door of our College at Rennes.

The porter, seeing him in such plight, clad in garments so incongruous, did not recognize him. The Father besought him to bring the Father Rector, that he might impart to him, he said, some news from Canada. The Father Rector was putting on the Sacerdotal vestments, in order to go and celebrate holy Mass, but the porter having told him that a poor man, come from Canada, was asking for him, that word "poor" touched him. "Perhaps," he said to himself, "he is in haste, and he may be in need." He then lays aside the sacred vestments with which he was partly robed; he goes to find him; the Father, without revealing his identity, offers him letters signed by the Governor of the Dutch; before reading these he puts various questions to the Father, without recognizing him; and then, at last, he asks him if he were indeed acquainted with Father Isaac Jogues. "I know him very well," he answers. "We have had word that he was taken by the Hiroquois; is he dead? is he still captive? Have not those Barbarians slain him?" "He is at liberty, and it is he, my Reverend Father, who speaks to you," and thereupon he falls upon his knees to receive his blessing. The Father Rector, overcome with an unaccustomed joy, embraces him, and has him enter the house; every one hastens thither; the joy and consolation of a deliverance so little expected interrupt their words. In fine, they regard him as a Lazarus raised from the dead,—who is destined to go and die for the last time in the country where he has already suffered so many deaths.

From Rennes he comes to Paris: the Queen having heard mention of his sufferings, says aloud: "Romances are feigned, but here is a genuine combination of great adventures." She wished to see him; her eyes were touched with compassion at the sight of the cruelty of the Hiroquois. He made no long sojourn in France; the spring of the year 1644, having come, he betook himself to la Rochelle in order to cross back to the country of his martyrdom,—where, having arrived, he was sent to

Montreal. Peace being made with the Hiroquois, the Father was taken from Montreal, to go and lay the foundations of a Mission in their country, which was named "The Mission of the martyrs." On the sixteenth of May, 1646, this good Father left three rivers in company with Sieur Bourdon, the engineer of Monsieur the Governor. They arrived (back) at three Rivers,—having accomplished their embassy,—the 29th of the month of June.

FATHER ISAAC JOGUES RETURNS FOR THE THIRD TIME TO THE COUNTRY OF THE HIROQUOIS, WHERE HE IS PUT TO DEATH

Hardly had the poor Father been refreshed among us two or three months, when he recommenced his expeditions; on the twenty-fourth of September, in the same year, 1646, he embarks with a young Frenchman,[1] in a canoe conducted by some Hurons, in order to return to the land of his crosses. He had strong premonitions of his death. We have learned that he was slain directly upon his entrance into that country full of murder and blood: here follows a letter announcing this:

"For the rest, I have not much to tell you, except how the French arrived, on the 17th of this present month of October, 1647, at the fort of the Maquois. The very day of their coming, they began to threaten them, saying: 'You will die to-morrow: be not astonished. But we will not burn you; have courage; we will strike you with the hatchet and will set your heads on the palings,' (that is to say, on the fence about their village), 'so that when we capture your brothers they may still see you.' You must know that it was only the nation of the bear which put them to death; the nations of the wolf and the turtle did all that they could to save their lives, and said to the nation of the bear: 'Kill us first.' But, alas, they are not in life for all that. Know, then, that on the 18th, in the evening, when they came to call Isaac to supper, he got up and went away with that

[1] Jean de la Lande. *See* p. 131, *note.*

Barbarian to the lodge of the bear.   There was a traitor with
his hatchet behind the door, who, on entering, split open his
head; then, immediately, he cut it off, and set it on the palings.
The next day, very early, he did the same to the other man, and
their bodies were thrown into the river.   Monsieur, I have
not been able to know or to learn from any Savage why they
have killed them."

Such is what the Dutch have written of the death of Father
Isaac Jogues.

[*Ibid.*, xxxi., *Doc.* lxiii.]

III

ACCOUNT OF RENÉ GOUPIL (DONNÉ)

By Father Isaac Jogues

René Goupil was a native of Anjou, who, in the bloom of his youth, urgently requested to be received into our Novitiate at Paris, where he remained some months with much edification. His bodily indispositions having taken from him the happiness of consecrating himself to God in holy Religion,— for which he had a strong desire,—he journeyed, when his health improved, to New France, in order to serve the society there, since he had not had the blessing of giving himself to it in old France. And, in order to do nothing in his own right, —although he was fully master of his own actions,—he totally submitted himself to the guidance of the superior of the Mission, who employed him two whole years in the meanest offices about the house, in which he acquitted himself with great humility and Charity. He was also given the care of nursing the sick and the wounded at the hospital, which he did with much skill—for he understood surgery well—as with affection and love, continually seeing our Lord in their persons. He left so sweet an odor of his goodness and his other virtues in that place, that his memory is still blessed there.

When we came down from the Hurons in July, 1642, we asked Reverend Father Vimont to let us take him with us, because the Hurons had great need of a Surgeon: he granted our request.

I cannot express the joy which this good young man felt when the superior told him that he might make ready for the journey. Nevertheless, he well knew the great dangers that await one upon the river; he knew how the Iroquois were enraged against the French. Yet that could not prevent him— at the least sign of the will of him to whom he had voluntarily committed all his concerns—from setting forth for 3 Rivers.

We departed thence on the 1st of August,—the day after the feast of Our Blessed Father. On the 2nd, we encountered the enemies, who, separated into two bands, were awaiting us with the advantage which a great number of chosen men, fighting on land, can have over a small and promiscuous band, who are upon the water in scattered canoes of bark.

Nearly all the Hurons had fled into the woods, and, as soon as they left us, we were seized. On this occasion his virtue was very manifest; for, as soon as he saw himself captured, he said to me: "O my father, God be blessed; he has permitted it, he has willed it—his holy will be done. I love it, I desire it, I cherish it, I embrace it with all the strength of my heart." Meantime, while the enemies pursued the fugitives, I heard his confession, and gave him absolution,—not knowing what might befall us after our capture. The enemies having returned from their hunt, fell upon us like mad dogs, with sharp teeth,—tearing out our nails, and crushing our fingers, which he endured with much patience and courage.

His presence of mind in so grievous a mishap appeared especially in this, that he aided me, notwithstanding the pain of his wounds, as well as he could, in the instruction of the captive Hurions who were not christians. While I was instructing them separately, and as they came, he called my attention to the fact that a poor old man named Ondouterraon, was among those whom they would probably kill on the spot,— their custom being always to sacrifice some one in the heat of their fury. I instructed this man at leisure, while the enemies were attending to the distribution of the plunder from 12 canoes, some of which were laden with necessaries for our Fathers among the Hurons. The booty being divided, they killed this poor old man,—almost at the same moment in which I had just given him a new birth through the salutory water of holy Baptism. We still had this consolation, during the journey that we made in going to the enemies' country, that we were together; on this journey I was witness to many virtues.

Upon the road he was always occupied with God. His

words and the discourses that he held were all expressive of submission to the commands of the Divine providence, and showed a willing acceptance of the death which God was sending him. He gave himself to him as a sacrifice, to be reduced to ashes by the fires of the Iroquois, which that good Father's hand would kindle. He sought the means to please him in all things, and everywhere. One day he said to me,— it was soon after our capture, while we were still on the way,— "My Father, God has always given me a great desire to consecrate myself to his holy service by the vows of Religion in his holy society; my sins have rendered me unworthy of this grace until this hour. I nevertheless hope that Our Lord will be pleased with the offering which I wish now to make him, by taking, in the best manner that I can, the vows of the society in the presence of my God and before you." This being granted to him, he uttered the vows with much devotion.

Covered with wounds as he was, he dressed those of other persons,—the enemies who had received some blow in the fight, as well as the prisoners themselves. He opened a vein for a sick Iroquois; and all that with as much charity as if he had done it to persons very friendly.

His humility, and the obedience which he rendered to those who had captured him, confounded me. Two Iroquois who conveyed us both in their canoe told me that I must take a paddle and use it; I would do nothing of the kind, being proud even in death. They addressed him in the same way, some time afterward, and immediately he began to paddle; and when these barbarians tried to drive me, by his example, to do the like, he, having perceived it, asked my pardon. I sometimes suggested to him, along the way, the idea of escaping, since the liberty they gave us furnished him sufficient opportunity for this; but as for myself, I could not leave the french and 24 or 25 huron captives. He would never do so,—committing himself in everything to the will of Our Lord, who inspired him with no thought of doing what I proposed.

On the lake we met 200 Iroquois, who came to Richelieu while the French were beginning to build the fort; these loaded us with blows, covered us with blood, and made us experience the rage of those who are possessed by the demon. All these outrages and these cruelties he endured with great patience and charity toward those who ill-treated him.

On approaching the first village, where we were treated so cruelly, he showed a most uncommon patience and gentleness. Having fallen under the shower of blows from clubs and iron rods with which they attacked us, and being unable to rise again, he was brought—as it were, half dead—upon the scaffold where we were already were, in the middle of the village; but he was in so pitiful a condition that he would have inspired compassion in cruelty itself. He was all bruised with blows, and in his face one distinguished nothing but the whites of his eyes; but he was so much the more beautiful in the sight of the Angels as he was disfigured, and similar to him of whom it is said: *Vidimus eum quasi leprosum*, etc.; *non erat ei species neque decor.*

Hardly had he taken a little breath, as well as we, when they came to give him 3 blows on his shoulders with a heavy club, as they had done to us before. When they had cut off my thumb,—as I was the most conspicuous,—they turned to him and cut his right thumb at the 1st joint,—while he continually uttered, during this torment, "JESUS, MARY, JOSEPH." During six days, in which we were exposed to all those who wished to do us some harm, he showed an admirable gentleness; he had his whole breast burned by the coals and hot cinders which the young lads threw upon our bodies at night, when we were bound flat on the earth. Nature furnished more skill to me than to him for avoiding a part of these pains.

After they had given us life,—at the very time when, a little before, they had warned us to prepare for being burned, —he fell sick, suffering great inconveniences in every respect, and especially in regard to the food, to which he was not accustomed. In that, one might say most truly, *Non cibus utilis aegro.* I could not relieve him,—for I was also very sick, and had none of my fingers sound or entire.

But this urges me to come to his death, at which nothing was wanting to make him a Martyr.

After we had been in the country six weeks,—as confusion arose in the councils of the Iroquois, some of whom were quite willing that we should be taken back,—we lost the hope, which I did not consider very great, of again seeing 3 Rivers that year. We accordingly counseled one another in the divine arrangement of things; and we were preparing for everything that it might ordain for us. He did not quite realize the danger in which we were,—I saw it better than he; and this often led me to tell him that we should hold ourselves in readiness. One day, then, as in the grief of our souls we had gone forth from the Village, in order to pray more suitably and with less disturbance, two young men came after us to tell us that we must return home. I had some presentiment of what was to happen, and said to him: "My dearest brother, let us commend ourselves to Our Lord and to our good mother the blessed Virgin; these people have some evil design as I think." We had offered ourselves to Our Lord, shortly before, with much devotion,—beseeching him to receive our lives and our blood, and to unite them with his life and his blood for the salvation of these poor peoples. We accordingly return toward the Village, reciting our rosary, of which we had already said 4 decades. Having stopped near the gate of the Village, to see what they might say to us, one of these two Iroquois draws a hatchet, which he held concealed under his blanket, and deals a blow with it on the head of René, who was before him. He falls motionless, his face to the ground, pronouncing the holy name of JESUS (often we admonished each other that this holy name should end both our voices and our lives). At the blow, I turn round and see a hatchet all bloody; I kneel down, to receive the blow which was to unite me with my dear companion; but, as they hesitate, I rise again, and run to the dying man, who was quite near. They dealt him two other blows with the hatchet, on the head, and despatched him,— but not until I had first given him absolution, which I had been wont to give him every two days, since our captivity; and this was a day on which he had already confessed.

It was the (29th) of September, the feast of st. Michael, when this Angel in innocence and this Martyr of Jesus Christ, gave his life for him who had given him his. They ordered me to return to my cabin, where I awaited, the rest of the day and the next day, the same treatment; and it was indeed the purpose of all that I should not long delay, since that one had begun. Indeed, I passed several days on which they came to kill me; but our Lord did not permit this, in ways which it would be tedious to explain. The next morning, I nevertheless went out to inquire where they had thrown that Blessed body, for I wished to bury it, at whatever cost. Certain Iroquois, who had some desire to preserve me, said to me: "Thou hast no sense! Thou seest that they seek thee everywhere to kill thee, and thou still goest out. Thou wishest to go and seek a body already half destroyed, which they have dragged far from here. Dost thou not see those young men going out, who will kill thee when thou shalt be outside the stockade?" That did not stop me, and Our Lord gave me courage enough to wish to die in this act of charity. I go, I seek; and with the aid of an Algonquin—formerly captured, and now a true Iroquois—I find him. The children, after he had been killed, had stripped him, and had dragged him, with a rope about his neck, into a torrent which passes at the foot of their Village. The dogs had already eaten a part of his loins. I could not keep back my tears at this sight; I took the body, and, by the aid of that Algonquin, I put it beneath the water, weighted with large stones, to the end that it might not be seen. It was my intention to come the next day with a mattock, when no one should be there, in order to make a grave and place the body therein. I thought that the corpse was well concealed; but perhaps some who saw us,—especially of the youths,— withdrew it.

The next day, as they were seeking me to kill me, my aunt [1]

---

[1] "The mother of his guard or host,—whom he called his 'aunt.' "—*Ibid., Relation of 1647*, xxxi., 83.

sent me to her field,—to escape, as I think; this caused me to delay until the morrow, a day on which it rained all night, so that the torrent swelled uncommonly. I borrowed a mattock from another cabin, the better to conceal my design; but, when I draw near the place, I no longer find that Blessed deposit. I go into the water, which was already very cold; I go and come,—I sound with my foot, to see whether the water has not raised and carried away the body; I find nothing. How many tears did I shed, which fell into the torrent, while I sang, as well as I could, the psalms which the church is accustomed to recite for the dead.

After all, I find nothing; and a woman of my acquaintance, who passed there and saw me in pain, told me, when I asked her whether she knew what they had done with him, that they had dragged him to the river, which was a quarter of a league from there, and which I was not acquainted with. That was false: the young men had taken away the body, and dragged it into a little wood near by,—where, during the autumn and winter, the Dogs, Ravens, and Foxes fed upon it. In the Spring, when they told me that it was there that they had dragged him, I went thither several times without finding anything. At last, the 4th time, I found the head and some half-gnawed bones, which I buried with the design of carrying them away, if I should be taken back to 3 Rivers, as they spoke of doing. I kissed them very devoutly, several times, as the bones of a Martyr of Jesus Christ.

I give him this title not only because he was killed by the enemies of God and of his Church, and in the exercise of an ardent charity toward his neighbor,—placing himself in evident peril for the love of God,—but especially because he was killed on account of prayer, and notably for the sake of the holy Cross.

He was in a Cabin where he nearly always said the prayers, —which little pleased a superstitious old man who was there. One day, seeing a little child of 3 or 4 years in the cabin,— with an excess of devotion and of love for the Cross, and with a simplicity which we who are more prudent than he, according to the flesh, would not have shown,—he took off his cap, put it on this child's head, and made a great sign of the cross upon its body. The old man, seeing that, commanded a young man of his cabin, who was about to leave for the war, to kill him,—which order he executed, as we have said.

Even the child's mother, on a journey in which I happened to be with her, told me that it was because of this sign of the Cross that he had been killed; and the old man who had given the command that he should be slain,—one day when they called me to his cabin to eat, when I had previously made the sign of the Cross,—said to me: "That is what we hate; that is why they have killed thy companion, and why they will kill thee. Our neighbors the Europeans do not do so." Sometimes, also, when I was praying on my knees during the hunt, they told me that they hated this way of doing, and on account of it they had killed the other Frenchman; and that, for this reason, they would kill me when I came back to the Village.

I ask Your Reverence's pardon for the haste with which I write this, and for the want of respect of which I am thus guilty. You will excuse me, if you please; I feared lest I should fail at this opportunity, to discharge a duty which I ought to have performed long ago.

[*Ibid.*, xxviii, *Doc.* lvii.]

IV

LETTER OF FATHER PAUL RAGUENEAU TO THE VERY REVEREND FATHER VINCENT CARAFFA, GENERAL OF THE SOCIETY OF JESUS, AT ROME

(*1649*)

[This is a letter, written by Ragueneau,[1] in the Huron country, March 1, 1649, to the father general of the Jesuits, giving in response to the latter's request, many details of the Huron mission. Affairs temporal are in a dangerous condition; for the constant attacks of the Iroquois have destroyed all the outlying Huron villages, and the mission is now forced to rely on its own strength for defense. So well has the mission been conducted, that it produces most of its own food. . . . It has every prospect of success, were it not for the raids of the Iroquois. In one of these (occurring in July, 1648), they take by storm the mission village of St. Joseph, which they burn down, and Father Antoine Daniel is slain by the enemy, while encouraging his flock,—the first martyr in that mission. *Ibid.*, xxxiii., 15.]

---

[1] Paul Ragueneau, born in Paris, March 18, 1608, became a Jesuit novice Aug. 21, 1626. His studies were pursued at Clermont and Bourges: he was also an instructor in the latter institution during 1628-32, among his pupils being "the great Condé." He came to Canada June 28, 1636, and labored in the Huron mission until its close—except during the year 1640-41; in the spring of the latter year, he, with Nicolet, held an ineffectual conference with the hostile Iroquois near Three Rivers. He was named by the Hurons Aondecheté.

Ragueneau was superior of the Huron mission from early in 1645 until its destruction in 1649; and superior of all the Canadian missions from 1650 to 1653.—*Ibid.*, ix., *note* 40.

Our Very Reverend Father in Christ:

Pax Christi

I have received, very Reverend Paternity, your letter dated January 20, 1647. If you wrote us last year, 1648, we have not yet received that letter. Your Paternity evinces pleasure in the news of the state of our Huron mission. Indeed (such is your Paternal love toward us), you even stoop to details and bid us inform you of everything.

There are here eighteen Fathers, rour coadjutors, twenty-three Données, seven servants (to whom alone wages are paid), four boys and eight soldiers. Truly, we are so threatened by the hostile rage of our savage enemies that, unless we wish our enterprise and ourselves to perish in an hour, it was quite necessary for us to seek the protection of these men, who devote themselves to both domestic duties and farm work, and also to building fortifications, and to military service. For since, until late years, our abode, which we call the Residence of Ste. Marie, was surrounded on every side by the numerous villages of our friends, the Hurons, we feared more for them than for ourselves from hostile attack: so during that time, however small our number, we lived in safety, without anxiety. But now, far different is the aspect of our affairs and of this whole region; for so crushed are our Hurons by disasters, that, their outposts being taken and laid waste with fire and sword, most of them have been forced to change their abodes, and retreat elsewhere; hence it has come to pass that at last we are devoid of the protection of others; and now we, stationed at the front, must defend ourselves with our own strength, our own courage, and our own numbers.

This our dwelling—or shall I say our fort?—of Sainte Marie, the French who are with us defend, while our Fathers sally forth, far and wide, scattered among the villages of the Hurons, and through the Algonquin tribes far distant from us,—each one watching over his own mission, and intent only upon the ministry of the word, leaving all temporal cares to those who remain at home. In truth, domestic matters keep so fortunate a course that, although our number has increased,

and we greatly desire new help to be sent us,—both of laymen and, especially, of our own fathers,—still in no wise is it
necessary to increase expenses. On the contrary, they are
lessening daily, and each year we ask for less temporal aid
to be sent us—so much so that we can, for the most part,
support ourselves upon that which is here produced. Verily,
there is not one of our brethren who does not feel in this
respect great relief from those distresses which were in former
years very burdensome, and seemed insurmountable. For we
have larger supplies from fishing and hunting than formerly;
and we have not merely fish and eggs, but also pork, and milk
products, and even cattle, from which we hope for great addition to our store. I write of these particulars, because your
Paternity so desired.

Christianity has certainly made progress here, in many ways,
beyond our expectation. We baptized, the past year, about
one thousand seven hundred,—not counting many whom we
shall mention below as baptized by Father Antoine Daniel,[1]
the number of whom could not be accurately given. Nor are
these, albeit barbarians, such Christians as one might be inclined to suppose, ignorant of things divine and not sufficiently
qualified for our mysteries. Many indeed understand religion,
and that profoundly; and there are some whose virtue, piety,
and remarkable holiness even the most holy Religious might

---

[1] Antoine Daniel was born at Dieppe, May 27, 1601; and, at the age of twenty,
entered the Jesuit novitiate at Rouen. He was, after 1650, a teacher and
preacher at the college of Eu, until his departure for Canada (1632), whither
he went with his brother, Captain Charles Daniel. He endeavored, with Brébeuf
and Davost, to go at once to the Huron country; but the savages refused to take
them, and they were compelled to wait for a more favorable opportunity. This
came a year later, when these three returned with the Hurons who had come
down to Three Rivers for trade. They established themselves at Ihonatiria, and
Daniel remained there until his death,—except during the two years 1636-38, when
he was at Quebec, attending to some Huron lads whom he had taken thither
to instruct in religion and in the ways of civilization. In the summer of 1648,
the Iroquois made a sudden raid, and, on July 4, surprised and utterly destroyed
the town of Teanaustayé (called by the missionaries St. Joseph). Daniel, after
doing all in his power to encourage and console his people, was murdered at the
church door by the Iroquois; his body, riddled with arrows, was thrown into
the flames that consumed the building. He was the second martyr among the
Jesuits sent to New France.—*Ibid.*, v., *note* 53.

without sin envy. One who is an eye-witness of these things cannot sufficiently admire the finger of God, and congratulate himself that so fortunate a field of labor, so rich in divine blessing, had fallen to his lot.

We maintain eleven missions—eight in the Huron language and three Algonquin. The work is divided between an equal number of Fathers who have had experience. Four, sent to us last year, devote their time to learning the language; and these we have assigned as helpers to the chief missionaries. Thus only three Fathers remain at home—one as spiritual Director, another as Procurator and minister, the third to look after the needs of the Christians, who come to us from every quarter. For out of our own poverty we minister to the poverty of the Christians, and heal their diseases both of soul and body, surely to the great advancement of Christianity. Last year, nearly six thousand partook of our hospitality. How strange it is that *in terra aliena, in loco horroris et vastae solitudinis,* we should seem to draw *mel de petra, oleumque de saxo durissimo*—thence to supply the needs, not merely of us who are strangers, but also of the natives themselves. I say these things that your Paternity may know the abundance of God's goodness toward us. For, while during this year famine has been heavy upon the villages on all sides of us, and now weighs upon them even more heavily, no blight of evil has fallen upon us; nay, we have enough provisions upon which to live comfortably during three years.

But one thing—the fear of war and the rage of foes— seems able to overthrow the happy state of this infant church, and stay the advance of Christianity; for it grows yearly, and it is clear that no help can come to us save from God alone. The latest disaster that befell our Hurons—in July of last year, 1648—was the severest of all. Many of them had made ready to visit our French people in the direction of Quebec, to trade; other tasks had drawn some away from their villages; while many had undertaken a hostile expedition in another direction; when suddenly the enemy came upon them, stormed two villages, rushed into them, and set them on fire. With their wonted cruelty they dragged into captivity mothers with their children, and showed no mercy to any age.

Of these villages, one was called Saint Joseph; this was one of our principal missions, where a church had been built, where the people had been instructed in Christian rites, and where the faith had taken deep root. In charge of this Church was Father Antoine Daniel, a man of great courage and endurance, whose gentle kindness was conspicuous among his great virtues. He had hardly finished the usual mass after sunrise; and the Christians, who had assembled in considerable numbers, had not yet left the sacred house, when, at the war-cry of the enemy, in haste and alarm they seized their weapons. Some rush into the fight, others flee headlong; everywhere is terror, everywhere lamentation.

Antoine hastened wherever he saw the danger most threatening and bravely encouraged his people—inspiring not only the Christians with Christian strength, but many unbelievers with faith. He was heard to speak of contempt for death, and of the joys of Paradise, with such ardor of soul that he seemed already to enjoy his bliss. Indeed, many sought baptism; and so great was the number that he could not attend to each one separately; but was forced to dip his handkerchief in the water and baptize by sprinkling the multitude who thronged around him.

Meantime, there was no cessation in the ferocious attack of the enemy, and everywhere resounded the noise of muskets. Many fell around him who received at the same instant the life-giving water of baptism, and the stroke of death. When he saw that his people had fled, he himself, intent upon the gain of souls,—mindful of the safety of others, but forgetful of his own,—hurried into the cabins to baptize the sick, the aged, and children, and filled them with his own zeal. At last, he betook himself to the church, whither the hope of eternal glory had brought many Christians, and the fear of hell-fire many catechumens. Never were there more earnest prayers, never stronger proofs of true faith and real penitence. To these he gives new life of baptism, those he releases from the bonds of sin; he sets all on fire with divine love. Almost his only words were: "Brothers, today we shall be in Paradise; believe this, hope this, that God may forever love you."

Already the foe had scaled the rampart, and throughout the village the torch had been applied, and the cabins were burning. The victors are informed that there is rich plunder, easy to get, if they will hasten to the church; that there numbers of old people, and women, and a band of children, are gathered. Thither they hurry with discordant shouts, after their manner. The Christians see the enemy approaching. Antoine bids them flee wherever escape is yet possible.

That he may delay the enemy, and, like a good shepherd, aid the escape of his flock, he blocks the way of the armed men and breaks their onset; a single man against the foe, but verily filled with divine strength, he, who during all his life had been as the gentlest dove, was brave as a Lion while he met death. Truly, I might apply to him that saying of Jeremias: "He hath forsaken his covert as the Lion, for the land is laid waste because of the wrath of the dove, and because of the fierce anger of the Lord." At last he fell, mortally wounded by a musket shot; and, pierced with arrows, he yielded to God the blessed life which he laid down for his flock, as a good Shepherd, calling upon the name of Jesus. Savagely enraged against his lifeless body, hardly one of the enemy was there who did not add a new wound to his corpse; until at length, the church having been set on fire, his naked body cast into the flames was so completely consumed that not even a bone was left: indeed, he could not have found a more glorious funeral pyre.

In thus delaying the enemy, he was serviceable to his flock, even after his death. Many reached places of safety; others the victors overtook, especially mothers—at every step delayed by the babes at their breasts, or by those whose childish years —as yet unaccustomed to prudent fear—betrayed their hiding places.

Antoine had just finished his fourteenth year at the Huron

mission, everywhere a useful man, and assuredly raised up for the salvation of those tribes; but certainly ripe for heaven, and the first man of our society to be taken from us. True, his death was sudden, but did not find him unprepared: for he had always so lived that he was ever ready for death. Yet the Divine Goodness toward him seems to have been remarkable; for he had finished, only the first day of July, eight days of continuous spiritual Exercises of the Society in this house of Sainte Marie; and on the very next day, without any delay, or even one day's rest, he hastened to his own mission. Verily he burned with a zeal for God more intense than any flame that consumed his body.

He was a native of Dieppe, born of worthy and pious Parents. He had entered the Society in 1621, at the age of twenty one years; he was admitted to the Profession of the four vows in 1640; and at last ended his life July fourth, 1648. He was indeed a remarkable man; and a truly worthy son of the society—humble, obedient, united with God, of never failing patience, and indomitable courage in adversity. Thus he left to us a shining example of all the virtues; to the savage Christians, an impression of exalted faith and piety; to all, even the unbelievers, heavy grief at his death. Now at last, he will be granted, we certainly hope, as a most powerful Advocate in heaven for all this country.

In fact, by one of our number (a man of eminent piety and of well-attested humility, Father Joseph Marie Chaumonot) he was seen once and again after death. But when first our Fathers were gathered in council, and planning, as is their wont, for the promotion of Christianity, father Antoine was seen to appear in their midst, to revive us all with his strong counsel, and with the divine spirit which filled him. He seemed to be about thirty, as far as could be judged by his face; which presented to the Fathers a noble aspect, quite unlike anything human. The Father was asked how the Divine Goodness could suffer the body of his servant to be so shamefully treated after death,—disfigured as if by disgraceful wounds,—and to be so consumed by fire that nothing, not even a handful of ashes, was left to us. "Great is the Lord," replied he, "and most worthy of Praise. He beheld this reproach of his servant; and, to compensate for this in Divine fashion, he granted me many souls from purgatory, to accompany my triumph in heaven."

To make an end of writing, without exceeding the limit of a letter, I will add—what should have been written first of all to Your Paternity—that such is the condition of this house, and indeed of the whole mission, that I think hardly anything could be added to the piety, obedience, humility, patience, and charity of our brethren, and to their scrupulous observance of the rules. We are all of one heart, one soul, one spirit of the society. Nay, what must seem more wonderful, out of all the men attached to the house, of condition and nature so varied,—servants, boys, données, soldiers,—there is not one who does not seriously attend to his soul's salvation; so that clearly vice is banished hence, here virtue rules, and this is seen to be the home of holiness. This surely is our rejoicing, our peace in war, and our great security; for, whatever may be the dispensation of divine Providence, in life or in death this will be our consolation, that we are the Lord's and ever shall be, as we are permitted to hope. That so it may be, we implore your Paternity's Benediction upon us and our mission; and I chiefly, though unworthiest of all,—

Your most Reverend Paternity's
Most humble and obedient son,
PAUL RAGUENEAU

From the Residence of Sainte Marie,
among the Hurons, new France,
March 1, 1649.
To our Most Reverend Father in Christ,
Vincent Caraffa, General of the
Society of Jesus, Rome.

[*Ibid.*, xxxiii., *Doc.* lxvii.]

V

A VERITABLE ACCOUNT OF THE MARTYRDOM AND BLESSED DEATH OF FATHER JEAN DE BREBOEUF AND OF FATHER GABRIEL L'ALEMANT, IN NEW FRANCE, IN THE COUNTRY OF THE HURONS, BY THE IROQUOIS, ENEMIES OF THE FAITH

[This is a vivid and sympathetic account of the martyrdom of Brébeuf and Gabriel Lalemant, written by Christophe Regnaut, one of the donnés in the Huron mission. Although he did not witness the tragedy, he obtained full particulars of it from the Christian Hurons taken captive by the Iroquois, who were present throughout the horrible torments inflicted upon the unfortunate Jesuits. He relates these in detail, and then describes the condition of the martyrs' remains, which he has helped to bring from St. Ignace to Ste. Marie, and afterwards carefully examines, finding that the appearance of the bodies fully confirms the statements of the Hurons. The bones of these victims are carried to Quebec, "where they are held in great veneration." *Ibid.*, xxxiv., 9.]

Father Jean de Breboeuf and Father Gabriel L'Alemant [1] had set out from our cabin, to go to a small Village, called

---

[1] Gabriel Lalemant, nephew of Jerome and Charles, was born at Paris, Oct. 10, 1610, the youngest of a family of six,—all of whom, except the second son, entered the religious life; as also did the mother, after Gabriel's death. He became a Jesuit novice March 24, 1630; he was an instructor at Moulins, 1632-35 and 1641-44, the intervening time being spent at Bourges and La Flèche; and, later, was prefect of the college at Bourges for two years. Departing thence in June, 1646, he came to Canada, where he spent two years in ministrations at the French settlements on the St. Lawrence. He arrived in the Huron country in August, 1648, and his martyrdom took place on March 17 following.—*Ibid.*, xxxiv, *note* 1.

St. Ignace, distant from our cabin about a short quarter of a league, to instruct the Savages and the new Christians of that Village. It was on the 16th Day of March, in the morning, that we perceived a great fire at the place to which these two good fathers had gone. This fire made us very uneasy; we did not know whether it were enemies, or if the fire had caught in some of the huts of the village. The Reverend Father Paul Ragueneau, our Superior, immediately resolved to send someone to learn what might be the cause. But no sooner had we formed the design of going there to see, than we perceived several savages on the road, coming straight toward us. We all thought it was the Iroquois who were coming to attack us; but, having considered them more closely, we perceived that they were hurons who were fleeing from the fight, and who had escaped from the combat. These poor savages caused great pity in us. They were all covered with wounds. One had his head fractured; another his arm broken; another had an arrow in his eye; another had his hand cut off by a blow from a hatchet. In fine, the day was passed in receiving into our cabins all these poor wounded people, and in looking with compassion toward the fire, and the place where were those two good Fathers. We saw the fire and the barbarians. but we could not see anything of the two Fathers.

This is what these savages told us of the taking of the Village of St. Ignace, and about Fathers Jean de Bréboeuf and Gabriel L'Allemant:

"The Iroquois came, to the number of twelve hundred men; took our village, and seized Father Bréboeuf and his companion; and set fire to all the huts. They proceeded to vent their rage on those two Fathers, for they took them both and stripped them entirely naked, and fastened each to a post. They tied both of their hands together. They tore the nails from the fingers. They beat them with a shower of blows from cudgels, on the shoulders, the loins, the belly, the legs and the face—there being no part of their body which did not endure this torment." The savages told us further, that, although Father de Bréboeuf was overwhelmed under the weight of these blows, he did not cease continually to speak of God, and to encourage all the new Christians who were captives like himself to suffer well, that they might die well, in order to go in company with him to Paradise. While the good Father was thus encouraging these good people, a wretched huron renegade,—who had remained a captive with the Iroquois, and whom Father de Bréboeuf had formerly instructed and baptized,—hearing him speak of Paradise and Holy Baptism, was irritated, and said to him, "Echon," that is Father de Bréboeuf's name in Huron, "thou sayest that Baptism and the sufferings of this life lead straight to Paradise; thou wilt go soon, for I am going to baptize thee, and to make thee suffer well, in order to go the sooner to thy Paradise." The barbarian, having said that, took a kettle full of boiling water, which he poured over his body three dif-- ferent times, in derision of Holy baptism. And, each time that he baptized him in this manner, the barbarian said to him, with bitter sarcasm, "Go to Heaven, for thou art well baptized." After that, they made him suffer several other torments. The 1st was to make hatchets red-hot, and to apply them to the loins and under the armpits. They made a collar of these red-hot hatchets, and put it on the neck of this good Father. This is the fashion in which I have seen the collar made for other prisoners: They make six hatchets red-hot, take a large withe of green wood, pass the 6 hatchets over the large end of the withe, take the two ends together, and then put it over the neck of the sufferer. I have seen no torment which more moved me to compassion than that. For you see a man, bound naked to a post, who, having this collar on his neck, cannot tell what posture to take. For, if he lean forward, those above his shoulders weigh the more on him; if he lean back, those on his stomach make him suffer the same torment; if he keep erect, without leaning to one side or the other, the burning hatchets, applied equally on both sides, give him a double torture.

After that they put on him a belt of bark, full of pitch

and resin, and set fire to it, which roasted his whole body. During all these torments, Father de Bréboeuf endured like a rock, insensible to fire and flames, which astonished all the blood-thirsty wretches who tormented him. His zeal was so great that he preached continually to these infidels, to try to convert them. His executioners were enraged against him for constantly speaking to them of God and of their conversions. To prevent him from speaking more, they cut off his tongue, and both his upper and lower lips. After that, they set themselves to strip the flesh from his legs, thighs and arms, to the very bone; and then put it to roast before his eyes, in order to eat it.

While they tormented him in this manner, those wretches derided him, saying, "Thou seest plainly that we treat thee as a friend, since we shall be the cause of thy Eternal happiness; thank us, then, for these good offices which we render thee, —for, the more thou shalt suffer, the more will thy God reward thee."

Those butchers, seeing that the good Father began to grow weak, made him sit down on the ground; and one of them, taking a knife, cut off the skin covering his skull. Another one of those barbarians, seeing that the good Father would soon die, made an opening in the upper part of his chest, and tore out his heart, which he roasted and ate. Others came to drink his blood, still warm, which they drank with both hands,—saying that Father de Bréboeuf had been very courageous to endure so much pain as they had given him, and that, by drinking his blood, they would become courageous like him.

This is what we learned of the Martyrdom and blessed death of Father Jean de Bréboeuf, by several Christian savages worthy of belief, who had been constantly present from the time the good Father was taken until his death. These good Christians were prisoners to the Iroquois, who were taking them into their country to be put to death. But our good God granted them the favor of enabling them to escape by the way; and they came to us to recount all that I have set down in writing.

Father de Bréboeuf was captured on the 16th day of March, in the morning, with Father Lalemant, in the year 1649. Father de Bréboeuf died the same day as his capture, about 4 o'clock in the afternoon. Those barbarians threw the remains of his body into the fire; but the fat which still remained on his body extinguished the fire, and he was not consumed.

I do not doubt that all I have just related is true, and I would seal it with my blood; for I have seen the same treatment given to Iroquois prisoners whom the huron savages had taken in war, with the exception of the boiling water, which I have not seen poured on any one.

I am about to describe to you truly what I saw of the Martyrdom and of the Blessed Deaths of Father Jean de Bréboeuf and of Father Gabriel L'alemant. On the next morning, when we had assurance of the departure of the enemy, we went to the spot to seek for the remains of their bodies, to the place where their lives had been taken. We found them both, but a little apart from each other. They were brought to our cabin, and laid uncovered upon the bark of trees,—where I examined them at leisure, for more than two hours, to see if what the savages had told us of their martyrdom and death were true. I examined first the Body of Father de Bréboeuf, which was pitiful to see, as well as that of Father L'alemant. Father de Bréboeuf had his legs, thighs and arms stripped of flesh to the very bone; I saw and touched a large number of great blisters, which he had on several places on his body, from the boiling water which these barbarians had poured over him in mockery of Holy Baptism. I saw and touched the wound from a belt of bark, full of pitch and resin, which roasted his whole body. I saw and touched the marks of burns from the Collar of hatchets placed on his shoulders and stomach. I saw and touched his two lips, which they had cut off because he spoke constantly of God while they made him suffer.

I saw and touched all parts of his body, which had received more than two hundred blows from a stick: I saw and touched the top of his scalped head: I saw and touched the opening which these barbarians had made to tear out his heart.

In fine, I saw and touched all the wounds of his body, as the savages had told and declared to us: we buried these precious Relics on Sunday, the 21st day of March, 1649, with much Consolation.

I had the happiness of carrying them to the grave, and of burying them with those of Father Gabriel l'alemant. When we left the country of the hurons, we raised both bodies out of the ground, and set them to boil in strong lye. All the bones were well-scraped and the care of drying them was given to me. I put them every day into a little oven which we had, made of clay, after having heated it slightly, and when in a state to be packed, they were separately enveloped in silk stuff. Then they were put into two small chests, and we brought them to Quebec, where they are held in great veneration.[1]

It is not a Doctor of the Sorbonne who has composed this, as you may easily see; it is a relic from the Iroquois, and a person who has lived more than thought,—who is, and shall ever be,

Sir,
Your Very Humble and very obedient servant,
CHRISTOPHE REGNAUT

[*Ibid.*, xxxiv., *Doc.* lxix.]

[1] *See* p. 98, *note.*

VI

OF THE REMOVAL OF THE HOUSE OF SAINTE MARIE TO THE ISLAND OF ST. JOSEPH: OF THE CAPTURE AND DEVASTATION OF THE MISSION OF SAINT JEAN, BY THE IROQUOIS, AND OF THE DEATH OF FATHER CHARLES GARNIER AND OF FATHER NOËL CHABANEL, WHO WERE MISSIONARIES THERE

(From the Relation of 1649-1650)

By Father Paul Ragueneau

In consequence of the bloody victories obtained by the Iroquois over our Hurons at the commencement of the spring of last year, 1649, and of the more than inhuman acts of barbarity practiced toward their prisoners of war, and the cruel torments pitilessly inflicted on Father Jean de Brébeuf and Father Gabriel Lallemant,—terror having fallen upon the neighboring villages,—all the inhabitants dispersed. These poor, distressed people forsook their lands, houses, and villages, in order to escape the cruelty of an enemy whom they feared more than a thousand deaths. Many, no longer expecting humanity from man, flung themselves into the deepest recesses of the forest, where, though it were with wild beasts, they might find peace. Others took refuge upon some frightful rocks that lay in the midst of a great Lake nearly four hundred leagues in circumference,—choosing rather to find death in the waters, or from the cliffs, than by the fires of the Iroquois. A goodly number having cast in their lot

with the people of the Neutral Nation, and with those living
on the Mountain heights, whom we call the Tobacco Nation,
the most prominent of those who remained invited us to join
them, rather than to flee so far away.

This was exactly what God was requiring of us,—that, in
times of dire distress, we should flee with the fleeing, accompanying them everywhere; that we should lose sight of
none of these Christians, although it might be expedient to
detain the bulk of our forces wherever the main body of
fugitives might decide to settle down.

We told off certain of our Fathers, to make some itinerant
Missions,—some, in a small bark canoe, for voyaging along
the coasts, and visiting the more distant islands of the great
Lake, at sixty, eighty, and a hundred leagues from us; others
to journey by land, making their way through forest-depths
and scaling the summits of mountains.

But on each of us lay the necessity of bidding farewell to
that old home of sainte Marie,—to its structures, which, though
plain, seemed, in the eyes of our poor Savages, master-works
of art; and to its cultivated lands, which were promising us an
abundant harvest.

It was between five and six o'clock, on the evening of the
fourteenth of June, that a part of our number embarked in a
small vessel we had built. I, in company, with most of the
others, trusted myself to some logs, fifty or sixty feet in
length, which we had felled in the woods, and dragged into
the water, binding all together, in order to fashion for ourselves a sort of raft that should float on that faithless element. We voyaged all night upon our great Lake, by dint
of arms and oars; and we landed without mishap, after a
few days, upon an island, where the Hurons were awaiting
us, and which was the spot we had fixed upon for a general
reunion, that we might make of it a Christian island.

The Hurons who were awaiting us on that Island, called
the Island of Saint Joseph,[1] had sown there their Indian corn;
but the Summer drouths had been so excessive that they lost

[1] Now Charity Island, in Lake Huron.

hope of their harvest, unless Heaven should afford them some favoring showers. On our arrival they besought us to obtain this favor for them; and our prayers were granted that very day.

These grand forests, which, since the Creation of the world, had not been felled by the hand of any man, received us as guests; while the ground furnished to us, without digging, the stone and cement we needed for fortifying ourselves against our enemies. In consequence, thank God, we found ourselves very well protected, having built a small fort according to military rules, which, therefore, could be easily defended, and would fear neither the fire, the undermining, nor the escalade of the Iroquois.

Moreover, we set to work to fortify the village of the Hurons, which was adjacent to our abode. We erected for them bastions, which defended its approaches,—intending to put at their disposal the strength, the arms, and the courage of our Frenchmen.

The War had already made its ravages, not only in the devastation which occurred in the preceding Winter, but in the number of massacres which happened all through the Summer, on the mainland in the vicinity of this Island. But that nothing might be lacking in the miseries of an afflicted people, all the days and nights of Winter were but nights of horror, passed in constant fear and expectation of a hostile party of Iroquois, of whom tidings had been received; these (it was said) were to come to us to sweep this Island, and to exterminate, with us, the remnants of a nation drawing to its end.

In the Mountains, the people of which we name the Tobacco Nation, we have had, for some years past, two missions; in each were two of our Fathers. The one nearest to the enemy was that which bore the name of Saint Jean; its principal village, called by the same name, contained about five or six hundred families. It was a field watered by the sweat of one of the most excellent Missionaries who had dwelt in these regions, Father Charles Garnier,—who was also to water it with his blood, since there both he and his flock have met death, he himself leading them even unto Paradise.

The day approaching in which God would make a Church triumphant of that which, up to that time, had always been in warfare, and which could bear the name of a Church truly suffering, we received intelligence of it, toward the close of the month of November, from two Christian Hurons, escaped from a band of about three hundred Iroquois, who told us that the enemy was still irresolute as to what measures he would take,—whether against the Tobacco Nation, or against the island on which we were. Thereupon, we kept ourselves in a state of defence, and detained our Hurons, who had purposed taking the field to meet that enemy.

At the same time we caused the tidings to be speedily conveyed to the people of the Tobacco Nation, who received it with joy, regarding that hostile band as already conquered, and as occasion for their triumph. They resolutely awaited them for some days; then, wearying because victory was so slowly coming to them, they desired to go to meet it,—at least, the inhabitants of the village of St. Jean, men of enterprise and valor. They hastened their attack, fearing lest the Iroquois should escape them, and desiring to surprise the latter while they were still on the road. They set out on the fifth day of the month of December, directing their route toward the place where the enemy was expected. But the latter, having taken a roundabout way, was not met; and, to crown our misfortune, the enemy, as they approached the village, seized upon a man and woman who had just come out of it. They learned from these two captives the condition of the place, and ascertained that it was destitute of the better part of its people. Losing no time, they quickened their pace that they might lay waste everything, opportunity so greatly favoring them.

It was on the seventh day of the month of last December, in the year 1649, toward three o'clock in the afternoon, that this band of Iroquois appeared at the gates of the village, spreading immediate dismay, and striking terror into all those

poor people,—bereft of their strength and finding themselves
vanquished; when they thought to be themselves the conquerors. Some took to flight; others were slain on the spot.
To many, the flames, which were already consuming some of
their cabins, gave the first intelligence of the disaster. Many
were taken prisoners, but the victorious enemy, fearing the
return of the warriors who had gone to meet them, hastened
their retreat so precipitately, that they put to death all the old
men and children, and all whom they deemed unable to keep
up with them in their flight.

It was a scene of incredible cruelty. The enemy snatched
from a Mother her infants, that they might be thrown into
the fire; other children beheld their Mothers beaten to death
at their feet, or groaning in the flames,—permission, in either
case, being denied them to show the least compassion. It was
a crime to shed a tear, these barbarians demanding that their
prisoners should go into captivity as if they were marching
to their triumph. A poor Christian Mother, who wept for
the death of her infant, was killed on the spot, because she
still loved, and could not stifle soon enough her Natural
feelings.

Father Charles Garnier was, at that time, the only one of our
Fathers in that mission. When the enemy appeared, he was
just then occupied with instructing the people in the cabins he
was visiting. At the noise of the alarm, he went out, going
straight to the Church, where he found some Christians. "We
are dead men, my brothers," he said to them. "Pray to God,
and flee by whatever way you may be able to escape. Bear
about with you your faith through what of life remains; and
may death find you with God in mind." He gave them his
blessing, then left hurriedly, to go to the help of souls. A
prey to despair, not one dreamed of defense. Several found
a favorable exit for their flight; they implored the Father
to flee with them, but the bonds of Charity restrained him.
All unmindful of himself, he thought only of the salvation
of his neighbor. Borne on by his zeal, he hastened every-

where,—either to give absolution to the Christians whom he met, or to seek, in the burning cabins, the children, the sick, or the catechumens, over whom, in the midst of the flames, he poured the waters of Holy Baptism, his own heart burning with no other fire than the love of God.

It was while thus engaged in holy work that he was encountered by the death which he had looked in the face without fearing it, or receding from it a single step. A bullet from a musket struck him, penetrating a little below the breast; another, from the same volley, tore open his stomach, lodging in the thigh, and bringing him to the ground. His courage, however, was unabated. The barbarian who had fired the shot stripped him of his cassock, and left him weltering in his blood, to pursue the other fugitives.

This good Father, a very short time after, was seen to clasp his hands, offering some prayer; then, looking about him, he perceived at a distance of ten or twelve paces, a poor dying Man,—who, like himself, had received the stroke of death, but had still some remains of life. Love of God, and zeal for Souls, were even stronger than death. Murmuring a few words of prayer, he struggled to his knees, and, rising with difficulty, dragged himself as best he might toward the sufferer, in order to assist him in dying well. He had made but three or four steps, when he fell again, somewhat heavily. Raising himself for the second time, he got, once more, upon his knees and strove to continue on his way; but his body, drained of its blood, which was flowing in abundance from his wounds, had not the strength of his courage. For the third time he fell, having proceeded but five or six steps. Further than this we have not been able to ascertain what he accomplished,—the good Christian woman who faithfully related all this to us having seen no more of him, being herself overtaken by an Iroquois, who struck her on the head with a war-hatchet, felling her upon the spot, though she afterward escaped. The Father, shortly after, received from a hatchet two blows upon the temples, one on either side, which penetrated to the brain. His body was stripped and left, entirely naked, where it lay.

Two of our Fathers, who were in the nearest neighboring mission, received a remnant of these poor fugitive Christians, who arrived all out of breath, many of them all covered with their own blood. The night was one of continual alarm, owing to the fear, which had seized all, of a similar misfortune. Toward the break of day, it was ascertained from certain spies that the enemy had retired. The two Fathers at once set out, that they might themselves look upon a spectacle most sad indeed, but nevertheless acceptable to God. They found only dead bodies heaped together, and the remains of poor Christians,—some who were almost consumed in the pitiable remains of the still burning village; others deluged with their own blood; and a few who yet showed some signs of life, but were all covered with wounds,—looking only for death, and blessing God in their wretchedness. At length, in the midst of that desolated village, they descried the body they had come to seek; but so little cognizable was it, being completely covered with its blood, and the ashes of the fire, that they passed it by. Some Christian savages, however, recognised their Father; who had died for love of them. They buried him in the same spot on which their Church had stood, although there no longer remained any vestige of it, the fire having consumed all.

The poverty of that burial was sublime, and its sanctity no less so. The two good Fathers divested themselves of part of their apparel, to cover therewith the dead; they could do no more, unless it were to return entirely unclothed.

It was truly a rich treasure to deposit in so desolate a spot, the body of so noble a servant of God; but that great God will surely find a way to reunite us all in Heaven, since it is for his sake alone that we are thus scattered, both during life and after death.

Dread lest the enemy, having made but a show of departure, might retrace his steps, constrained all that escort of love to set out again that same day, and, without losing time, to return, as speedily as possible, to the place whence they had departed,—without food or drink; by roads difficult of passage; and at a most fatiguing season, as the snow had already covered the ground.

Two days after the taking and burning of the village, its inhabitants returned,—who, having discovered the change of plan which had led the enemy to take another route, had had their suspicions of the misfortune that had happened. But now they beheld it with their own eyes; and at the sight of the ashes, and the dead bodies of their relatives, their wives, and their children, they maintained for half the day a profound silence,—seated, after the manner of savages, upon the ground, without lifting their eyes, or uttering even a sigh, —like marble statues, without speech, without sight, and without motion. For it is thus that the Savages mourn,—at least the men and the warriors,—tears, cries and lamentations befitting, so they say, the women.

Father Charles Garnier was born in Paris, in the year 1605, and entered our Society in 1624; he was thus but little over 44 years of age on the 7th of December, 1649,—the day on which he died in labors which were truly Apostolic, and in which he had lived since the year 1636, when he left France and went up to the country of the Hurons.

From his infancy, he entertained the most tender sentiments of piety, and, in particular, a filial love toward the most holy Virgin, whom he called his Mother. "It is she," he would say, "who has carried me in her arms all through my youth, and who has placed me in the Society of her Son." He had made a vow to uphold, until death, her Immaculate Conception. He died on the eve of that august Festival, that he might go to solemnize it yet more gloriously in Heaven.

From the time of his Novitiate, he seemed an Angel, his humility being so uncommon that he was held before all others as a mirror of sanctity. He had experienced the greatest difficulties in obtaining permission from his father to enter our Society; but these were very much enhanced when, ten years after that first separation, it became necessary to reconcile that father to a second, of a still more painful kind. This was his departure from France, to go into these Missions at the end of the world,—our Superiors having expressed their wish that his Father should yield consent to this, on account of the peculiar obligations which our Society was under to him. It required a whole year to contend with all the struggles of nature in the mind of his good father, who could not hear of so cruel a separation. He employed therein friends, tears, prayers, and continual mortifications. At length, he succeeded in obtaining this great boon from Heaven, and with so much joy in his heart, that he looked upon that day as the happiest of his entire life.

As soon as he came among the Hurons, we had in him an indefatigable worker, replete with every gift of Nature, and of Grace that could make an accomplished Missionary. He had mastered the language of the Savages so thoroughly that they themselves were astonished at him. He worked his way so far into their hearts, and with such a power of eloquence, as to carry them away with him. His face, his eyes,—even his laugh, and every movement of his body,—preached sanctity. His heart spoke yet louder than his words, and made itself heard, even in his silence.

His mortification was equal to his love. He sought it day and night; always lay upon the bare ground, and bore constantly upon his body some portion of that Cross which during life he held most dear, and on which it was his desire to die. Every time that he returned from his Mission rounds, he never failed to sharpen freshly the iron points of a girdle all covered with spur-rowels, which he wore next to his skin. In addition to this, he would very often use a discipline of wire, armed, besides, with sharpened points. His daily fare differed in no way from that of the Savages,—that is to say, it was the scantiest that a miserable beggar would expect in France. During that last year of famine, acorns and bitter roots were, to him, delicacies,—not that he was insensible to their bitterness, but that love gave a relish to them. And yet he had ever been the cherished child of a rich and noble house, and the object of all a Father's endearments,—brought up, from the cradle, on other foods than those of Swine. But so far was he from regarding himself as wretched in this great surrender of everything, where he was; or from wishing to say, in the words of the Prodigal son, *Quanti mercenarii in domo Patris mei abundant panibus, ego autem hîc fame pereo,* that, on the contrary, he esteemed himself happy in suffering all things for God.

In his latest letters, addressed to me three days before his death, in response to a request which I made to him touching the state of his health,—asking if it would not be right that he should quit for a time his Mission, in order to come once more to see us, and recruit a little his strength,—he answered me by urging, at great length, many reasons which disposed him to remain at his Mission, but reasons which gathered their force only from the spirit of charity and truly Apostolic zeal with which he was filled.

"It is true," he added, "that I suffer something in regard to hunger, but that is not to death; and, thank God, my body and my spirit keep up in all their vigor. I am not alarmed on that side; but what I should fear more would be that, in leaving my flock in the time of their calamities, and in the terrors of war,—in a time when they need me more than ever,—I would fail to see the opportunities which God gives me of losing myself for him, and so render myself unworthy of his favors. I take only too much care of myself," added he, "and if I saw that my powers were failing me, I should not fail, since your Reverence bids me, to come to you; for I am at all times ready to leave everything, to die, in the spirit of obedience, where God wills; but otherwise, I will never come down from the Cross on which his goodness has placed me."

These great aspirations after sanctity had grown with him from his infancy. For myself, having known him for more than twelve years,—in which he opened to me all his heart, as he did to God himself,—I can truly say that, in all those years, I do not think that, save in sleep, he has spent a single hour without those burning and vehement desires of progressing more and more in the ways of God, and of helping forward in them his fellow creatures. Outside of these considerations, nothing in the world affected him,—neither relatives, nor friends, nor rest, nor consolation, nor hardships, nor fatigues. God was his all; and, apart from Him, all else was to him as nothing.

During the prevalence of contagious diseases,—when they shut on us everywhere the doors of the cabins, and talked of nothing but massacring us,—not only did he go unswervingly, where he felt there was a soul to gain for Paradise; but, by an excess of zeal, and an ingenuity born of Charity, he found means of opening all the ways that had been closed against him, and of breaking down, sometimes forcibly, all that opposed his progress.

His strongest inclination was to aid the most depraved, however repulsive the disposition that any one might possess, however vile and insolent he might be. He felt for all alike, with the bowels of a Mother,—not omitting any act of corporal Mercy which he could perform for the salvation of souls. He has been seen to dress ulcers so loathsome, and which emitted a stench so offensive, that the Savages, and even the nearest relatives of the sick man, were unable to endure them. He alone would handle these, wiping off the pus and cleansing the wound, every day, for two or three months together, with an eye and a countenance that betokened only charity,—though he often saw very clearly that the wounds were incurable. "But," said he, "the more deadly they are, the stronger inclination have I to undertake the care of them,—that I may lead these poor people even to the gate of Paradise, and keep them from falling into sin at a time which is for them the most perilous in life."

He tied himself neither to his work nor to persons, to places nor employments; but, regarding equally in everything the will of God, wherever he might be; whatever occupation obedience might appoint to him, from that very moment he betook himself to it with courage and constancy, and as a man who had no other thought in the world save that of finding God where, at the time, it was willed that he should seek him. Often was he called upon to leave the care of Missions, where his whole heart lay, to till the ground; to harness himself to some conveyance and drag it over the snows, like a horse at the plough; to care for the sick; to take charge of the cooking; or to go up and down in the forest in quest of some wild grapes, achieving ten or twelve leagues in finding his load,—to procure from it, after protracted labors, scarcely as much wine as would be needed for the celebration of a few Masses during the remainder of the year. In everything, he was indifferent to himself; and, to look at him, one would think that he had no inclination save for that which one saw him doing, and that that was the real occupation to which God had called him. "We shall do nothing," he used to say, "for the salvation of souls if God do not take sides with us. When it is he who sets us apart to this, by the direction of obedience, he binds himself to aid us in it; and with him assisting us, we shall accomplish that which he expects of us. But when it happens that we set our hearts on any particular employment, be it the holiest on earth, God does not bind himself to second our efforts, but leaves us to ourselves; and, of ourselves, what can we accomplish save a nothing, or the sin which lowers us beneath a nothing?"

There yet remains a little word addressed by him, from the Island of saint Joseph, to his two brothers,—that is, the Reverend Father Henry de St. Joseph, of the Order of the Carmelites, and the Reverend Father Joseph, of Paris, a Capuchin. That letter discloses to us the temper of his heart, and the presentiment he had of his death. "This little word," he wrote, "is to encourage us, all three, to hasten on in the love of our holy Master; for I can hardly think that some one of us three may not be very near the close of his career. Let us redouble then our zeal, hasten our steps, redouble our prayers, each for the others, and make a new protestation that he whom our Lord shall first of us three call to himself shall intercede for the two who remain,—to obtain for them, from Our Lord, his holy love, a perfect union with him, and the grace of final perseverance. I make then, the first, this protestation: and I fervently beseech Our Lord that he will possess our three hearts, and make them one with his own, both now and in eternity." This was the manner of speech of a Saint, who loved his brothers as a Saint, and as Saints.

OF THE DEATH OF FATHER NOËL CHABANEL

Here is the sixth victim whom God has taken to himself from those of our Society whom he has called to this mission of the Hurons,—there having been, as yet, not one of us who has died there without shedding his blood, and consummating the sacrifice in its entirety.

Father Noël Chabanel was the Missionary companion of Father Charles Garnier; and when the village of saint Jean was taken by the Iroquois, there were but two days in which they were separated, in accordance with the orders which they had received,—our Fathers and I having thought it wiser not to keep two Missionaries exposed to danger; considering, besides, that the famine in that quarter was so severe that sufficient food for both could not be obtained. But it was not God's will that, having lived and been yoked together in the same Mission, they should be separated in death.

This good Father, then, returning whither obedience recalled him, had passed through the mission of saint Matthias, where were two others of our Fathers, and had left them on the morning of the seventh day of December. Having travelled six leagues over a most difficult road, he found himself overtaken by night in the thick of the forest, being in the company of seven or eight Christian Hurons. His men were resting, and asleep; he only was watching and in prayer. Toward midnight, he heard a noise, accompanied with cries,— partly of a victorious force who occupied that road; partly, also, of captives, taken that very day in the village of saint Jean, who were singing, as was their custom, their war-song.

On hearing the noise, the Father awoke his men, who fled at once into the forest, and eventually saved themselves,— scattering, some here, some there; and taking their route toward the very place from which the enemy had come out, though a little at one side of it.

These Christians, escaped from the peril, arrived at the Tobacco Nation, and reported that the Father had gone some little way with them, intending to follow them; but that, becoming exhausted, he had fallen on his knees, saying to them, "It matters not that I die; this life is a very small consideration; of the blessedness of Paradise, the Iroquois can never rob me."

At daybreak, the Father, having altered his route, desirous of coming to the Island where we were, found himself checked at the bank of a river, which crossed his path. A Huron reported the circumstance, adding that he had passed him, in his canoe, on this side of the stream; and that, to render his flight more easy, the Father had disburdened himself of his hat, and of a bag that contained his writings; also of a blanket, which our Missionaries use as robe and cloak, as mattress and cushion, for a bed, and for every other convenience,—even for a dwelling place, when in the open country, and when they have, for a time, no other shelter. Since then, we have been unable to learn any other news of the Father.

Of the manner of his death we are uncertain,—whether he may have fallen into the hands of the enemies, who actually slew on the same road some thirty persons; or that, having missed his way in the forest, he may have died there, partly from hunger, partly from cold, at the foot of some tree at which weakness obliged him to halt. But, after all, it seems to us most probable that he was murdered by that Huron,— once a Christian, but since an Apostate,—the last to see him, and who, to enjoy the possessions of the Father, would have killed him, and thrown his body into the River. Had we been inclined to pursue this matter further, I feel sure that we would have discovered proofs sufficient to convict this murderer; but, in such general misery, we judged it wiser to smother our suspicions; and we closed our own eyes to what we were well pleased was not evident. It is enough for us that God's purposes should have been served.

Father Noël Chabanel had come to us from the Province of Toulouse, in the year 1643, having been received into our society as early as the year 1630; when he was only seventeen years of age. God had given him a strong vocation for these countries; but, once here, he had much to contend with; for, even after three, four, and five years of effort to learn the language of the Savages, he found his progress so slight, that hardly could he make himself understood even in the most ordinary matters: This was no little mortification to a man who burned with desire for the conversion of the Savages, who, in other ways was deficient neither in memory nor mind, and who had made this manifest enough by having for some years successfully taught Rhetoric in France.

In consequence of this, the temper of his mind was so opposed to the ways and manners of the Savages, that he saw in them scarce anything that pleased him; the sight of them, their talk, and all that concerned them, he found irksome. He could not accustom himself to the food of the Country; and residence in the Missions did such violence to his entire nature that he encountered therein extraordinary hardships, without any consolation,—at least of the character that we call sensible. There, one must always sleep on the bare ground, and live from morning to night in a little hell of smoke; in a place where often, of a morning, one finds himself covered with the snows that drift on all sides into the cabins of the Savages; where vermin abound; where the senses, each and all, are tormented both night and day. One has never anything but water to quench his thirst; while the best food usually eaten there is only a paste made with meal of Indian corn boiled in water. One must work there incessantly, though always so poorly nourished; never have one moment in the day in which to retire to any spot that is not public; have no other room, no other apartment, no other

closet, in which to prosecute his studies. One has not even
any other light than that of a smoky fire,—surrounded at the
same time, by ten or fifteen persons, and children of all ages,
who scream, weep, and wrangle; who are busied about their
cooking, their meals, their work, about everything, in a word,
that is done in a house.

When God, besides all this, withdraws his sensible graces,
and hides himself from a person who longs only for him,—
when he leaves him a prey to sorrow, to disgusts, and repug-
nances of Nature,—these are trials that are not within the
compass of ordinary virtue; and the love of God must be
strong in a heart, if it is not to be stifled by them. Join to
these the continual sight of dangers, in which one finds himself
at every moment, of attack by a savage Enemy who often
will subject you to the sufferings of a thousand deaths, ere
death itself ensues; who uses only fire, and flames, and un-
heard of cruelties. Doubtless a courage is needed worthy
of the children of God, if one is not to lose heart in the midst
of such abandonment.

It has been in this abandonment that God has willed to
put to the test, for five or six years, the fidelity of this good
Father; but assuredly the Devil never having got the better
of him upon that account, although he represented to him
every day that, by returning to France, he would find there
the joy, the repose, and comfort which during all his past
life he had received; that there he would not lack employment better suited to his disposition, employment in which
so many Saintly souls nobly practice the virtue of Charity
in a zeal for Souls, and expend their lives for the salvation
of their fellow-men. Never, for all that, would he break
away from the Cross on which God had placed him; never
did he ask that he might come down from it. On the contrary, in order to bind himself to it more inviolably, he obliged
himself, by a vow, to remain there till death, so that he might
die upon the Cross. These are the terms of the vow, as he
conceived it, and its very words.

Domine Jesu Christe, qui me Apostolorum Sanctorum hujus vineae Huronicae adjutorem, licet indignissimum, admirabili dispositione tuae paternae Providentiae voluisti: Ego, Natalis Chabanel, impulsus desiderio serviendi Spiritui tuo sancto, in promovendâ barbarorum Huroniae, ad tuam fidem conversione; Voveo, coram sanctissimo Sacramento pretiosi Corporis et Sanguinis tui, Tabernaculo Dei cum hominibus, perpetuam stabilitatem in hac Missione Huronicâ: omnia intelligendo juxta Societatis, et Superiorum ejus interpretationem, et dispositionem. Obsecro te igitur, suscipe me in servum hujus Missionis perpetuum, et dignum effice tam excelso ministerio, Amen. Vigesimâ die Junii, 1647.

"*Jesus Christ, my Savior, who by a wonderful dispensation of your Paternal Providence have willed that I, although altogether unworthy, should be a Coadjutor of the Holy Apostles in this vineyard of the Hurons; impelled by the desire of ministering to the purpose which your holy Spirit hath respecting me, that I should help forward the conversion to the faith of the barbarians of this Huron country: I, Noël Chabanel,—being in the presence of the most holy Sacrament of your Body and your precious Blood, which is the tabernacle of God among men,—make a vow of perpetual stability in this Mission of the Hurons; understanding all things as the Superiors of the Society expound them, and as they choose to dispose of me. I conjure you, therefore, O my Savior, to be pleased to receive me as a perpetual servant of this Mission, and to make me worthy of so lofty a ministry. Amen.*"

He made this vow on the feast of Corpus Christi, in the year 1647; and although, since that time, these rebellions of Nature have constantly tasked his virtue, grace has always been the mistress; and God has granted him the perseverance he so ardently desired.

The last time that he parted from us, to go to the Mission where he died,—embracing and bidding the last farewell to that one of our Fathers who was charged with the direction of his soul,—he said to him, "My dear Father, may it be for good and all, this time, that I give myself to God; and may I belong to him." But he uttered these words with so strong an emphasis, and a countenance so bent upon true sanctity, as sensibly to affect the Father to whom he was speaking; and who, chancing at that very hour to meet one of his friends, could not refrain from saying to him: "Verily, I have just been deeply moved! That good Father has but now spoken to me with the look and voice of a victim who immolates himself. I know not what God wills, but I see that he is fashioning a great Saint."

In truth, God was preparing him for the sacrifice, and affording him some kind of presentiment of it. He had said to one of his friends: "I do not know what is working within me, or what God wills to do with me; but in one respect I feel entirely changed. I am naturally very timorous; but, now that I am going to a most dangerous post, and, as it seems to me, death is not very far away, I no longer feel any fear. This frame of mind springs not from myself."

When he set out from the Mission of saint Matthias, on the very day of his death, he said, speaking to the Father, who was embracing him: "I am going whither obedience calls me; but whether I shall succeed or not in obtaining from the Superior that he send me back to the Mission that was allotted to me, God must be served until death."

We shall see in the following letter,—which he wrote to the Reverend Father Pierre Chabanel, his brother Religious of our Society,—his appreciation of suffering.

"Judging from human appearances," said he, "Your Reverence has been very near to possessing a brother a Martyr; but alas; in the mind of God, to merit the honor of Martyrdom, a virtue of another stamp than mine is needed. The

Reverend Father Gabriel Lallemant, one of the three whom our Relation mentions as having suffered for Jesus Christ, had taken, for a month before his death, my place in the village of saint Louys,—while I, as being more robust of body, was sent upon a Mission more remote and more laborious, but not so fruitful in Palms and Crowns as that of which my cowardice has, in the sight of God, rendered me unworthy. It will be when it shall please the divine Goodness, provided that I strive to realize, in my person, *Martyrem in umbrâ et Martyrium sine sanguine.* The ravages of the Iroquois throughout this country will perhaps, some day, supply what is wanting, through the merits of those many Saints with whom I have the consolation of leading so peaceful an existence in the midst of such turmoil and continual danger to life. The Relation will dispense me from adding anything at present, as I have neither paper nor leisure, save so much as are needed to entreat Your Reverence, and all our Fathers of your Province, to remember me at the holy Altar as a victim doomed, it may be, to the fires of the Iroquois. *Ut merear tot Sanctorum patrocinio victoriam in tam forti certamine.*"

These are his words, worthy of a man who was only awaiting the moment of the sacrifice.

[*Ibid.*, xxxv., *Doc.* lxxiv.]

VII

RELATION OF WHAT OCCURRED IN THE MISSION OF THE FATHERS OF THE SOCIETY OF JESUS, IN THE COUNTRY OF NEW FRANCE, FROM THE SUMMER OF THE YEAR 1653 TO THE SUMMER OF THE YEAR 1654

By François Le Mercier

MY REVEREND FATHER:

Pax Christi.

I have waited until this day, the twenty-first of the month of September, before taking my pen in hand to inform Your Reverence of the condition in which we are,—having been unable to do so sooner, because we did not know it ourselves. Our minds have been so divided during the past year that, to tell the truth, we have enjoyed Peace while thinking we were at war. Therein God has blessed our administration; and from the plots of treachery entertained by the Iroquois, our enemies, he has derived their welfare and ours. Such are the hopes given us in this matter by the fortunate results of a journey which one of our Fathers has recently made to that country. It was Father Simon le Moine,[1] who was sent thither in the beginning of July, and left us in suspense until his return, a few days ago, at which we were filled with a joy that was all the greater as we had reason to fear that he had been cruelly burnt,—which fate has already befallen several of our Fathers at the hands of these wretches. But God guided all the Father's steps in the heart of the Iroquois Nation. He found there a captive Church, composed of our old time Hurons. He converted a great Iroquois Captain, the Chief of eighteen hundred men, whom he was leading

[1] *See p. 138, note.*

244

to a new war. Finally the Father received presents from the most important nation; it is centrally situated among the other Iroquois nations, who are inviting us to go and instruct them. We gave them our word that next Spring we would go and dwell there, building a house like the one we used to have among the Hurons before the war had driven us thence.

The enterprise of establishing a Mission next Spring in the heart of the Iroquois Nation obliges us to ask Your Reverence for the aid of six of our Fathers, for we are too few. Monsieur de Lauson, our Governor, intends to send thither a number of picked Frenchmen for starting a new settlement; while we shall send some of our Fathers and some workmen to build the first Church there in honor of the most Blessed Virgin. The expense will be excessive; but as it is an affair of God more than ours, his Providence will provide for it. Even if we should be obliged to set out, as we often did in our Huron missions, with only a staff in hand, and only our trust in God for maintenance, Our Fathers are all resolved to make the attempt. There will be a great deal to do, and much more to suffer, and everything to fear; for we have to deal with Barbarous Nations, who breathe only blood and have drunk that of the Martyrs.

JOURNEY OF FATHER SIMON LE MOINE TO THE COUNTRY OF THE IROQUOIS, IN JULY, AUGUST, AND SEPTEMBER

On the second days of the month of July (1654), Father Simon le Moine set out from Quebec on his journey to the Onnontaehronnon Iroquois. Passing by three Rivers, he proceeded thence to Montreal, where a young man of stout heart and long a resident here, very piously joined him. For greater ease I will follow the Father's journal.

"On the 17th of July, St. Alexis's day, we set out from home with that great saint of many travels, toward a land unknown to us.

"On the 18th, following constantly the course of the River saint Lawrence, we encounter nothing but breakers and impetuous floods thickly strewn with rocks and shoals.

"The 19th. The River continues to increase in width and forms a lake, pleasant to the sight, and eight or ten leagues in length. In the evening, a swarm of troublesome mosquitoes gave us warning of rain, which drenched us all night long. It is a pleasure, sweet and innocent beyond conception, to have, under these conditions, no shelter but the trees planted by nature since the creation of the world.

"The 20th. We saw nothing but islands, of the most beautiful appearance in the world, intercepting here and there the course of this very peaceful river. The land toward the North appears to us excellent. Toward the rising sun is a chain of high mountains which we named after saint Margaret.

"The 21st. The islands continue. Toward evening we break our bark canoe. It rains all night, and the bare rocks serve us as bed, mattress and everything else. He who has God with him, rests calmly anywhere.

"The 22nd. The rapids, which for a time are not navigable, compel us to shoulder our little baggage and the canoe that bore us. On the other side of the rapids I caught sight of a herd of wild cows proceeding in a very calm and leisurely manner. Sometimes there are seen four or five hundred of them together in these regions.

"On the 23rd and 24th of the month, our pilot having injured himself, we were forced to halt, becoming a prey to the mosquitoes, and to wait patiently—a task often more difficult than facing death itself, because of the annoyances from which, day or night, there is no respite.

"The 25th. The river is becoming so extremely rapid that we are compelled to leap into the water and drag our canoe after us among the rocks, like a horseman who alights and leads his horse by the bridle. In the evening we arrive at the mouth of lake saint Ignace, where eels abound in prodigious numbers.

"The 26th. A high wind, accompanied by rain, forces us

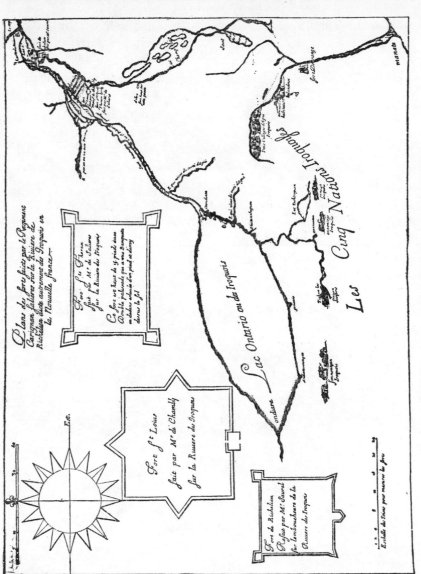

THE IROQUOIS COUNTRY, AND PLANS OF FORTS ON RIVER RICHELIEU.

[From the "Relation" of 1664-65.]

to land, after proceeding four leagues. A cabin is soon made; bark is stripped from neighboring trees and thrown over poles planted in the ground on either side, and made to meet in the form of an arbor; and there you have your house complete. Ambition gains no entrance to this palace, and it is every whit as acceptable to us as if its roof were of gold.

"The 27th. We coast along the shores of the lake, everywhere confronted by towering rocks, now appalling, and now pleasing to the eye. It is wonderful how large trees can find root among so many rocks.

"The 28th. Nothing but thunder and lightning and a deluge of rain, forcing us to seek the shelter of our canoe, which, turned bottom upward over our heads, serves us as a house.

"On the 29th and 30th of July, the wind-storm continues, and checks our progress at the mouth of a great lake called Ontario; we call it the lake of the Iroquois, because they have their villages on its southern side. The Hurons are on the other side, farther inland. This lake is twenty leagues in width, and about forty in length.

"On the 31st, the day of saint Ignatius, we are obliged by the rain and wind to penetrate through pathless wastes,— crossing long islands, and shouldering our baggage, our provisions, and the canoe. This road seems long to a poor man who is thoroughly fatigued.

"On the first day of the month of August, some Iroquois fishermen, perceiving us from a distance, come trooping up to receive us. One of them hastens forward, running half a league to be the first to tell us the news, and inform us of the condition of the country. He is a Huron captive and a good Christian, whom I formerly instructed during a winter that I spent with the Savages. This poor lad could not believe that I was his pastor, whom he had never hoped to see again. We land at a little fishing village, and there is zealous strife as to who shall carry all our baggage. But alas! I find almost none but Huron women, Christians for the most part,—formerly rich and enjoying their ease; but now reduced to servitude by their captivity. They ask me to pray to God, and I have the consolation of confessing there at my leisure our former host of the tobacco Nation, Hostagehtak. His feelings and his devotion bring tears to my eyes. He is a fruit of the labors of Father Charles Garnier, that holy Missionary whose death was so precious in the sight of God.

"The second day of August. We walk about twelve or fifteen leagues through the woods, and camp where night overtakes us.

"On the 3rd, toward noon, we found ourselves on the banks of a river, a hundred or a hundred and twenty paces in width, on the other side of which there was a fishing hamlet. An Iroquois, to whom I had formerly shown some kindness at Montreal, took me across in his canoe; and then, as a mark of honor, carried me on his shoulders, not allowing me to set foot in the water. All received me with joy, and these poor people enriched me with their poverty. I was escorted to another village, a league distant, where a young man of importance entertained me at a feast because I bear his Father's name, 'Ondessonk.' The Captains, each in his turn, came and made us their speeches. I baptized some little skeletons who, perhaps, were only waiting for this drop of the precious blood of Jesus Christ.

"The 4th. They ask me why we are dressed in black, and I take occasion to speak to them concerning our mysteries; they listen very attentively. A little dying child is brought to me, and I name it Dominique. The time is now past when these little innocents are hidden from our sight. I was regarded as a great medicine-man, although I had, as my sole remedy, only a bit of sugar to give to those feeble creatures. We pursue our journey, finding our dinner awaiting us midway. The nephew of the first Captain of the country is to lodge me in his cabin, being sent by his uncle to escort us, and bringing us all that the season could furnish them in the way of the choicest delicacies,—above all, some bread made of fresh Indian corn; and some ears, which we roasted in the fire. On this day we again sleep at the sign of the beautiful star.

"The 5th. We had four leagues to cover before arriving at the chief village, Onnontagué. The roads are full of people going and coming, who are out to greet me. One calls me a brother, another an uncle, another a cousin; never have I had so many kinsfolk. At a quarter of a league from the village, I began a harangue which brought me into high favor: I called by name all the Captains, families, and persons of importance—speaking slowly, and in the tone of a Captain. I told them that Peace was attending my course, that I was dispelling war in the more distant nations, and that joy was accompanying me. Two Captains made me their harangue upon my entrance, but with a joy and a light in their countenances that I had never seen in savages. Men, women, and children—all showed me respect and love.

"At night I caused the chiefs to assemble in order to give them two presents. The purpose of the first was to wipe their faces, so that they might look on me with favor, and that I might never see any sign of sadness on their brow. The second was to remove any gall still remaining in their hearts. After several more exchanges of courtesy, they withdrew to consult together; and at length responded to my presents with two others, richer than mine.

"On the 6th, I received calls from different quarters to administer my medicine to some little weak emaciated children, and I baptized some of them. I heard the confessions of some of our old Huron Christians, and found that God is everywhere, and that he is pleased to work in person in hearts where the faith has held sway. He builds himself a temple there, where he is worshipped in spirit and in truth— for which may he be forever blessed.

"In the evening our host drew me aside and said to me, with a great show of affection, that he had always loved us; and that at last his heart was content, as he saw that all the troops of his nation asked only for Peace. He added that the Sonnontoehronons had come, a short time before, to exhort them to take some wise action in this matter on the side of Peace, making some fine presents for this purpose; that the Onioenhronnons had brought three collars, with the same object in view; that the Anniehronnons would doubtless follow the others; and that therefore I was to be of good cheer; since I bore with me the welfare of all the land.

"On the 7th, a good Christian woman, Terese by name, a Huron captive, wishing to pour out her heart to me away from all noise and in quiet, invited me to go and see her in an outlying cabin where she dwelt. This good Christian had with her a young captive of the Neutral Nation, between fifteen and sixteen years old, whom she loved as her own daughter. She had instructed her so well in the mysteries of the faith that I was utterly surprised. 'Well, my sister,' I said to her, 'why hast thou not baptized her, since she has as strong a faith as thou thyself, and since she wishes to die a Christian?' 'Alas! my brother,' that captive made answer, 'I did not think it was permitted me to baptize except in danger of death. Baptize her now thyself since thou dost deem her worthy, and give her my name.' That was the first baptism of a grown person performed at Onnontagué, for which we are indebted to the Piety of a Huron woman. When God prepares a soul, the consummation of its salvation is soon accomplished.

"Almost at the same time I was summoned to a sick man who was reduced to a skeleton,—an ulcer, caused by an ill-dressed gunshot wound, eating away his flesh. But the words of heaven found no entrance to that heart, all swelled up as it was with pride.

"The 8th. I baptize three little dying children. Some come and confess. I inquire after all our old acquaintances in order to learn their fortunes. I had orders to ascertain what had become of a young Huron woman, a Christian, named Caterine Skouatenhré, whom we used to call 'the Nun'; Her sister told me she had died while praying to God, never having forgotten him in the whole course of her illness, which had been long.

"On the 9th, toward noon, there comes a direful report of the murder of three of their hunters at the hands of the cat

Nation, a day's journey from here. That means that a war is kindled in that direction.

"On the tenth day of August, the envoys from the three neighboring Nations having arrived, after the customary summons of the captains, to the effect that all should assemble in Ondessonk's cabin, I opened the proceedings with a public prayer, which I offered on my knees and in a loud voice, using the Huron tongue throughout. I appealed to the great master of heaven and earth, that he might inspire us to act for his glory and our own good; I cursed all the Demons of hell, since they are spirits of discord; and I prayed the guardian Angels of the entire country to speak to the hearts of my hearers, when my words should strike their ears.

"I astonished them greatly when they heard me name them all by Nations, bands, and families, and each person individually who was of some little consequence—all by the help of my written list, which was to them a thing full of both charm and novelty. I told them that in my speech I had nineteen words to lay before them.

"First, I said that Onnontio—Monsieur de Lauson, Governor of New France—was speaking through my mouth, and in his person the Hurons and the Algonquins, as well as the French, since all three Nations had Onnontio for their great Captain. A large Porcelain collar, a hundred little tubes or pipes of red glass, which constitute the diamonds of the country, and a moose-skin, somewhat worn,—these three presents accompanied one word only.

"My second was to cut the bonds of the eight captives from Sonnontouan, who had been taken by our Allies, and brought to Montreal.

"The third was to break also the bonds of those members of the Wolf Nation who had been captured at the same time.

"The fourth, to thank the people of Onnontagué for bringing back our captive to us.

"The fifth present was to thank the people of Sonnontouan for rescuing him from his position on the scaffold.

"The sixth was for the Onioenhronon Iroquois, because they too had helped in this.

"The seventh, for the Onneiochronnons, in return for breaking the bonds that had held him captive.

"The purpose of the eighth, ninth, tenth, and eleventh presents was to give to each of these four Iroquois Nations a hatchet, to be used in the New war in which they were engaged with the Cat Nation.

"The twelfth present was intended to renew the courage of the Sonnontoehronnons, who had lost some of their number in this war.

"The thirteenth was to strengthen their palisade,—that is, enable them to maintain a strong defense against the enemy.

"The fourteenth, to paint their faces; for it is the custom of the warriors here never to go into battle without having their faces painted,—some with black, some with red, and some with various other colors,—each having in this matter his own style of livery, so to speak, which he retains through life.

"The fifteenth, to harmonise all their thoughts, for which purpose alone I made three presents,—a porcelain collar, some little glass Tubes, and a moose-skin.

"With the sixteenth, I opened Annonchiassé's door to all the Nations,—thus indicating that they would be welcome in our cabin.

"With the seventeenth, I exhorted them to become instructed in the truths of our faith, making three presents to accompany this word.

"With the eighteenth, I asked them to lay no more ambuscades in future for the Algonquins and Huron Nations when they should wish to visit us in our French settlements. I made three gifts with this request.

"Finally, with the nineteenth present, I wiped away the tears of all the young warriors, caused by the death of their great Captain Annenneraes, who had been taken captive by the Cat Nation not long before.

"At each of my presents they uttered a loud shout of applause from the depths of their chests, in evidence of their delight. I was occupied fully two hours in delivering my entire harangue, which I pronounced in the tone of a Captain,—walking back and forth, as is their custom, like an actor on a stage.

"After that they gathered together by Nations and bands, calling to them an Anniehronnon who by good luck happened to be present. They consulted together for more than two hours longer, when they at length called me back and gave me a seat of honor among them.

"That one of the Captains who is the tongue of the Country and acts as its orator, repeated faithfully the substance of all that I had said. Then they all began to sing to express their joy; and told me that I might, for my part, pray to God, which I did very willingly.

"After these songs, he addressed me in the name of his nation. 1. He thanked Onnontio for the good will he entertained toward them, in token whereof he produced two large Porcelain collars.

"2. In the name of Anniehronnon Iroquois, he thanked us for causing the lives of five of their allies, of the Wolf Nation, to be spared,—therewith, two more collars.

"3. In the name of the Sonnontoehronnon Iroquois, he thanked us for rescuing from the flames five of their people, and this with two more collars. Each present was followed by applause from the whole assembly.

"Another Captain, of the Nation of the Onneiocronnons, arose. 'Onnontio,' said he, addressing Monsieur de Lauson, our absent Governor, 'Onnontio, thou art the support of the earth; thy spirit is a spirit of Peace, and thy words soften the most rebellious hearts.' After other praises, which he uttered in a tone animated with affection and respect, he displayed four large collars, with which to thank Onnontio for encouraging them to make a spirited fight against their new enemies of the cat Nation, and for exhorting them never to wage war again with the French. 'Thy voice, Onnontio,' said he, 'is wonderful, for it produces in my heart, at the same

time, two wholly opposite emotions. Thou givest me courage
to fight, and thou softenest my heart with thoughts of peace.
Thou are both peaceable and yet very warlike—beneficent to
those thou lovest, and terrible to thy enemies. We all wish
thee to love us, and we shall love the French for thy sake.'

"To conclude these thanksgivings, the Onnontaerrhonnon
Captain took the word. 'Listen, Ondessonk,' he said to me:
'Five whole Nations address thee through my mouth; I have
in my heart the sentiments of all the Iroquois Nations, and
my tongue is faithful to my heart. Thou shalt tell Onnontio
four things, which are the gist of all our deliberations in
Council.

" '1. It is our wish to acknowledge him of whom thou has
told us, who is the master of our lives, and who is unknown
to us.

" '2. The May-tree for all matters of concern to us is
to-day planted at Onnontagué.' He meant that that would be
thenceforth the scene of the assemblies and parleys relating
to the Peace.

" '3. We conjure you to choose a site that will be advantageous to yourselves, on the shores of our great lake, in order
to build thereon a French settlement. Place yourselves in
the heart of the country, since you are to possess our hearts.
Thither we will go to receive instruction, and thence you will
be able to spread out in all directions. Show us Paternal care,
and we will render you filial obedience.

" '4. We are involved in new wars, wherein Onnontio
gives us courage; but for him we shall have only thoughts
of Peace.'

"They had reserved their richest presents to accompany
these last four words; but I am sure that their countenances
spoke more eloquently than their tongues, and joy was de-
picted on their faces, with so much kindness that my heart
was deeply moved.

"On the eleventh day of August, there was nothing but
feasting and rejoicing on every hand. At night, however, a
disaster befell us: a cabin having caught fire,—we know not

how,—a furious wind carried the flames to the others; and in less than two hours more than twenty of them were reduced to ashes, while the rest of the village was in danger of destruction. Nevertheless, God maintained the spirits of all in the joy of the preceding day, and kept their hearts as calm toward me as if this misfortune had not occurred.

"The 12th. Our captive Christian woman, wishing to confess before my departure, gave me some occupation, or, rather, the rest that I was desiring. I baptised a little girl of four years who was dying: I recovered from the hands of one of these barbarians the new testament of the late Father Jean de Brébeuf, whom they cruelly put to death five years ago, and another little book of devotion that had been used by the late Father Charles Garnier, whom these very people killed four years ago. These two Fathers were at their Missions when that blessed death overtook them, as a reward for the labors of many years, which they had spent in holy service in all these regions. As for myself, who had been a witness to the sanctity of their lives and the glory of their deaths, I shall all my life attach greater value to these two little books, their beloved relics, than if I had found some mine of gold or silver.

"The 13th. In regard to the conflagration that had occurred, in order to follow the custom of friends on such occasions, I convoked the council, and gave the people two presents to console them. Accordingly, in the name of Achiendassé (that is the name of the superior general of all the Missions of our Society in these regions), I began by planting for them the first stake for a new cabin; this corresponds to our french custom of laying the foundation-stone of a new building. The purpose of my second present was to throw down the first piece of bark that was to cover the cabin. This mark of affection gratified them; and three of their Captains thanked me for it publicly in speeches, that one would not believe could emanate from the intellect of those whom we call savages.

"The 14th. A young Captain, chief of a levy of eighteen hundred men who were to set out as soon as possible to prosecute the war against the cat Nation, begged me urgently for baptism. For several days I had been giving him instruction, and, as I wished to make him prize this mark of grace by deferring it until some future journey, he said to me, 'How now, my brother? If from this day forth I possess the Faith, cannot I be a Christian? Hast thou power over death to forbid its attacking me without orders from thee? Will our enemies' arrows become blunted for my sake? Dost thou wish me, at each step that I take in battle, to fear hell more than death? Unless thou baptize me, I shall be without courage, and shall not dare to face the conflict. Baptize me, for I am determined to obey thee; and I give thee my word that I will live and die a Christian.'

"The 15th. Early in the morning, I lead my Catechumen aside, and, seeing his heart piously inclined toward baptism, give him the name of my dear travelling companion, Jean Baptiste. He embraces me, pours out his heart to me in love, and solemnly declares that Jesus shall be his only hope and his all.

"Meanwhile the others seek for me everywhere, that I may give the Farewell feast; all the people of importance, both men and women, are invited into our cabin, in my name, according to the custom of the country, to honor my departure.

"We take our leave well attended, after the public proclamations of the Captains as to who shall carry our little baggage.

"Half a league from there, we meet a number of elders, all members of the council, who are waiting for me in order to bid me Farewell, in the hope that I shall return; and they evince an ardent desire to see this hope fulfilled.

"The 16th. We arrive at the entrance to a little lake in a great basin that is half dried up, and taste the water from a spring of which these people dare not drink, as they say there is an evil spirit in it that renders it foul. Upon tasting of it, I find it to be a spring of salt water; and indeed we made some salt from it, as natural as that which comes from the sea, and are carrying a sample of it to Quebec. This lake is very rich in Salmon-trout and other fish.

"The 17th. We enter their river and, a quarter of a league from there, on the left, we come to that of Sonnontouan which swells the current of the former and leads, they say, to Onioen and to Sonnontouan in two days' journey. Proceeding three leagues from that point, by a very easy route, we leave on the right hand the River Oneiout, which appears very deep to us. Finally, a good league further down, we come to a shoal which gives its name to a fishing village. There I find some of our Christian Hurons of both sexes, whom I have not yet seen; I hear their confessions, with much satisfaction on both sides.

"The 18th. While my boatmen were repairing their canoes, one of those good women had me baptize her child, two years of age, in order that, as she said, he might go to heaven to join his little sister, who had been baptized on a previous occasion, and had been slain by these people. I baptized another little innocent who was gasping in death.

"The 19th. We push forward down the same River, which is of a fine width and deep throughout, with the exception of some shoals where we must step into the water and drag the canoe after us, lest the rocks break it.

"The 20th. We arrive at the great lake Ontario, called the lake of the Iroquois.

"The 21st. This lake is in violent commotion, owing to the furious winds that followed a rainstorm.

"The 22nd. Coasting quietly along the shores of this great lake, my boatmen shoot at and kill a large Stag. My companion and I content ourselves with looking at them while they broil their steaks, it being Saturday, a day of abstinence for us.

"The 23rd. We arrive at the spot which is to become our dwelling place and the site of a French settlement. There are beautiful prairies here and good fishing; it is a resort for all Nations.[1] I find some new Christians who confess.

[1] The route followed by Le Moyne on his return may be roughly indicated thus. Starting from their village, a little S. E. of Manlius, the party probably followed the main trail, leading to the Senecas, as far west as the Onondaga River. Descending this stream to Onondaga Lake, which is but an expansion of

"On the 24th and 25th we were detained by the wind. On the 26th, our boatmen having embarked before the storm had subsided, one of our canoes sprang a leak, and narrowly escaped drowning; but at last we took refuge on an island, where we dried ourselves at our leisure.

"The 27th. Toward evening, a slight calm gives us time to regain the mainland:

"The 28th and 29th. Hunting detains my boatmen, who are in the best humor in the world; for flesh is the Paradise of a man of flesh.

"On the 30th and on the last day of the month of August, the rain and wind greatly annoy poor travelers who, after toiling during the day, are badly used all night.

"September the first. I never saw so many deer: but we had no desire to hunt them, though my companion killed three almost in spite of himself. What a pity! for we left all the venison there, except some of the more delicate portions, and the skins.

"On the second of the month, while proceeding across vast prairies, we see in different places herds of wild cattle; their horns resemble in many respects the antlers of a stag.

"The 3rd and 4th. Our success in the chase does not abate, game and venison appearing to follow us everywhere. Herds of twenty cows leap into the water, almost as if to come and meet us, and our men, for sheer sport, kill some of them with their hatchets.

"The 5th. We cover in one day the same distance that we scarcely accomplished in two long days' journey on our way up, through rapids and breakers.

the river, they halted near one of the salt springs of that region, north of the present Syracuse. Continuing down this lake and stream, they reached the Seneca River, which from that point receives the name of Oswego River. Three leagues below the mouth of the Onondaga, they passed its junction with the Oneida; the fishing village where they soon after halted was probably near the present village of Phenix. Still descending the Oswego, they apparently followed it to its place of discharge into Lake Ontario,—coasting the eastern shore of which, they came (Aug. 23) to the "place assigned for our residence, and for a French settlement." This last location is not satisfactorily identified; it may have been either the mouth of the Salmon River, or Sachett's Harbor—both good landing-places, and points of strategic importance.—*Ibid.*, xli., *note* 6.

"The 6th. Our Sault St. Louis frightens my men. They put me ashore four leagues above the settlement of Montreal, and God gives me strength enough to reach that place before noon and to celebrate Holy Mass, of which I have been deprived during my entire journey.

"The 7th. I pass on, and go down toward three Rivers, whither my boatmen wish to go.

"We arrived at Quebec only on the eleventh day of the month of September of this year, 1654."

[*Ibid.*, xli., *Doc.* lxxxvi.]

VIII

*RELATION OF WHAT OCCURRED IN THE MIS-
SION OF THE FATHERS OF THE SOCIETY
OF JESUS, IN THE COUNTRY OF NEW
FRANCE, IN THE YEARS 1655 AND 1656*

[The *Relation* of 1655-56 is written by Jean de
Quen, in the absence of his superior (Le Mercier) at
the Onondaga mission recently begun by the Jesuits.
This enterprise is fully described in the journal of
Father Dablon, who, with Chaumonot, began the mis-
sion in the preceding autumn. A prefatory note by
De Quen outlines the chief events of the year. The
Relation proper begins with an account of Le Moyne's
second voyage to the Mohawk country (August to No-
vember, 1655). Soon after Le Moyne's departure, an
Onondaga deputation, "representing all the upper Iroquois Nations," arrives at Quebec to confirm the peace.
They ask for a French colony in their country and for
Christian teachers. After careful consideration it is decided to send back Dablon and Chaumonot with these
envoys.—*Ibid.* xlii., 9.]

My Reverend Father:
   Pax Christi:
   As the weeks are composed of both days and nights; the
Seasons of heat and cold, of rain and shine; so also we may
say our year has been but a mingling of joys and sorrows, of
successes and failures.
   For twenty years past, vessels have not reached this country so early, or in greater number. Five or six at a time were
seen anchored in the roadstead at Kebec,—and that at the
beginning of June,—to our own delight and that of the en-

tire country. But, not finding in the vessels a single one of our Fathers come to help us in the conquest of souls, we were very keenly disappointed.

In the month of September of last year, 1655, two of our Fathers went up to the country of the Onontaeronon Iroquois, to start a new Mission among people who, after killing, slaughtering, burning, and eating us, came to solicit our services. During the entire Winter, we were apprehensive of the failure of this enterprise; but last Spring the return of one of the two Fathers, accompanied by several Iroquois Captains, changed this fear into some confidence, which led us to hope for success in the undertaking.

This hope was notably increased by the zeal and courage exhibited by four of our Fathers, two of our Brethren, and fifty young Frenchmen, who went to lay the foundations of a new Church in a place where the Evil One and cruelty have reigned, perhaps ever since the Deluge. The Onontaeronon Iroquois, who had come to visit us, exulted with joy on seeing us favor their purpose; and their delight, as shown in word and look, overflowed into our own hearts. But this joyous mood soon became clouded by the massacre or capture of seventy-one Christian Hurons, killed or seized by the Agneronon Iroquois on the Island of Orleans, two leagues from Kebec. Ours was a mingled portion of good and ill, of joy and sorrow.

Toward the end of August, we perceived fifty canoes and two hundred and fifty Savages approaching, laden with treasures of the country. They were coming to trade with the French, and to ask for Fathers of our Society to go and teach them in their dense Forests, five hundred leagues distant from Kebec. In the face of so pleasant a day, we forgot all the unpleasant nights of the past. Two of our Fathers and one of our Brethren embarked with thirty Frenchmen; but the Agneronons—whom we call the lower Iroquois, and who have never consented to make peace with our Allies—cut the thread of our hopes in a moment by attacking these unfortunate people, on their return, and killing one of the two Fathers who were going to preach the Gospel to them in their country.

You see plainly with what truth we can say that the days of this past year have been *boni et mali*—"good and evil," like the days of Job. Yet, let us say rather, that they have all been good, since they have been filled with Crosses. We are not startled at the sight of our own blood. Our small number causes us grief and sadness; we cry for help and succor; and we believe that Your Reverence will hear our appeal, and that you will send us, by the next ship, six valiant Fathers, men of courage, who are not afraid to face a thousand deaths, which danger must every day be undergone in seeking Barbarians in the lairs of their vast forests.

JOURNEY OF FATHER SIMON LE MOYNE TO THE AGNIERONNON IROQUOIS

In the summer of last year, 1655, it was thought necessary to send a Father of our society into the country of the Agnieronnon Iroquois, in order that we might by this show of friendship and confidence, confirm the peace with them. The lot having fortunately fallen upon Father Simon le Moyne, he left Montreal on this errand, on the seventeenth day of August, with twelve Iroquois and two Frenchmen.

At the time when Father Simon le Moyne was sent to the Agieronnon Iroquois—who are nearer Montreal than Kebec, and who, while making Peace with us, have never desisted from their hostile designs on the Algonquins and Hurons,— the Onontaeronnon Iroquois, who are more distant, came on an embassy representing all the upper Iroquois Nations, to confirm the Peace, not only with the French but also with the Algonquins and the Hurons.

The delegation consisted of eighteen men, who came to Kebec by way of Montreal and three Rivers, to see Monsieur de Lauson, governor of the country and also the Algonquin and Huron Savages living there.

A great group assembled on the date fixed for the council,—Sunday the twelfth of September, 1655, at noon. In the midst of this assembly the chief Ambassador, who acted as spokesman, displayed twenty-four collars of porcelain—the pearls and diamonds of this country, in the Savages' eyes. A response in kind to all these presents would have been necessary, had we not purposed sending to their country two of our Fathers to enlist their more cordial support, and to spare no effort in promoting so important an enterprise. This blessed lot fell on Fathers Joseph Chaumont[1] and Claude Dablon,[2] of whom the former knows the language and commands the sympathies of the Savages; while the latter has recently come from France, with heart and soul bent on this Mission. Our minds had been greatly divided regarding the propriety of exposing our Fathers to this new risk before the return of Father Simon le Moyne, who was still in the hands of the

[1] Pierre Joseph Marie Chaumonet was born March 9, 1611, in a village of Burgundy, France. While a lad, he wandered into Italy, and finally, at the age of twenty-one, resolved to enter the Jesuit order at Rome. In 1639 he was assigned to the Canadian mission, and immediately went to the Huron country. When the Hurons were dispersed by the Iroquois (1649) . . . he followed his disciples in their flight to Isle St. Joseph (now Charity Island), Lake Huron. Finding this retreat no longer safe from their enemies, the Hurons, in the March following, were established on the isle of Orleans by the Jesuits, on an estate purchased by them from Eléenore de Grandmaison. This colony was under Chaumonet's care. In September, 1655, Chaumonet went with Dablen to the Onondaga mission, and labored among the Iroquois tribes during the next three years. Returning to Quebec, he again took charge of his Huron colony,—remaining in this post thirty-five years longer. In the autumn of 1692, he was compelled to give up his charge, by a lingering illness which finally ended his life, Feb. 21, 1695.—*Ibid.*, xviii., *note* 1.

[2] Claude Dablon was born at Dieppe, Jan. 21, 1619. He entered the Jesuit novitiate Sept. 17, 1639; his studies were pursued at Paris, La Flèche, and Eu. Joining the Canadian missions in 1655, he was immediately sent with Chaumonot to Onondaga, where he labored until the abandonment of the French settlement there (March, 1658). He remained at Quebec until May, 1661, when he went with Druillettes on a mission to the Cree tribes about Hudson Bay; at the end of a year they returned to Canada. Dablon apparently remained in the St. Lawrence settlements until the summer of 1668, when he went with Marquette to minister to the Algonkin tribes about Lake Superior. While engaged in these labors, Dablon was appointed (1670) superior of all the Canadian missions, and rector of the College of Quebec; but he could not reach the St. Lawrence until the following year. He died at Quebec in 1697.

Dablon, as superior, edited the *Relations* of 1671 and 1672, and compiled others covering the period of 1673-79; he also edited the papers of the explorer Marquette.—*Ibid.*, xli., *note* 13.

Agnieronnon Iroquois. For nothing would have been more in accord with the disposition of those Nations,—treacherous as they are, and having such an advantage over us in the possession of men whom they well knew to be dear and precious to us,—than to fall upon us and our Hurons and Algonquins, when we were no longer fearing them and when thoughts of Peace had, in most minds, displaced hostile distrust. Nevertheless, Monsieur our Governor was of the opinion that we must risk all for the sake of winning all, and it was to be feared that, if we allowed this opportunity to pass by, our course would cause a rupture of the Peace, as showing too evident distrust on our part. His council agreed with him; the Fathers, likewise, upon whom this blessed lot had fallen, doubted not that it was their duty to depart upon this mission, since they were undertaking it for the glory of God and for the salvation of souls whose Angels were calling us to their aid, and in whose behalf the charity of Jesus Christ must solicit our help.

Finally, on the nineteenth of September, our Fathers and these Ambassadors left us. I cannot more faithfully set forth the successive events of their journey, and the fruits which God has reaped therefrom, than by giving the journal sent us by Father Dablon.

JOURNEY OF FATHERS JOSEPH CHAUMONT AND CLAUDE DABLON TO ONONTAGUE, A COUNTRY OF THE UPPER IROQUOIS

The people named Agneronnons are called the Iroquois of the lowlands, or the Lower Iroquois; while we speak of the Onontaeronons, and other Nations near these, as the Iroquois of the highlands, or the Upper Iroquois, because they are situated nearer the source of the great Saint Lawrence river and inhabit a country full of mountains. Onontaé—or as other pronounce it, Onontagué—is the chief town of the Onontaeronons; and thither our course was directed.

Having, then, left Kebec on the 19th of September, 1655,

and Montreal on the 7th of October, we ascended the Saint Louys rapids.

On the 9th, we crossed the Lake named after Saint Louys, and situated in the very middle of the bed of the Saint Lawrence river. This great stream forms lakes in some places, by expanding its waters over flats and shallows, and then gathering them together again into its channel.

On the 13th, we made small progress, because our provisions failing, our hunters and fishers went to seek their living and ours in the woods and streams.

The 14th. Both fishing and hunting failing, our provisions being very short, and our appetite sharpened by hunger, we devoured a wild cow, or species of hind,—these animals having horns like the stag's, and not like those of our European bull. That poor animal had drowned, and her flesh smelled very badly: but appetite is an excellent cook, who although he flavored this dish with neither salt, pepper, nor cloves, yet made us relish it highly.

The 15th. God made us pass from scarcity to abundance by giving our hunters eight bears. Straightway, we saw almost all our men turned butchers and cooks, while all around us was to be seen nothing but meat, fat and skins.

Early on the 24th, we reached Lake Ontario, at the entrance to which five stags were killed, toward evening. Nothing further was needed to arrest our company's progress. It is pleasant to see the herds of cows or deer swimming from isle to isle. Our hunters cut them off, on their return to the mainland, and lined the entire shore with them, leading them to death whithersoever they chose.

Toward 9 o'clock on the morning of the 29th, we arrived at Otihatangué, where we were offered the kettle of welcome, and all crowded around to see us eat. This was our first lodging in the country of the Onontaeronnons, who received us with profuse demonstrations of friendship. A score of Hurons, who were here fishing, showed their joy at seeing Father Chaumonot, some throwing themselves upon his neck, others inviting him to a feast, and still others sending him presents.

On the 30th, we left the water, and prepared for our trip overland to Onontagué. In the afternoon, there appeared 60 Oneoutchoueronon Warriors, on their way to fight the so called Neds perces, beyond the rapids. They were led by Atondato- chan, the same who came to Montreal in the second Embassy sent by the village of Oneout. He is a man of fine appear- ance, and an eloquent speaker. He begged us to stay here one day longer, that he might learn our errand.

These Warriors, having all assembled on the 31st, Father Chaumonot, after the ceremonies customary on such occasions, addressed Atondatochan; he said, first, that he congratulated himself and thanked God at seeing that great man, whose voice had rung out so loud at Montreal that it was still to be heard there, so great was its strength. In the second place, he said he was led to visit that country in order to secure the fulfill- ment of his promise, to speak from that time but the same language, to have but one Sun, and one heart,—in short, to be thenceforth brothers. These two clauses were received with the customary applause, and the faces of all showed how much they enjoyed this speech. In the third place, as the report had spread hither that peace had been concluded between the French and Annieronons without including the Algonquins and Hurons, the Father added that he had come to negotiate a genuine peace between all parties. And, in the fourth place, he presented 1500 porcelain beads, in order to solicit kind treat- ment for the two Frenchmen who were among those whom they were going to fight. He also prayed the maker of all things to watch over Atondatochan's expedition. We had de- termined to make him a considerable present to induce him to stop his soldiers; but learned privately that we would cer- tainly have been refused, because of their keen resentment at the loss of some of their number, which they are bent on revenging at any cost.

After the Father had spoken for half an hour, the Chief began the song of response; and all commenced to sing; in wondrous harmony; in a manner somewhat resembling our plain-chant.

The first song said that it would take all the rest of the day to thank the Father for so good a speech as he had made them.

The second was to congratulate him upon his journey and his arrival.

They sang a third time to light him a fire, that he might take possession of it.

The fourth song made us all relatives and brothers; the fifth hurled the hatchet into the deepest abyss, in order that peace might reign in all these countries; and the sixth was designed to make the French masters of the river Ontiahantagué. At this point the Captain invited the Salmon, brill, and other fish, to leap into our nets, and to fill that river for our service only. He told them that they should consider themselves fortunate to end their lives so honorably; named all the fishes of that river, down to the smallest, making a humorous address to each kind; and added a thousand things besides, which excited laughter.

The seventh song pleased us still more, its purpose being to open their hearts, and let us read their joy at our coming. At the close of their songs, they made us a present of two thousand porcelain beads.

Then the Father raised his voice, and told the Chief that his fine powers of speech would ever increase in volume; that, hitherto, they had resounded through all the confines of Lake Ontario, but, in future, they would speed across the greatest of all lakes, and be heard as thunder throughout France. At this the Captain and all his followers were extremely pleased. They then invited us to a feast which concluded the ceremonies.

We started overland for Onontagué on the 1st of November, meeting on the way a good Huron woman named Therese Oionhaton. This poor woman, upon learning of the Father's arrival, came from her home, three leagues distant, to wait for him as he passed. Her joy was great at seeing the black gowns once more before her death. The Father asked her whether the child whom she held in her arms were Baptized, and by whom. She replied that she herself had Baptized it, with these words: "Jesus, take pity on my child. I Baptize thee, little one, that thou mayest be blessed in Heaven." Thereupon the Father instructed her, Confessed her, and comforted her.

On the 5th of November, 1655, as we were continuing our journey, a Captain of note named Gonaterezon, came a good league to meet us. He made us halt, pleasantly congratulated us upon our arrival, put himself at the head of our Company, and gravely led us to a spot a quarter of a league from Onontagué, where the Elders of the country awaited us. When we had seated ourselves beside them, they offered us the best dishes they had, especially some Squashes cooked in embers. While we were eating, one of the elders, a Captain named Okonchiarennen, arose, imposed silence, and harangued us a good quarter of an hour. He said, among other things, that we were very welcome; our coming had been earnestly desired and long awaited; and, since the young men, who breathed only war, had themselves asked for and procured peace, it was for them, the Elders, to lay aside their arms and to ratify and embrace it in all sincerity, as they did. Courage, then, we were to take possession of our domains, and enter our new home with all assurance.

After the speaker had dilated upon this theme, and spoken in what seemed a rather affected manner, the Father made answer, that his speech was a very agreeable draught to us, and took away all the fatigue of our journey; that he came on Onnontio's behalf, to satisfy their demands; and that he doubted not that they would be content when they learned his errand. All the People listened with attention and admiration, delighted to hear a Frenchman speak their language so well.

Then he who had introduced us arose, gave the signal, and led us through a great crowd of people, some of whom were drawn up in rows to see us pass through their midst, while others ran after us, and still others offered us fruit, until we came to the village, the streets of which were carefully cleaned and the cabin-roofs crowded with children. At length, a large cabin which had been prepared for us received us, and also all the people it could hold.

Very late that evening, the Elders held a Council on our cabin, where one of them, after greeting us on behalf of the nation, made us two presents. One of these was 500 porcelain beads, to wipe our eyes, wet with tears shed over the murders committed in our country that year; and, as grief causes loss of voice, having, he said, clearly perceived our weakness of utterance upon our arrival, he added a second present of 500 beads, to strengthen our lungs, to remove the phlegm from our throats, and to make our voices clear, free and strong. The Father thanked them for their good will, saying that Onnontio and Achiendasé—the names of Monsieur the Governor and of the Father Superior of our Missions, respectively —had their eyes turned toward Onontagué, in order to see our condition from Kebec. He then presented to them 2000 beads, that they might open the door of the cabin where they had lodged us, in order that all the French might see the kind treatment we received, the beautiful mats upon which we reposed, and the pleasant faces greeting. They were delighted with this compliment.

On the 7th, Sunday, a secret Council of 15 Captains was held, to which he (the Father) was called. In this Assembly, they said to the Father: 1, That Agochiendagueté— who is, as it were, the King of this country—and Onnontio had voices of equal power and firmness, and that nothing could sever so suitable a tie, which held them in such close union. 2, That they would give some of their most active young men to conduct home the Huron Ambassadors who had come with us to treat of Peace. Thirdly, they begged that Onnontio might be informed that, even if some one of their own people should be ill-treated or even killed by the Annieronnons, yet that would not hinder the alliance; and they desired the same assurance on Onnotio's part, in case any ill befell the French from the same quarter. In the fourth place, as they had learned that the most acceptable thing they could do, in On-

natio's eyes, would be to inform him that Autumn that they
had erected a Chapel for the Believers, they said that, to please
him, they would take steps to that end at the earliest possible
moment.   In reply to this Clause, the Father took the word,
and told them that they had discovered how to win the heart
and the entire good will of Monsieur the Governor.   All gave
a shout of approval, with which the Council ended.

THE FATHERS TREAT WITH THESE PEOPLE

All the first day was spent, partly in feasting, partly in negotiating peace for the Algonquins; and, as this was the most
difficult matter, it demanded the most serious deliberation.
For that reason, the Father notified the Elders that he had a
private communication to make to them.   When they were
assembled, he addressed them to the following effect: 1. The
Huron question being closed, he said no more about it; but he
assured them that the Algonquins would send an Embassy
the next Spring, if they saw their minds inclined to peace.
2. When the Hurons should have planted their Villages near
us, the Algonquins also would wish to visit us.   In the third
place, in order to be fully assured of the Onnontaeronnons' desire for peace, the Algonquins hoped to see some of their captive nephews returned, since they themselves had so freely
released their prisoners, at the request of the Governor of
Montreal, and had sent them back with presents,—to which,
however, no response had ever been made.   In the fourth
place, if they wished the peace to be general, they must cease
to raise the hatchet against the Nation of the Nez percez.   The
answer was, that they would deliberate on these four points.

On the evening of the same day, some thirty Elders, who
had gathered in our cabin, invited the Father, as if by way
of diverting him, to tell them something entertaining.   For
a full hour the Father talked to them on St. Paul's Conversion,
with which they were so delighted that they begged him to
continue,—and, above all, to tell them something about the beginning of the world.   He did so; and he also preached on

the chief mysteries of our Religion, with such success that, at the close, one of the company began to pray in public to the maker of all things; while two others asked what they must do to become believers.

On the eleventh, while the Father was laboring to restore the ancient foundations of the Huron church, the others visited the salt Spring, four leagues distant and near the lake called Gannentae.[1] This is the site chosen for the French settlement, on account of its central position among the four Iroquois Nations, being accessible to them by canoe, over river and Lakes which make communication free and very easy.

THE FATHERS MAKE THEIR PRESENTS

On Monday, November 15th, between nine and ten o'clock in the morning,—after a little dying infant had been secretly sent to Paradise by the waters of Baptism,—all the elders and people assembled in a public place, in compliance with our request, as we wished to satisfy the general curiosity. We began, as on the preceding day, with public prayers. Then the Father adopted the people of Oiogoen as his children. After this, he displayed a large porcelain collar, saying that his mouth was Onnontio's, and the words he was about to utter were the words of the French, Hurons, and Algonquins, who all spoke through him.

The first present was intended to hush the cries heard everywhere by the Father, and to wipe away the tears that he saw coursing down their cheeks. But, since it did not suffice to wipe them away, and as he could not dry up this stream while the source was still running, he offered a second present to calm their minds, the seat of all these griefs; and, as the seat

---

[1] Gannentae was the Indian name of the place where the Jesuits established this first Onondaga mission. J. S. Clark thus describes the location (*Cayuga History*, p. 33, *note*): "It was then about twelve miles from the main village of the Onondagas (then south of the present Manlius). The 'Jesuits' Well' still exists, with its accompanying salt fountains, and may be found just north of the railroad bridge on lot 106. This was the first Catholic chapel erected in the present territory of the State of New York."—*Ibid.*, xli., *note* 16.

of the mind is in the head, he made them a crown of the prof-
fered collar, which he put on the head of each one successively.
At first, they were surprised at the novelty; they were pleased,
however, when they saw the Father holding a little Kettle, full
of excellent beverage, of which he made them all drink, as a
third present—in order to dispel their grief and apply the
remedy to their very hearts and bowels. This was accompanied
by a beautiful collar. And, in order to wipe away the blood,
and implant joy in every breast, leaving no trace of sadness
anywhere, the Father presented four Beaver-skins to the four
Iroquois Nations, one for each.

The 9th present affected them even more. He brought
forward a small tree, whose upper branches bore the names
of their deceased Captains, and were lopped off to signify their
death; but the tree had many other branches, strong and in
full leaf, representing their children, through whom these departed Heroes would be restored to life in the persons of their
descendants. This tree attracted much more attention than the
beads accompanying it.

The two following gifts were to assure them that Annenrai
and Tehaionhacoua, two famous Captains killed in war,—the
former of whom had taken an oath of fidelity before the
Governor of Montreal, and the latter had died invoking
Heaven,—to give assurance, I say, that these two brave men
were not dead, but continued as firmly united with the French
as the collars, presented in their name, were inseparably attached to each.

The eleventh present pleased them still more; for the
Father, drawing out his handkerchief, showed them therein,
on the one side the ashes of a certain Teotegouisen, buried at
three Rivers, and on the other those of the French; and, mix-
ing them together, he declared that the Iroquois and the
French were but one, both before and after death. He added
a second collar to the one accompanying these ashes, to restore
that man to life. Here the applause was very great, and they
were eager to see and hear what would follow. The most
beautiful collar of all was produced by the Father, when he

said that all he had thus far offered was but a lenitive and slight alleviation for their woes; He could not prevent them from being ill, or from dying, but he had a very sovereign remedy for all sort of afflictions. That was properly what brought him to their country, and they had given excellent proof of their good sense in going down to Kebec in quest of him. This great remedy was the Faith, which he came to proclaim to them, and which they would doubtless receive with a favor equal to their wisdom in asking for it. The Father then preached in what was really the Italian style, having a sufficient space for walking about and for proclaiming with pomp the word of God. After that, it can, I think, be said to have been announced to all the Peoples of those countries. Though he could have, as recompense for all these labors, only the consolation of having preached Jesus Christ before so fine an audience, he would have reason to be fully satisfied. At any rate his sermon was attentively followed, cries of approval being heard from time to time.

The addition of another present was necessary, to exonerate the Faith from the calumnies circulated against it by the devil's agents. In order to impress his meaning upon their minds, he showed them a fair sheet of white paper, symbolizing the integrity, innocence, and purity of the Faith; and another, all soiled and blackened, whereon were written the calumnies uttered against it. The latter sheet was torn and burnt according as these lies were answered or refuted. The Father proceeded with so much zeal and ardor, and with such torrent of forceable words, that all appeared very deeply moved.

As a relief to all this, there followed the present of the Ursuline Mothers of Kebec, who made a cordial offer to receive into their house the little girls of the country, for education in piety and in the fear of God. Then came the present of the Hospital Mothers who had quite recently built a large and splendid hospital, for the careful reception and charitable nursing of any sick of their Nation who might be at Kebec.

With the seventeenth present we asked that a chapel might

be erected as soon as possible, in which we might perform our functions with freedom and propriety; and with the eighteenth, that the supplies be provided necessary for us during our Winter's labors among them.

The four following were a pledge, that in the following Spring, some young Frenchmen would come, and they must then launch their canoes and go to receive them; and that these upon their arrival, would erect a palisade for the public defence. They were also advised to prepare at the same time the Mat for receiving the Algonquins and the Hurons who would follow the French. At this news, a shout, louder than usual, was given in expression of their sentiments.

To please the Onnontagueronnons, the next two presents were an invitation to the two other Nations to move their Villages nearer, in order the better to share the advantage of the vicinity of the French. We were obliged to add a present exhorting them to stay the Annieronnons' hatchet; and another to unite their minds, that henceforth they might be as one.

The first of the four following, which were offered in behalf of the Algonquins, was a pledge that the latter would send an Embassy the coming Spring; the second, that, when the French and Hurons should have become settled, the Algonquins would probably follow them; the third, that they would like to see again some of their captive nephews; while the fourth was to remind them of the presents given by the Ondataouaouats, upon delivering thirteen prisoners to the French of Montreal.

We felt obliged to make one more present, of considerable value, for a young Frenchman named Charles Garmant, who has been for some years among the Oneioutchronnons.[1] The Chief of that Nation was addressed by the Father, and told that he had too much sense not to see what course to pursue in the matter; that he, the Father, would not picture to him the pleasure he would afford Onnontio and all the French, by restoring their brother to them; that he saw well enough

---

[1] Charles Garman (Garemand) was captured by the Iroquois in June, 1653, at which time he was eight years old.—*Ibid.*, xlii., *note* 5.

what joy his relatives would feel at his return; and, therefore all that was left to his discretion.

With the present next to the last, the Father cleared his path for walking, with head erect, through all the Iroquois Villages, and gave them the like liberty to traverse the entire country of the French.

Finally, the last present was given in order to recapitulate all that had been said, and to impress it firmly on their minds, that their ears should never again open to any calumnies invented by the enemies of the public peace.

The Council closed with repeated applause on both sides, and a brief reply that on the following day a fuller response would be rendered.

It is past belief how the Father's speech and his engaging ways charmed these people. "Though he had spoken till evening," said some, "our ears would never have been full, and our hearts would still have been hungry for his words." Others added that the Dutch had neither sense nor tongues; they had never heard them mention Paradise or Hell; on the contrary, they were the first to incite them to wrong doing. The rest expressed themselves in some other way, but all were unanimous in saying in their own tongue, *Nunquan sic loquutus est homo*—which appears plainly in this issue; for the chief of the deputies from Oiogoen came to the Father, after the Council, to say that he wished to adopt him as his brother—a mark of great confidence with these Peoples.

In the afternoon, when the Father had retired to a neighboring wood, in order to say his prayers in quiet, four Iroquois women went in quest of him for the purpose of being instructed: and before evening, nine of them did the same, among whom was the sister of the chief of all the Captains.

REPLY TO THE FATHERS' PRESENTS

The sixteenth day was still more successful than those preceding, being appointed for receiving a reply to our presents; and this reply was as favorable as could be desired by the most zealous adherents of our Faith. They began their acknowledgements with six airs, or chants, which savored nothing of the Savage; and expressed very naively, by the variation of tones, the different passions which they sought to portray.

The first chant was composed of these words: *Oh, the beautiful land, the beautiful land, that the French are to occupy!* Agochiendaguesé, represented by an Elder, who continued just as if the chief himself were speaking, began alone; then all the rest repeated his exact words and tones, harmonizing remarkably well.

In the second chant, the Chief intoned the words, *Good news, very good news;* and the others repeated them in the same tone. Then he resumed; *In very truth, my brother, in very truth, we are speaking together; in very truth, we have a message from Heaven.*

The third chant had an ornament, in the form of a very musical refrain, and was as follows: *My brother, I salute thee; my brother, be welcome. Ai, ai, ai, hi. O the beautiful voice, O the beautiful voice that thou hast! Ai, ai, ai, hi. O the beautiful voice, O the beautiful voice, that I have! Ai, ai, ai, hi.*

The fourth chant had another ornament; the Musicians, namely, beat time by striking their feet, hands, and pipes against their mats. This they did in such perfect accord that the sound, so regular, blended with their voices and became a harmony pleasing to the ear. The words were as follows: *My brother, I salute thee; again I salute thee. In all sincerity, and without simulation, I accept the Heaven that thou has shown me; yes, I approve it, I accept it.*

The fifth time, they sang as follows: *Farewell, war; farewell hatchet! We have been fools till now, but in the future we will be brothers; yes, we will really be brothers.*

The final song was composed of these words: *Today the great peace is made. Farewell war; Farewell arms! For the affair is entirely beautiful. Thou upholdest our Cabins when thou comest among us.*

These songs were followed by four beautiful presents. With

the first, Agochiendaguesé, after a long speech testifying his gratitude that he and Onnontio were now but one, said that since the Hurons and Algonquins were Onnontio's children, they must be his also; he therefore adopted them by offering the first two presents, which he cast at the Father's feet.

The third and most beautiful of all the presents offered was a collar of seven thousand beads, which, however, was as nothing compared with his words. "It is the present of the Faith," said he; "it is to tell thee that I am really a Believer, and to exhort thee not to weary in teaching us. Continue to visit our Cabins, and have patience with our dullness in learning the Prayer. In a word, impress it well upon our minds and hearts."

Thereupon, wishing to make a striking display of his ardor, he took the Father by the hand, raised him and led him out before all the company, and threw himself on his neck in close embrace. Then, holding the beautiful collar in his hand, he made for him a belt with it,—declaring before heaven and earth his determination to embrace the Faith as he embraced the Father, and calling all the spectators to witness that this girdle, with which he encircled the Father so closely, symbolized his own future close union with the Believers. He protested and swore again and again that he was sincere in his words.

The Father made the hearers redouble their shouts of approval, as often as this chief promised to become a believer. Was not that a sight to draw tears from the eyes of the most hardened—to see the head of an infidel Nation making public profession of the Faith and all his people applauding his action? I pray all who shall read this to lift up their hearts to God in behalf of these poor Barbarians.

The fourth and last present was little in comparison with the preceding, its purpose being merely to inform the Father that the kettle of the war against the Cat Nation was over the fire; that hostilities would be opened toward Spring; and that the Huron Ambassadors would be dismissed the next day, with an escort of fifteen of the Country's leading men.

After this Captain had finished speaking, the Chief Deputy from Oiogoen arose and made a speech of thanks, of much wit and eloquence, which lasted a good half-hour. The pith of his polite address was, that he and all his Nation deemed themselves greatly obliged to Onnontio for the honor of adoption by him; that they would never become unworthy of that high distinction, or fail to do honor to so illustrious a connection; and that, furthermore, brilliant as it was, it did honor to Onnontio, since neither the speaker nor his people had even been adopted except by people of rank; yet that this adoption of them by Onnontio crowned all the glory which they derived from all their previous ties and alliances.

To show his joy over this glory, the Deputy began a song, which was as pleasing as it was new. All present sang with him, but in a different and heavier tone, beating time on their mats; while the man himself danced in the midst of them all, performing strange antics,—keeping his whole body in motion; making gestures with his hands, feet, head, eyes and mouth,— and all this so exactly in the time of both his own singing and that of the others, that the result was admirable. He sang these words: *A, a, ha, Gaianderé, gaianderé;* that is, translated into Latin, *Io, io, triumphe.* And then, *E, e, he, Gaianderé, gaianderé; O, o, ho, Gaianderé, gaianderé.* He explained what he meant by his *Gaianderé*, which signifies, among the natives, "something very excellent." He said that, what we call the Faith, would be called by them *Gaianderé*; and, to explain it better, he offered his first piece of porcelain.

He offered the second in behalf of the Onneioutchronnon, because as they both were twin brothers, he thought that he, too, ought to thank Onnontio, since he shared the happiness of being adopted by him.

The third was an assurance that the present offered by us the day before, to unite the minds of the Anniehronnons with those of the four other Nations, would be effectual.

The fourth pleased us greatly, being given in declaration that not only the Father, but also his two children, would all become sincere believers,—meaning, that both the Onnontagueronnon, who is the father, and the Oiogeon and Onneiout, who are his children, would embrace the Faith.

With the fifth, he adopted the Hurons and Algonquins as his brothers; and with the sixth, promised that the three Nations should unite, and go, the following Spring, to bring the French and the Savages who should desire to come into their Country.

It was necessary to make a reply to all of this, which the Father did in two words, each accompanied by a present. One was to repair the rents made in our Cabin by the people who crowded it every day, and who could not see their fill of us; and the other was to clean the mat on which future Councils between their Country and the French and their Allies were to be held.

This beautiful day closed with the teaching of a score of people of the Village, who presented themselves anew in order to pray.

On the seventeenth, after celebrating holy Mass, we were taken out to make measurements for a chapel. It was erected on the following day, which, by good omen, was the day of the Dedication of saint Peter and saint Paul. It is true that all our marble and precious metals were only bark. Upon its completion, it was consecrated by the Baptism of three children, to whom the way to Heaven was opened under that bark roof just as well as it is to those who are held over fonts whose arches are of gold and silver.

[*Ibid.*, xlii., *Doc.* xc.]

IX

JOURNEY OF THE FATHERS OF OUR SOCIETY, AND OF SOME FRENCHMEN, TO THE COUNTRY OF THE UPPER IROQUOIS, CALLED ONNONTOERONNONS

(From the Relation of 1656-1657)

Preceded by a letter written to Reverend Father Louys Cellot, Provincial of the Society of Jesus in the Province of France, by Father François Le Mercier

MY REVEREND FATHER:

Pax Christi:

After addressing all our vows to Heaven to implore its aid, we have recourse to your Reverence to ask your holy blessing, before embarking on the most dangerous and likewise the most glorious enterprise that can be undertaken in this country. We are on the eve of our departure to go and collect what remains of the blood of the Son of God among these peoples, where we have had the happiness of shedding our own and of carrying the light of the Faith to them; although their sole design hitherto has been to extinguish it; that is, we go to establish ourselves among the Iroquois. I think that, in mentioning these Barbarians, I say all that can be said; for their name alone shows the risk which we run and the glory which will accrue to God from the execution of that design.

We are not ignorant of the fact that these Savages have eaten us with relish and have drunk with pleasure the blood of the Fathers of our Society; that their hands and their lips are still wet with it, and that the fires in which they roasted their limbs are not yet quite extinguished. We have not forgotten the conflagrations that they have kindled to consume

280

our houses, and the cruelty that they have practiced on our bodies, which still bear its marks. We know that their whole policy consists in knowing well how to plot treachery, and to conceal all their plans for it; that no Nero or Diocletian ever declared himself so strongly against the Christians as these bloodthirsty Savages have done against us; and that the faith would at the present moment be received among many infidel Nations, had they not surpassed in rage and fury the greatest persecutors of JESUS CHRIST. We have not yet been able to dry the tears in which, for six years, our eyes have been bathed when we cast them upon the flourishing condition of the Huron Church before these Oppressors had sapped its foundations,—making Martyrs of its Pastors, and Saints of most of its members; and leaving but a very pitiful remnant, who have sought refuge under the wing of the French, the only asylum left them in their misfortune. We see that, ever since that first havoc, they have always pushed on their conquests, and have made themselves so redoubtable in this country that everything gives way before their arms. They still have strength in their hands, and perhaps treachery in their hearts; and our allies are so weakened and so reduced in numbers, that barely enough remain to preserve the names of many very populous and very important nations. Notwithstanding all that, we consider ourselves so convinced of the will of God,—who, of old, turned his greatest persecutors into his most illustrious Apostles—that we have no doubt that, at the present time, he opens the door to his Preachers, that they might go and plant the faith in the very heart of his enemies, triumph over their barbarity, change these Wolves and Tigers into Lambs, and bring them into the fold of JESUS CHRIST.

It is not without reason that we conceive such bright hopes. The manifestations of Divine providence and the means employed by its guidance, which has so well directed matters to the point at which they have now arrived, compel us to admit that we cannot, without extreme cowardice, disappoint the expectations that God has caused to arise for us where we least expected them. For what power other than his could force these peoples, inflated with pride on account of their victories, not only to come and seek a peace with us of which they seem to have no need, but also to place themselves un-armed in our hands, and throw themselves at our feet,— begging us to accept them as our friends, when we were so weak that we could no longer withstand them as enemies? They had but to continue, to massecre the remainder of the French Colony, for they met with hardly any resistance, either from the French or from the Savages, our Confederates; and nevertheless, for over three years, they incessantly sent pres-ents and embassies to ingratiate themselves with us, and to solicit us to make peace. Old and young, women and children, place themselves at our mercy; they enter our forts; they act confidently with us, and spare no effort to open their hearts to us, and to make us read therein that all their solicitations are as sincere as they are pressing.

They are not content with coming to us, but for a long time they invite us to go to them, and offer us the finest land that they have, and that is to be found in this New world. Neither the necessities of trade nor the hopes of our protection induce them to do all that; for they have hitherto had and still enjoy both those things with the Dutch, much more advan-tageously than they can ever hope to do with the French. But it is the act of God; he has, doubtless, lent an ear to the blood of the Martyrs, which is the seed of Christians, and which now causes them to spring up in this land that was watered by it. For, not only have those greatest enemies of the Faith given presents to declare that they wish to embrace it; not only have they asked for Preachers to instruct them, and publicly pro-fessed in open Council that they were Believers; but the Fathers of our Society who have passed the last winter with them have also observed so many good dispositions for the planting of a new Church among them,—not only from the miraculous things that have happened there, as Your Rever-ence will see in the Journal, but also from the numerous first-fruits already consecrated to heaven,—that we depart, with all confidence, to cause the name of JESUS CHRIST to resound in those lands where the Devil has always been master from the beginning of the world.

If those people are so anxious to have us in their country, we feel no less eagerness to leave ours and to go among them. And this is another proof of the will of God, who disposes all things so opportunely that I find myself equally and agreeably importuned from two very different directions,—on one side, by the Iroquois, who urge us; on the other, by our Fathers and Brethren, who eagerly ask to be allowed to join the party. The desire of the former and the zeal of the latter compel me to satisfy them all; and, although the former have hitherto manifested nothing but cruelty, the latter feel only an affection for them, which makes them hold life cheap, and lavish it generously, for the salvation of those who have so often sought to put them to death.

Divine providence also manifests itself by giving us at this moment a goodly number of our Fathers, who not only have the courage to expose themselves to everything, but also possess the capacity of teaching those Barbarians,—whose language, as well as that of many other Nations still more remote, is not very different from that of the Hurons. It is this that revives their fervor and gives to old men, broken down after glorious labors, the courage to desire to go among those peoples, and to spend the remainder of their lives, with the same zeal that they manifested fifteen or twenty years ago when they labored in the Huron Missions.

It is true that the stumbling-block which might hinder our design lies with the lower Iroquois, called Anniengehronnons, with whom we do not go to dwell. They may presume that, if we unite ourselves so closely with the four Upper Nations, it will be to place ourselves in a position to fear them no longer. But, even if they should oppose our establishment, we far prefer to have them alone for enemies than the Four Nations together; these would become irritated if we refused them our friendship, and—seeing themselves disappointed in their just expectations, and so manifestly deceived after such solemn promises, so frequently reiterated both here and in their country, to go and settle in their land—that they would make us experience the baleful effects of that vexation. Thus, a refusal or delay would be followed by the total ruin of this New France, which, after being reduced to extremities by a single Nation, could not long withstand the efforts of five together, if they conspired against her. The blessing of peace, which we are beginning to enjoy, is so sweet and so necessary for the publication of the Faith that, even if there were great danger, we would willingly immolate ourselves, as public victims, to avert the storm which would inevitably burst upon our French, and to ward off the misfortunes which would accompany a war more dangerous than those that preceded it. But, even if we had not all those moral assurances that God has touched the hearts of the Iroquois, we should consider ourselves sufficiently compelled to devote our sweat and our blood to the last drop.

Such is the state of affairs; and such are the effects of so many prayers, mortifications, fasts, alms, and good works, which have been performed in both Frances, and have caused so great a design to be conceived. But, as the undertaking is arduous, and difficult of execution, we beg those pious souls to continue their fervor, so that God may continue to pour his blessings on this country. And, for my part, I beg Your Reverence and all our Fathers and Brethren of your Province to lift your hands to heaven, while we go to declare war against Infidelity, and to fight the Devil in the very heart of his country. I am, with all possible respect and submission,

Your Reverence's
Very humble and very obedient
servant in Our Lord,
Francois le Mercier,
From Montreal, this   of the Society of Jesus.
6th of June, 1656.

AS these people had asked for us, we sent, in the year 1655, two Fathers of our Society to their country, to ascertain their dispositions toward the Faith and their inclinations toward the

French. After associating with them for about six months,—as set forth in the Relation of last year,—one of the two came down to Quebec. Although he spoke favorably of the good will of those Iroquois, nevertheless he did not efface from our minds the distrust of their perfidy and treachery that we had conceived. Thus, when it became necessary to cast the bell, as the saying is, and to decide upon the establishment of a Mission and a residence in their country, we found ourselves extremely perplexed, as also did Monsieur our Governor. We were aware that falsehood, deceit, and treachery were almost as natural to these people as life itself. We knew how much they were addicted to bloodshed, fire, and carnage. We remembered our poor Huron churches and the cruelties they had practiced on our worthy Algonquins. We had before our eyes the horrible tortures which they had inflicted upon several of our Fathers. The fury that animates these Barbarians whispered in our ears that they were preparing the same for us. However, we resolved to grant to those people what they so urgently asked, and to establish ourselves in the heart of their country.

No sooner said than done. A goodly number of French prepared to embark, with Father René Menard, Father Claude d'Ablon, Father Jacques Fremin, Brother Ambroise Broar, and Brother Joseph Boursier,—whom Reverend Father François le Mercier, Superior of the Missions of our Society in these countries, took with him to wage war against the Demons in their very stronghold. But let us follow with eye and mind him who has traced their journey for us on paper, and who was one of the party.[1]

We started from Quebec on the 17th of May, 1656. Our Main body comprised four Nations,—some French; some Onnontoeronnons who had come for us; some Sonnontoeronnons, who had come to contract an alliance with us; and some Hurons. We filled two large shallops and several canoes. Many looked upon us with compassion and with trembling hearts, as so many victims destined to the fires and the fury of the Iroquois. . . .

---

[1] Doubtless Father Dablon. See p. 263, *note* 2.

On the eleventh of July, we reached the entrance to Lake Gannentaa,[1] on the shores of which we intended to establish our residence. Here the Elders, who knew that this was the spot upon which Fathers Chaumont and d'Ablon had decided, awaited our arrival with a great multitude of people.

The Elders had caused two scaffolds to be erected, from which to pay us their compliments aloud, and to deliver to us their harangues. It is the custom of these peoples to entertain during a portion of the night those who come to visit them,— either with compliments, or with speeches seasoned with the graces of the country, or with their songs and dances. But when they saw us so fatigued after so long a journey, they told us they would withdraw, in order that their civilities might not disturb our rest,—to which they said they wished to contribute, by singing around our cabins the softest and most agreeable airs.

On the morning of the following day, we chanted the *Te Deum* in thanksgiving for our happy arrival, and took possession of the whole country in the name of JESUS CHRIST, —dedicating and consecrating it to him at the holy Sacrifice of the Mass.

On Monday, the seventeenth, we set to work in good earnest, to build lodgings for ourselves, and a good Redout for the soldiers, which we erected on an eminence commanding the Lake and all the surrounding places. While the workmen were so employed, our Father Superior went with fifteen of our best soldiers to the Village of Onnontaghé, five short leagues from our residence. The people, who had been notified of the coming of the French, came forth in crowds to meet us. At the entrance to the Village, our soldiers fired a fine salvo, which delighted all the spectators. We were conducted to the Cabin of one of the principal and most renowned Captains of the country, where everything was prepared for our reception in their fashion. Fruit was brought to us from all sides; there was nothing but feasting; and for ten days all the game and fish of the village were used in regaling the French.

---

[1] *See* p. 271, *note.*

Some time afterward, another squad of French in fine attire marched in, with the drum beating. Never were seen so many bright faces; it seemed as if the hearts of the Savages were leaping out of their eyes. If, after all that, they betray and massacre us, I will accuse them, not of dissimulation, but of frivolity and inconstancy, which in a short time can change the affection and confidence of those Barbarians into fear, hatred and treachery.

These people had called together all the States of the country, or rather all the allied Nations. That great council was held on the 24th of the month of July, when all the Nations placed in the hands of Achiendasé (who is our Father Superior) the settlement of the difficulty between the Sonnontoueronnons and the Annioronnons, which was soon ended. They then, with manifestations of extraordinary good will, agreed that we should establish ourselves and reside in their country. Finally, each one deposited his presents in the war-kettle.

Now, as these people are great haranguers and frequently make use of allegorics and metaphors, our Fathers adapt themselves to this custom of theirs to win them to God. They are delighted when they see that we succeed as well as they.

We had so well displayed, arranged and disposed our presents, that they made a wonderful show; but Father Joseph Chaumont, who speaks Iroquois as well as the natives of the country, seemed to add to their value in interpreting their meaning.

It will not be out of place to observe, in passing, that these presents consist entirely of porcelain collars, beads, arquebuses, powder and lead, coats, hatchets, kettles, and other similar articles. Before giving an explanation of them, our Fathers and our French knelt down, removed their hats, clasped their hands, and intoned aloud the *Veni Creator* at full length. This astonished and delighted the spectators, to whom we explained that we never dealt with any matter of importance without first asking the assistance of the Spirit who governs the whole world.

Then Father Joseph Chaumont arose and explained the

meaning of the eight or ten presents. In distributing these presents he included the Algonquins and the Hurons, that they might form but one heart and one people with all those nations. He proclaimed that, as Onontaghé was the Parliament of the whole country and Agochiendagueté the most esteemed in all those regions, Achiendasé, as the mouth of Onontio,[1] came to unite with him, to help him in raising up the houses that had been overthrown, in maintaining what was in good condition, and in defending the country against the disturbers of the peace. While the Father explained all these matters, he was listened to with admiration and with the acclamations of all these peoples, who were delighted to see us so well versed in their ways.

He gave a present to return thanks that they had shared with Onnontio the spoils taken from their enemies; for they had sent him two children, whom they had taken and brought hither from the Cat Nation.

He gave two others; one, in acknowledgment of their reception of us into their country, which was as courteous as the invitation had been urgent; and the other, to induce them to place in the water the canoe, that it might carry news of us to Quebec.

Finally the Father assumed a louder tone, and exclaimed: "It is not for purposes of trade that you see us appear in your country. Your furs are of too little value in our eyes to induce us to undertake so long, so difficult, and so dangerous a journey. Keep your beaver-skins, if you choose, for the Dutch; even those which may come into our hands will be used for your good. We seek not perishable things. For the Faith, we have left our country; For the Faith, we have quitted the great ships of the French to embark in your small canoes; for the Faith, we have given up fine houses, to lodge in your bark cabins; for the Faith, we deprive ourselves of the delicate viands we might have enjoyed in France, to eat your boiled meal and

---

[1] *Agochiendagueté;* title of Onondago chief. *Achiendasé;* Huron-Iroquois appellation of Jesuit superior. *Onontio;* Huron-Iroquois name for the governors of New France.

other food, which the animals in our country would hardly touch." Then, taking up a very fine collar of porcelain beads, artistically made, he continued: "For the sake of the Faith, I hold this rich present in my hand, and I open my mouth to remind you of the word you pledged us when you came down to Quebec to conduct us to your country. You solemnly promised to lend ear to the words of the great God. They are in my mouth; listen to them; I am but his spokesman."

These and many other words, full of fire and uttered with the most Christian vehemence, caused these poor Barbarians such astonishment, that they seemed quite beside themselves; their minds wavered between joy and fear. For my part, I must admit that what I saw and heard on that occasion surpasses anything that can be said or written of it.

On the 27th of July, we returned to the shores of the Lake, where a considerable portion of our French were engaged in erecting a residence, which we shall call Sainte Marie of Gannentaa. We had built a Chapel at Onontaghé, to which some of our Fathers were attached, while the others went through the cabins. The French, at sainte Marie of Lake Gannentaa, worked at all the trades practiced in a city, in order to provide a lodging for all of us, and to protect us in the midst of these barbarous Nations. All this was done, not without trouble. It was necessary to work hard, to sleep little, to lie on the earth, sheltered by miserable pieces of bark, to be pestered night and day by little flies or gnats, which attack one on all sides and at all hours. All that, added to change of air and the great fatigues of the journey, so affected our constitutions, at the hottest seasons of the year, that we all fell sick. It was pitiful to see sometimes as many as twenty heaped almost on top of the other, at a time and in a country where we had no other succor than that of Heaven. But he who caused our wounds soon applied a good dressing to them. At the height of our misery and privations, he sent us so much game and so many fish in our Lake before the usual season, that the sick were relieved, and those who were cured were sustained in doing their work. He so touched the hearts of these people that they brought us some of their dainties, such as the beans and squashes of the country, which are firmer and better than those of France. They also gave us fresh ears of their corn, which are not disagreeable. Thus, we all escaped with a few attacks of tertian fever, which caused us to experience every possible kindness at the hands of the savages during our illness.

News has come to us here that the Dutch wish to bring us some horses and other commodities, as they are glad that we dwell in these countries.

A former Captain of Oiogoen, an intelligent man engaged in public affairs, came to see us on behalf of the whole of his Nation. He requested Achiendasé to give them some of our Fathers, assuring him that they would erect a Chapel for them, and that the people desired to be instructed in our belief. He was given Father René Menard and two Frenchmen, notwithstanding our great scarcity of workmen. Father Joseph Chaumont is to accompany him as far as Oiogoen; from there he will go to Sonnontouan, to lay from afar the foundations of a fine Mission, and to sow the seeds of a great harvest, which we hope to gather, if it please God to preserve peace for us and to send us workmen.

[*Ibid.*, xliii., xliv., *Doc.* xcvi.]

X

LETTER OF FATHER CLAUDE CHAUCHETIERE,[1] RESPECTING THE IROQUOIS MISSION OF SAULT ST. FRANÇOIS XAVIER, NEAR MONTREAL

Sault St. François Xavier,
this 14th of October, 1682.

My Reverend Father:

Pax Christi:

In answer to Your Reverence's letter respecting what you have asked me, I will say that we are in a part of the country where the climate is not as good as in france, although, thanks be to God, I am in very good health. We are in a very high and beautiful location, with a fine view, 60 leagues Distant from Quebec,—which is called "the Iroquois mission." It is the finest mission in Canada, and, as regards piety and devotion, resembles one of the best churches in France.

The river St. Lawrence here forms a Lake two leagues wide; and The place where we are is so high that the waters of this great river fall here with a loud roar, and roll over many Cascades, which frighten one to look at. The water foams As you see it do under a mill-Wheel. We nevertheless readily pass over it every day in our bark canoes. And I cannot help saying that one must be crazy to run the rapids as we do without fear of being drowned.

[1] Claude Chauchetiére was born at Poitiers Sept. 7, 1645, and on his nineteenth birthday began his novitiate in the Jesuit order at Bordeaux. He studied philosophy at Poitiers during 1665-67; and was then an instructor at Tulle, La Rochelle, and Saintes, respectively. Completing his studies at Poitiers (1673-78), he was sent to the Canada mission. After a year of preparation, he was assigned (1670) to the Sault St. Louis mission where he remained fifteen years. In 1694, he went to the Montreal residence, spending another fifteen years; and finally died at Quebec in 1709. He wrote a life of the Iroquois maiden, Catherine Tegakwita. —*Ibid.*, lx., *note* 34.

We have a large farm, on which we keep oxen, cows, and poultry, and gather corn for our subsistance. It is sometimes necessary to take charge of all temporal as well as spiritual matters, now that Father Fremin has gone down in an Infirm condition to Quebec, as well as Father Cholenec. Some savages get their land Plowed, and harvest french wheat, Instead of indian corn. It is impossible to describe their Joy when They can harvest 20 or 30 minots of french wheat, and are able to eat bread from time to time. But as this sort of grain costs them too much labor, their usual occupation is to Plow the soil in order to plant indian corn in it. If The savages were fed, they would work much more than they do.

Our village grows larger every year, while the Lorette mission, where father chaumont is, steadily diminishes. That of the mountain does not decrease, neither does it Increase much; but ours grows continually. We think that in two or three years all the aniez will be in this Place. More than eighty have settled here recently. We have a chapel 25 feet Wide, and nearly 60 feet Long. We have three Bells, with which we produce a very agreeable Carillon; and The savages will soon have another bell, weighing two hundred livres, to complete the harmony.

From eight o'clock Until eleven, which is the hour for our repast, my occupation consists in visiting the savages, or in working to make Books for them (because, as their nature is very fickle,—of which They themselves complain,—they must be often visited, either to give them suitable encouragement, or to prevent and appease their disputes, or to prepare the newcomers for receiving the sacraments). There are sixty Cabins —that is to say, from one hundred and twenty to 150 families, as there are at least two in each Cabin. To perform these visits with profit demands all the time of one missionary; another would be required for the children, and one for those who are more advanced, who need to be Instructed in virtue.

My work is made easier this way; I sketch upon paper The truths of The Gospel and The practises of virtue Invented by Monsieur de Nobletz. Another Book Contains colored pictures of The Ceremonies of the mass applied to the passion of our lord; another Contains Pictures showing The torments of hell; another The Creation of the world. The savages Read these with pleasure and profit, and these Books are Their mute teachers.

You will be pleased to hear from me respecting the austerities practised by certain savage women—Although there may be some indiscretion in their doing so; but it will show you their fervor. More than 5 years ago some of them learned, I know not how, of the pious practises followed by the nuns in Montreal who are hospital sisters. They heard of disciplines, of iron girdles, and of hair shirts. This religious life began to please them very much, and three of them formed an association, in order to commence a sort of Convent; but we stopped them, because we did not Think that The time had come for this. However, even if they were not cloistered, they at least observed Chastity; and one of them died with the reputation of sanctity, 3 years Ago next spring. They, and some others who imitated them, would be admired in france, if what they do were known there.

The first who began made her first attempt about Christmas in The year 1676, when she divested herself of her clothing, and exposed herself to The air at the foot of a large Cross that stands beside our Cemetery. She did so at a time when the snow was falling, although she was pregnant; and the snow that fell upon her back caused her so much suffering that she nearly died from it—as well as her child, whom the cold chilled in its mother's womb. It was her own idea to do this —to do penance for her sins, she said. She has had four companions in her fervor, who have since imitated her. Two of them made a hole in the ice, in the depth of winter, and Threw themselves into The water, where they remained during the time that it would take to say a Rosary slowly and sedately. One of the the two, who Feared that she would be found out, did not venture to Warm herself when she returned to her cabin, but lay down on her mat with lumps of ice adhering to her shoulders. There have been several other Inventions of similar mortifications, which men and women have discovered for the purpose of tormenting themselves, and which constitute their usual penance. But we have made them give up whatever was excessive.

During the past two years, Their fervor has greatly augmented since God has removed from this world one of these devout savage women who live like Nuns, and she died with the reputation of sanctity. We cease not to say masses to thank God for the graces that we believe we receive, every Day, through her Intercession. Journeys are continually made to her tomb; and the savages, following her example, have become better Christians than they were. We daily see wonders worked through her Intercession. Her name was Catherine Tegaskouita.[1] During her lifetime she had made an agreement with a friend to make each other suffer, because she was too weak to do so by herself, owing to her Continual illness. She had begged her companion to do her the Charity of severely chastising her with Blows from a whip. This they did for a year, without anyone knowing it, and for that purpose they withdrew, every sunday, into a Cabin in the middle of the Cemetery; and there, taking in their hands willow shoots, they mingled prayers with penance. Finally, when one of the two saw that her companion had fallen sick at the end of The year, she was pressed by scruples to reveal The matter, and to ask whether she had not sinned in what she had done.

At that time people here used only willow shoots, or Thorns, which here are very long; but since they have heard of the disciplines, of iron girdles, and of similar Instruments of penance, The use of these Daily becomes more general. And,

---

[1] Catherine Tegakwita was one of Lamberville's converts at the Mohawk village of Gandaouagué, where she received baptism in 1675. Two years later, she left her own country, and went to make her abode at the Iroquois mission of St. François Xavier du Sault. There her great industry in toil, with continual austerities and mortifications gradually reduced her strength, until a protracted illness caused her death April 17, 1680. Her virtues and sanctity were regarded as so unusual that her grave became a place for pilgrimage, where miracles have been ever since recorded; and various efforts have been made to secure her canonization. Father Claude Chauchetière wrote her biography, and painted her portrait.—*Ibid.,* lxii., *note* 18.

as The men have found that the women use them, they will not
Let themselves be outdone, and ask us to permit them to use
these every Day; but we will not allow it.

The women, to the number of 8 or 10, Began The practice;
and The wife of the dogique—that is to say, of him who Leads
the Singing and says The prayers—is among the number. She
it is who, in her husband's absence, also causes The prayers to
be said aloud, and Leads The Singing; and in this capacity she
assembles the devout women of whom we have spoken, who
call themselves sisters. They tell One another their faults,
and deliberate together upon what must be done for The relief of the poor in the Village—whose number is so great that
there are almost as many poor as there are Savages.

The sort of monastery that they maintain here has its
rules. They have promised God never to put on their gala-
dress (for savage women have some taste and take pride in
adorning themselves with porcelain beads; with vermilion,
which they apply to their Cheeks; and with earrings and
bracelets). They assist One another in the fields; They meet
together to incite one another to virtue; and one of them had
been received as a nun in The hospital of monreal.

There are married people here who have for a long time
lived as brother and sister. There are aged women, veterans in
the faith, who Instruct the others as missionaries would do,
and God thereby supplies the want of these which we experience. There are many women who have shared Their
fields,—thus, as it were, taking The bread from their own
mouths to give it to the new-comers,—who are not yet in a
position to do anything for them in return,—in order to win
them to God. When there are widows and sick persons,
the Captains make their families work, for the love of God, at
building Cabins for those who have none. Some live in the
woods in the same state of Innocence as do those in the village; and they return with consciences as pure as When they
went away. And I may state, without exaggeration, that when
they return we do not find in many of them matter for absolution; and yet They are sufficiently enlightened to accuse

themselves of the least Imperfections,—Such as Slight distractions during their prayers, petty acts of Impatience, some instance of forgetfulness, and things which, in their case, are often virtues. Modesty is natural to Them. When They pray or Sing in The church, they do so with so much devotion that all the french settlers here who see them are impressed by it, and say that they are more devout than we allege. I was forgetting to tell you that, when They are in the woods, they have the sundays and feast days marked by small Lines to the number of seven, one for each Day of the week: we mark Crosses upon the lines that indicate the feast-days and The sundays, and they observe these very exactly.

We have here no other demon to Contend against than liquor and drunkenness, which make a hell of all the Iroquois villages, wherein life is a continual suffering. The french are the cause of its giving us much trouble here; for, in order to strip the Savages to their very Shirts, they follow them everywhere, to make them drink and become intoxicated.

If you wish me to tell you something about the manner in which the savages dress—although, had I time, I would prefer painting some for you—you must know that it is not Wanting in taste, especially on feast-Days. The women have no other Head-dress than their hair, which they part over the middle of the head, and then tie behind with a sort of Ribbon, which they make out of eel-skin painted a bright red. I myself have often been deceived, and have taken it for a real Ribbon. They grease Their hair, which thereby becomes as Black as Jet. As for The men, They are ridiculous in dressing Their Hair, and there is not one who does not do it up in a special fashion. On sundays and feast-days, the men and women wear fine white chemises; and The women take wonderful care to clothe themselves so modestly that there is nothing indecorous or uncovered about them,—for they closely fasten the chemise. This falls over a petticoat, consisting of a blue or red Blanket, a brasse or more Square, which they fold in two, and simply gird around the waist; and The Chemise, which falls over this sort of petticoat, reaches only to the knees.

The savages have often asked us if there were any vanity in dress. They are not accustomed to wear these except in going to church, on Communion and feast-Days. On other Days They are poorly but modestly clad.

I would like to give you a more exact description of their consciences, of which you may have a fair Idea from what I have said. But, besides the fact that it would take too Long, and that I shall send something about it to one of my brothers, I would Fear that it might perhaps be thought somewhat exaggerated.

The savage women sometimes propound to us doubts in spiritual matters, as difficult as those that might be advanced by the most cultured persons in france. The knowledge of the cases of conscience often renders us good service here; without it we would be in danger of making many mistakes respecting proximate occasions, the baptism of adults, and marriages. In truth, the working of The Holy ghost seems admirable in these minds, which have been trained amid the forests and the woods.

When I Read Them Your Letter on sunday, as I preached to them, They wept while listening to me; and the dogique then spoke to them in a very pathetic manner. They often ask me whether any prayers are said for them in france, and I assure them that there are. From time to time, They deplore the misfortunes of their birth; and, after they become Christians, they live like angels, fearing to fall into the evil ways from which faith and Christianity have withdrawn Them.

[*Ibid.*, lxii., *Doc.* clii.]

PART IV

THE EXPANSION WESTWARD OF NEW
FRANCE, AND THE JESUIT MISSIONS

1659—1763

I

RELATION OF WHAT OCCURRED IN THE MISSION OF THE FATHERS OF THE SOCIETY OF JESUS, IN THE COUNTRIES OF NEW FRANCE, FROM THE SUMMER OF THE YEAR 1659 TO THE SUMMER OF THE YEAR 1660

By Father Jerome Lalemant

[A chapter is devoted to an account of the Algonkin tribes, who have fled westward from the Iroquois. This is taken from a narrative by one of the Fathers (probably Druillettes), who had recently met, far up the Saguenay, a converted Indian, who has spent the last two years in wandering through the region of Lake Superior and Hudson Bay, and describes to the Father what he has seen there. The Algonkins have fled to those shores for refuge. The mines of the region are described. Indian reports of a western sea lead to some curious speculations regarding the water-route to China and Japan which was then a general article of belief. . . . This account is supplemented by information obtained from Radisson and Grosseilliers, who have just returned from another long voyage to the West. They encountered in Northeastern Illinois, the fugitive remnant of the Tobacco tribe, who have there taken refuge from the Iroquois. The explorers visit the Sioux tribes. All this news of many tribes who dwell in the darkness of paganism rouses new hopes in the Jesuits; and they long to go thither with the torch of the gospel.—*Ibid.*, xlv., 16.]

301

OF THE CONDITION OF THE COUNTRY IN GENERAL

The Ocean which separates us from France sees on its eastern side, only rejoicing, splendor, and bonfires; but on its western, nothing but war, slaughter, and conflagrations.

What consoles us is our full assurance that people do not regard us merely as do those who, being themselves in port or on shore, contemplate with compassion the wreck of a poor vessel shattered by the storm, and even shed some tears over it. But we promise ourselves much more, knowing the prayers, and all sorts of good works which are being performed for the conversion of our Savages; and learning of the good purposes with which God has inspired many persons of merit, for accomplishing the destruction of the Iroquois.

That means to open a door, high and wide, for proclaiming the Faith and giving the Preachers of the Gospel access to people of great extent, in regard to both the territories which they occupy, and the diversity of nations composing them— all of whom are four or five hundred leagues distant from us in the forests, shunning the common enemy. Were it not for the latter, they would come and enrich this country with their furs, and we should visit them and enrich Heaven with the glorious spoils that we should wrest from the powers of Hell.

We know—and we will state the facts more fully—that there are tribes of the same language, both stationary and wandering, as far as the North sea, on whose shores these nations border; and that there are others, very recently discovered, extending as far as the South sea. They stretch out their arms to us, and we ours to them, but on both sides they are too short to unite across such a distance; and when, finally, we are on the point of embracing each other, the Iroquois steps in between and showers blows upon both of us.

We know that very far beyond the great lake of the Hurons —when the Iroquois did not molest our mission, and before he had expelled us from them by the murder of our Fathers, —we know that some remnants of the wreck of that Nation rallied in considerable numbers beyond the lakes and mountains frequented by their enemies, and that but recently they sent a deputation hither to ask back again their dear old Pastors. But these good pastors are slain on the way, by the Iroquois, their guides are captured and burned, and all the roads are rendered impossible.

We even know that among the Iroquois the Faith is in a vigorous condition, although they do not possess it in their own persons, but in those of numerous captives. These only long to have us with them, or to be themselves with us. Finally we know that, whithersoever we go in the forests, we find some fugitive Church, or else some infant one; everywhere we find children to send to heaven, and adults to instruct; but everywhere, too, we find the Iroquois, who, like an obtrusive phantom, besets us in all places. They prevent the tribes from five or six hundred leagues about us from coming down hither, laden with furs that would make this country overflow with immense riches—as was done in a single journey which some of those Nations undertook this year —although secretly, and, as it were, by stealth, from fear of their foes.

What gives the enemy this advantage over us is, that all the rural settlements outside Quebec are without defense, and are distant from one another as much as eight or ten leagues on the banks of the great river. In each house there are only two, three, or four men, and often only one, alone with his wife and a number of children, who may all be killed or carried off without anyone's knowing aught about it in the nearest house. They come like Foxes through the woods. They attack like lions. They take flight like birds, disappearing before they have really appeared.

I say nothing of the losses that France would suffer if these vast regions should pass from her control. The foreigner would reap a great advantage, to the detriment of French navigation.

Of the five tribes constituting the entire Iroquois nation, that which we call the Agnieronnons has been so many times

at both the top and the bottom of the wheel, within less than
sixty years, that we find in history few examples of similar
revolutions. We cannot go back very far in our researches
in their past history, as they have no Libraries other than the
memory of their old men; and perhaps we should find nothing
worthy of publication. What we learn from these living
books is that, toward the end of the last century, the Agnieronnons were reduced so low by the Algonkins that there seemed
to be scarcely any more of them left on earth. Nevertheless, this scanty remnant, like a noble germ, so increased in a
few years as to reduce the Algonkins in turn. But this condition did not last long, for the Andastogehronnons waged
such energetic warfare against them during ten years that they
were overthrown for the second time, and so humiliated that
the mere name Algonkin made them tremble.

That was at the time when the Dutch took possession of these
regions and conceived a fondness for the beavers of the natives, some thirty years ago; and in order to secure a greater
number, they furnished those people with firearms, with which
it was easy to conquer their conquerors. That is what has
rendered them formidable everywhere; it has also put into
their heads that idea of sovereign sway to which they aspire,
mere barbarians although they are.

But what is more astonishing is, that they actually hold dominion for five hundred leagues around, although their numbers are very small; for, of the five Nations constituting the
Iroquois, the Agnieronnons do not exceed five hundred men
able to bear arms, who occupy three or four wretched Villages.

It is beyond doubt that, if the Anieronnons were defeated
by the French, the other Iroquois Nations would be glad to
compromise with us. Then those fair Missions would be re-
vived at Onnontagué, at Oiogoen, and in all the other remaining Iroquois Nations, where we have already sown the
first seeds of the faith. Moreover the great door would be
open toward the tribes of the North, and toward those newly
discovered ones of the West, all of whom we embrace under

the general name of Algonkins. But it is a subject of too wide a scope, and demands a separate Chapter.

OF THE CONDITION OF THE ALGONKIN COUNTRY, AND OF SOME NEW DISCOVERIES

I cannot more clearly describe the condition of the Nations of the Algonkin tongue than by giving the simple account of what one of our Fathers [1] has learned about them,—who has been, this year, on the Saguenay River of Tadoussac,—as Providence gave him opportunities for this during that journey.

As those Nations are very widely extended over five or six hundred leagues of forest, facing toward the East, those dwelling in the uttermost parts of the West, and those of the North, lying between the two others. Of those of the East he says nothing that has not been given in the preceding Relations; of the two other groups he speaks as follows:

"On the thirtieth of July of the year one thousand six hundred and sixty, ascending the Saguené to the distance of thirty-two leagues from Tadoussac, I encountered eighty Savages; and among them was one named Awatanik, a man of importance because he was a Captain in rank, and much more so because he had received holy Baptism ten years before in the country of the Nipisiriniens. The glorious Archangel, whose name he bears, seems to have taken pleasure in leading this man, as if by the hand, and conducting him here to us, to show us the way which will take us to the North sea—where various Algonkin Nations have sought a retreat fleeing from the Iroquois, who also prevents us from going in search of them by the ordinary route of the great River. I will give an account of the various routes, and some incidents of his journey.

"He started, in the month of June of the year one thousand six hundred and fifty-eight, from the lake of the Ouinipegouek, which is strictly only a large bay in lake Huron. It

[1] Probably Father Druillettes.

is called by others 'the lake of the stinkards,' not because it is salt, like the water of the Sea,—which the Savages call Ouinipeg, or 'stinking water,'—but because it is surrounded by sulphurous soil, whence issue several springs which convey into this lake the impurities absorbed by their waters in the places of their origin.[1]

"He passed the remainder of that summer and the following winter near the lake which we call Superior, from its position above that of the Hurons, into which it empties by a water fall that has also given it its name; and, as our traveler halted there for some time, let us pause a while with him to note the peculiarities of the place.

"This lake, which is more than eighty leagues long by forty wide in certain places, is studded with Islands picturesquely distributed along its shores. The whole length of its coast is lined with Algonkin Nations, fear of the Iroquois having forced them to seek there an asylum. It is also enriched in its entire circumference with mines of lead in a nearly pure state; with copper of such excellence that pieces as large as one's fist are found, all refined; and with great rocks, having whole veins of turquoise.[2] The people even strive to make us believe that its waters are swollen by various streams which roll along with the sand grains of gold in abundance—the refuse, so to speak, of the neighboring mines. What inclines us to believe this, is that, when the foundations of saint Joseph's Chapel were dug on the shore of lake Huron,—which is nothing but the discharge of lake Superior,—the workmen found a vein, as large as one's arm, of these grains of gold, the sand that was mixed with the vein being so little in quantity as to be almost imperceptible in comparison with the rest. But the workmen, who knew that there were mines of copper in those regions, being persuaded that it was from a brass mine (in ignorance that brass is a composition), filled in the

---

[1] Reference is here made to Lake Nipissing.

[2] The "turquoises" described by the Indian were amethysts, which are abundant in the rocks of that region. The alleged grains of gold were doubtless iron pyrites. "St. Joseph's chapel" evidently refers to the mission of that name at the Huron villages of Ihonatiria and Toanché.—*Ibid.,* xlv., *note* 20.

foundations which they had dug, without knowing that they were sealing up a treasure there.

"But there are riches of another nature. The Savages dwelling about that end of the lake which is farthest distant from us, have given us entirely new light, which will not be displeasing to the curious, touching the route to Japan and China for which so much search has been made. For we learn from these people that they find the Sea on three sides, toward the South, toward the West, and toward the North, so that, if this is so, it is a strong argument and a very certain indication that these three seas, being thus contiguous, form in reality but one sea, which is that of China. For,—that of the South, which is the Pacific sea and is well enough known, being connected with the North sea, which is equally well known, by a third Sea, the one about which we are in doubt,— there remains nothing more to be desired than the passage into this great sea, at once a Western and an Eastern sea.

"Now we know that, proceeding Southward for about three hundred leagues from the end of the lake Superior, of which I have just spoken, we come to the bay of St. Esprit,[1] which lies on the thirtieth degree of latitude and the two hundred and eightieth of longitude, in the Gulf of Mexico, on the coast of Florida; and in a Southwesternly direction from the same extremity of lake Superior, it is about two hundred leagues to another lake, which empties into the Vermilion sea on the coast of New Grenada, in the great South Sea. It is from one of these two coasts that the Savages who live some sixty leagues to the West of our lake Superior obtain European goods, and they even say that they have seen some Europeans there.

"Moreover, from this same lake Superior, following a River toward the North, we arrive, after eight or ten days' journey, at Hudson Bay,[2] in fifty-five degrees of latitude. From this place, in a Northwesterly direction, it is about forty leagues by land to Button Bay, where lies port Melson, on the fifty-

---

[1] The name St. Esprit appears on the Franquelin map (1684) at what is now Mobile Bay. The early Spanish explorers applied the same name to either Matagorda or Galveston Bay.—*Ibid.*, xlv., *note* 21.

[2] Hendrik Hudson discovered the bay which bears his name, Aug. 3, 1610. In

seventh degree of latitude and the two hundred and seventieth of longitude; the distance thence to Japan is to be reckoned at only one thousand four hundred and twenty leagues, there being only seventy-one degrees of a great circle intervening. These two Seas, then, of the South and of the North, being known, there remains only that of the West, which joins them, to make only one from the three; and it is the fresh knowledge that we have gained from a Nation which, being situated at about the forty-seventh degree of latitude and the two hundred and seventy-third of longitude, assures us that ten days' journey Westward lies the Sea, which can be no other than the one we are looking for,—it is this knowledge that makes us believe that the whole of North America, being thus surrounded by the sea on the east, South, West and North, must be separated from Groeslande (Greenland) by some strait, of which a good part has already been discovered; and that it only remains now to push on some degrees farther, to enter nothing less than the Japan sea. In order to make the passage of Hudson strait, this is to be attempted only in the months of August and September; for during these months only, the passage is less blocked with ice.

"But enough for the present. If the Iroquois permit, we shall be fully able to go and enlighten ourselves more clearly concerning this discovery, which, being known to us only through the medium of Savages, does not give us all the information we might desire. Let us follow our guide, who, after wintering in the place I have just described, left it in the following spring. Advancing by short stages because of his family, who accompanied him, after covering about a hundred leagues' distance, he arrived at the great bay of the North, along which he found various Algonkin Nations who have settled on the shores of that sea.

"This bay is Hudson Bay, of which we have just been speaking. In the middle of it our Savage saw a large Island

1612-13, Sir Thomas Button, an English commander, visited Hudson Bay, wintered on its shores, and thoroughly explored the bay and Southampton Island. He discovered the Nelson River, and at its mouth, which he called Port Nelson, he made his winter abode.—*Ibid.*, xlv., *note 22*.

which takes its name from the white bears inhabiting it. These are water rather than land animals, since they leave the sea but rarely, and generally live on fish, whereas black Bears feed usually only on flesh, and do not leave the land. The white Bears' greatest dainty,—excepting the Bustards, on which they make war as skilfully as do the most expert men,—are the little Whales. These, from a natural antipathy, devour in turn those animals by which their own young are devoured. If, as sometimes happens, these white Bears, coming together toward Springtime, are borne out into the open sea on some block of ice that has become detached from the shore, about the month of June, it is then a fine sight to see these new Argonauts voyaging at the mercy of winds and storms, and contending for their lives against the hunger that assails them on those floating icebergs, or against the Whales that wait to devour them when hunger shall force them to leap into the water and fish for sea-wolves or sea-dogs. They often pass whole months in this perilous seafaring, until at length, by a stroke of good luck, their vessel is wrecked by running aground somewhere; for then these animals leap ashore, utterly famished, and make ample amends for the fast they have endured, devouring everything in their path, and sparing neither man nor beast to satisfy their ravenous hunger.

"But let us return to our Pilgrim. On his way, he met with various Nations, whose names have already been recorded. He noticed especially the Kilistinons, who are divided among nine different residences, some of a thousand, others of fifteen hundred men; they are settled in large villages, where they leave their wives and children while they chase the Moose and hunt the Beaver. The skin of the latter is of so little value to them since the Iroquois has prevented its sale, that they broil the Beavers over the fire, as is done with Swine in France, to render them eatable the more quickly. After visiting these tribes, our man betook himself to the Pitchibourenik, a people dwelling at the entrance to the Bay, whither the Hurons and Nipisiriniens formerly were wont to go for trade; and whence they procured a great abundance of Beavers in exchange for hatchets, cleavers, knives, and other like commodities, which they carried thither. During a certain part of the year, the abundance of Deer is still greater in these regions than that of Beavers; indeed it is so enormous that they provision themselves therewith for a year—either by smoking the flesh, which is their most usual method, or by letting it freeze. For toward those Northern regions nothing decays or becomes tainted during the greater part of the year; and, indeed, a little father Northward human bodies lose none of their beauty for a long time after death, being as rosy and as intact thirty years after their decease as during their lifetime. And so it is said in those countries that the dead are in good health, but the living fall ill. Icebergs are seen there some of twenty-two brasses, others of three hundred or three hundred and sixty feet.

"These become detached from the shore, and break sometimes with such violence that, on falling into the sea, they arouse by this downfall, storms that have put vessels in danger of being sunk; they, possibly, caused the destruction of the one whose wreck the Savages have seen on their coast.

"What excites my especial admiration in this unfortunate land is to see how Providence fails its creatures in nothing, supplying the defects of some by aid from others, in a way one would never imagine. When one views the shores of this sea almost destitute of trees,—whether from the severity of the cold, which prevents their growth, or because the rocks with which these regions are almost entirely covered cannot provide nourishment for large forests,—who would not think it contrary to God's will that these lands should be inhabited by man, since they are so destitute of the conveniences of human life? Nevertheless, Nations are found peopling these rocks and occupying this soil which is most sterile and most hard-favored by nature. But how can people live there without fire, when the cold is so intense? God has provided for that; he gives them their store of wood every year, and uses the stags as beasts of burden to carry it to them. This fuel consists of the wood or horns of the stags themselves. You may believe what you choose; but we are assured that these peoples have no better fire than that which they make with the wood of these great animals, which must be in prodigious numbers to supply with their antlers the branches of oaks and of other trees suitable for burning.

"But let us not leave our guide, who is coasting along the entire bay. It does not fare ill with him, for he declares that he has no lack of game, large and small; and that a man in his company killed one of those white Bears of which we have made mention. We did not learn from him whether its flesh is as good as that of the wild geese, Swans, and Ducks, that are found in the same region in the month of May, as well as countless numbers of little tufted birds and swallows, and likewise martins, white hares and black foxes. If powder for hunting runs short, one can resort to fishing for trout and salmon, which these Savages well know how to catch, not with lines, but with the harpoon simply.

"After our Algonkin had visited all the Nations surrounding the Bay, and had laden himself with various presents sent by those peoples to the French and Algonkins of these regions, —to attract them to their Bay, in order that they might all fortify themselves there against the Iroquois,—he left the seacoast to proceed inland and seek a road to Tadoussac, through vast forests which were unknown to him. As he was advancing through the woods, without compass and without taking altitude, he learned of the three Rivers, one of which leads straight to our village of three Rivers. This route he would not take, although it is much shorter and surer, but, at the same time, much more exposed to the Iroquois. The two other Rivers flow into lake St. Jean, whence the river Saguené takes its rise. He chose the more remote of these two Rivers as the safer one,—the other being not very far from the country where three Nations were overthrown by the Iroquois, two or three years ago, and compelled to seek a refuge with other more distant ones. The names of these latter are the Kepatawangachik, the Outabitibek, and the Ouakwiechiwek.

"Finally, he reached a spot thirty-two leagues from Tadoussac, where he entertained me with an account of his adventures and travels, and began to tell me in advance the condition to which the Iroquois had reduced the Algonkin Nations toward Lake Superior and the lake of the Ouinipeg. But scarcely had I returned to Quebec when I found two Frenchmen [1] there who had but just arrived from those upper countries with three hundred Algonkins, in sixty canoes loaded with furs. Following is an account of what they saw with their own eyes; it will give us a view of the condition of the Algonkins of the West, as we have until now mentioned those of the North.

"They passed the winter on the shores of lake Superior. Continuing their circuit, they were much surprised, on visiting the Nadwechiwec, to see women disfigured by having the ends of their noses cut off down to the cartilage; in that part of the face, then, they resemble death's heads. Moreover,

[1] The two Frenchmen here referred to were Radisson and Groseilliers, who had just returned from their second western voyage, after an absence of two years. See Radisson's account of this expedition, in his *Voyagés* (Prince Soc.), pp. 134-172.—*Ibid.*, xlv., *note* 23.

Medard Chouart, sieur des Groseilliers: from Brie, in France, was born in 1621 or 1625. He came to Three Rivers in 1641 and later spent some time in the Huron country. Sulte claims that in 1645, he was sent to the Lake Superior region by the Jesuits, in whose service he was. Returning thence, he became a soldier in the Quebec garrison, and then a pilot on the St. Lawrence; and a year later married Helene, daughter of Abraham Martin. She died in 1651, leaving a son, and in 1653, he took for his second wife Marguerite, sister of his friend, Radisson. These two adventurous men made various important explorations together, and were the original promoters of the Hudson's Bay Company. Regarding the first of these voyages, there has been much uncertainty and discussion; they journeyed westward in the summer of 1659 and spent the winter near Lake Pepin, among the Sioux tribes then located southwest of Lake Superior. On this voyage, they gained information which led them to plan further explorations northward; and, after several unsuccessful attempts to secure aid for this enterprise, they finally obtained ships and men from Charles II. of England, in the spring of 1668. Radisson's ship was driven back by a storm, but that of Groseilliers succeeded in reaching Hudson's Bay, the objective point of this expedition. In consequence, an English fort was established that year, at the mouth of Rupert's River; and in the following year, Radisson took possession of Port Nelson in the name of the English king; and would seem then to have gone to France. Five years later they returned to Canada, and Groseilliers remained for a time with his family at Three Rivers. In 1681, the two friends commanded another expedition to Hudson's Bay, this time to establish a French post there; but two years later, they returned to Europe, and were induced by England to re-enter the service of the Hudson's Bay Company. Radisson went back to the Bay, and spent several years there; but Groseilliers apparently remained and died in England.—*Ibid.*, xxviii., *note* 32.

they have a round portion on the top of their heads torn away. Making inquiry as to the cause of this ill-treatment, they learned, to their admiration, that it is the law of the country which condemns to this punishment all women guilty of adultery, in order that they may bear, graven on their faces, the penalty and shame of their sin. What renders this custom the more admirable is that, although each man in that country has seven or eight wives, the temptation is, consequently, much stronger among those poor creatures,—some of whom are always more cherished than others,—yet the law is more strictly executed there than it would be perhaps in the most highly civilized Cities, if it should be established therein.

"But we must take leave of these people, and enter the territories of another Nation, which is warlike and which with its bows and arrows has rendered itself redoubtable among the upper Algonkins as the Iroquois among the lower; and so it bears the name of Poualak, which means 'Warriors.'

"As wood is scanty in supply and small in size in their country, nature has taught them to make fire with coal from the earth and to cover their cabins with skins. Some of the more ingenious make themselves buildings of loam, very nearly as the swallows build their nests; and they would sleep not less comfortably under these skins and this mud than do the great ones of the earth under their golden canopies, if they did not fear the Iroquois, who come in search of them from a distance of five or six hundred leagues."

But if the Iroquois goes thither, why shall not we also? If there are conquests to make, why shall not the faith make them, since it makes them in all parts of the world?

[*Ibid.*, xlv., *Doc.* cii.]

II

JOURNAL OF FATHER CLAUDE ALLOUEZ'S VOYAGE INTO THE OUTAOUAC COUNTRY

(From the Relation of 1666-1667)

[Le Mercier gladly announces that "this year has passed in perfect peace," owing to the chastisement administered to the Iroquois by the French troops. The opening chapter of the *Relation* reviews the changes wrought in Canada by the new policy of Louis XIV, which is now developing that colony into "a veritable New France." Tracy has returned to France; but Courcelles governs the country with vigor and discretion. Talon, the Intendant, is using every means for developing all the resources of the country and extending its commerce. He is promoting the fisheries, and finding a market for their products, especially in the West Indies. He is opening the mines; he orders lands to be cleared, and the timber manufactured into staves, boards, etc.; he has begun ship-building. . . . Allouez has returned from his two years' mission among the Ottawas; he has travelled nearly 2,000 leagues in the wilderness of the great Northwest.—*Ibid.*, l., 16.]

Two years ago and more, Father Claude Allouez[1] set out for that great and arduous Mission, in behalf of which he has

[1] Claude Jean Allouez was was born at St. Didier, France, June 6, 1622. At the age of seventeen, he entered the Jesuit novitiate at Toulouse. Departing (1658) for Canada, he served at Three Rivers and other St. Lawrence settlements, for seven years. In August, 1665, he went to labor among the Ottawas of Lake Superior, and other Western tribes. Twenty-five years were spent by him in these Western missions; his death occurred Aug. 27 or 28, 1689, while engaged in missionary work. See Dablen's circular letter announcing Allouez's death in Margry's *Découvertes et Établissements des Français* (Paris, 1876); this missionary is therein styled "a second Xavier," and credited with having instructed more than 100,000 savages and baptized over 10,000.—*Ibid.*, xliv., *note* 10.

journeyed, in all his travels, nearly two thousand leagues through these vast forests,—enduring hunger, nakedness, shipwreck, weariness by day and night, and the persecution of the Idolators; but he has also had the consolation of bearing the torch of the faith to more than twenty different infidel Nations.

We cannot gain a better knowledge of the fruits of his labors than from the Journal which he was called upon to prepare. He begins as follows:

"On the eighth of August, in the year 1665, I embarked at three Rivers with six Frenchmen, in company with more than four hundred Savages of various nations, who, after transacting the little trading for which they had come, were returning to their own country.

"The Devil offered all conceivable opposition to our journey, making use of the false prejudice held by these savages, that Baptism causes their children to die. One of their chief men declared to me, in arrogant and menacing terms, his intention, and that of his people, to abandon me on some desert Island if I ventured to follow them farther. We had proceeded as far as the rapids of the river des prairies, where the breaking of the Canoe that bore me made me apprehensive of the threatened disaster. We promptly set about repairing our little vessel: and, although the Savages did not trouble themselves either to aid us or to wait for us, we were so expeditious as to join them near the long Sault, two or three days after we started.

"But our Canoe, having been once broken, could not long be of service, and our Frenchmen, already greatly fatigued, despaired of being able to follow the Savages, who were thoroughly accustomed to such severe exertions. Therefore, I resolved to call them all together, in order to persuade them to receive us separately into their Canoes,—showing them that our own was in so bad a condition as to be thenceforth useless to us. They agreed to this; and the Hurons promised, although with much reluctance, to provide for me.

"On the morrow, accordingly, when I came down to the water's edge, they at first received me well, and begged me to wait a very little while, until they were ready to embark.

After I had waited, and when I was stepping down into the water to enter their Canoe, they repulsed me with the assertion that their was no room for me, and straightway began to paddle vigorously, leaving me all alone with no prospect of human succor. I prayed God to forgive them, but my prayer was unanswered; for they were subsequently wrecked, and the divine Majesty turned my abandonment one the part of men to the saving of my life.

"Finding myself, then, entirely alone, forsaken in a strange land,—for the whole fleet was already a good distance away,— I had recourse to the blessed Virgin, in whose honor we had performed a novena which gained for us from that Mother of Mercy a very manifest daily protection. While I was praying to her I saw, quite contrary to my hopes, some Canoes in which were three of our Frenchmen. I hailed them, and resuming our old Canoe, we proceeded to paddle with all our strength, in order to overtake the fleet. But we had long since lost sight of it, and knew not whither to go, it being very difficult to find a narrow detour which must be taken in order to gain the portage of Cat Rapids (as that part is called). We would have been lost had we missed this narrow channel; but it pleased God to guide us directly, and almost without our realizing it, to this portage. Here, as I saw two more Canoes belonging to the Savages, I leaped into the water, and hastened to intercept them by land on the other side of the portage, where I found six Canoes. 'How is this?' I said to them; 'do you thus forsake the French? Know you not that I hold Onnontio's voice in my hands, and that I am to speak for him, through the presents he entrusted to me, to all your nations?' These words forced them to give us aid, so that we joined the bulk of the fleet toward noon.

"Upon landing, I spoke to them all, and threatened them with the displeasure of Monsieur de Tracy,[1] whose spokes-

---

[1] Alexander de Prouville, marquis de Tracy, was born in 1603. He was a lieutenant-general in the French Army, and achieved notable successes against the Dutch in Cayenne, and in the adjacent islands. In Nov., 1663, he was appointed governor-general of all French possessions in the Americas, and soon afterward left France to visit those regions. He did not reach Canada until June, 1665.

man I was. Fear of disobliging that great Onnontio impelled one of the chief men among them to take the word and harangue long and forcibly to persuade us to turn back. The weakness of this discontented man was turned to account by the evil spirit for closing the way against the Gospel. None of the others were better disposed; so that, although our Frenchmen found places for themselves without much difficulty, no one would be burdened with me—all declaring that I had neither skill at the paddle, nor strength to carry loads on my shoulders.

"In this abandoned state I withdrew into the woods, and, after thanking God for making me so acutely sensible of my slight worth, confessed before his divine Majesty that I was only a useless burden on the earth. My prayer ended, I returned to the water's edge, where I found the disposition of that Savage who had repulsed me with such contempt entirely changed; for, unsolicited, he invited me to enter his Canoe, which I did with much alacrity, fearing he would change his mind.

"No sooner had I embarked than he put a paddle in my hand, urging me to use it, and assuring me it was an honorable employment, and one worthy of a great Captain. I willingly took the paddle and, offering up to God this labor in atonement for my sins, and to hasten the poor Savages' conversion, I imagined myself a malefactor sentenced to the Galleys; and, although I became entirely exhausted, yet God gave me sufficient strength to paddle all day long, and often a good part of the night. But this application did not prevent my being commonly the object of their contempt and the butt of their jokes: for, however much I exerted myself, I accomplished nothing in comparison with them, their bodies being large and strong, and perfectly adapted to such labors. The slight esteem in which they held me caused them to steal from me every article of my wardrobe that they could; and I had much difficulty in

His vigorous and resolute measures against the Mohawks brought peace to the harassed Canadian colonies, and so alarmed the savages that they did not venture to disturb them for years afterward. In Aug., 1667, Tracy returned to France, where he died three years later.—*Ibid.*, xlix., *note* 11.

retaining my hat, the wide rim of which seemed to them peculiarly fitted for defense against the excessive heat of the sun. And when evening came, as my Pilot took away a bit of blanket that I had, to serve him as a pillow, he forced me to pass the night without any covering but the foliage of some tree.

"When hunger is added to these discomforts, it is a severe hardship, but one that soon teaches a man to find a relish in the bitterest roots and the most putrid meat. We were forced to accustom ourselves to eat a certain moss growing upon the rocks. It is a sort of shell-shaped leaf which is always covered with caterpillars and spiders; and which, on being boiled, furnishes an insipid soup, black and viscous, that rather serves to ward off death than to impart life.

"One morning, we found a stag that had been dead four or five days. It was a lucky accident for poor starvelings. I was given a piece of it, and although its offensive odor deterred some from eating any, hunger made me take my share; but my mouth had a putrid taste, in consequence, until the next day.

"Amid all these hardships, whenever we came to any Rapids, I carried as heavy burdens as I could; but I often succumbed under them, and that made our Savages laugh and mock me, saying they must call a child to carry me and my burden. Our good God did not forsake me utterly on these occasions, but often wrought on some of the men so that, touched with compassion, they would, without saying anything, relieve me of my chapel or some other burden, and would help me to journey a little more at my ease.

"We endured these hardships for nearly two weeks; and after passing the Nipissirinien Lake, as we were descending a little River, we heard cries of lamentation and death-songs. Approaching the spot whence came these outcries, we saw eight young Savages of the Outaouacs, frightfully burned by a direful accident, a spark having by inadvertence fallen into a keg of powder. Four among them were completely scorched, and in danger of dying. I comforted them and prepared them for

Baptism, which I would have conferred had I had time to see them sufficiently fitted for it; for, despite this disaster, we had to keep on our way, in order to reach the entrance to the Lake of the Hurons, which was the rendezvous of all these travelers.

"Toward the beginning of September, after coasting along the shores of the Lake of the Hurons, we reached the Sault; for such is the name given to a half-league of rapids that are encountered in a beautiful river which unites two great Lakes— that of the Hurons, and Lake Superior.

"This River is pleasing, not only on account of the Islands intercepting its course and the great bays bordering it, but because of the fishing and hunting, which are excellent there. We sought a resting place for the night on one of these Islands, where our Savages thought they would find provision for supper upon their arrival; for, as soon as they had landed, they put the kettle on the fire, expecting to see the Canoe laden with fish the moment the net was cast into the water! But God chose to punish their presumption, and deferred giving any food to the starving men until the following day.

"On the second of September, then, after clearing this Sault,—which is not a waterfall, but merely a very swift current impeded by numerous rocks,—we entered Lake Superior, which will henceforth bear Monsieur de Tracy's name, in recognition of indebtedness to him on the part of the people of those regions.

"The form of this lake is nearly that of a bow, the Southern shore being much curved and the Northern nearly straight. Fish are abundant there, and of excellent quality; while the water is so clear and pure that objects at the bottom can be seen to the depth of six brasses.

"One often finds at the bottom of the water pieces of pure copper, of ten and twenty livres' weight. I have several times seen such pieces in the Savages' hands; and since they are superstitious, they keep them as so many divinities, or as presents which the gods dwelling beneath the water have given them, and on which their welfare is to depend. For this reason they preserve these pieces of copper, wrapped up, among their most precious possessions. Some have kept them for more than fifty years; others have had them in their families from time immemorial, and cherish them as household gods.

"For some time, there had been a sort of great rock, all of copper, the point of which projected from the water; this gave the passers-by the opportunity to go and cut off pieces from it. When, however, I passed that spot, nothing more was seen of it; and I think that the storms—which here are very frequent, and like those at sea—have covered the rock with sand. Our Savages tried to persuade me that it was a divinity, who had disappeared for some reason they do not state.[1]

"This Lake is, furthermore, the resort of twelve or fifteen distinct nations—coming, some from the North, others from the South, and still others from the West; and they all betake themselves either to the best parts of the shore for fishing, or to the Islands, which are scattered in great numbers all over the Lake. These peoples' motive in repairing hither is partly to obtain food by fishing, and partly to transact their petty trading with one another, when they meet. But God's purpose was to facilitate the proclaiming of the Gospel to wandering and vagrant tribes—as will appear in the course of this Journal.

"Having, then, entered Lake Tracy, we spent the whole month of September in coasting along its southern shore— where, finding myself alone with our Frenchmen, I had the consolation of saying holy Mass, which I had been unable to do since my departure from three Rivers.

"We then crossed the Bay named for saint Theresa by the late Father Menard. There this brave missionary spent a winter, laboring with the same zeal which afterward made him sacrifice his life in quest for souls. I found, at no great

[1] The copper of Lake Superior was well-known among the Algonkin tribes when the French began to settle in Canada, and early writers frequently mention the mines of that region. In 1768, the English government was petitioned for the grant of "all the copper mines circumjacent to Lake Superior," for sixty miles inland. . . . In 1843, the so-called "copper rock of Lake Superior" was transported from its original locality on the Ontonagon River. Its weight was estimated at 6,000 to 7,000 pounds, and its purity at 95 percent. It was placed in the Smithsonian Institute at Washington, D. C.—*Ibid.*, l., *note* 28.

distance thence, some remnants of his labors, in the persons of two Christian women who had always kept the faith, and who shone like two stars amid the darkness of that infidelity. I made them pray to God, after I had refreshed their memory concerning our mysteries."

Following is what Father Allouez relates concerning the customs of the Outaouacs and other peoples, which he has studied very carefully,—not trusting the account given him by others, but having been himself an eye-witness and observer of everything described in this manuscript.

"There is here," he says, "a false and abominable religion, resembling in many respects the beliefs of some of the ancient Pagans. The Savages of the regions recognize no sovereign master of Heaven and Earth, but believe there are many spirits-some of whom are beneficent, as the Sun, the Moon, the Lake, Rivers, and Woods; others malevolent, as the adder, the dragon, cold, and storms. And, in general, whatever seems to them either helpful or hurtful they call a Manitou, and pay it the worship and veneration which we render only to the true God.

"These divinities they invoke whenever they go out hunting, fishing, to war, or on a journey—offering them sacrifices, with ceremonies appropriate only for Sacrificial priests.

"One of the leading old men of the Village discharges the function of Priest, beginning with a carefully prepared harangue addressed to the Sun—if the eat-all feast, which bears a certain resemblance to a holocaust, is held in its honor. During this invocation, all the Guests eat even to the last morsel; after which a man appointed for the purpose takes a cake of tobacco, breaks it in two, and throws it into the fire. Everyone cries aloud as the tobacco burns and the smoke rises aloft; and with these cries the sacrifice ends.

"I have seen an idol set up in the middle of a village; and to it, among other presents, ten dogs were offered in sacrifice, in order to prevail on this false god to send elsewhere the disease that was depopulating the Village.

"As, moreover, these people are of gross nature, they

recognize no purely spiritual divinity, believing that the Sun is a man, and the Moon his wife; that snow and ice are also a man, who goes away in the spring and comes back in the winter; that the evil spirit is in adders, dragons, and other monsters; that the crow, the kite, and some other birds are genii, and speak just as we do; and that there are even people among them who understand the language of birds, as some understand a little that of the French.

"They believe, moreover, that the souls of the Departed govern the fishes in the lake; and thus, from earliest times, they have held the immortality, and even the metempsychosis, of the souls of the dead fishes, believing that they pass into other fishes' bodies. Therefore they never throw their bones into the fire, for fear that they will offend these souls, so that they will cease to come into their nets.

"They hold in very special veneration a certain fabulous animal which they have never seen except in dreams, and which they call Missibizi, acknowledging it to be a great genius, and offering it sacrifices in order to obtain good sturgeon-fishing.

"They also say that the little nuggets of copper which they find at the bottom of the water in the Lake, or in the Rivers emptying into it, are the riches of the Gods who dwell in the depths of the earth.

"The fountain-head of their Religion is libertinism; and all these various sacrifices end ordinarily in debauches, indecent dances, and shameful acts of concubinage. All the devotion of the men is directed toward securing many wives, and changing them whenever they choose; that of the women, toward leaving their husbands; and that of the girls, toward a life of profligacy.

"Let us say something about the art of Medicine in vogue on this country. Their science consists in ascertaining the cause of the ailment and applying the remedies.

"They deem the most common cause of illness to come from failure to give a feast after some successful fishing or hunting excursion; for then the Sun, who takes pleasure in feasts, is angry with the one who has been delinquent in his duty, and makes him ill.

"Besides this general cause of sickness, there are special ones, in the shape of certain little spirits, malevolent in their nature, who thrust themselves of their own accord, or are sent by some enemy, into the parts of the body that are most diseased. Thus, when any one has an aching head, or arm, or stomach, they say that a Manitou has entered this part of the body, and will not cease its torments until it has been drawn or driven out.

"The most common remedy, accordingly, is to summon the Juggler, who comes attended by some old men, with whom he holds a sort of consultation on the patient's ailment. After this, he falls upon the diseased part, applies his mouth to it, and, by sucking, pretends to extract something from it, as a little stone, or a bit of string, or something else, which he has concealed in his mouth beforehand, which he displays, saying, 'There is the Manitou; now thou are cured, and it only remains to give a feast.'

"The Devil, bent on tormenting those poor blinded creatures even in this world, has suggested to them another remedy, in which they place great confidence. It consists in grasping the patient under the arms, and making him walk barefoot over the live embers in the cabin; or, if he is so ill that he cannot walk, he is carried by four or five persons, and made to pass slowly over all the fires, a treatment which often enough results in this, that the greater suffering thereby produced cures, or induces unconsciousness of, the lesser pain which they strive to cure.

"After all, the commonest remedy, as it is the most profitable for the Physician, is holding of a feast to the sun, which is done in the belief that this luminary, which takes pleasure in liberal actions, being appeased by a magnificent repast, will regard the patient with favor, and restore him to health."

After a hard and fatiguing journey of five hundred leagues, the Father, in founding the Missions of which we are about to speak, found opportunity to exercise the zeal which had made him eagerly undergo so many fatigues. Let us begin with the Mission of Saint Esprit, which is the place of his abode. He speaks as follows:

"This part of the lake where we have halted is between two large villages, and forms a sort of centre for all the Nations of these regions, because of its abundance of fish, which constitute the chief part of these peoples' sustenance.

"Here we have erected a little Chapel of bark, where my entire occupation is to receive the Algonquin and Huron Christians, and instruct them; baptize and catechise the children; admit the Infidels, who hasten hither from all directions, attracted by curiosity; and make them see the truths of our faith.

"I have hung up in the Chapel various pictures, as of Hell and of the Universal Judgement, which furnish me themes for instruction well adapted to my Hearers. God blesses these beginnings; for the young people's debauches are no longer so frequent, and the young girls, who formerly did not blush at the most shameless acts, hold themselves in restraint, and maintain the modesty so becoming to their sex."

[Allouez's journal is continued, forming nearly the whole of the *Relation*. He relates his work among the Ottawa tribes. The savages have lost their former dread of baptism as causing death; they now imagine that this rite will cure sickness, and raise up the dying. The Father ministers especially to the sick and the dying; he finds only four adults who are worthy of baptism.

Allouez next mentions his labors among the Pottawattomies. These people he has met at Lake Superior, whither they resort. Bands of the Sacs and Foxes also sojourn near Chequamegon, to whom Allouez preaches the faith.

The seed of the true religion has been carried among the Illinois tribes by some of their own people, whom Allouez has instructed. He regards that nation as offering a most promising field for missionary labor; he finds them friendly, and more inclined than other tribes to recognise a Supreme Being. He describes a ceremony peculiar to them, the calumet dance.

He meets also some wandering Sioux and Cree savages: regarding all these distant tribes he gives much curious information. The crees invite him to spend the winter with them, but he cannot leave his present field to do so.

Le Mercier concludes, from Allouez's report, that missionaries to the Northwest should have a fixed residence, with men to work for their maintenance and to erect chapels for religious services. This is Allouez's own plan, to execute which he descends to Quebec for aid.—*Ibid.* li., 1 ff.]

[*Ibid.*, l., li., *Doc.* cxxi.]

III

TAKING POSSESSION, IN THE KING'S NAME, OF ALL THE COUNTRIES COMMONLY INCLUDED UNDER THE DESIGNATION OUTAOUAC

(From the Relation of 1671-1672. By Father Claude Dablon)

It is well to afford a general view of all these Outaouac territories, not only for the purpose of designating the places where the Faith has been proclaimed by the planting of Missions, but also because the King,[1] by very recently taking possession of them with a ceremony worthy of the eldest son of the Church, put all these tribes under the protection of the Cross before receiving them under his own—as will be set forth in the account to be given of that act of taking possession.

By glancing, as one can, at the Map of the lakes, and of the territories on which are settled most of the tribes of these regions, one will gain more light upon all these Missions than by long descriptions that might be given of them.

The reader may first turn his eyes to the Mission of Sainte Marie du Sault, three leagues below the mouth of Lake superior. He will find it situated on the banks of the river by which this great Lake discharges its waters, at the place called the Sault, very advantageous in which to perform Apostolic functions, since it is the great resort of most of the Savages of these regions, and lies in the almost universal route of all who go down to the French settlements. It was also on this spot that all these lands were taken possession of in his Majesty's name, in the presence and with the approval of fourteen Nations who had come hither for that purpose.

[1] Louis XIV (Le Grand).

Toward the other end of the same lake is found the Mission of Saint Esprit, covering both the district known as Chagaoumigong point and the neighboring islands. It will be easy to recognise the rivers and routes leading to various Nations, either stationary or nomadic, located in the vicinity of this same lake, who are somewhat dependent on this Mission of saint Esprit in the matter of trade, which draws them to our Savages' abode.

For it is a Southward course that is taken by the great river called by the natives Missisipi, which must empty somewhere in the region of the Florida sea, more than four hundred leagues hence. Fuller mention of it will be made hereafter. Beyond that great river lie the Villages of the Ilinois, a hundred leagues from saint Esprit point. Still farther away is situated another Nation, of an unknown tongue, beyond which, it is said, lies the Western sea. Again, proceeding toward the West-Northwest, we find the people called Assinipoulac, not far from the North sea, two weeks' journey from the Mission of saint Esprit.

The reader will also be enabled—on his journey, so to speak—to note all the places on this Lake where copper is said to be found. For the slabs and huge lumps of this metal which we have seen; that great rock of copper, seven or eight hundred livres in weight, seen near the head of the Lake by all who pass; and, furthermore, the numerous pieces found at the water's edge in various places,—all seem to force upon us the conviction that somewhere there are parent mines not yet discovered.

Toward the South, on the other side of the Lake, are the territories formerly occupied by various Nations of the Hurons and Outaouacs, who had stationed themselves at some distance from one another, as far as the famous Island of Missilimakinac.[1] In the neighborhood of this island, various

[1] Such an allusion, and at so early a date, sufficiently indicates the importance of Mackinac Island to both Indians and white men. It was, until the day of railroads, the central point for all travel on the upper Great Lakes, and for a vast extent of wilderness and half settled country beyond. . . . Not until 1670 is Mackinac (Michillimackinac) mentioned in the *Relations,* although Ménard

Peoples used to make their abode, who now fully intend to return thither if they see that peace is firmly established. It is for this reason that we have already begun to found there the Mission of St. Ignace.

Thence one enters the Lake called Mitchiganous, to which the Ilinois have given their name. Between this lake of the Ilinois and Lake Superior is seen a long bay called the bay des Puans, at the head of which is the Mission of saint François Xavier.

Finally, the remaining tribes, farther distant toward the South and Southwest, are either beginning to draw near to us,— for already the Ilinois have reached the bay mentioned above, or else are waiting until we can advance to them. All these matters will be treated more in detail, touching upon what has been found most rare and curious among those newly-discovered countries and Peoples. But first let us see how the King took possession of them this year, and subjected them to Jesus Christ's dominion before placing them under his own.

It is not our present purpose to describe this ceremony in detail, but merely to touch on matters relating to Christianity and the welfare of our missions, which are going to be more flourishing than ever after what occurred to their advantage on this occasion.

When Monsieur Talon,[1] our Intendant, returned from

and Allouez must have seen it in their early voyages. The reason for this is suggested in our text; the tribes who had dwelt there had been, long before, driven thence by the fierce Iroquois, and that region was practically deserted until 1670—when the Hurons on Superior, in fear of the Sioux, retreated to the North shore of Mackinac Island. Here Marquette continued his missionary labors with them, at the site of the present St. Ignace.—*Ibid.*, lv., note 3.

[1] Jean Baptiste Talon was born in Picardy, in 1625. He held various government positions in France, until he was appointed (March, 1665) intendant of justice, police, and finance in the French colonies of North America. In this position he displayed great executive ability, energy, and honesty, and did much for the development and prosperity of Canada—carrying out the policy recently devised by Louis XIV. He sent Albanel to Hudson Bay, and St. Lusson to the upper Great Lakes, and thus opened the way for the exploration of the great Northwest. His health giving way in 1668, he returned to France, but, after two years' stay there, resumed his office in New France, where he remained until 1672, after which he held a post of honor in the king's own household.— *Ibid.*, xlix., note 14.

Portugal, and after his shipwreck, he was commanded by the King to return to this country; and at the same time received his Majesty's orders to exert himself strenuously for the establishment of Christianity here, by aiding our Missions, and to cause the name and the sovereignty of our invincible Monarch to be acknowledged by even the least known and the most remote Nations. These commands, reinforced by the designs of the Minister,—who is ever equally alert to extend God's glory, and to promote that of his King in every land,—were obeyed as speedily as possible. Monsieur Talon had no sooner landed that he considered means for insuring the success of these plans,—choosing to that end sieur de saint Lusson,[1] whom he commissioned to take possession, in his place and in his Majesty's name, of the territories lying between the East and the West, from Montreal as far as the South sea, covering the utmost extent and range possible.

For this purpose, after wintering on the Lake of the Hurons, Monsieur de saint Lusson repaired to sainte Marie du Sault early in May of this year, sixteen hundred and seventy-one. First, he summoned the surrounding tribes living within a radius of a hundred leagues, and even more; and they responded through their Ambassadors, to the number of fourteen Nations. After making all necessary preparations for the successful issue of the whole undertaking to the honor of France, he began, on June fourth of the same year, with the most solemn ceremony ever observed in these regions.

For, when all had assembled in a great public council, and a height had been chosen well adapted to his purpose,—overlooking, as it did, the Village of the people of the Sault,—he caused the Cross to be planted there, and then the King's standard to be raised, with all the pomp that he could devise.

The Cross was publicly blessed, with all the ceremonies of the Church, by the Superior of these Missions; and then, when it had been raised from the ground for the purpose of plant-

---

[1] Simon Francois Daumont sieur de Lusson, was a French gentleman who had probably come to Canada with Talon in 1670. He was sent then to the Northwest—partly to take possession of that region for France, partly to search for copper mines.—*Ibid.*, lv., *note* 4.

ing it, the *Vexilla* was sung. Many Frenchmen there present at the time joined in this hymn, to the wonder and delight of the assembled Savages; while the whole company was filled with a common joy at the sight of this glorious standard of JESUS CHRIST, which seemed to have been raised so high only to rule over the hearts of all these poor peoples.

Then the French Escutcheon, fixed to a Cedar pole, was also erected, above the Cross, while the *Exaudiat* was sung, and prayer for his Majesty's Sacred person was offered in that far-away corner of the world. After this, Monsieur de saint Lus-son, observing all the forms customary on such occasions, took possession of those regions, while the air resounded with repeated shouts of "Long live the King!" and with the dis-charge of musketry,—to the delight and astonishment of all those peoples, who had never seen anything of the kind.

After this confused uproar of voices and muskets had ceased, perfect silence was imposed upon the whole assemblage; and Father Claude Allouez began to Eulogize the King, in order to make all those Nations understand what sort of a man he was whose standard they beheld, and to whose sovereignty they were that day submitting. Being well versed in their tongue and in their ways, he was so successful in adapting himself to their comprehension as to give them such an opinion of our incomparable Monarch's greatness that they have no words with which to express their thoughts upon the subject.

"Here is an excellent matter brought to your attention, my brothers," said he to them, "a great and important matter, which is the cause of this council. Cast your eyes upon the Cross raised so high above your heads; there it was that JESUS CHRIST, the son of God, making himself man for the love of men, was pleased to be fastened and to die, in atonement to his Eternal Father for our sins. He is the master of our lives, of Heaven, of Earth, and of Hell. Of him I have always spoken to you, and his name and word I have bourne into all these countries.

"But look likewise at that other post, to which are affixed the armorial bearings of the great Captain of France whom we call King. He lives beyond the sea; he is the Captain of the greatest Captains, and has not his equal in the world. All the Captains you have ever seen, or of whom you have ever heard, are mere children compared with him. He is like a great tree, and they, only like little plants that we tread under foot in walking.

"You know about Onnontio, that famous Captain of Quebec. You know and feel that he is the terror of the Iroquois, and that his very name makes them tremble, now that he has laid waste their country and set fire to their Villages. Beyond the sea there are ten thousand Onnontios like him, who are only the Soldiers of that Great Captain, our Great King, of whom I am speaking. When he says, 'I am going to war,' all obey him; and those ten thousand Captains raise Companies of a hundred soldiers each, both on sea and on land. Some embark in ships, one hundred or two hundred in number, like those you have seen at Quebec. Your Canoes hold only four or five men—or, at the very most, ten or twelve. Our ships in France hold four or five hundred, and even as many as a thousand.

"Other men make war by land, but in such vast numbers that, if drawn up in double file, they would extend farther than from here to Mississaquenk, although the distance exceeds twenty leagues. When he attacks, he is more terrible than the thunder; the earth trembles, the air and the sea are set on fire by the discharge of his Cannon; while he has been seen amid his squadrons, all covered with the blood of his foes, of whom he has slain so many with his sword that he does not count their scalps, but the rivers of blood which he sets flowing. So many prisoners of war does he lead away that he makes no account of them, letting them go about whither they will, to show that he does not fear them. No one now dares make war upon him, all nations beyond the sea having most submissively sued for peace. From all parts of the world people go to listen to his words and to admire him, and he alone decides all the affairs of the world.

"What shall I say of his wealth? You count yourselves

rich when you have ten or twelve sacks of corn, some hatchets, glass beads, kettles, or other things of that sort.   He has towns of his own, more in number than you have people in all these countries five hundred leagues around; while in each town there are warehouses containing enough hatchets to cut down all your forests, kettles to cook all your moose, and glass beads to fill all your cabins.   His house is longer than from here to the head of the Sault,"—that is, more than half a league,— "and higher than the tallest of your trees; and it contains more families than the largest of your villages can hold."

The Father added much more of this sort, which was received with wonder by those people, who were all astonished to hear that there was any man on earth so great, rich, and powerful.

Following this speech, Monsieur de Saint Lusson took the word, and stated to them in martial and eloquent language the reasons for which he had summoned them,—and especially that he was sent to take possession of that region, receive them under the protection of the great King whose Panegyric they had just heard; and to form thenceforth but one land of their territories and ours.   The whole ceremony was closed with a fine bonfire, which was lighted toward evening, and around which the *Te Deum* was sung to thank God, on behalf of those poor ·peoples, that they were now the subjects of so great and powerful a Monarch.

[*Ibid.*, lv., *Doc.* cxxvii.]

IV

OF THE FIRST VOYAGE MADE BY FATHER MARQUETTE [1] TOWARD NEW MEXICO, AND HOW THE IDEA THEREOF WAS CONCEIVED

[One of the most valuable and important documents in our series is the journal of Father Marquette, describing the voyage in which he and Joliet discovered and explored the Mississippi River. It is prefaced with a brief note by Dablon, which mentions Marquette's early desire to carry the gospel to the Southern tribes, and his opportunity for doing so when Joliet is chosen by Frontenac and Talon to explore the then unknown water routes beyond Lake Michigan.— *Ibid.*, lix., 14.]

The Father had long premeditated This Undertaking, influenced by a most ardent desire to extend the Kingdom of Jesus Christ, and to make him Known and adored by all the peoples of that country. He saw himself, As it were, at the door of these new Nations when, as early as the year 1670, he was laboring in the Mission at the point of st. Esprit, at the extremity of lake superior, among the outaouacs; he even saw occasionally various persons belonging to these new peoples from whom he obtained all the Information that he could. This induced him to make several efforts to commence this undertaking, but ever in vain; and he even lost all hope of

[1] Father Jacques Marquette: born at Laon, June 10, 1637: entered the Order at Nancy, Oct. 8, 1654; arrived at Quebec, Sept. 20, 1666; died near the present site of Ludington, Mich., May 18, 1675. His remains were transferred two years later and buried in Mission chapel near Point St. Ignace, at the head of East Moran Bay. There they were discovered, Sept. 3, 1877, by V. R. Fr. E. Jacker. The little monument erected at the spot covers part of his remains; but the larger portion are preserved at Marquette College, Milwaukee.—*Ibid.*, lxxi., p. 150.

succeeding therein, when God brought about for him the following opportunity.

In the year 1673, Monsieur The Count De Frontenac,[1] Our Governor, and Monsieur Talon, then Our Intendant, Recognizing the Importance of this discovery,—either that they might seek a passage from there to the sea of China, by the river that discharges into the Vermillion, or California Sea; or because they desired to verify what has for some time been said concerning the 2 Kingdoms of Theguaio And Quiuira, which Border on Canada, and in which numerous gold mines are reported to exist,—these Gentlemen, I say, appointed at the same time for This undertaking Sieur Jolyet,[2] whom they considered very fit for so great an enterprise; and they were well pleased that Father Marquette should be of the party.

[1] Louis de Buade, Count de Frontenac. was born in 1620. His natural preference was for military life, and at the age of fifteen he was sent to Holland, where he served under the prince of Orange. The greater part of his life was spent in active military service, although at times he was attached to the Royal court. His marriage was unhappy, and his only son died at an early age. In 1672, he received the appointment of governor of New France, an office he filled with great ability, but his fiery headstrong disposition soon involved him in quarrels with the Jesuits, fur traders, and civil authorities and even the Sulpitians. He was recalled in 1682. His successors, however, lacked his foresight and energy. The Iroquois tribes who had been kept in subjection under Frontenac's administration soon regained their arrogance. In 1689 they made a raid on Montreal Island, burning and ravaging the settlements and threatening the town. In this critical state of affairs, the king sent Frontenac back to Canada as the one man who could rescue it from peril. Returning in 1689, he at once began vigorous military operations against the Iroquois and against the English colonies as their allies. In 1696, Frontenac, notwithstanding his advanced age, led in person an expedition into the enemy's country, which resulted in the destruction of the leading Onondaga and Oneida villages. This blow crushed the power of the Iroquois, and saved Canada. He died Nov. 28, 1698, to the deep regret of most of the Canadians.—*Ibid.*, lv., *note* 11.

[2] Louis Joliet was a son of Jean Joliet, and was baptized in September, 1645, at Quebec. A student at the Jesuit college there until 1666, he had taken minor orders, and was preparing for priesthood. In 1666 and 1667, he is mentioned as "clerk of the church" at the seminary of Quebec; and, apparently in the latter year, he abandoned the ecclesiastical life. In October, 1667 (according to Sulte), he went to France, where he spent a year; and in 1669 he was sent with Jean Péré, by Talon in search of copper-mines at Lake Superior. Returning from this expedition, he met, in September of that year, La Salle and his Sulpitian companions, near the western end of Lake Ontario. Joliet was present at Saulte Ste. Marie when St. Lusson took possession of that region for France (June 4, 1671), and he was sent by Frontenac to explore the Mississippi region, in company with the Jesuit Marquette, whose mission at Pt. St. Ignace he reached in December, 1672. In the following May, they began their voyage, which lasted

They were not mistaken in the choice they made of Sieur Jolyet, For he is a young man, born in this country, who possesses all the qualifications that could be desired for undertaking. He has experience and Knows the Languages spoken in the Country of the Outaouacs,[1] where he has passed several years. He possesses Tact and prudence, which are the chief qualities necessary for the success of a voyage as dangerous as it is difficult. Finally, he has the Courage to dread nothing where everything is to be Feared. Consequently, he has fulfilled all The expectations entertained of him; and if, having passed through a thousand dangers, he had not unfortunately been wrecked in the very harbor, his Canoe having been upset below sault st Louys, near Montreal,—where he lost both his men and his papers, and whence he escaped only by a sort of Miracle,—nothing would have been left to be desired in the success of his Voyage.

SECTION 1ST. DEPARTURE OF FATHER JACQUES MARQUETTE FOR THE DISCOVERY OF THE GREAT RIVER CALLED BY THE SAVAGES MISSISIPI, WHICH LEADS TO NEW MEXICO.

The feast of the IMMACULATE CONCEPTION of the BLESSED VIRGIN—whom I have always Invoked since I have been in this country of the outaouacs, to obtain from God the grace of being able to visit the Nations who dwell along the

five months. Joliet's papers were lost on the return voyage; but a letter from Frontenac to Colbert, dated Nov., 1674, says of the explorer: "He left with the Fathers at Saulte Ste. Marie, in Lake Superior, copies of his journals; these we cannot get before next year." Unfortunately these copies also appear to have been lost.

In 1679, he made a voyage to Hudson Bay, at the demand of the farmers of revenue in Canada. With Jacques de Lalande, he obtained, in the same year, the grant of Isles Mingan, on the north shore of the St. Lawrence, where valuable fisheries were located; and in 1680 was granted, to Joliet alone, the island of Anticosti, also noted for its extensive fisheries. This latter concession was specifically made as a reward for his discoveries in the above voyages. For many years, he lived at Anticosti with his family. In April, 1697, he also obtained the seigniory of Joliet in Beauce county, Quebec. In 1680, he was appointed hydrographer for the king. The English invasion of Canada in 1690 caused him great losses; and it is claimed that, at his death (about 1700), he was actually suffering from poverty.—*Ibid.,* l., *note* 19.

[1] *See* p. 314, ff.

Missisipi River—was precisely the Day on which Monsieur Jollyet arrived with orders from Monsieur the Count de frontenac, Our Governor, and Monsieur Talon, Our Intendant, to accomplish This discovery with me. I was all the more delighted at This good news, since I saw that my plans were about to be accomplished; and since I found myself in the blessed necessity of exposing my life for the salvation of all these peoples, and especially of the Ilinois, who had very urgently entreated me, when I was at the point of st. Esprit, to carry the word of God to Their country.

We were not long in preparing all our Equipment, although we were about to Begin a voyage, the duration of which we could not foresee. Indian Corn, with some smoked meat, constituted all our provisions; with these we Embarked—Monsieur Jollyet and myself, with 5 men—in 2 Bark Canoes, fully resolved to do and suffer everything for so glorious an Undertaking.

Accordingly, on the 17th day of may, 1673, we started from the Mission of st. Ignace at Michilimakinac, where I Then was. The Joy that we felt at being selected for This Expedition animated our Courage, and rendered the labor of paddling from morning to night agreeable to us. And because We were going to seek Unknown countries, we took every precaution in our power, so that, if our Undertaking were hazardous, it should not be foolhardy. To that end, we obtained all the Information that we could from the savages who had frequented those regions; and we even traced out from their reports a Map of the whole of that New country; on it we indicated the rivers which we were to navigate, the names of the peoples and of the places through which we were to pass, the Course of the great River, and the direction we were to follow when we reached it.

Above all, I placed our voyage under the protection of the Blessed Virgin Immaculate, promising her that, if she granted us the favor of discovering the great River, I would give it the Name of the Conception, and that I would also make the first Mission that I should establish among Those New peoples,

bear the same name. This I have actually done, among the
Ilinois.

SECTION 2ND. *THE FATHER VISITS, IN PASS-*
ING, THE TRIBES OF THE FOLLE AVOINE.
WHAT THAT FOLLE AVOINE IS. HE ENTERS
THE BAY DES PUANTS; SOME PARTICULARS
ABOUT THAT BAY. HE ARRIVES AMONG
THE FIRE NATION.

With all these precautions, we Joyfully Plied our paddles
on a portion of Lake huron, on That of the Illinois and on
the bay des Puants.

The first Nation that we came to was That of the folle
avoine. I entered Their River, to go and visit these peoples
to whom we have preached The Gospel for several years,—
in consequence of which, there are several good christians
among Them.

The wild oat, whose name they bear because it is to be
found in their country, is a sort of grass, which grows naturally in the small Rivers with muddy bottoms, and in Swampy
Places. It greatly resembles the wild oats that Grow amid our
wheat. The ears grow upon hollow stems, joined at Intervals; they emerge from the Water about the month of June,
and continue growing until they rise About two feet above it.
The grain is not larger than That of our oats, but it is twice as
long, and The meal therefrom is much more abundant. The
Savages Gather and prepare it for food as Follows. In The
month of September, which is the suitable time for The harvest, they go in Canoes through These fields of wild oats;
they shake its Ears into the Canoe, on both sides, as they pass
through. The grain falls out easily, if it be ripe, and they
obtain their supply In a short time. But, in order to clean
it from the straw, and to remove it from a husk in which
it is Enclosed, they dry it in the smoke, upon a wooden grating,
under which they maintain a slow fire for some Days. When
The oats are thoroughly dry, they put them in a Skin made
into a bag, thrust It into a hole dug into the ground for This

purpose, and tread it with their feet—so long and so vigorously that The grain separates from the straw, and is very easily winnowed. After this, they pound it to reduce it to flour,—or even, without pounding it, they Boil it in water and season it with fat. Cooked in This fashion The wild oats have almost as delicate a taste as rice has when no better seasoning is added.

I told these peoples of the folle avoine of My design to go and discover Those Remote nations, in order to Teach them the Mysteries of Our Holy Religion. They were Greatly surprised to hear it, and did their best to dissuade me. They represented to me that I would meet Nations who never show mercy to Strangers, but Break Their heads without any cause; and that war was kindled Between Various peoples who dwelt upon our Route, which Exposed us to the further manifest danger of being killed by the bands of Warriors who are ever in the Field. They also said that the great River was very dangerous, when one does not know the difficult Places; that it was full of horrible monsters, which devoured men and Canoes Together; that there was even a demon, who was heard from a great distance, who barred the way, and swallowed up all who ventured to approach him; Finally that the Heat was so excessive In those countries that it would Inevitably Cause Our death.

I thanked them for the good advice that they gave me, but told them that I could not follow it, because the salvation of souls was at stake, for which I would be delighted to give my life; that I scoffed at the alleged demon; that we would easily defend ourselves against those marine monsters; and, moreover, that We would be on our guard to avoid the other dangers with which they threatened us. After making them pray to God, and giving them some Instruction, I separated from them. Embarking then in our Canoes, We arrived shortly afterward at the bottom of the Bay des puantz, where our Fathers labor successfully for the Conversion of these peoples, over two thousand of whom they have baptized while they have been there.

This bay bears a Name which has a meaning not so offensive in the language of the Savages; For they call it *la bayé sallée* ["salt bay"] rather than Bay des Puans,—although with Them this is almost the same and this is also The name which they give to the Sea. This led us to make very careful researches to ascertain whether there were not some salt-Water springs in This quarter, As there are among the hiroquois, but we found none. We conclude, therefore, that This name has been given to it on account of the quantity of mire and Mud which is seen there, whence noisome vapors Constantly arise, Causing the loudest and most Continual Thunder that I have ever heard.

The Bay is thirty leagues in depth and eight in width at its Mouth; it narrows gradually to the bottom, where it is easy to observe a tide which has its regular ebb and flow, almost Like That of the Sea. This is not the place to inquire whether these are real tides; whether they are Due to the wind, or to some other cause; whether there are winds, The precursors of the Moon and attached to her suite, which consequently agitate the lake and give it an apparent ebb and flow whenever the Moon ascends above the horizon. What I can positively state is, that, when the water is very Calm, it is easy to observe it rising and falling according to the Course of the moon; although I do not deny that This movement may be Caused by very Remote Winds, which, pressing on the middle of the lake, cause the edges to Rise and fall in the manner which is visible to our eyes.

We left This bay to enter the river that discharges into it; it is very beautiful at its Mouth, and flows gently; it is full Of bustards, Ducks, Teal and other birds, attracted thither by the wild oats of which they are very fond. But after ascending the river a short distance, it becomes very difficult of passage, on account of both the Currents and the sharp Rocks, which cut the Canoes and the feet of Those who are obliged to drag them, especially when the Waters are low. Nevertheless, we successfully passed Those rapids; and on approaching Machkoutens, the fire Nation, I had the Curiosity to drink the mineral Waters of the River that is not far from that village. I also took time to look for a medicinal plant which a savage, who knows its secret, showed to Father Alloues with many Ceremonies. Its root is employed to Counteract snakebites, God having been pleased to give this antidote Against a poison which is very common in these countries. It is very pungent, and tastes like powder when crushed with the teeth; it must be masticated and placed upon the bite inflicted by the snake. The reptile has so great a horror of it that it even flees from a Person who has rubbed himself with it. The plant bears several stalks, a foot high, with rather long leaves; and a white flower which greatly resembles the wall flower.[1] I put some in my canoe, in order to examine it at leisure while we continued to advance toward Maskoutens, where we arrived on The 7th of June.

SECTION 3RD. DESCRIPTION OF THE VILLAGE OF MASKOUTENS; WHAT PASSED THERE BETWEEN THE FATHER AND THE SAVAGES. THE FRENCH BEGIN TO ENTER A NEW AND UNKNOWN COUNTRY, AND ARRIVE AT MISSISIPI.

Here we are at Maskoutens. This Word may, in Algonquin, mean, "the fire Nation,"—which, indeed, is the name given to this tribe. Here is the limit of the discoveries which the french have made, For they have not yet gone any further.

This Village Consists of three Nations who have gathered there—Miamis, Maskoutens, and Kikabous. The former are the most civil, the most liberal, and the most shapely. They wear two long locks over their ears, which give them a pleasing appearance. They are regarded as warriors, and rarely undertake expeditions without being successful. They are very docile, and listen quietly to What is said to Them; and they appeared so eager to Hear Father Alloues when he Instructed

[1] The description here given is insufficient for the identification of the plant. Various plants have been regarded as specifics for the bites of venomous serpents, especially *Aristolochia serpentaria* and *Polygala Senega;* but their virtues have apparently been somewhat exaggerated.—*Ibid.,* vol. lix., *note* 18.

them that they gave Him but little rest, even during the night. The Maskoutens and Kikabous are ruder, and seem peasants in comparison with the others. As Bark for making Cabins is scarce in this country They use Rushes; these serve Them for making walls and Roofs, but do not afford them much protection against the winds, and still less against the rains when they fall abundantly. The Advantage of Cabins of this kind is, that they make packages of Them, and easily transport them wherever they wish, while they are hunting.

When I visited them, I was greatly Consoled at seeing a handsome Cross erected in the middle of the village, and adorned with many white skins, red Belts, and bows and arrows, which these good people had offered to the great Manitou (This is the name which they give to God). They did this to thank him for having had pity On Them during the Winter, by giving Them an abundance of game When they Most dreaded famine.

I took pleasure in observing the situation of this village. It is beautiful and very pleasing; For, from an Eminence upon which it is placed, one beholds on every side prairies, extending farther than the eye can see, interspersed with groves or with lofty trees. The soil is very fertile, and yields much indian corn. The savages gather quantities of plums and grapes, wherewith much wine could be made, if desired.

No sooner had we arrived than we, Monsieur Jollyet and I, assembled the elders together; and he told them that he was sent by Monsieur Our Governor to discover New countries, while I was sent by God to Illumine them with the light of the holy Gospel. He told them that, moreover, The sovereign Master of our lives wished to be known by all the Nations; and that in obeying his will I feared not the death to which I exposed myself in voyages so perilous. He informed them that we needed two guides to show us the way; and We gave them a present, by it asking them to grant us the guides. To this they very Civilly consented; and they also spoke to us by means of a present, consisting of a Mat to serve us as a bed during the whole of our voyage.

On the following day, the tenth of June, two Miamis who were given us as guides embarked with us, in the sight of a great crowd, who could not sufficiently express their astonishment at the sight of seven frenchmen, alone in two Canoes, daring to undertake so extraordinary and so hazardous an Expedition.

We knew that, at three leagues from Maskoutens, was a River, which discharged into Missisipi. We knew also that the direction we were to follow in order to reach it was westsouthwesterly. But the road is broken by so many swamps and small lakes that it is easy to lose one's way, especially as the River leading thither is so full of wild oats that it is difficult to find the Channel. For this reason we greatly needed our two guides, who safely Conducted us to a portage of 2,700 paces, and helped us to transport our Canoes to enter That river; after which they returned home, leaving us alone in this Unknown county, in the hands of providence.[1]

Thus we left the Waters flowing to Quebec, 4 or 500 Leagues from here, to float on Those that would thenceforward Take us through strange lands. Before embarking thereon, we Began all together a new devotion to the blessed Virgin Immaculate, which we practised daily, addressing to her special prayers to place under her protection both our persons and the success of our voyage; and, after mutually encouraging one another, we entered our Canoes.

The River on which we embarked is called Meskousing. It is very wide; it has a sandy bottom, which forms various shoals that render its navigation very difficult. It is full of Islands Covered with Vines. On the banks one sees fertile land, diversified with woods, prairies, and Hills. There are oak, Walnut and basswood trees; and another kind, whose branches are armed with long thorns. We saw there neither feathered game nor fish, but many deer and a large number of cattle. Our Route lay to the southwest, and, after navigating about 30 leagues, we saw a spot presenting all the ap-

---

[1] Reference is here made to the Fox-Wisconsin portage. The name "Meskousing" is but one of the numerous variants of "Wisconsin."—*Ibid.*, lix., *note* 20.

pearances of an iron mine; and, in fact, one of our party who had formerly seen such mines, assures us that The One which We found is very good and very rich. It is Covered with three feet of good soil, and is quite near a chain of rocks, the base of which is covered by very fine trees. After proceeding 40 leagues on This same route, we arrived at the mouth of our River, and, at 42 and a half degrees of latitude, We safely entered Missisipi on the 17th of June, with a Joy that I cannot Express.

SECTION 4TH. OF THE GREAT RIVER CALLED MISSISIPI; ITS MOST NOTABLE FEATURES; OF VARIOUS ANIMALS, AND ESPECIALLY THE PISIKIOUS OR WILD CATTLE, THEIR SHAPE AND NATURE; OF THE FIRST VILLAGES OF THE ILINOIS, WHERE THE FRENCH ARRIVED.

Here we are, then, on this so renowned River, all of whose peculiar features I have endeavored to note carefully. The Missisipi River takes its rise in various lakes in the country of the Northern nations. It is narrow at the place where Miskous empties; its Current, which flows southward, is slow and gentle. To the right is a large Chain of very high Mountains, and to the left are beautiful lands; in various Places, the stream is Divided by Islands. On sounding we found ten brasses of Water. Its Width is very unequal; sometimes it is three-quarters of a league, and sometimes it narrows to three arpents. We gently followed its Course, which runs toward the south and southeast, as far as the 42nd degree of Latitude. Here we plainly saw that its aspect was completely changed. There are hardly any woods or mountains; The Islands are more beautiful, and are Covered with finer trees. We saw only deer and cattle, bustards and Swans without wings, because they drop Their plumage in This country. From time to time, we came upon monstrous fish, one of which struck our Canoe with such violence that I Thought that it was a great tree, about to break the Canoe to pieces.[1]   On another occasion, we saw on The water a monster with the head of a tiger, a sharp nose Like That of a wildcat, with whiskers and straight, Erect ears; The head was grey and the Neck quite black; but We saw no more creatures of this sort. When we cast our nets into the water we caught a Sturgeon, and a very extraordinary Kind of fish.   It resembles the trout, with This difference, that its mouth is larger.   Near its nose— which is smaller, as are also the eyes—is a large Bone shaped Like a woman's busk, three fingers wide and a cubit long, at the end of which is a disk as Wide As one's hand.   This frequently causes it to fall backward when it leaps out of the water.   When we reached the parallel of 41 degrees 28 minutes, following The same direction, we found that Turkeys had taken the place of game; and the pisikious,[2] or wild cattle, That of the other animals.

We call them "wild cattle," because they are very similar to our domestic cattle.   They are not longer, but are nearly as large again, and more Corpulent.   When Our people killed one, three persons had much difficulty in moving it.   The head is very large; The forehead is flat, and a foot and a half Wide between the Horns, which are exactly like Those of our oxen, but black and much larger.   Under the Neck They have a Sort of large dewlap, which hangs down; and on The back is a rather high hump.   The whole of the head, The Neck, and a portion of the Shoulders, are Covered with a thick Mane Like That of horses; It forms a crest a foot long, which makes them hideous, and, falling over the eyes, Prevents them from seeing what is before Them.   The remainder

---

[1] "This was probably the cat fish of the Mississippi. They sometimes grow enormously large, and strike with great force any object that comes their way."— B. F. French's note, *Desc. of Miss. Valley*, p. 17.—*Ibid.*, lix., *note* 21.

[2] The terms *vache sauvage, boeuf sauvage*, and sometimes buffe and buffle, were applied to the buffalo, the moose and the elk, whence has arisen much confusion in regard to the former habitat of the buffalo. But examination of the fossil remains of this animal indicates that the buffalo was not found east of Hudson's Bay and the Great Lakes, or the Alleghanies. Boucher makes a definite statement on this point: "As for the animals called Bufles, they are only found in the country of the Outaouacs, some four or five hundred leagues from Quebec, toward the West and North."—*Ibid.*, ix., *note* 33.

of the Body is covered with a heavy coat of curly hair, almost Like That of our sheep, but much stronger and Thicker. It falls off in the Summer, and The skin becomes as soft As Velvet. At that season, the savages Use the hides for making fine Robes, which they paint in various Colors. The flesh and the fat of the pisikious are Excellent, and constitute the best dish at feasts. Moreover, they are very fierce; and not a year passes without their killing some savages. When attacked, they catch a man on their Horns, if they can, toss Him in the air, and then throw him on the ground, after which they trample him under foot, and kill him. If a person fire at Them from a distance, with either bow or a gun, he must, immediately after the Shot, throw himself down and hide in the grass; For if they perceive Him who has fired they Run at him and attack him. As their legs are thick and rather Short, they do not run very fast, As a rule, except when angry. They are scattered about the prairie in herds; I have seen one of 400.

We continued to advance, but, As we knew not whither we were going,—for we had proceeded over One hundred leagues without discovering anything except animals and birds,—we kept well on our guard. On this account, we make only a small fire on land, toward evening, to cook our meals; and, after supper, we remove Ourselves as far from it as possible, and pass the night in our Canoes, which we anchor in the river at some distance from the shore. This does not prevent us from always posting one of the party as a sentinel, for fear of surprise. Proceeding still in southerly and south-south-westerly direction, we find ourselves at the parallel of 41 degrees, and as low as 40 degrees and some minutes,—partly southeast and partly southwest,—after having advanced over 60 leagues since We Entered the River, without discovering anything.

Finally on the 25th of June, we perceived on the water's edge some tracks of men, and a narrow and somewhat beaten path leading to a fine prairie. We stopped to Examine it; and, thinking that it was a road which Led to some village of savages, We resolved to go and reconnoiter it. We therefore left our two Canoes under the guard of our people, strictly charging Them not to allow themselves to be surprised, after which Monsieur Jollyet and I undertook this investigation— a rather hazardous one for two men who exposed themselves, alone, to the mercy of a barbarous and Unknown people. We silently followed The narrow path, and, after walking About 2 leagues, We discovered a village on the bank of a river, and two others on a Hill distant about half a league from the first. Then we Heartily commended ourselves to God, and, after imploring his aid, we went farther without being perceived, and approached so near that we could even hear the savages talking. We therefore Decided that it was time to reveal ourselves. This we did by Shouting with all Our energy, and stopped, without advancing any further. On hearing the shout, the savages quickly issued from their Cabins, And having probably recognized us as frenchmen, especially when they saw a black gown,—or, at least, having no cause for distrust, as we were only two men, and had given them notice of our arrival,— they deputed four old men to come and speak to us. Two of these bore tobacco-pipes, finely ornamented and adorned with various feathers. They walked slowly, and raised their pipes toward the sun, seemingly offering them to it to smoke,— without, however, saying a word. They spent a rather long time in covering the short distance between their village and us. Finally, when they had drawn near, they stopped to Consider us attentively. I was reassured when I observed these Ceremonies, which with them are performed only among friends; and much more so when I saw them Clad in Cloth, for I judged thereby they were our allies. I therefore spoke with them first, and asked them who they were. They replied that they were Ilinois; and, as a token of peace, they offered us their pipes to smoke. They afterward invited us to enter their Village, where all the people impatiently awaited us. These pipes for smoking tobacco are called in This country Calumets. This word has come so much into use that, in order to be understood, I shall be obliged to use it, as I shall often have to mention these pipes.

SECTION 5TH. HOW THE ILINOIS RECEIVED THE FATHER IN THEIR VILLAGE

At the door of the Cabin in which we were to be received was an old man, who awaited us in a rather surprising attitude, which constitutes a part of the Ceremonial that they observe when they receive Strangers. This man stood erect, and stark naked, with his hands extended and lifted toward the sun, As if he wished to protect himself from its rays, which nevertheless shone upon his face through his fingers. When we came near him, he paid us This Compliment: "How beautiful the sun is, O frenchman, when thou comest to visit us! All our village awaits thee, and thou shalt enter all our Cabins in peace." Having said this, he made us enter his own, in which were a crowd of people: they devoured us with their eyes, but, nevertheless, observed profound silence. We could, however, hear these words, which were addressed to us from time to time in a low voice: "How good it is, My brothers, that you should visit us."

After We had taken our places, the usual Civility of the country was paid to us, which consisted in offering us the Calumet. This must not be refused, unless one wishes to be considered an Enemy, or at least uncivil; it suffices that one make a pretense of smoking. While all the elders smoked after Us, in order to do us honor, we received an invitation on behalf of the great Captain of all the Ilinois to proceed to his Village where he wished to hold a Council with us. We went thither in a large Company, For all these people, who had never seen any frenchmen among Them, could not cease looking at us. They Lay on The grass along the road; they proceeded us, and then retraced their steps to come and see us Again. All this was done noiselessly, and with marks of great respect for us.

When we reached the Village of the great Captain, We saw him in the entrance of his Cabin, between two old men,—all

three erect and naked, and holding their Calumet turned toward the sun. He harangued us In a few words, congratulating
us upon our arrival. He afterward offered us his Calumet, and
made us smoke while we entered his Cabin, where we received
all their usual kind Attentions.

Seeing all assembled and silent, I spoke to them by four
presents that I gave them. By the first, I told them that
we were journeying peacefully to visit the nations dwelling
on the River as far as the Sea. By the second, I announced
to them that God, who had Created them, had pity on Them,
inasmuch as, after they had so long been ignorant of him,
he wished to make himself Known to all the peoples; that I
was Sent by him for that purpose; and that it was for Them
to acknowledge and obey him. By the third, I said that the
great Captain of the French informed them that he it was
who restored peace everywhere; and that he had subdued The
Iroquois. Finally, by the fourth, we begged them to give us
all The Information that they had about the Sea, and the
Nations through Whom we must pass to reach it.

When I had finished my speech, the Captain arose, and,
resting His hand upon the head of a little Slave whom he
wished to give us, he spoke thus: "I thank thee, Black Gown,
and thee, O frenchman,"—addressing himself to Monsieur
Jollyet,—"for having taken so much trouble to come to visit
us. Never has the earth been so beautiful, or the sun so
Bright, as today; Never has our river been so Calm, or so
clear of Rocks, which your canoes have Removed in passing;
never has our tobacco tasted so good, or our corn appeared so
fine, as We now see Them. Here is my son, whom I give
thee to Show thee my Heart. I beg thee to have pity on
me, and on all my Nation. It is thou who Knowest the great
Spirit who has made us all. It is thou who speakest to Him,
and who hearest his word. Beg Him to give me life and
health, and to come and dwell with us, in order to make us
Know him." Having said this, he placed the little Slave near
us, and gave us a second present, consisting of an altogether
mysterious Calumet, upon which they place more value than

upon a Slave. By this gift, he expressed to us The esteem that he had for Monsieur Our Governor, from the account which we had given of him; and, by a third, he begged us on behalf of all his Nation not to go farther, on account of the great dangers to which we Exposed ourselves.

I replied that I Feared not death, and that I regarded no happiness greater than that of losing my life for the glory of Him who has made all. This is what these poor people cannot Understand.

The Council was followed by a great feast, Consisting of four dishes, which had to be partaken of in accordance with all their fashions. The first course was a great wooden platter full of sagamité,—that is to say, meal of indian corn boiled in water, and seasoned with fat. The Master of Ceremonies filled a Spoon with sagamité three or four times, and put it to my mouth As if I were a little Child. He did The same to Monsieur Jollyet. As a second course, he caused a second platter to be brought, on which were three fish. He took some pieces of them, removed the bones therefrom, and, after blowing upon them, to cool Them he put them in our mouths As one would give food to a bird. For the third course, they brought a large dog, that had just been killed; but, when they learned that we did not eat this meat, they removed it from before us. Finally, the 4th course was a piece of wild ox, The fattest morsels of which were placed in our mouths.

After this feast, we had to go to visit the whole village, which Consists of fully 300 Cabins. While we walked through the Streets, an orator Continually harangued to oblige all the people to come to see us without Annoying us. Everywhere we were presented with Belts, garters, and other articles made of the hair of bears and cattle, dyed red, Yellow, and gray. These are all the rarities they possess. As they are of no great Value, we did not burden ourselves with Them.

We Slept in the Captain's Cabin, and on the following day we took Leave of him promising to pass again by his village, within four moons. He Conducted us to our Canoes, with nearly 600 persons who witnessed our Embarkation, giving us every possible manifestation of the joy that Our visit had caused them. For my own part, I promised, on bidding them Adieu, that I would come the following year, and reside with Them to instruct them. But, before quitting the Ilinois country, it is proper that I should relate what I observed of their Customs and usages.

SECTION 6TH. OF THE CHARACTER OF THE ILINOIS; OF THEIR HABITS AND CUSTOMS: AND OF THE ESTEEM THAT THEY HAVE FOR THE CALUMET, OR TOBACCO-PIPE, AND OF THE DANCE THEY PERFORM IN ITS HONOR.

When one speaks the word "Ilinois" it is as if one said in their language, "the men,"—As if the other Savages were looked upon by them merely as animals. It must also be admitted that they have an air of humanity which we have not observed in the other nations that we have seen upon our route. The shortness Of my stay among Them did not allow me to secure all the Information that I would have desired; among all Their customs, the following is what I have observed.

They are divided into many villages, some of which are quite distant from that of which we speak, which is called peouarea. This causes some difference in their language, which, on the whole, resembles allegonquin, so that we easily understood each other. They are of a gentle and tractable disposition; we Experienced this in the reception which they gave us. They have several wives, of whom they are Extremely jealous; they watch them very closely, and cut off their noses or ears when they misbehave. I saw several women who bore the marks of their misconduct. Their Bodies are shapely; they are active and very skillful with their bows and arrows. They also use guns, which they buy from our savage allies who Trade with our french. They use them especially to inspire, through their noise and smoke, terror in their Enemies; the latter do not use guns, and have never seen any, since they live too Far toward the West. They are warlike, and make themselves dreaded by the Distant tribes to the south and west, whither they go to procure Slaves; these they barter, selling them at a high price to other Nations, in exchange for other Wares. Those very Distant Savages against whom they war, have no Knowledge of Europeans; neither do they know anything of iron, or of Copper, and they have only stone Knives. When the Ilinois depart to go to war, the whole village must be notified by a loud Shout, which is uttered at the doors of their Cabins, the night and The Morning before their departure. The Captains are distinguished from the warriors by wearing red Scarfs. These are made, with considerable Skill, from the Hair of bears and wild cattle. They paint their faces with red ocher, great quantities of which are found at a distance of some days' journey from the village. They live by hunting, game being plentiful in that country, and on indian corn, of which they always have a good crop; consequently, they have never suffered from famine. They also sow beans and melons, which are Excellent, especially those that have red seeds. Their Squashes are not of the best; they dry them in the sun, to eat them during The winter and spring. Their Cabins are very large, and are Roofed and floored with mats made of Rushes. They make all Their utensils of wood, and Their Ladles out of the heads of cattle, whose Skulls they know so well how to prepare that they use these ladles with ease for eating their sagamité.

They are liberal in cases of illness, and Think that the effect of the medicines administered to them is in proportion to the presents given to the physician. Their garments consist only of skins; the women are always clad very modestly and very becomingly, while the men do not take the trouble to cover themselves. I know not through what superstition some Ilinois, as well as some Nadouessi, while still young, assume the garb of women, and retain it throughout their lives. There is some mystery in this, For they never marry and glory in demeaning themselves to do everything that

the women do. They go to war, however, but can use only
clubs, and not bows and arrows, which are the weapons proper
to men. They are present at all the juggleries, and at the
solemn dances in honor of the Calumet; at these they sing,
but must not dance. They are summoned to the Councils,
and nothing can be decided without their advice. Finally,
through their profession of leading an Extraordinary life,
they pass for Manitous,—that is to say, for Spirits—or persons of Consequence.[1]

There remains no more, except to speak of the Calumet.
There is nothing more mysterious or more respected among
them. Less honor is paid to the Crowns and scepters of Kings
than the Savages bestow upon this. It seems to be the God
of peace and of war, the Arbiter of life and of death. It
has but to be carried upon one's person, and displayed, to
enable one to walk safely through the midst of Enemies—
who, in the hottest of the Fight, lay down Their arms when
it is shown. For That reason, the Illinois gave me one, to
serve as a safe guard among all the Nations through whom
I had to pass during my voyage. There is a Calumet for
peace, and one for war, which are distinguished solely by the
Color of the feathers with which they are adorned; Red
is a sign of war. They also use it to put an end to Their
disputes, to strengthen Their alliances, and to speak to
Strangers. It is fashioned from red stone,[2] polished like

[1] The custom here described appears to have been prevalent among the Southern and Western tribes, and is mentioned by many travelers and writers, even
down to comparatively recent times. . . . Charlevoix and Long, among others,
suppose that the assumption of feminine garb and occupations by men proceeded
from a superstition or a dream, or was the observance of some religious rite;
some other writers assert that these men were set aside for infamous purposes
—a statement apparently verified by much evidence, especially as this class of
men were held in utmost contempt, even among savages. They were called by
the French *bardache* (a word originally from arabic *bardaj*, "slave"), or *berdache;*
the English corruption of this word, "berdash" (a word used, in various forms,
as early as 1548), is everywhere in use in the West and North, to designate the
men referred to.—*Ibid.,* lix., *note* 26.

[2] The redstone of which the calumet was made has been, from an early period,
obtained by the Indians from the celebrated "Pipestone Quarry," in Pipestone
county in the southwestern corner of Minnesota. This place was first described
by George Catlin, who visited it in 1836. . . . The stone was named in honor of
him, "Catlinite."—*Ibid.,* lix., *note* 27.

marble, and bored in such a manner that one end serves as a receptacle for the tobacco, while the other fits into the stem; this is a stick two feet long, as thick as an ordinary cane, and bored through the middle. It is ornamented with the heads and necks of various birds, whose plumage is very beautiful. To these they also add large feathers,—red, green, and other colors,—wherewith the whole is adorned. They have a great regard for it, because they look upon it as the calumet of the Sun; and, in fact, they offer it to the latter to smoke when they wish to obtain a calm, or rain, or fine weather. They scruple to bathe themselves at the beginning of Summer, or to eat fresh fruit, until after they have performed the dance, which they do as follows:

The Calumet dance, which is very famous among these peoples, is performed solely for important reasons; sometimes to strengthen peace, or to unite themselves for some great war; at other times, for public rejoicing. Sometimes they thus do honor to a Nation who are invited to be present; sometimes it is danced at the reception of some important personage, as if they wished to give him the diversion of a Ball or a Comedy. In Winter, the ceremony takes place in a Cabin; in summer, in the open fields. When the spot is selected, it is completely surrounded by trees, so that all may sit in the shade afforded by their leaves, in order to be protected from the heat of the Sun. A large mat of rushes, painted in various colors, is spread in the middle of the place, and serves as a carpet upon which to place with honor the God of the person who gives the Dance; for each has his own God, which they call their Manitou. This is a serpent, a bird, or other similar thing, of which they have dreamed while sleeping, and in which they place all their confidence for the success of their war, their fishing, and their hunting. Near this Manitou, and at its right, is placed the Calumet in honor of which the feast is given; and all around it a sort of trophy is made, and the weapons used by the warriors of those Nations are spread, namely: clubs, war-hatchets, bows, quivers, and arrows.

Everything being thus arranged, and the hour of the Dance drawing near, those who have been appointed to sing take the most honorable place under the branches; these are the men and women who are gifted with the best voices, and who sing together in perfect harmony. Afterward, all come to take their seats in a circle under the branches; but each one, on arriving, must salute the Manitou. This he does by inhaling the smoke, and blowing it from his mouth upon the Manitou, as if he were offering to it incense. Everyone at the outset, takes the Calumet in a respectful manner, and, supporting it with both hands, causes it to dance in cadence keeping good time with the air of the songs. He makes it execute many differing figures; sometimes he shows it to the whole assembly, turning himself from one side to the other. After that, he who is to begin the Dance appears in the middle of the assembly, and at once continues this. Sometimes he offers it to the sun, as if he wished the latter to smoke it; sometimes he inclines it toward the earth; again, he makes it spread its wings, as if about to fly; at other times, he puts it near the mouths of those present, that they may smoke. The whole is done in cadence; and this is, as it were, the first Scene of the Ballet.

The second consists of a Combat carried on to the sound of a kind of drum, which succeeds the songs, or even unites with them, harmonizing very well together. The Dancer makes a sign to some warrior to come to take the arms which lie upon the mat, and invites him to fight to the sound of the drums. The latter approaches, takes up the bow and arrows, and the war-hatchet, and begins the duel with the other, whose sole defense is the Calumet. This spectacle is very pleasing, especially as all is done in cadence; for one attacks, the other defends himself; one strikes blows; the other parries them; one takes to flight, the other pursues; and then he who was fleeing faces about, and causes his adversary to flee. This is done so well—with slow and measured steps, and to the rhythmic sound of the voices and drums—that it might pass for a very fine opening of a Ballet in France. The third Scene consists of a lofty Discourse, delivered by

him who holds the Calumet; for, when the Combat is ended
without bloodshed, he recounts the battles at which he has
been present, the victories that he has won, the names of
the Nations, the places, and the Captives whom he has made.
And, to reward him, he who presides at the Dance makes
him a present of a fine robe of Beaver-skins, or some other
article.   Then, having received it, he hands the Calumet
to another, the latter to a third, and so on with all the others,
until everyone has done his duty; then the President presents the Calumet itself to the Nation that has been invited
to the Ceremony, as a token of the everlasting peace that is
to exist between the two peoples.

Here is one of the Songs that they are in the habit of
singing.   They give it a certain turn which cannot be sufficiently expressed by Note, but which nevertheless constitutes
all its grace.

Ninahani, ninahani, ninahani, nani ongo.[1]

[1] Martin, in Douniol edition (t. ii, p. 273) gives the entire chant (of which but
one sentence is found in the Montreal MS.), with both words and musical notation. He gives as his authority "a manuscript preserved by the Jesuits, at Paris,
in which appear the notation of the song in the calumet dance, and the beginning
of the seventh section." The song is as follows:

Cf. illustrated description of calumet dance, as practiced among the **Omaha**
Indians, given in *U. S. Bur. Ethnol. Rep.*, 1881-82, pp.   276-282.—*Ibid.*,
lix., *note* 29.

*SECTION 7TH. DEPARTURE OF THE FATHER FROM
THE ILINOIS: OF THE PAINTED MONSTERS
WHICH HE SAW UPON THE GREAT RIVER
MISSISIPI: OF THE RIVER PEKITANOUI. CON-
TINUATION OF THE VOYAGE.*

We take leave of our Ilinois at the end of June, about
three o'clock in the afternoon. We embark in the sight of
all the people, who admire our little Canoes, for they have
never seen any like them.

We descend, following the current of the river called Pekitanoui, which discharges into the Mississipy, flowing from the
Northwest. I shall have something important to say about
it, when I shall have related all that I have observed along
this river.

While passing near the rather high rocks that line the river,
I noticed a simple which seem to me very Extraordinary.
The root is like small turnips fastened together by little
filaments, which taste like carrots. From this root springs
a leaf as wide As one's hand, and half a finger thick, with
spots. From the middle of this leaf spring other leaves,
resembling the sconces used for candles in our halls; and
each leaf bears Five or six yellow flowers shaped like little
Bells.

We found quantities of mulberries, as large as Those of
france; and a small fruit which we at first took for olives,
but which tasted like oranges; and another fruit as large As
a hen's egg. We cut it in halves, and two divisions appeared,
in each of which 8 to 10 fruits were encased; these are shaped
like almonds, and are very good when ripe. Nevertheless,
The tree that bears them has a very bad odor and its leaves
resemble Those of the walnut-tree. In These prairies there
is also a fruit similar to Hazel-nuts but more delicate; The
leaves are very large, and grow from a stalk at the end of
which is a head similar to That of a sunflower, in which all
its Nuts are regularly arranged. These are very good, both
Cooked and Raw.

While Skirting some rocks, which by Their height and Length inspired awe, We saw upon one of them two painted monsters which at first made Us afraid, and upon Which the boldest savages dare not Long rest their eyes. They are as large As a calf; they have Horns on their heads Like those of a deer, a horrible look, red eyes, a beard Like a tiger's, a face somewhat like a man's, a body Covered with scales, and so Long A tail that it winds all around the Body, passing above the head and going back between the legs, ending in a Fish's tail. Green, red, and black are the three Colors composing the Picture. Moreover, these 2 monsters are so well painted that we cannot believe that any savage is their author; for good painters in france would find it difficult to paint so well,—and, besides, they are so high up on the rock that it is difficult to reach that place Conveniently to paint them. Here is approximately The shape of these monsters, As we have faithfully Copied it.[1]

While conversing about these monsters, sailing quietly in clear and calm Water, we heard the noise of a rapid, into which we were about to run. I have seen nothing more dreadful. An accumulation of large and entire trees, branches, and floating islands, was issuing from the mouth of the river pekistanouï, with such impetuosity that we could not without great danger risk passing through it. So great was the agitation that the water was very muddy, and could not become clear.

Pekitanouï[2] is a river of Considerable size, coming from the Northwest, from a great Distance; and it discharges into the Missisipi. There are many villages of savages along this river, and I hope by its means to discover the vermilion or California sea.

---

[1] Parkman says (*Lasalle*, p. 59, *note* 1): "The rock where these figures were painted is immediately above the city of Alton (Ill.). The tradition of their existence remains, although they are entirely effaced by time. In 1867, when I passed the place, a part of the rock had been quarried away."—*Ibid.*, lix., *note* 33.

[2] *Pekitanouï:* the Missouri River. "The name here given by Marquette meaning 'muddy water,' prevailed till Marest's time (1712). A branch of Rock river is still called Pekatonica. The *Récollets* called the Missouri, the River of Ozages." Shea's note in *Disc. of Miss. Valley*, p. 58.—*Ibid.*, lix., *note* 31.

Judging from the Direction of the course of the Missisipi, if it Continue the same way, we think that it discharges into the mexican gulf. It would be a great advantage to find the river Leading to the southern sea, toward California; and, As I have said, this is what I hope to do by means of the Pekitanouï, according to the reports made to me by the savages. From them I have learned that, by ascending this river for 5 or 6 Days, one reaches a fine prairie, 20 or 30 Leagues Long. This must be crossed in a Northwesterly direction, and it terminates at another small river,—on which one may embark, for it is not very difficult to transport Canoes through so fine a country as that prairie. This 2nd River Flows toward The southwest for 10 or 15 Leagues, after which it enters a Lake, small and deep [the source of another deep river—*Substituted by Dablon*], which flows toward the West, where it falls into The sea.[1] I have hardly any doubt that it is The vermillion sea, and I do not despair of discovering It some day, if God grant me the grace and The health to do so, in order that I may preach The Gospel to all The peoples of this new world who have so Long Groveled in the darkness of infidelity.

Let us resume our Route, after Escaping As best We could from the dangerous rapid Caused by The obstruction which I have mentioned.

*SECTION 8TH: OF THE NEW COUNTRIES DISCOV-
ERED BY THE FATHER. VARIOUS PARTICULARS.
MEETING WITH SOME SAVAGES. FIRST NEWS
OF THE SEA AND OF EUROPEANS. GREAT DAN-
GER AVOIDED BY MEANS OF THE CALUMET.*

After proceeding about 20 Leagues straight to the south, and a little less to the southeast, we found ourselves at a

---

[1] This supposition of Marquette's has been confirmed by later explorations, which show that the head waters of the Platte, tributary to the Missouri, closely approach those of the Colorado, which falls into the Gulf of California.—*Ibid.*, lix., *note* 34.

river called ouaboukigou, The mouth of which is at the 36th degree of latitude. Before reaching it, we passed by a Place that is dreaded by the Savages, because they believe that a manitou is there,—that is to say a demon—that devours travelers; and The savages, who wished to divert us from our undertaking, warned us against it. This is the demon; there is a small cove, surrounded by rocks 20 feet high, into which The whole Current of the river rushes; and, being pushed back against the waters following It, and checked by an Island near by, the Current is Compelled to pass through a narrow Channel. This is not done without a violent Struggle between all these waters, which force one another back, or without a great din, which inspires terror in the savages, who fear everything. But this did not prevent us from passing, and arriving at Waboukigou.[1] This river flows from the lands of the East, where dwell the people called Chaouanons in so great numbers that in one district there are as many as 23 villages, and 15 in another, quite near one another. They are not at all warlike, and are the nations whom the Iroquois go so far to seek, and war against without any reason; and because these poor people cannot defend themselves, they allow themselves to be captured and taken Like flocks of sheep, and innocent though they are, they nevertheless sometimes experience The barbarity of the Iroquois, who cruelly burn Them.

A short distance above the river of which I have just spoken are cliffs, on which our frenchmen noticed an iron mine, which they consider very rich. There are several veins of ore, and a bed a foot thick, and one sees large masses of it united with Pebbles. A sticky earth is found there, of three different colors,—purple, violet, and Red. The water in which the latter is washed assumes a bloody tinge. There is also very heavy red sand. I placed some on a paddle, which was dyed

[1] *Ouaboukigou* (Ouabouskigou, on the maps of both Joliet and Marquette); corrupted by the French into Ouabache, and Anglicized as Wabash. By early writers and map-makers the name was applied to both the present Wabash river and the Ohio below their junction: it was also called by the French Riviere de St. Jerome.—*Ibid.*, lix., *note* 35.

with its color—so deeply that The water could not wash it away during the 15 days while I used it for paddling.

Here we Began to see Canes, or large reeds, which grow on the banks of the river; their color is a very pleasing green; all the nodes are marked by a Crown of Long, narrow, pointed leaves. They are very high, and grow so thickly that The wild cattle have some difficulty in forcing their way through them.

Hitherto, we had not suffered any inconvenience from mosquitoes; but we were entering into their home, as it were. This is what the savages of this quarter do to protect themselves against them. They erect a scaffolding, the floor of which consists only of poles, so that it is open to the air in order that the smoke of the fire made underneath may pass through, and drive away those little creatures, which cannot endure it; the savages lie down upon the poles, over which the bark is spread to keep off rain. These scaffoldings also serve them as a protection against The excessive and Unbearable heat of this country; for they lie in the shade, on the floor below, and thus protect themselves against the sun's rays, enjoying the cool breeze that circulates freely through the scaffolding.

With the same object, we were compelled to erect a sort of cabin on The water, with our sails as a protection against the mosquitoes and the rays of the sun. While drifting down with The current, in this condition, we perceived on land some savages armed with guns, who awaited us. I at once offered them my plumed calumet, while our frenchmen prepared for defense, but delayed firing, that The savages might be the first to discharge their guns. I spoke to them in huron, but they answered me by a word which seemed to me a declaration of war against us. However, they were as frightened as we were; and what we took for a signal for a battle was an Invitation that they gave us to draw near, that they might give us food. We therefore landed, and entered their Cabins, where they offered us meat from wild cattle and bear's grease, with white plums, which are very good. They have guns, hatchets, hoes, Knives, beads, and flasks of double glass, in which they put Their powder. They wear Their hair long, and tattoo their bodies after the hiroquois fashion. The women wear headdresses and garments like those of the huron women. They assured that we were no more than ten days' journey from The sea; that they bought cloth and all other goods from the Europeans who lived to The east, that these Europeans had rosaries and pictures; that they played upon Instruments; that some ot them looked Like me, and had been received by these savages kindly. Nevertheless, I saw none who seemed to have received instruction in the faith; I gave Them as much as I could, with some medals.

This news animated our courage, and made us paddle with Fresh ardor. We thus push forward, and no longer see so many prairies, because both shores of The river are bordered with lofty trees. The cottonwood, elm, and basswood trees there are admirable for Their height and thickness. The great numbers of wild cattle, which we heard bellowing, lead us to believe that The prairies are near. We also saw Quail on the water's edge. We killed a little parroquet, one half of whose head was red, The other half and The Neck was yellow, and The whole body green. We had gone down to near the 33rd degree of latitude having proceeded nearly all the time in a southerly direction, when we perceived a village on The water's edge called Mitchigamea. We had recourse to our Patroness and guide, The Blessed VIRGIN IMMACULATE; and we greatly needed her assistance, For we heard from afar The savages who were inciting one another to the Fray by their Continual yells. They were armed with bows, arrows, hatchets, clubs and shields. They prepared to attack us, on both land and water; part of them embarked in great wooden canoes—some to ascend, others to descend the river, in order to Intercept us and surround us on all sides. Those who were on land came and went, as if to commence The attack. In fact, some Young men threw themselves into The water, to come and seize my Canoe; but the current compelled Them to return to land. One of them then hurled his club, which passed over without striking us. In vain I showed The calumet, and made them signs that we were not coming to war against them. The alarm continued, and they were already preparing to pierce us with arrows from all sides, when God suddenly touched the hearts of the old men, who were standing at the water's edge. This no doubt happened through their sight of our Calumet, which they had not clearly distinguished from afar; but as I did not cease displaying it, they were influenced by it, and checked the ardor of their Young men. Two of these elders even,—after casting into our canoe, as if at our feet, Their bows and quivers, to reassure us—entered the canoe, and made us approach the shore, whereon we landed, not without fear on our part. At first, we had to speak by signs, because none of them understood the six languages which I spoke. At last, we found an old man who could speak a little Ilinois.

We informed them, by our presents, that we were going to the sea. They understood very well what we wished to say to Them, but I know not whether they apprehended what I told them about God, and about matters pertaining to their salvation. This is a seed cast into the ground, which will bear fruit in its time. We obtained no other answer than that we would learn all that we desired at another large village, called Akamsea, which was only 8 or 10 leagues lower down. They offered us sagamité and fish, and we passed The night among them, with some anxiety.

SECTION 9TH: RECEPTION GIVEN TO THE FRENCH IN THE LAST VILLAGE WHICH THEY SAW. THE MANNERS AND CUSTOMS OF THOSE SAVAGES. REASONS FOR NOT GOING FARTHER.

We embarked early on the following day, with our interpreter; a canoe containing ten savages went a short distance ahead of us. When we arrived within half a league of the Akamsea, we saw two canoes coming to meet us. He who commanded stood upright, holding in his hand The calumet, with Which he made various signs, according to the custom of the country. He joined us, singing very agreeably, and gave us tobacco to smoke; after that, he offered us sagamité, and bread made of indian corn, of which we ate a little. He then preceded us, after making us a sign to follow Him slowly. A place had been prepared for us under The scaffolding of the chief of the warriors: it was clean, and carpeted with fine rush mats. Upon These we were made to sit, having around us the elders, who were nearest to us; after them, The warriors; and, finally, all The common people in a crowd. We fortunately found there a Young man who understood Ilinois much better than did The Interpreter whom we had brought from Mitchigamea. Through him, I spoke at first to the whole assembly by The usual presents. They admired what I said to Them about God and the mysteries of our holy faith. They manifested a great desire to retain me among them, that I might instruct Them.

We afterward asked them what they knew about the sea. They replied that we were only ten days' journey from it— we could have covered the distance in 5 days; that they were not acquainted with The Nations who dwelt There, because Their enemies prevented Them from Trading with those Europeans; that the hatchets, Knives, and beads that we saw were sold to Them partly by Nations from The east, and partly by an Ilinois village situated at four days' journey from their village westward. They also told us that the savages with guns whom we had met were Their Enemies, who barred Their way to the sea, and prevented Them from becoming acquainted with the Europeans, and from carrying on any trade with them; that, moreover, we exposed ourselves to great dangers by going farther, on account of the continual forays of their enemies along the river,—because, as they had guns and were very warlike, we could not without manifest danger proceed down the river, which they constantly occupy.

During this conversation, food was continually brought to us in large wooden platters, consisting sometimes of sagamité, sometimes of whole corn, sometimes of a piece of dog's flesh.

The entire day was spent in feasting. These people are very obliging and liberal with what they have; but they are wretchedly provided with food, for they dare not go and hunt wild cattle, on account of Their Enemies. It is true that they have abundance of indian corn, which they sow at all seasons. We saw at the same time some that was ripe, some other that had only sprouted, and some again in the Milk, so that they sow it three times a year. They cook it in great earthen jars, which are well made.[1] They also have plates of baked earth which they use in various ways. The men go naked, and wear Their hair short; they pierce their noses, from which, as well as from Their ears, hang beads. The women are clad in wretched skins; they knot Their hair in two tresses which they throw behind their ears, and have no ornaments with which to adorn themselves. Their feasts are given without any ceremony. They offer the Guests large dishes, from which all eat at discretion and offer what is left to one another. Their language is exceeding difficult, and I could succeed in pronouncing only a few words notwith-standing all my efforts. Their Cabins, which are made of bark, are Long and Wide; they sleep at the two ends, which are raised two feet above the ground. They keep Their corn in large baskets made of Canes, or in gourds as large as half-barrels. They know nothing of the Beaver. Their wealth consists in the skins of wild cattle. They never see snow in their country, and recognize The winter only through The rains, which there fall more frequently than in summer. We ate no other fruit there than watermelons. If they knew how to till their soil, they would have fruits of all kinds.

In the evening, the elders held a secret council, in regard to the design entertained by some to break our heads and rob us; but the Chief put a stop to all these plots. After sending for us, he danced the calumet before us, in the manner I

---

[1] Regarding the pottery manufactured by the tribes of this region . . . it is probable that the earthen jars and vessels used by the Arkansas tribes at the time of Marquette's visit did not essentially differ, in form, process of manufacture, or use, from the specimens now on our museum shelves, obtained from mounds.— *Ibid.*, lix., *note* 40.

have already described, as a token of our entire safety; and, to relieve us of all fear, he made me a present of it.

Monsieur Jolliet and I held another Council, to deliberate upon what we should do—whether we should push on, or remain content with the discovery which we had made. After attentively considering that we were not far from the gulf of Mexico, the basin of which is at a latitude of 31 degrees 60 minutes, while we were at 33 degrees 40 minutes, we judged that we could not be more than 2 or 3 days' journey from it; and that, beyond a doubt, the Missisipi river discharges into the florida or Mexican gulf, and not to The east in Virginia, whose sea-coast is at 34 degrees latitude,—which we had passed, without, however, having yet reached the sea,— or to the west in California, because in that case our route would have been to The west, or the west-southwest, whereas we had always continued It toward the south. We further considered that we exposed ourselves to the risk of losing the results of this voyage, of which we could give no information if we proceeded to fling ourselves into the hands of the Spaniards who, without doubt, would at least have detained us as captives. Moreover, we saw very plainly that we were not in a condition to resist Savages allied to The Europeans, who were numerous, and expert in firing guns, and who continually infested the lower part of the river. Finally, we had obtained all the information that could be desired in regard to this discovery. All these reasons induced us to decide upon Returning; this we announced to the savages, and, after a day's rest, made our preparations for it.

SECTION 10TH. RETURN OF THE FATHER AND OF THE FRENCH. BAPTISM OF A DYING CHILD

After a month's Navigation, while descending Missisipi from the 42nd to the 34th degree, and beyond, and after preaching the Gospel as well as I could to the Nations that I met, we start on the 17th of July from the village of the akensea, to retrace our steps. We therefore reascend the

Missisipi which gives us much trouble in breasting its Currents. It is true that we leave it, at about the 38th degree, to enter another river, which greatly shortens our road, and takes us with but little effort to the lake of the Ilinois.

We have seen nothing like this river that we enter, as regards its fertility of soil, its prairies and woods; its cattle, elk, deer, wildcats, bustards, swans, ducks, parroquets, and even beaver. There are many small lakes and rivers. That on which we sailed is wide, deep, and still, for 65 leagues. In the Spring and during part of The Summer there is only one portage of half a league. [1] We found on it a village of Ilinois called Kaskasia, consisting of 74 Cabins. They received us very well, and obliged me to promise that I would return to instruct them. One of the chiefs of this nation, with his young men, escorted us to the Lake of the Ilinois, whence at last, at The end of September, we reached the bay des puantz, from which we had started in the beginning of June.

Had this voyage resulted in the salvation of even one soul, I would consider all my troubles well rewarded, and I have reason to presume that such is the case. For, when I was returning, we passed through the Ilinois of Peouarea,[2] and during three days I preached the faith in all their Cabins; after which, while we were embarking, a dying child was brought to me at The water's edge, and I baptized it shortly before it died, through an admirable act of providence for the salvation of that Innocent soul.

[*Ibid.*, lix., *Doc.* cxxxvi.]

___

[1] Reference is here made to the Illinois River; from its upper waters the traveler obtained access to Lake Michigan by several portages. That between its northern fork (the Des Plaines River) and the Chicago River was, owing to the southward current along the west shore of Lake Michigan, the usual route on the outward voyage from Mackinac and other northern points.—*Ibid.*, lix., *note* 41.

[2] These villages of the partly nomadic Illinois savages were not situated at the places afterward known by their names. The Kaskaskia village is placed by Shea (*Disc. of Miss. Valley*, p. 74, *note*), "near Rockport" (by which he apparently means the so-called "Starved Rock," on which La Salle built Fort St. Louis); and Parkman locates it (*Lasalle*, pp. 65, 156), "about seven miles below the site of the present town of Ottawa" (Ill.).—*Ibid.*, lix., *note* 42.

V

UNFINISHED JOURNAL OF FATHER JACQUES MARQUETTE, ADDRESSED TO THE REVEREND FATHER CLAUDE DABLON, SUPERIOR OF THE MISSIONS

[This is Marquette's (unfinished) journal of his second voyage to the Illinois tribes—a journey with a pathetic ending, for he dies on the way, while striving to reach Mackinac. Departing from De Pere, October 25, 1674, accompanied by two Frenchmen, he enters the waters of Lake Michigan via the portage at Sturgeon Bay. There they fortunately meet a party of Illinois Indians, who desire the Father to go under their escort. Now begins a long and tedious voyage, so interrupted by storms and severe cold that it is not until December 4 that the party reach Chicago River. The Father is again ill, and finds himself unable to proceed further.

In February Marquette's health begins to improve. The last week in March brings a south wind and the river opens. This gives them an opportunity to resume their journey; but it is not until April 8 that they reach the Illinois village. Marquette's journal ends upon the 6th, while he and his men are awaiting favorable weather to descend the Des Plaines River.—*Ibid.*, lix., 17.]

My Reverend Father:

Pax Christi.

Having been compelled to remain at st. Francois throughout the summer on account of an ailment of which I was cured in the month of september, I waited there the return of our people from down below, in order to learn what I was to do with regard to my wintering. They brought me orders to proceed to the mission of La Conception among the Illinois. After complying with Your Reverence's request for copies of my journal concerning the missisipi River, I departed with Pierre Porteret and Jacque [*blank space in Ms*], on the 25th of october, 1674, about noon. The wind compelled us to pass the night at the outlet of the River, where the Poutewatamis were assembling; for the elders would not allow them to go in the direction of the Ilinois, lest the young men, after collecting robes with the goods that they brought from below, and after hunting Beaver, might seek to go down in the spring; because they have reason to fear the nadouessi.

26th of october   On passing the village, we found only two cabins of savages, who were going to spend the winter at la gasparde. We learned that 5 canoes of Poutewatamis, and 4 of Ilinois, had started to go to the Kaskaskia.

27   We were delayed in the morning by rain; in the afternoon, we had fine, calm weather, so that at sturgeon bay we joined the savages, who traveled ahead of us.

28   We reached the portage. A canoe that had gone ahead prevented us from killing any game. We began our portage and slept on the other shore, where the stormy weather gave us much trouble. Pierre did not arrive until an hour after dark, having lost his way on a path where he had never been. After the rain and thunder, snow fell.

29   Being compelled to change our camping-ground, we continue to carry our packs. The portage covers nearly a league, and is very difficult in many places. The Ilinois assemble in the evening in our cabin, and ask us not to leave them, as we may need them, and they know the lake better than we do. We promise them this.

30   The Ilinois women complete our portage in the morning. We are delayed by the wind. There are no animals.

31   We start, with tolerably fair weather, and sleep at a small river. The road by land from sturgeon bay is very difficult.

Last autumn, we were traveling not far from it when we entered the forest.

After I said holy mass, we came for the night to a river, *November 1* whence one goes to the Poutewatamis by a good road. Chachagwessiou, an Ilinois greatly esteemed among his nation, partly because he engages in the fur trade, arrived at night with a deer on his back, of which he gave us a share.

After holy mass, we travel all day in very fine weather. 2 We kill two cats, which are almost nothing but fat.

While I am ashore, walking on fine sand—the whole water's 3 edge being covered with grass similar to that which is hauled up by the nets at St. Ignace,—I come to a river which I am unable to cross. Our people enter it, in order to take me on board; but we are unable to go out, on account of the waves. All the other canoes go on, excepting one, which came with us.

We are delayed. There seems to be an Island out in the 4 lake, for the game go there at night.

We had considerable difficulty in getting out of the River 5 at noon. We found the savages in a river, where I seized the opportunity of instructing the Ilinois, on account of a feast that nawaskingwe had just given to a wolfskin.

We performed a good day's journey. While the savages 6 were hunting, they discovered some tracks of men, and this compelled us to stay over on the following day.

We landed about 2 o'clock, because there was a good camp- 9 ing ground. We were detained there for 5 days, on account of the great agitation of the lake, although without any wind; and afterward of the snow, which was melted on the following day by the sun, and a breeze from the lake.

After proceeding a sufficient distance, we camp at a favor- 15 able place, where we are detained 3 days. Pierre mends a savage's gun. Snow falls at night, and thaws during the day.

We sleep near the bluffs, and are very poorly sheltered. 20 The savages remain behind while we are delayed 2 days and a half by the wind. Pierre goes into the woods, and finds the prairie 20 leagues from the portage. He also goes through a fine canal which is vaulted, as it were, to the height of a man, in which there is water a foot deep.

23 After embarking at noon we experience some difficulty in reaching a river. Then the cold began, and more than a foot of snow covered the ground; it has remained ever since. We were delayed for three days, during which Pierre killed a deer, 3 bustards, and 3 Turkeys, which were very good. The others proceeded to the prairies. A savage discovered some cabins, and came to get us. Jacques went there on the following day with him; 2 hunters also came to see me. They were maskoutens, to the number of 8 or 9 cabins, who had separated from the others in order to obtain subsistence. With fatigues almost impossible to frenchmen, they travel throughout the winter over very bad roads, the land abounding in streams, small lakes, and swamps. Their cabins are wretched; and they eat or starve, according to the places where they happen to be. Being detained by the wind, we noticed that there were great shoals out in the lake, over which the waves broke continually. Here I had an attack of diarrhoea.

27 We had some trouble in getting out of the river; then, after proceeding about 3 leagues, we found the savages, who had killed some cattle, and 3 ilinois who had come from the village. We were delayed there by a wind from the land, by heavy waves from the lake, and by cold.

We went ahead of the savages so that I might celebrate *December* 1 holy mass.

3 After saying holy mass, we embarked, and were compelled to make for a point, so that we could land, on account of floating masses of ice.

4 We started with a favoring wind, and reached the river of the portage, which was frozen to the depth of half a foot; there was more snow there than elsewhere, as well as more tracks of animals and Turkeys.

Navigation on the lake is fairly good from one portage to the other, for there is no crossing to be made, and one can land anywhere, unless one persist in going on when the waves are high and the wind is strong. The land bordering it is of no value, except on the prairies. There are 8 or 10 quite fine rivers. Deer-hunting is very good, as one goes away from the Poutewatamis.

As we began yesterday to haul our baggage in order to 12 approach the portage, the Ilinois who had left the Poutewatamis arrived, with great difficulty. We were unable to celebrate holy mass on the day of the Conception, owing to the bad weather and cold. During our stay at the entrance of the river, Pierre and Jacques killed 3 cattle and 4 deer, one of which ran some distance with its heart split in 2. We contented ourselves with killing 3 or 4 turkeys, out of the many that came around our cabin because they were almost dying of hunger. Jacques brought in a partridge that he had *Partridge* killed, exactly like those of France except that it had two ruffs, as it were, of 3 or 4 feathers as long as a finger, near the head, covering the 2 sides of the neck where there are no feathers.

Having encamped near the portage, 2 leagues up the river, 14 we resolved to winter there, as it was impossible to go farther, since we were too much hindered and my ailment did not permit me to give myself much fatigue. Several Ilinois passed yesterday, on their way to carry furs to nawaskingwe; we gave them one of the cattle and one of the deer that Jacque had killed on the previous day. I do not think that I have ever seen any savages more eager for French tobacco than they. They came and threw beaver-skins at our feet, to get some pieces of it; but we returned these, giving them some pipefuls of the tobacco because we had not yet decided whether we would go farther.

Chachagwessiou and the other Ilinois left us, to go and 15 join their people and give them the goods that they had brought, in order to obtain their robes. In this they act like the traders, and give hardly any more than do the French. I instructed them before their departure, deferring the holding of a council until the spring, when I should be in their village. They traded us 3 fine robes of ox-skins for a cubit of tobacco; these were very useful to us during the winter.

Being thus rid of them, we said the Mass of the Conception. After the 14th, my disease turned into a bloody flux.

30   Jacque arrived from the Ilinois village, which is only six leagues from here; there they were suffering from hunger, because the cold and snow prevented them from hunting. Some of them notified la Toupine and the surgeon that we were here; and, as they could not leave their cabin, they had so frightened the savages, believing that we would suffer from hunger if we remained here, that Jacque had much difficulty in preventing 15 young men from coming to carry away all our belongings.

January
1675
16   As soon as the 2 frenchmen learned that my illness prevented me from going to them, the surgeon came here with a savage, to bring us some blueberries and corn. They are only 18 leagues from here, in a fine place for hunting cattle, deer, and turkeys, which are excellent there. They had also collected provisions while waiting for us—; and had given the savages to understand that their cabin belonged to the black gown; and it may be said that they have done and said all that could be expected from them. After the surgeon had spent some time here, in order to perform his devotions, I sent Jacque with him to tell the Ilinois near that place that my illness prevented me from going to see them; and that I would even have some difficulty in going there in the spring, if it continued.

24   Jacque returned with a sack of corn and other delicacies, which the French had given him for me. He had also brought the tongues and flesh of two cattle, which a savage and he had killed near here. But all the animals feel the bad weather.

26   3 Ilinois brought us, on behalf of the elders, 2 sacks of corn, some dried meat, pumpkins, and 12 beaver-skins; 1st, to make me a mat; 2nd, to ask me for powder; 3rd, that we might not be hungry; 4th, to obtain a few goods. I replied; 1st, that I had come to instruct them, by speaking to them of prayer, etc.; 2nd, that I would give them no powder, because we sought to restore peace everywhere, and I did not wish them to begin war with the muiamis; 3rd, that we feared not

hunger; 4th, that I would encourage the french to bring them goods, and that they must give satisfaction to those who were among them for the beads which they had taken as soon as the surgeon started to come here. As they had come a distance of 20 leagues I gave them, in order to reward them for their trouble and for what they had brought me, a hatchet, 2 knives, 3 clasp-knives, 10 brasses of glass beads, and 2 double mirrors, telling them that I would endeavor to go to the village,—for a few days only, if my illness continued. They told me to take courage, and to remain and die in their country and that they had been informed that I would remain there for a long time.

Since we addressed ourselves to the Blessed Virgin Im- *February 9* maculate, and commenced a novena with a mass,—at which Pierre and Jacque, who do everything they can to relieve me, received communion,—to ask God to restore my health, my bloody flux has left me, and all that remains is a weakness of the stomach. I am beginning to feel much better, and to regain my strength. Out of a cabin of Ilinois, who encamped near us for a month, a portion have again taken the road to the Poutewatamis, and some are still on the lake-shore, where they wait until navigation is open. They bear letters for our Fathers of st. François.

We have had opportunity to observe the tides coming in *20* from the lake, which rise and fall several times a day; and, although there seems to be no shelter in the lake, we have seen the ice going against the wind. These tides made the *Tides* water good or bad, because that which flows from above comes from the prairies and small streams. The deer which are plentiful near the lake-shore, are so lean that we had to abandon some of those which we had killed.

We killed several partridges, only the males of which had *March 23* ruffs on the neck, the females not having any. These partridges *Partridges* are very good, but not like those of france.

The north wind delayed the thaw until the 25th of March, *30* when it set in with a south wind. On the very next day, game began to make its appearance. We killed 30 pigeons, which I found better than those down the great river; but they are smaller, both old and young. On the 28th, the ice broke up, and stopped above us. On the 29th, the waters rose so high that we had barely time to decamp as fast as possible, putting our goods in the trees, and trying to sleep on a hillock. The water gained on us nearly all night, but there was a slight freeze, and the water fell a little, while we were near our packages. The barrier has just broken, the ice has drifted away; and, because the water is already rising, we are about to embark to continue our journey.

The blessed Virgin Immaculate has taken such care of us during our wintering that we have not lacked provisions, and have still remaining a large sack of corn, with some meat and fat. We also lived very pleasantly, for my illness did not prevent me from saying holy mass every day. We were unable to keep Lent, except on Fridays and saturdays.

31   We started yesterday and traveled 3 leagues up the river without finding any portage. We hauled our goods probably about half an arpent. Besides this discharge, the river has another one by which we are to go down. The very high lands alone are not flooded. At the place where we are, the water has risen more than 12 feet. This is where we began our portage 18 months Ago. Bustards and ducks pass continually; we contented ourselves with 7. The ice, which is drifting down, keeps us here, as we do not know in what condition the lower part of the river is.

April 1   As I do not yet know whether I shall remain next summer in the village, on account of my diarrhoea, we leave here part of our goods, those with which we can dispense, and especially a sack of corn. While a strong south wind delays us, we hope to go tomorrow to the place where the French are, at a distance of 15 leagues from here.

9   Strong winds and the cold prevent us from proceeding. The two lakes over which we passed are full of bustards, geese, ducks, cranes, and other game unknown to us. The rapids are quite dangerous in some places. We have just met the surgeon, with a savage who was going up with a

canoe-load of furs; but, as the cold is too great for persons who are obliged to drag their canoes in the water, he has made a cache of his beaver-skins, and returns to the village tomorrow with us. If the French procure robes in this country, they do not disrobe the savages, so great are the hardships that must be endured to obtain them.

[Addressed: †
"To My Reverend Father, Father Claude Dablon, Superior of the Missions of the Society of Jesus in new france. Quebec."]

[Endorsed: "Letter and Journal of the late Father Marquette."]

Endorsed: ["Everything concerning Father Marquette's voyage."]

[*Ibid.*, lix., *Doc.* cxxxvii.]

VI

ACCOUNT OF THE SECOND VOYAGE AND THE DEATH OF FATHER JACQUES MARQUETTE. BY FATHER CLAUDE DABLON

[In this document Dablon briefly relates the second voyage of Marquette, adding details of his death, and of the removal (1677) of his bones to Mackinac. After reaching the Illinois village, the Father holds (three days before Easter), a great council, where over 1,500 men are present, besides the women and children. He sets out for Mackinac, hoping to reach the mission house there in time to die within its walls; but his strength fails so rapidly that he is obliged to land near Ludington, Michigan, where he dies on the same day (May 18, 1675). His faithful companions there inter his body, which is removed two years later, by some of his Ottawa disciples, to the St. Ignace mission at Mackinac.—*Ibid.*, lix., 18.]

The mission of the Ilinois was founded in the year 1674, after the first voyage which father jacques marquet made to discover new territories and new peoples who are on the great and famous river missisipi.

The year following he made a second voyage in order to establish there the mission: it is that one which we are about to relate.

SECTION 1ST. NARRATIVE OF THE 2ND VOYAGE
THAT FATHER MARQUET MADE TO THE
ILINOIS. HE REACHES THEM, NOTWITHSTAND-
ING HIS ILLNESS. AND BEGINS THE MISSION
OF LA CONCEPTION.

Father Jacques marquette, having promised the Ilinois on
his first voyage to them, in 1673, that he would return to
them the following year, to teach them the mysteries of
our religion, had much difficulty in keeping his word. The
great hardships of his first voyage had Brought upon him a
bloody flux, and had so weakened him that he was giving up
the hope of undertaking a second. However, his sickness
decreased; and, as it had almost entirely Abated by the close
of the summer in the following year, He obtained the permission of his superiors to return to the Ilinois and there
begin that fair mission.

He set out for that purpose, in the month of november of
the year 1674, from the bay des puants, with two men, one
of whom had made the former voyage with him. During
a month of navigation on the lake of the Ilinois, he was tolerably well; but, as soon as the snow Began to fall, he was
again seized with his bloody flux, which compelled him to
halt in the river which Leads to the Ilinois. It was there that
they constructed a Cabin in which to pass the winter, amid such
inconveniences that, his malady increasing more and more, he
saw clearly that God was granting to him the favor which he
had so many times besought from him; and he even told his
two Companions very plainly that he would certainly die of
that malady, and during that voyage. Duly to prepare his
soul, despite the severe disposition of his Body, he began this
so severe winter sojourn by the retreat of st. ignatius, which
he performed with every feeling of devotion, and many
Celestial Consolations; and then he passed the whole of the
remaining time in holding communion with all Heaven,—
having, in these deserts, no intercourse with the earth except,
with his two Companions. He Confessed them and adminis-

tered Communion to them twice in the week, and exhorted them as much as his strength permitted him. A short time after christmas, that he might obtain the favor of not dying without having taken possession of his Dear mission, he invited his Companions to make a novena in honor of the immaculate conception of the blessed virgin. His prayer was answered, against all human probability; and his health improving, he prepared himself to go to the village of the Ilinois as soon as navigation should open,—which he did with much Joy, setting out for that place on the 29th of march. He spent eleven Days on the Way, during which time he had occasion to suffer much, both from his own Illness, from which he had not entirely recovered, and from the very severe and unfavorable weather.

On at last arriving at the village, he was received as an angel from Heaven. After he had assembled at various times the Chiefs of the nation, with all the old men, that he might sow in their minds the first seeds of the gospel, and after having given Instruction in the Cabins, which were always filled with a great crowd of people, he resolved to address all in public, in a general assembly which he called together in the open Air, the Cabins being too small to contain all the people. It was a beautiful prairie, close to a village, which was Selected for the great Council; this was adorned, after the fashion of the country, by Covering it with mats and bearskins. Then the father, having directed them to stretch out upon Lines several pieces of chinese taffeta, attached to these four large Pictures of the blessed Virgin, which were visible on all sides. The audience was Composed of 500 chiefs and elders, seated in a circle around the father, and of all the Young men, who remained standing. They numbered more than 1,500 men, without counting the women and children, who are always numerous,—the village being Composed of 5 or 600 fires. The father addressed the whole body of people, and conveyed to them 10 messages, by means of ten presents which he gave them. He explained to them the principal mysteries of our Religion, and the purpose that had brought him to their country. Above all, he preached to them Jesus Christ, on the very eve (of that great day) on which he had died upon the Cross for them, as well as for all the rest of mankind; then he said holy mass. On the third Day after, which was easter sunday, things being prepared in the same mannér as on Thursday, he celebrated the holy mysteries for the 2nd time; And by these two, the only sacrifices ever offered there to God, he took possession of that land in the name of Jesus Christ, and gave to that mission the name of the Immaculate Conception of the blessed virgin.

He was listened to by all these peoples with universal Joy; and they prayed him with most earnest Entreaty to come back to them as soon as possible, since his sickness obliged him to return. The father, on his Side, expressed to them the affection which he felt for them, and the satisfaction that they had given him; and pledged them his word that he, or some other of our fathers would return to Carry on that mission so happily Inaugurated. This promise he repeated several times, while parting with them to go upon his Way; and he set out with so many tokens of regard on the part of Those good peoples that, as a mark of honor they chose to escort him for more than 30 leagues on the Road, vying with each other in taking Charge of his slender baggage.

SECTION 2ND. THE FATHER IS COMPELLED TO LEAVE HIS ILINOIS MISSION. HIS LAST ILLNESS. HIS PRECIOUS DEATH IN THE HEART OF THE FOREST.

After the Ilinois, filled with great esteem for the gospel, had taken Leave of the father, he Continued his journey, and shortly after reached the lake of the Ilinois, upon whose waters he had to journey nearly a hundred leagues, by an unknown route whereon he had Never before traveled; for he was obliged to coast along the southern Shore of the lake, having come by the northern. But his strength was so

rapidly diminishing that his two men despaired of being able
to bring him alive To the end of their journey. Indeed, he
became so feeble and exhausted that he was unable to assist or
even to move himself, and had to be handled and carried about
like a child.

Meanwhile, he Preserved in that condition an admirable
equanimity, resignation, Joy, and gentleness, consoling his dear
Companions and encouraging them to suffer patiently all the
hardships of that voyage, in the assurance that God would not
abandon them after his death. It was during this voyage that
he began to make more special preparation for death. He held
Communion, sometimes with our Lord, sometimes with his
holy mother, or with his guardian angel, or with all paradise.
He was often heard repeating These words: *Credo quod re-
demptor meus vivit;* or, *maria, mater gratiae, mater dei, memento mei.* In addition to the spiritual exercise, which was
read to him every Day, he requested toward the close that
they would read to him his meditation preparatory for death,
which he carried about with him. He recited every Day his
breviary; and although he was so low that his sight and
strength were greatly enfeebled, He continued to do so to the
last day of his life, despite the remonstrance of his companions.

Eight Days before his death, he was thoughtful enough to
prepare the holy water for use during the rest of his illness,
in his agony, and at his burial; and he Instructed his Companions how it should be used.

The evening before his death, which was a friday, he told
them, very Joyously that it would take place on the morrow.
He conversed with them during the whole Day as to what
would need to be done for his burial; about the manner in
which they should inter him; of the spot that should be
chosen for his grave; how his feet, his hands, and his face
should be arranged; how they should erect a Cross over his
grave. He even went so Far as to counsel them, 3 hours
before he expired, that as soon as he was dead they should
take the little Hand-bell of his Chapel, and sound it while
he was being put under ground. He spoke of all these things

with so great tranquility and presence of mind that one might have supposed that he was concerned with the death and funeral of some other person, and not with his own.

Thus did he converse with them as they made their way upon the lake,—until, having perceived a river, on the shore of which stood an eminence that he deemed well suited to be the place of his interment, he told them that That was the place of his last repose. They wished, however, to proceed farther, as the weather was favorable, and the day was not far advanced; but God raised a Contrary wind, which compelled them to return, and enter the river which the father had pointed out. They accordingly brought him to the land, lighted a little fire for him, and prepared for him a wretched Cabin of bark. They laid him down therein, in the least uncomfortable way that they could; but they were so stricken with sorrow that, as they have since said, they hardly knew what they were doing.

The father, being thus Stretched on the ground in much the same way as was st. francis xavier, as he had always so passionately desired, and finding himself alone in the midst of These forests, for his companions were occupied with the disembarkation, he had leisure to repeat all the last acts in which he had continued during these last Days.

His dear companions having afterward joined him, all disconsolate, he Comforted them, and inspired them with the confidence that God would take care of them after his death, in these new and unknown countries. He gave them the last Instructions, thanked them for all the charities which they had exercised in his behalf during the whole journey, and entreated pardon for the trouble that he had given them. He charged them to ask pardon for him also, from all our fathers and brethren who live in the country of the outaouacs. Then he undertook to prepare them for the sacrament of penance, which he administered to them for the last time. He gave them also a paper on which he had written all his faults since his own last Confession, that they might place it in the hands of the father superior that the latter might be enabled to pray to God for him in a more special manner. Finally, he promised not to forget them in Paradise; and, as he was very Considerate, knowing that they were much fatigued with the hardships of the preceeding Days, he bade them go and take a little repose. He assured them that his hour was not yet so very near, and that he would awaken them when the time should come—as, in fact, 2 or 3 hours afterward he did summon them, being ready to enter into the agony.

They drew near to him, and he embraced them once again, while they burst into tears at his feet. Then he asked for holy water and his reliquary; and having himself removed his Crucifix, which he carried always suspended round his neck, he placed it in the hands of one of his Companions, begging him to hold it before his eyes. Then, feeling that he had but a short time to live, he made a last effort, Clasped his hands, and, with a steady and fond look upon his Crucifix, he uttered aloud his profession of faith, and gave thanks to the divine majesty for the great favor which he accorded him of dying in the Society, of dying in it as a missionary of Jesus Christ,—and, above all, of dying in it, as he had always prayed, in a Wretched cabin in the midst of the forests and bereft of all human succor.

After that, he was silent, communing within himself with God. Nevertheless he let escape from time to time these words, *Sustinuit anima mea in verbo ejus;* or these, *Mater Dei, memento mei*—which were the last words he uttered before entering his agony, which was, however, very mild and peaceful.

He prayed his companions to put him in mind, when they should see him about to expire, to repeat frequently the names of Jesus and mary, if he could not himself do so. They did as they were bidden; and, when they Believed him to be near his end, one of them Called aloud, "Jesus, Mary!" The dying man repeated the words distinctly, several times; and as if, at These sacred names, Something presented itself to him, he Suddenly raised his eyes above his Crucifix, holding them Riveted on that object, which he appeared to regard with pleasure. And so, with a countenance beaming and all aglow, he expired without any Struggle, and so gently that it might have been regarded as a pleasant sleep.

His two poor Companions, shedding many tears over him, composed his Body in the manner which he had prescribed to them. Then they carried him devoutly to burial, ringing the while the little Bell as he had bidden them; and planted a large Cross near his grave, as a sign to passers-by.

When it became a question of embarking, to proceed on their journey, one of the two, who for some Days had been so Heartsick with sorrow, and so greatly prostrated with an internal malady, that he could no longer eat or breathe except with difficulty, bethought himself, while the other was making all preparations for embarking, to visit the grave of his good father, and ask his intercession with the glorious virgin, as he had promised, not doubting in the least that he was in Heaven. He fell, then, upon his knees, made a Short prayer, and having reverently taken some earth from the tomb, he pressed it to his breast. Immediately his sickness Abated, and his sorrow was changed into a Joy which did not forsake him during the remainder of his journey.

SECTION 3RD. WHAT OCCURRED AT THE REMOVAL OF THE BONES OF THE LATE FATHER MAR-QUETTE, WHICH WERE TAKEN FROM HIS GRAVE ON THE 19TH OF MAY, 1677, THE SAME DAY AS THAT ON WHICH HE DIED IN THE YEAR 1675. A BRIEF SUMMARY OF HIS VIRTUES.

God did not permit that a deposit so precious should remain in the midst of the forest, unhonored and forgotten. The savages named Kiskakons, who have been making public profession of Christianity for nearly ten years, and who were instructed by father Marquette when he lived at the point of st. Esprit, at the extreme of lake superior, carried on their last winter's hunting in the vicinity of the lake of the Ilinois.

As they were returning in the spring; they were greatly
pleased to pass near the grave of their good father, whom
they tenderly loved; and God also put it into their hearts to
remove his bones and bring them to our church at the mission
of st. Ignace at missilmakinac, where those savages make their
abode.

They repaired then, to the spot, and resolved among themselves to act in regard to the father as they are Wont to do
toward Those for whom they profess great respect. Accordingly, they opened the grave, and uncovered the Body;
and, although the Flesh and Internal organs were all Dried
up, they found it entire, so that not even the skin was in any
way injured. This did not prevent them from proceeding to
dissect it, as is their custom. They cleansed the bones and
exposed them to the sun to dry; then, carefully laying them
in a box of birch-bark, they set out to bring them to our mission
of st. Ignace.

There were nearly 30 Canoes which formed, in excellent
order, that funeral procession. There were also a goodly number of iroquois, who United with our algonkin savages to
lend more honor to the ceremonial. When they drew near
our house, father nouvel, who is its superior, with father
piercon, went out to meet them, accompanied by the frenchmen and savages who were there; and having halted the Procession, he put the usual questions to them, to make sure
that It was really the father's body which they were bringing. Before conveying it to land, they Intoned the *de pro-
fundis* in the presence of the 30 Canoes, which were still on the
water, and of the people who were on the shore. After that,
the Body was carried to the church, care being taken to observe all that the ritual appoints in such ceremonies. It remained exposed under the pall, all that Day, which was
whitsun-monday, the 8th of June; and on the morrow, after
having rendered to it all the funeral rites, it was lowered
into a small Vault in the middle of the church, where it rests
as the guardian angel of our outaouas missions. The savages
often come to pray over his tomb. Not to mention more than

this instance, a young girl, aged 19 or 20 years, whom the late father had Instructed, and who had been baptized in the past year, fell sick, and applied to father nouvel to be bled and to take certain remedies. The father prescribed to her, as sole medicine, to come for 3 days and say a *pater* and three *ave's* at the tomb of father marquette. She did so, and before the 3rd Day was cured, without bleeding or any other remedies.

Father Jaques marquette, of the province of champagne, died at the age of 38 years, of which 21 were passed in the Society—namely, 12 in france and 9 in Canada. He was sent to the missions of the upper algonquins, who are called outaouacs; and labored therein with the Zeal that might be expected from a man who had proposed to himself st. francis xavier as the model of his life and death. He resembled that great Saint, not only in the variety of barbarian languages which he mastered, but also by the range of his Zeal, which made him carry the faith To the ends of this new world, and nearly 800 leagues from here into the forests, where the name of Jesus Christ had never been proclaimed.

He always entreated God that he might end his life in these laborious missions, and that, like his dear st. xavier, he might die in the midst of the woods bereft of everything. Every Day, he Interposed for that end both the merits of Jesus Christ and the intercession of the virgin Immaculate, for whom he entertained a singular tenderness.

Accordingly, he obtained through such powerful mediators that which he solicited with so much earnestness; since he had, like the apostle of the Indies, the happiness to die in a wretched cabin on the shore of lake Ilinois, forsaken by all the world.

We might say much of the rare virtues of this noble missionary; of his Zeal, which prompted him to carry the faith so far, and proclaim the gospel to so many peoples who were unknown to us; of his gentleness, which rendered him beloved by all, and made him all things to all men—a frenchman with the french, a huron with the hurons, an algonquin with the algonquins; of the childlike Candor with which he disclosed his heart to his superiors, and even to all kinds of persons, with an ingenuousness which won all Hearts; of his angelic Chastity; and of his uninterrupted union with God.

But that which Apparently predominated was a devotion, altogether rare and singular, to the blessed virgin, and particularly toward the mystery of her immaculate conception. It was a pleasure to him him speak or preach on that subject. All his conversations and letters contained something about the blessed virgin Immaculate—for so he always called her. From the age of 9 years, he Fasted every saturday; and from his tenderest Youth Began to say the little office of the Conception, Inspiring everyone with the same devotion. Some months before his death, he said every Day with his two men a little corona of the immaculate conception which he had devised as follows: After the Credo, there is said once the *pater* and *ave*, and then 4 times these words: *Ave filia Dei patris, ave mater filii Dei, ave sponsa spiritus sancti, ave templum totius trinitatis; per sanctam virginitatem et immaculatam conceptionem tuam, purissima virgo, emunda Cor et Carnem meam; in nominee patris, et filii, et spiritus sancti,*— concluding with the *gloria patri*, the whole repeated three times.

He Never failed to Say the mass of the Conception,—or, at least, when he could do so, the prayer of the Conception. He hardly meditated upon anything else Day and night. That he might leave us an ever-enduring testimony of his sentiments, it was his desire to bestow on the mission of the Ilinois the name of la Conception.

So tender a devotion toward the mother of God merited some singular grace; and she accorded him the favor that he had always requested—to die on a saturday. His companions never doubted that she appeared to him at the hour of his death, when, after pronouncing the names of Jesus and mary, he Suddenly raised his eyes above his Crucifix, holding them fixed on an object which he regarded with extreme pleasure and a Joy that showed itself upon his features; and they had at that time, the impression that he had rendered up his soul into the hands of his good mother.

One of the last letters that he wrote to the father superior of the missions before his great voyage, is sufficient evidence that such were his sentiments. He Begins it thus: "The Blessed virgin immaculate has obtained for me the favor of reaching this place in good health, and with the resolve to correspond to the intentions which God has respecting me, since he has assigned me to the voyage toward the south. I have no other thought than that of doing what God wills. I dread nothing—neither the nadoissis, nor the reception awaiting me among the nations, dismay me. One of two Things will happen: either God will punish me for my crimes and cowardice, or else he will give me a share in his Cross, which I have not yet carried since my arrival in this country. But this Cross has been perhaps obtained for me by the blessed virgin immaculate, or it may be death itself, that I may cease to offend God. It is that for which I try to hold myself in readiness, surrendering myself altogether into his hands. I entreat Your Reverence not to forget me, and to obtain for me of God that I may not remain ungrateful for the favors which he heaps upon me."

There was found among his papers a Manuscript entitled "The Directing care of God over a missionary," in which he shows the excellence of that vocation, the advantages which it affords for self-sanctification, and the care that God takes of Gospel laborers. One sees in this little abstract the spirit of God which possessed him.

[*Ibid.,* lix., *Doc.* cxxxviii.]

VII

REVEXUES OF THE JESUITS IX CAXADA

1701

[This is a formal declaration, made by the Jesuit Superior at Quebec, of the revenues and estates belonging to the Jesuits in Canada, in October, 1701. Their total income, as here given, amounts to a little more than 13,000 livres a year. This list is followed by a statement of the expenditures which are necessary for their work; the support of forty-eight priests and nine donnes, "almost all of whom are aged and worn out in the missions", besides the wages of fourteen hired servants; the maintenance of the college, residences, and chapels; traveling expenses, and alms to the poor. The order also has to carry a debt of 6,000 livres.— *Ibid.*, lxv., 18.]

We, the undersigned, Religious of the Society of Jesus in Canada, in obedience to the order of his majesty which has been made known to us by Monsieur the Chevalier de Calliere, governor and lieutenant-general in all northern new france, and by Monsieur de Champigny, intendant of the country, do Certify that our fixed Revenues and Perquisites, with both our Taxes and obligations, are as follows:

The King, in his liberality gives us in Canada, for the maintenance of our missions among all the foreign nations of this country, in an extent of 7 to 800 leagues, a pension from the state of   5,000 livres
And, besides, in a gratuity from the custom-duties   315   "

Item, for the 3rd Instructor at the College of
Quebec ....   400 livres
There is also a charitable donation, a gift
made by his majesty to the Abnaquis and the
iroquois converted to the faith, to assist the
orphans, widows, old people, And poor, from
which neither we nor the missionaries who have
charge of Those savages have profited in any
manner. This gift and alms amounts to.....   1,500   "

THE REVENUE FROM OUR OWN PROPERTY AT QUEBEC

Our house in the lower town is rented at...   300   "
That in the upper town is rented at.......   120   "
Our mill close by the College may, unless
there be unusual expenses, yield a revenue of..   300   "
A little piece of land opposite quebec, at
Coste de lauzon   30   "
The Estate of nostre Dame des anges, where
there are mills and farms, *cens et rentes*, and
tolls upon the little River St. Charles.......   1,205   "
The Siegniory of Sillery, on account of the
rents from the tenants, the eel-fisheries, and
a mill, about...........................   250   "
The Estate of St. gabriel, the soil of which
is almost everywhere sterile and unprofitable,
about   40   "
The Seigniory of Batiscan, in seigniorial rents
and for the mill, about.................   300   "
Cap de la Magdelaine, which is a sandy piece
of land, without trees for firewood, sterile,
and abandoned by nearly all the inhabitants who
had established themselves there, may yield..   160   "
The Little piece of land at three Rivers,
about   60   "

La Prairie de la magdelaine, and [the parish]
of St. lambert, where there is a mill and domain,
and rents from some tenants who have remained and are almost all Ruined by the iro-
quois war . . . .   385 livres

The Perquisates in either *lots* [*lods*] *et
ventes,* or old debts, or similar matters   280   "

Our revenue in france, expenses and charges
defrayed, which we receive here, may amount,
at the most, to   4,000   "

Thus all the Revenues of the jesuit fathers of
Canada may amount to   13,145   "

It is True that, when the years are good, this may be increased by 1,000 livres, or thereabout; but, when they are bad,
—either through the seasons, or through war, which causes
everything to become dear in distant countries,—the revenues
diminish accordingly, and the expenses greatly increase.

THE EXPENDITURES

From the above Revenues we must feed, clothe, and furnish with necessaries our fathers and brethren who are here,—
forty-eight Religious, and nine perpetual domestics called
"donnez," almost all of whom are aged and worn out in the
missions; so are also most of the fathers, who have grown
old and are Broken down by the arduous labors of such missions. We have also in our missions at least fourteen men as
hired servants, to take the missionaries in canoes to the remote
places where the savages live, to furnish them with wood, and
to help them in other like ways.

There must be added the maintenance of our sacristies, and
of our churches or chapels in the missions, and the repairs of
our buildings; the expenses for all the journeys of the missionaries coming and going; and, above all, the great outlays
for carrying to the missionaries at 3, 4, and 500 leagues from
quebec, all their necessaries, and the alms to the poor, both

french and Savages. Thus we have only a very moderate amount with which to provide for so many expenses; and, besides more than 6,000 livres that we actually owe, we have to pay annually an amortisable rent of 1,000 livres.

Our principal establishments are: the College of Quebec, where there are 18 Religious; It is to this place that those whom the severe fatigues of these missions have rendered unfit for service retire.

The Residence of montreal, where there are four Religious.

The mission of the iroquois of the sault, near montreal, where there are four fathers.

That of St. Francois de salle, composed of abnaquis, loups, and sokokis, where there are 2 priests, jesuit missionaries.

The mission of the abnaquis of acadia, near the English, where there are three missionary fathers. In the missions of the outaois, islinois, miamis, scioux, and other nations, to the frontier of the mississipy region, there are eleven jesuit priests and four brethren.

At the mission of laurette, where dwell the remnant of the huron nation, one jesuit priest.

Moreover, two and sometimes three fathers from the College of Quebec leave in the spring for the missions of the Papinachois, of tadoussac, of Chikoutimy, of the mistassins, and of lake St. John, and do not return until far into the autumn; and often some one of them even spends there the winter also. Done at Quebec, this 4th of October, 1701; and in testimony of the above, we have signed the present declaration as exact and true. Signed, therefore, martin bouvart, rector of the College of quebec, and superior of the missions of the Society of Jesus in new france; françois Vallant, and pierre Rafaix.

[*Ibid.*, lxv., *Doc.* clxxvi.]

VIII

*A LETTER, ADDRESSED TO REVEREND FATHER
JEAN DE LAMBERVILLE, REGARDING
THE ILLINOIS MISSIONS*

MY REVEREND FATHER:

I send to Your Reverence The invoice of this year, 1702, for The Ilinois missions, and for The 3 fathers who are there now. I beg you not to be surprised if it be somewhat large. It is to supply clothes and provisions for three fathers, besides Brother guibort and perhaps Brother gillet, who are in need of everything; and to begin at last to supply, once for all, The principal items of all that is required for 3 missions—which have always been borrowing; which have always lacked most of the necessary articles; And wherein The missionaries have done nothing but languish. Father bineteau died there from exhaustion; but, If he had had a few drops of spanish wine, for which he asked us during his last illness, and some little dainties,—such as sugar, or other things,—or had we been able to procure some Fresh food for him, he would perhaps be still alive. Father pinet and father marest are wearing out their strength; and they are 2 saints, who take pleasure in being deprived of everything—in order, they say, that they may soon be nearer paradise. But they do not fail to tell me and to write me that I must bring some little comforts for the sick, and that these languish because they are in need of everything; and they tell the truth. For my part I am in good health, but I have no cassock, etc.; I am in a sorry plight, and the others are hardly less so.

Three winter cassocks.

3 pairs of winter hose.

3 lined cloaks.

3 summer cassocks; 3 pairs of winter and 3 of summer breeches.

3 pairs of summer hose.

3 pairs of cloth breeches for winter.

6 pairs of breeches of black duck or strong linen.

12 hempen shirts, lined; calico handkerchiefs; Cap linings.

4 hats; 3 hoods; 3 pairs of mittens.

One Livre of black Wool.

Half a livre of black and other silk.

One Livre of fine white thread.

2 livres of black thread. 1 livre of twine for Nets. 3 Lines; 3 whip—[lashes?]

3 livres of coarse white thread.

6 pairs of Shoes.

3 pairs of double-soled slippers.

3 pieces of white thread galloon.

One thousand pins.

One Ream of good and strong paper, of large size.

One Ream of small-sized paper. 3 good razors, with a whetstone.

3 sticks of spanish wax. 3 half-double caps.

12 [small] towels and 6 [small] napkins.

3 covered bowls for The sick.

12 pewter spoons, with knives and forks.

[*illegible*—6 case-knives?] in 6 sheaths.

3 deep pewter basins with a narrow edge.

6 plates.

3 tinned kettles with lids, and strong, to hold 6 pots [1] each.

One Syringe; one livre of Theriac; ointment, plasters, alum, vitriol, aniseed, medicines, and pastils.

One host-Iron, and shape for cutting the wafers.

50 livres of flour, in a Barrel. 3 Tin boxes.

One minot of Salt, in a Barrel.

A jar of oil.

A Barrel of 15 pots of vinegar.

---

[1] The *pot* is a measure containing two pints,—the French pint, however, being equivalent to .934 of a litre, or 1.64 English pints. *Ibid.*, xxxii., *note* 4.

30 livres of Sugar.

Rice, raisins, prunes.

25 pots of spanish wine, In 2 kegs.

25 pots of brandy.

9 livres of pepper.

One Livre of nutmegs and cloves.

Six pairs of half-worsted hose. [Material for making] awnings as a protection against the gnats that infest the mississipi.

One piece of strong sail cloth.

One livre or 2 of cotton candle-wicking.

Indian ink and cotton (*illegible*).

A thousand nails, large, medium-sized, and small.

150 livres of powder.

50 livres of assorted shot, large and small.

50 livres of Bullets; [500 gun-flints].

Ten livres of vermillion.

Ten livres of large glass Beads—black, white and Striped.

Ten livres of small glass Beads—white, green, and transparent.

One gross of large Clasp-knives, with horn handles.

One gross of round buckles, both large and medium-sized.

One gross of small metal plates.[1]

Six gross of small belts.

Six gross of finger-Rings.

3 gross of awls.

One thousand needles.

Six boxes of gun-flints.

Twenty gun-screws.

One dozen [wooden?] combs.

3 dozen Spools of fine iron wire, or Else a roll of fine wire.

Six Bars of soap.

Three dozen hatchets, medium-sized, large, and small.

Three dozen medium-sized hoes.

Three hatchets [*illegible*], 3 mattocks.

---

[1] *Platins* apparently refers to metal plates used as looking glasses—of which the Indians, like all other savages, are very fond. *Ibid.*, lxvi., *note* 5.

One dozen trade shirts—large, medium-sized, and small.
Six blue capotes—large, medium-sized, and small.
Six ells of stuff for capotes, to make Breech-clouts.
Thirty livres of good tobacco.
Three dozen wax candles, and
Six livres of Wax tapers for the 3 missionaries.

The same is needed in proportion for each mission; and a chapel, with all its accessories, is required for The missionary to the Scious, since a father will be sent there; and he has need of a man, if Monsieur Le Sueur does not defray all His expenses. Your Reverence will see Him about it. You will find this a very long list, but Nothing can be Omitted from it if you wish the missionaries to have any comfort. Since it costs nothing for The fort to the Missionaries of quebec—who have Received through Monsieur d'Iberville 10 times more than they asked—we Shall not be in a worse condition; and he has written to me that we should bring out engagés [hired men] from France, whom we could get There cheaper than here, and whose passage would cost us nothing.[1]

[*Ibid.*, lxvi., *Doc.* clxxviii.]

[1] This letter is unsigned, but it was probably written by Father Jacques Gravier, who succeeded Father Allouez in the Illinois mission, in 1688, and labored there till 1705,

IX

LETTER BY REVEREND FATHER ÉTIENNE DE CARHEIL TO MONSIEUR LOUIS HECTOR DE CALLIERES, GOVERNOR

(1702)

[Étienne de Carheil was born at Carentoir, France, in November, 1633, and began his novitiate in the Jesuit college at Paris, Aug. 30, 1653. He was ordained in 1666 and immediately set out for Canada. After two years at Quebec, spent in preparation for mission-work, he was sent to Cayuga, where he labored until 1683; he was then, like other missionaries to the Iroquois, compelled to leave that field, through the growing hostility of the savages; and, in 1686 was assigned to the mission among the Hurons and Ottawas at Mackinac. The establishment of Detroit (1701) by La Mothe Cadillac, the French commander at Mackinac, drew away the Hurons from the latter post, and Carheil could no longer remain there. He had, moreover, provoked the enmity of Cadillac, and also of the fur-traders, by his opposition to the brandy traffic, so prevalent at all the trading-posts and so demoralizing to both French and Indians. This and the practical abandonment of Mackinac obliged Carheil to return to Quebec in 1703. . . . Carheil's letter to Callières, the governor (dated at Michillimackinac, Aug. 30, 1702), complaining of the disorders there, will be given in this series. (See below.)—*Ibid.* l., *note* 21.]

At Michilimakina,
the 30th of August, 1702.

MONSEIGNEUR:

Could I have Believed that my going down below would have been of any greater use to you than have been all the letters that I have Written to you continually, during fifteen entire years,—for the purpose of informing you exactly, as in God's sight, according to Truth, according to my conscience, of all That was absolutely necessary for the advancement of our missions and for the welfare of the Colony,—I would not have failed to go down; and I would have made it my duty to go to explain to you verbally what I might not have sufficiently made known in my letters.

But even if I had Never Written to you, It was only necessary to have seen all That is to be seen every day at Montreal, and That you yourself have only too often seen, to enable you to carry back to france enough to give Information to his majesty, and to constrain him to succor our missions. These are reduced to such an extremity that we can no longer maintain them against an infinite multitude of evil acts—acts of brutality and violence; of injustice and impiety; of lewd and shameless conduct; of contempt and insults.

If his majesty desire to save our missions and to support the Establishment of Religion, as we have no Doubt he does, we beg him most humbly to Believe What is most true, namely; that there is no other means of doing so than to abolish completely the two Infamous sorts of Commerce which have brought the missions to the brink of destruction, and which will not long delay in destroying these if they be not abolished as soon as possible by his orders, and be prevented from ever being restored. The first is the Commerce in brandy; the second is the Commerce of the savage women with the french. Both are carried on in an equally public manner, without our being able to remedy the evil, because we are not supported by the Commandants. They—far from attempting, when we undertake to remonstrate with them, to check these trades—themselves carry them on with greater freedom than do their

Subordinates and so sanction them by their example. So much is this the case that all the villages of our savages are now only Taverns, as regards drunkenness; and sodoms, as regards immorality—from which we must withdraw, and which we must abandon to the just Anger and vengeance of God.

You see by this that, in whatever manner the french trade is Established among our savages, if it be desired to still retain us among them, we must be delivered from the Commandants and from their garrisons. These, far from being necessary, are on the contrary, so pernicious that we can truly say that they are the greatest scourge of our missions. All the pretended service which it is sought to make people believe that they render to the King is reduced to 4 chief occupations, of which we beg you to Inform His majesty.

The first consists in keeping a public Tavern for the sale of brandy, wherein they trade it Continually to the savages, who do not cease to become intoxicated, notwithstanding our efforts to prevent it. The second occupation of the soldiers consists in being sent from one post to another by the Commandants in order to carry their wares and their brandy thither, after having made arrangements together; and none of them have any other object than That of assisting one another in their Traffic.

Their third occupation consists in making of their fort a place that I am ashamed to call by its proper name, where the women have found out that their bodies might serve in lieu of merchandise and would be still better received than Beaver-skins; accordingly, that is now the most usual and most Continual Commerce, and that which is most extensively carried on. Whatever efforts the missionaries may make to denounce and abolish it, this traffic increases, instead of diminishing, and grows daily more and more. All the soldiers keep open house in their dwellings for all the women of their acquaintance. From morning to night, they pass entire Days there, one after another—sitting by their fire, and often on their beds, engaged in conversations and actions proper to their commerce. This generally ends only at night, because the crowd is too great during the day to allow of their concluding it then—although they frequently arrange among themselves to leave a house empty, so as not to defer the conclusion until night.

The 4th occupation of the soldiers is gambling, which at the times when the traders assemble sometimes proceeds to such excess that they are not satisfied with passing the whole day, but they also spend the whole night in this pursuit. But what makes their misconduct on This score still worse is, that so persistent an attachment to the game is hardly ever unaccompanied by the general Intoxication of all the players; and drunkenness is nearly always followed by quarrels that arise among them.

If occupations of this kind can be called the king's service, I admit that they have always rendered him one of Those four services. But I have observed none other than those four; and consequently, if such services be not considered necessary to the King, there has never been hitherto any necessity for keeping them here: and after they are recalled, there is no necessity of sending them back. For in reality the Commandants come here solely for the purpose of trading in concert with their soldiers, without troubling themselves about anything else. They have no intercourse with the missionaries, except with regard to Matters wherein they consider the latter useful for the furtherance of their own temporal affairs; and beyond that they are hostile to the fathers as soon as these undertake to oppose the misconduct, which being in accord neither with the service of God nor the service of the King, is nevertheless advantageous to the trade of the Commandants.

It is also important that you should be informed of an abuse that the Commandants have introduced with respect to the savages, which has produced among them only bad results. It is this, that—not Content with the Constant profit which they derive from the trade—They have found means to convince the Court that it is necessary to supply them with considerable funds for the purpose of making presents to the savages—either to interest them in our concerns, our designs, and our undertakings, or to reward them when they render

services that may be deemed worthy of recompense.   This is
truly a fine pretext; but it is certain that never was anything
less needed with regard to the savages.   The sole effect which
this has produced upon the savages has been, to teach them
to be exacting in requiring that they be solicited; to make it
necessary that all their actions and all their emotions be purchased by dint of presents:

But with all This, all the presents that are given them are
almost nothing in Comparison with the fund supplied by the
Court to the Commandants for that purpose.   The gifts are
reduced almost entirely to the single expenditure of tobacco—
which is the most usual present, because the savages are passionately fond of it.   However, what remains of the fund is
much greater and more considerable than the amount spent
in giving them presents, and it is greatly to be feared that the
Commandants turn it to their own benefit and that by careful
Economy They keep the best part of it for their own use.

It is the Commandants, it is the Garrisons, who, uniting
with the brandy traders have completely desolated the missions
by almost universal drunkenness and Lewdness; the civil
authorities not only tolerate but permit these, inasmuch as,
while able to Prevent them, they do not.

In whatever light we may consider the Commerce carried
on, as regards either the Common interest of Canada, or the
advancement of Christianity, It would be Infinitely more advantageous for both if the savages themselves went down annually for that purpose to Montreal, than it would be to send
the french here to trade, in the way they come every Year.
You ask, what would be best; to restore the 25 Permits without any posts, or to Establish posts without the 25 Permits.[1]
I frankly admit that I am very much embarrassed to answer
because I know not very well to what kind of posts you are

[1] For many years, since at least 1660,—the fur trade had been illegally carried
on by wandering Canadian trappers and voyageurs, who were commonly termed
"wood-rangers." Laws against this illicit traffic were enacted by the French
government, but they were seldom effective; and it was openly charged that the
Canadian governors and other officials were in collusion with them. In May,
1681, royal edicts granted amnesty to those who had disobeyed these laws; the

pleased to refer. Are they posts solely of traders, without garrisons and without commandants; or posts that would be occupied at the same time by persons employed in Trading, and by Commandants with their garrisons, who would watch over their *safety?*

I know too well the young men of Canada to whom the permits would be granted, to be able to Consent to their restoration. They are young men who have become accustomed, by more than 15 years of Impunity, to the Commerce of brandy and to that with women. There can be no hope of their abstaining from either in the future. Even if They who govern the country should put an end to the Commerce in brandy, and Consequently to the Drunkenness of the savages, could they prevent That with women—which is still more harmful, more pernicious, more fatal to our missions than that in brandy? It is impossible for us to apply a remedy for this evil, because they all Alike hide it under the decent pretext of their necessities—which, although innocent in themselves, are not in their case.

Their first necessity consists in having women whom they Employ in pounding corn and doing their Cooking, and whom they detain under that pretext in their houses, when they wish and as long as they wish. The second consists in having some to cut wood for them, and to carry it to their dwellings to Heat them. The third consists in having laundresses who, at the same time when, on the one hand, they wash their linen, on the other defile their bodies and blacken their souls by the most shameful brutishness. The 4th consists in having some women who make savage shoes, Garters [leggings?], and pouches, according to their fashion and other similar articles. There are also some other necessities, less common and less usual than those 4 which are the chief ones, of which they

governor was authorized to grant 25 licenses for the fur trade, forbidding all other persons to engage therein. Each licensed person was allowed to send out twenty-five canoes, with three men to each canoe. These licenses also proved inadequate to suppress illegal traffic, and they were revoked by the king in 1696. They were restored in 1716, again revoked in 1719, and reissued in 1726.—*Ibid.,* lxv., *note* 37.

make use to lure the women to their houses, and to give themselves a pretext for going to theirs if it pleases them. These provide for the men an ever-ready excuse for exculpating themselves, and for removing suspicions when they are found there, —although, in reality, they entice and keep them there only with the intention of doing with them what is most immoral and most Criminal. It is enough that, after pounding their corn for them at their homes, after cutting their wood for them in the forest, after washing their linen on the shore of the lake, after making shoes for them in their own cabins, the women should carry all those articles to the persons who have employed them, in order to receive payment therefor, and to withdraw at once without remaining any longer in their houses. All else is but a proximate occasion for sin.

Moreover, lewdness has become Established and not only through the liberty that the french have taken of admitting to their houses the savage women at all hours; but What has most contributed to Establish it is the liberty, which they themselves have taken, of going to seek those women in their villages; many of the most dissolute do not hesitate to leave the french houses, and to go to live with the women in their cabins. This is an evil that has Begun only since the departure of Monsieur de ladurantaye, whose successors have not been as Chaste as he was; as a result of this, one of them has more than one child in the village.

Here is another evil in connection with This matter, which is all the greater because it is Made more visible by trying to Hide it. It is that there are several who are addicted to such excessive and Continual lewdness that, as they cannot bear to have any other Company that That of the women who are necessary to their passions, They build separate houses for themselves alone,—where, Remaining solitary as regards the french, They are Never so as regards the women, at the times suitable for their Commerce. You see very well that this is not an evil that can be tolerated, so scandalous is it. Traders— who are associated together, and have Common interests— should not live thus, separated from one another, lest while dwelling alone, accidents might happen to them which they fear not, but which they should Fear, and which everyone should Dread for them. May we therefore be delivered forever from Those solitaries and their Solitudes.

Finally, the most scandalous Evil of all, and that which needs to be the most strenuously opposed, is that the traders have become so accustomed to have women for their Use in the trading-places, and these have become so necessary to them, that they cannot do without them even on their journeys. I do not refer to Those who are taken with their husbands, because there is nothing in This that is not decent; I refer to single women, women without husbands, women who are mistresses of their own Bodies, women who can dispose of them to these men, and whom the latter know to be willing to do so,—in a word, They are the prostitutes of Montreal, who are alternately brought here and taken back; and They are all the prostitutes of this place, who are carried in the same way from here to Montreal, and from Montreal here. The pretext that they usually allege for taking women in preference to men on their journeys is, that women cost them less than men, and are satisfied with lower wages. They speak the truth; but the very fact of their being Satisfied with less wages is a manifest proof of their dissoluteness. If they Were wise would they not ask to be paid the same as men, since they perform the same services—and frequently do more, by Cutting wood for them and by Cooking their food, which men will not do? Therefore that is not their sole Reason for taking women; but the reason is that The women, Being depraved, want them as men; and they, on their part, want them as women, on all their journeys,—after which If they quit one another, They separate from these only to seek others.

I ask you here, Monseigneur, whether you Consider that all These evils respecting which I have just submitted our complaints, can be abolished by restoring the 25 permits. If they can be abolished, then restore the Permits; and assure us that the Evils are abolished, by measures that will be certain to produce their effect. But if, on the contrary, you do not consider that they can be abolished, you should at the same time Consider that the 25 Permits must by no means be restored, since their Restoration would infallibly Cause that of lawlessness.

Now suppose that, for the Reasons given Above, neither the garrisons with their Commandants nor the 25 Permits are Reestablished in our missions; and that the Trade of the savages cannot be Reestablished or permanently fixed with certainty at montreal. There would remain, then, no other measure for the Company to adopt than to send and maintain in our missions up here Selected persons, sober and virtuous, Intelligent, and well versed in everything connected with That trade,—and finally, such as would be fully disposed to live on terms of mutual Agreement with all the missionaries. These men should be sent, in whatever number the Company might Deem necessary and sufficient for carrying on its Trade, for attaching thereto the Savages, and for retaining them in it both by their presence and that of their wares; and by the sight, the transportation, and the Continual Sale of these wares among them. The French should be stationed in a good fort, always well provisioned, and well supplied with arms for its defense,—where Those who would have charge of the Trade would on Such occasions occupy the position of Commandants, while the others would take the place of the garrisons.

Such, monseigneur, is What we Consider the best that can be done for our missions, and the best that can be done in the Interest of the Company—which, by That means, would be sure to obtain exclusive possession of all the Beaver-skins. For there would no longer be either Commandants or garrisons— who, in spite of all the precautions that may be taken, nevertheless succeed in obtaining a considerable portion of the peltries, by an Infinite number of hidden ways, and by secret intelligence with the savages.

As Regards the detroit Establishment, I have nothing to tell you about it of my own knowledge; for I have no Information concerning it, except through the reports of the french and the savages who talk with us here about it. Judging from their reports, it does not seem to them to be an advantageous Establishment. They are not Satisfied with it, for various very Important reasons—which I have pointed out to the Reverend father superior, in What I Write for my Justification against the charges brought by Monsieur de la Motte, who Continues to persecute me. . . .

I remain, with all the esteem and all the Respect that you deserve,

> Monseigneur,
> > your very humble and very obedient servant,
> > > signed, Étienne de Carheil,
> > > > of the Society of Jesus.

In speaking of the detroit Establishment, I forgot to tell you that, during the whole time while the war lasted, the savages desired That Establishment at detroit; because They always supposed that the destruction of the Iroquois was desired, and that by his Destruction They would peacably enjoy all the lands in his Country. But since they have found that, far from wishing to destroy him, we thought only of sparing and Preserving him; of befriending him, by giving him land in what they considered As their own country; and by Restoring the fort of Cataracouy for his benefit,—They have completely Changed their minds, and no longer look upon Detroit in any other light than That of an Enemy's country, where they can have no Wish to dwell, and where there can be no security for them. And assuredly they cannot think or judge otherwise; so that those of the huron nation who remain Here, and who do not wish to go to detroit, mistrust Those who have gone to Settle there, and Think that they intend to go there in order to Surrender to the Iroquois, so as to join in the Trade with the English.

[*Ibid.*, lxv., *Doc.* clxxvii.]

X

LETTER FROM FATHER LE PETIT, MISSIONARY, TO FATHER D'AVAUGOUR, PROCURATOR OF THE MISSIONS IN NORTH AMERICA

(1730)

[A letter from Mathurin le Petit to D'Avaugour (dated at New Orleans, July 12, 1730), gives a report of the Louisiana missions. The event of most importance therein is the terrible massacre by the Natches Indians (October 28, 1729) of the French people settled among them, over two hundred in number. The relation of this is preceded by an account of these savages, their character, customs, and religion.

The Natches tribe "is the only one on this continent which appears to have any regular worship." They worship the sun, and their chief of highest rank styles himself "Brother of the Sun"—arrogating to himself therewith despotic authority. At his death, his servants are strangled, that they may follow him in that capacity to the other world. . . . Having furnished this preliminary information, Le Petit narrates the particulars of the terrible vengeance taken by these savages for the injustice shown them by a tyrannical French commandant. They form a conspiracy, even with other tribes, to exterminate the French settlers; "and in less than two hours they massacred more than two hundred of the French."—*Ibid.*, lxviii., 12.]

My Reverend Father: At New Orleans.
           The 12th of July, 1730.
    The peace of Our Lord.

You cannot be ignorant of the sad event which has desolated that part of the French Colony established at *Natchez,* on the right bank of the Mississippi river, at the distance of a hundred and twenty leagues from its mouth. Two of our Missionaries who were engaged in the conversion of the Savages, have been included in the almost general massacre which this barbarous Nation made of the French, at a time too when they had not the least reason to suspect their perfidy. A loss so great as this infant mission has sustained, will continue for a long time to excite our deepest regrets.

This Nation of Savages inhabits one of the most beautiful and fertile countries in the world, and is the only one on this continent which appears to have any regular worship. Their Religion in certain points is very similar to that of the ancient Romans. They have a temple filled with Idols, which are different figures of men and of animals, and for which they have a most profound veneration. Their Temple in shape resembles an earthen oven, a hundred feet in circumference. They enter it by a little door about four feet high, and not more than three in breadth. No window is to be seen there. The arched roof of the edifice is covered with three rows of mats, placed one upon the other, to prevent the rain from injuring the masonry. Above on the outside are three figures of eagles made of wood, and painted red, yellow, and white. Before the door is a kind of shed with folding doors, where the Guardian of the Temple is lodged; all around it runs a circle of palisades, on which are seen exposed skulls of all the heads which their Warriors had brought back from the battles in which they had been engaged with the enemies of their Nation.

In the interior of the Temple are some shelves arranged at a certain distance from each other, on which are placed cane baskets of an oval shape, and in these are enclosed the bones of their ancient Chiefs, while by their side are those of their victims who had caused themselves to be strangled, to follow their masters into the other world. Another separate shelf supports many flat baskets very gorgeously painted, in which they preserve their Idols. These are figures of men and women made of stone or baked clay, the heads and the tails of extraordinary serpents, some stuffed owls, some pieces of crystal, and some jaw-bones of large fish. In the year 1699, they had there a bottle and the foot of a glass, which they regarded as very precious.

In this Temple they take care to keep up a perpetual fire, and they are very particular to prevent its ever blazing; they do not use anything for it but dry wood of the walnut or oak. The old men are obliged to carry, each one in his turn, a large log of wood into the enclosure of the palisade. The number of the Guardians of the Temple is fixed, and they serve by the quarter. He who is on duty is placed like a sentinel under the shed, from whence he examines whether the fire is not in danger of going out. He feeds it with two or three large logs, which do not burn except at the extremity, and which they never place one on the other, for fear of their getting into a blaze.

Of the women, the sisters of the great Chief alone have liberty to enter within the temple. The entrance is forbidden to all others, as well as to the common people, even when they carry something there to feast to the memory of their relatives, whose bones repose in the Temple. They give the dishes to the Guardian, who carries them to the side of the basket in which are the bones of the dead; this ceremony lasts only during one moon. The dishes are afterward placed on the palisades which surround the Temple, and are abandoned to the fallow-deer.

The Sun is the principal object of veneration to these people; as they cannot conceive of anything which can be above this heavenly body, nothing else appears to them more worthy of their homage. It is for the Same reason that the Chief of this Nation, who knows nothing on earth more dignified than himself, takes the title of brother of the Sun, and the credulity of the people maintains him in the despotic authority which he claims. To enable them better to converse together, they raise a mound of artificial soil, on which they build his cabin, which is of the same construction as the Temple. The door fronts the East, and every morning the great Chief honors by his presence the rising of his elder brother, and salutes him with many howlings as soon as he appears above the horizon. Then he gives orders that they shall light his calumet; he makes him an offering of the first three puffs which he draws; afterwards raising his hand above his head, and turning from the East to the West, he shows him the direction which he must take in his course.

There are in his cabin a number of beds on the left hand at entering; but on the right is only the bed of the great Chief, ornamented with different painted figures. This bed consists of nothing but a mattress of canes and reeds, very hard, with a square log of wood, which serves for a pillow. In the middle of the cabin is seen a small stone, and no one should approach the bed until he has made a circuit of this stone. Those who enter salute by a howl, and advance even to the bottom of the cabin, without looking at the right side, where the Chief is. Then they give a new salute by raising their arms above the head, and howling three times. If it be any one whom the Chief holds in consideration, he answers by a slight sigh and makes a sign to him to be seated. He thanks him for his politeness by a new howl. At every question which the Chief puts to him, he howls once before he answers, and when he takes his leave, he prolongs a single howl until he is out of his presence.

When the great Chief dies, they demolish his cabin, and then raise a new mound, on which they build the cabin of him who is to replace him in this dignity, for he never lodges in that of his predecessor. The old men prescribe the Laws for the rest of the people, and one of their principles is to have a sovereign respect for the great Chief, as being the brother of the Sun and the master of the Temple. They believe in the immortality of the soul, and when they leave this world they go, they say, to live in another, there to be recompensed or punished. The rewards to which they look forward, consist principally in feasting, and their chastisement in the privation of every pleasure. Thus they think that those who have been the faithful observers of their laws will be conducted into

a region of pleasures, where all kinds of exquisite viands will
be furnished them in abundance that their delightful and tranquil days will flow on in the midst of festivals, dances, and
women; in short, they will revel in all imaginable pleasures.
On the contrary, the violators of their laws will be cast upon
the lands unfruitful and entirely covered with water, where
they will not have any kind of corn, but will be exposed entirely
naked to the sharp bites of the mosquitoes, and that all Nations will make war upon them, that they will never eat meat,
and have no nourishment but the flesh of crocodiles, spoiled
fish and shell-fish.

These people blindly obey the least wish of their great Chief.
They look upon him as absolute master, not only of their
property but also of their lives, and not one of them would
dare to refuse him his head, if he should demand it; for whatever labors he commands them to execute, they are forbidden
to exact any wages. The French, who are often in need of
hunters or of rowers for their long voyages, never apply to
any one but their great Chief. He furnishes all the men they
wish, and receives payment, without giving any part to those
unfortunate individuals, who are not permitted even to complain. One of the principal articles of their Religion, and particularly for the servants of the great Chief, is that of honor-
ing his funeral rites by dying with him, that they may go to
serve him in the other world. In their blindness they willingly
submit to this law, in the foolish belief that in the train of
their Chief they will go to enjoy the greatest happiness.

To give an idea of this bloody ceremony, it is necessary to
know that as soon as an heir presumptive has been born to the
great Chief, each family that has an infant at the breast is
obliged to pay him homage. From all these infants they choose
a certain number whom they destine for the service of the
young Prince, and as soon as they are of a competent age,
they furnish him with employments suited to their talents.
Some pass their lives in hunting, or in fishing, to furnish supplies for the table; others are employed in agriculture, while
others serve to fill up his retinue. If he happen to die, all

these servants sacrifice themselves with joy to follow their dear master. They first put on all their finery, and repair to the place opposite to the Temple, where all the people are assembled. After having danced and sung a sufficiently long time, they pass around their neck a cord of buffalo hair with a running knot, and immediately the Ministers appointed for the executions of this kind, come forward to strangle them, recommending them to go to rejoin their master, and render him in the other world services even more honorable than those which had occupied them in this.

The principal servants of the great Chief having been strangled in this way, they strip the flesh off their bones, particularly those of their arms and thighs, and leave them to dry for two months, in a kind of tomb, after which they are placed in the Temple by the side of the bones of their master. As for the other servants their relatives carry them home with them, and bury them with their arms and clothes.

The same ceremony is observed in like manner on the death of the brothers and sisters of the great Chief. The women are always strangled to follow the latter, except when they have infants at the breast, in which case they continue to live, for the purpose of nourishing them. And we often see many who endeavor to find nurses, or who themselves strangle their infants, so that they shall not lose the right of sacrificing themselves in the public place, according to the ordinary ceremonies, and as the law prescribes.

This Government is hereditary; it is not, however, the son of the reigning Chief who succeeds his father, but the son of his sister, or the first Princess of the blood. This policy is founded on the knowledge they have of the licentiousness of their women. They are not sure, they say, that the children of the Chief's wife may be of the blood Royal, whereas the son of the sister of the Chief must be, at least on the side of the mother. The Princesses of the blood never espouse any but men of obscure family, and they have but one husband, but they have the right of dismissing him whenever it pleases them, and of choosing another among those of the Nation, provided he has not made any other alliance among them. If the husband has been guilty of infidelity, the Princess may have his head cut off in an instant; but she is not herself subject to the same law, for she may have as many Lovers as she pleases, without the husband having any power to complain. In the presence of his wife he acts with the most profound respect, never eats with her, and salutes her with howls, as is done by her servants. The only satisfaction he has is, that he is freed from the necessity of laboring, and has entire authority over those who serve the Princess.

In former times the Nation of the *Natchez* was very large. It counted sixty Villages and eight hundred Suns or Princes; now it is reduced to six little Villages and eleven Suns. In each of these Villages there is a Temple where the fire is always kept burning as in that of the great Chief, whom all the other Chiefs obey.

The great Chief nominates to the most important offices of the State; such are the two war-Chiefs, the two Masters of ceremony for the worship of the Temple, the two Officers who preside over the other ceremonies which are observed when foreigners come to treat of peace, another who has the inspection of the public works, four others charged with the arrangement of the festivals with which they publicly entertain the Nation, and such Strangers as come to visit them. All these Ministers, who execute the will of the great Chief are treated with the same respect and obedience as if he personally gave the orders.

Each year the people assemble to plant one vast field with Indian corn, beans, pumpkins, and melons, and then again they collect in the same way to gather the harvest. A large cabin situated on a beautiful prairie is set apart to hold the fruits of this harvest. Once in the summer, toward the end of July, the people gather by order of the great Chief, to be present at a grand feast which he gives them. This festival lasts for three days and three nights, and each one contributes what he can to furnish it; some bring game, others fish, etc. They have almost constant dances, while the great chief and his sister are in an elevated lodge covered with boughs, from whence they can see the joy of their subjects. The Princes, the Princesses and those who by their office are of distinguished rank, are arranged very near the Chief, to whom they show their respect and submission by an infinite variety of ceremonies.

The great chief and his sister make their entrance in the place of the assembly on a litter borne by eight of the greatest men; the Chief holds in his hand a great scepter ornamented with painted plumes, and all the people dance and sing about him in testimony of the public joy. The last day of this Feast he causes all his subjects to approach, and makes them a long harangue, in which he exhorts them to fulfill all their duties to Religion; he recommends them above all things to have a great veneration for the spirits who reside in the Temple, and carefully to instruct their children. If anyone has distinguished himself by some act of zeal, he is then publicly praised. Such a case happened in the year 1702. The Temple having been struck by lightning and reduced to ashes, seven or eight women cast their infants into the midst of the flames to appease the wrath of Heaven. The great Chief called these heroines, and gave them great praises for the courage with which they had made the sacrifice of that which they held most dear; he finished his panegyric by exhorting the other women to imitate so beautiful an example in similar circumstances.

The fathers of the families do not fail to carry to the Temple the first of their fruits, their corn and the vegetables. It is the same even with presents which are made to this Nation; they are immediately offered at the gate of the Temple, when the guardian, after having displayed and presented them to the spirits, carries them to the house of the great chief, who makes a distribution of them as he judges best, without any person testifying the least discontent.

They never plant their fields without having first presented the seed in the Temple with the accustomed ceremonies. As soon as these people approach the Temple, they raise their arms by way of respect, and utter three howls, after which they place their hands on the earth, and raise themselves again

three times with as many reiterated howls. When any one
has merely to pass before the Temple, he only pauses to salute
it by his downcast eyes and raised arms. If a father or mother
see their son fail in performance of this ceremony, they will
punish him immediately with repeated blows of a stick.

Such are the ceremonies of the *Natchez* Savages with regard to their Religion. Those of marriage are very simple.
When a young man thinks of marrying he has only to address
himself to the father of the girl, or if she have none, to her
eldest brother, and they agree on a price, which he pays in
skins or merchandise. When a girl has lived a licentious life,
they make no difficulty in receiving her, if there is the least
idea that she will change her conduct when she is married.
Neither do they trouble themselves as to what family she
belongs, provided that she pleases them. As to the relatives
of the girl, their only care is to inform themselves whether he
who asks her is an able hunter, a good warrior, and an excellent
workman. These qualities diminish the price which they have
a right to ask on marriage.

When the parties have agreed, the future husband goes
to the chase with his friends and when he has sufficient either
of game or fish, to feast the two families who have contracted
the alliance, they assemble at the house of the parents of the
girl. They particularly serve the newly married pair, who eat
from the same dish. The repast being ended, the bridegroom
smokes the calumet toward the parents of his wife, and then
toward his own parents, after which all the guests retire. The
newly married people remain together until the next day, and
then the husband conducts his wife to the residence of her
father-in-law, where they live until the family has built for
him a cabin of his own. While they are constructing it, he
passes the whole day in the chase to furnish food, which he
gives to those who are employed in this work.

The laws permit the *Natchez* to have as many wives as they
choose, nevertheless, the common people generally have but
one or two. This however is not the case with the chiefs, their

number is greater, because having the right to oblige the people to cultivate their fields, without giving them any wages, the number of their wives is no expense to them.

The marriage of the Chiefs is made with less ceremony. They content themselves with sending to fetch the father of the girl whom they wish to espouse, and they declare to him that they will give her the rank of their wives. They do not fail however, as soon as the marriage is consummated, to make a present to the father and mother. Although they have many wives, they keep but one or two in their own cabins; the rest remain at houses of their parents, where they go to see them when they wish.

At certain periods of the moon these savages never live with their wives. Jealousy has so little part in their hearts, that they find no difficulty in lending their wives to their friends. This indifference to the conjugal union results from the liberty they have in changing it when it seems good to them, provided that their wives have never borne children to them, for if any have been born of the marriage, nothing but death can separate them.

When this nation sends out a detachment for war, the Chief of the party erects two kinds of poles painted red from the top to the bottom, ornamented with red plumes, and arrows and tomahawks, also painted red. These poles are pointed to the side to which they are to carry the war. Those who wish to join the party, after having ornamented and daubed themselves in different colors, come to harangue the war-Chief. This harangue, who one makes after another, and which lasts nearly half an hour, consists of a thousand protestations of service, by which they assure him that they ask for nothing more than to die with him, that they are charmed to learn from so able a warrior the art of taking scalps, and that they fear neither the hunger nor the fatigues to which they are going to be exposed.

When a sufficient number of braves have presented themselves to the war-Chief he causes to be made at his house a beverage which they call the "war medicine."[1] This is an emetic which they make from a root they boil in large kettles full of water. The warriors, sometimes to the number of 300, having seated themselves about the kettle, they serve each with two pots of it. The ceremony is to swallow them with a single effort, and then to throw them up immediately by the mouth, with efforts so violent that they can be heard at a great distance.

After this ceremony, the war-Chief appoints the day of departure, that each one may prepare provisions necessary for the campaign. During this time, the warriors repair evening and morning to the place before the Temple, where, after having danced and related in detail the brilliant actions in which their bravery was conspicuous, they chant their death songs.

When on the war-path, they march in single file; four or five men who are the best walkers lead the way, and keep in advance of the army a quarter of a league, to observe everything, and give immediate notice. They encamp every evening an hour before sunset, and lie down about a large fire, each one with his arms near him. Before they encamp, they take the precaution to send out twenty warriors to the distance of half a league around the camp, for the purpose of avoiding all surprise. They never post sentinels during the night, but as soon as they have supped, they extinguish all fires.

As the War-chiefs always carry with them their idols, or what they call their spirits, well secured in some skins, at night they suspend them from a small pole painted red, which they erect in a slanting position, so that it may be bent on the side of the enemy. The warriors before they go to sleep, with war-club in hand, pass one after the other in a dance before

---

[1] Gatschet says that this war-medicine, or "war-physic," was a decoction of the button snakeroot; but he neglects to state whether he means *Liatris* or *Eryngium*, to both of which genera the above popular name is applied. The custom of drinking this medicine is mentioned also by Charlevoix. Gayarre says that it was "a fermented liquor, made with leaves of the cassia berry tree."—*Ibid.*, lxviii., *note* 15.

these pretended spirits, at the same time uttering the fiercest threats toward the side on which are their enemies.

The *Natchez*, like all the other Nations of Louisiana, distinguish by particular names those who have killed a greater or less number of the enemy. The old war-Chiefs distribute these names according to the merit of the warriors. To deserve the title of a great man-slayer, it is necessary to have taken 10 slaves or to have carried off 20 scalps. When a person understands their language, the name itself of a warrior enables him to learn all his exploits. Those who, for the first time, have taken a scalp or made a captive, do not sleep at their return with their wives, and do not eat any meat; they ought not to partake of anything but fish and thickened milk. This abstinence lasts for six months. If they fail to observe it, they imagine that the soul of him whom they have killed will cause them to die through sorcery, that they will never again obtain any advantage over their enemies, and that the slightest wounds they may receive will prove fatal.

They take extreme care that the great Chief shall not in anyway expose his life when he goes to war. If, carried away by his valor, he should happen to be killed, the Chiefs of the party and the other principal warriors would be put to death on their return; but executions of this kind are almost without example, on account of the precautions they take to preserve him from this evil.

When one of these Savages dies, his relatives come to mourn his death during an entire day, they then array him in his most beautiful dresses, they paint his face and his hair, and ornament him with plumes, after which they carry him to a grave prepared for him, placing by his side his arms, a kettle and some provisions. For the space of a month, his relatives come at dawn of day and at the beginning of the night, to weep for half an hour at his grave. The nearest relatives continue this ceremony for three months.

When any foreign Nation comes to treat of peace with the *Natchez* savages, they send their couriers to give notice of the day and hour when they shall make their entrance. The great

Chief orders the Masters of ceremony to prepare all things for
this grand occasion. They begin by naming those who during
each day should support the strangers, for the expense never
falls upon the Chief, but always on his subjects. Then they
clear the roads, they sweep the cabins, they arrange the seats
on a large hall which is on the mound of the great Chief by
the side of his cabin. His throne, which is on an elevation,
is painted and ornamented, and the bottom is furnished with
beautiful mats.

On the day that the Ambassadors are to make their entrance,
all the Nation assembles. The Masters of the ceremony place
the Princes, the Chiefs of the Villages, and the old Chiefs of
quality near the great Chief, on particular seats. When the
Ambassadors arrive, they stop and chant the song of peace.
The ambassage ordinarily consists of thirty men and six women.
Six of the best made, who have the finest voices, march in
front. They are followed by the others who chant in like
manner, regulating the cadence with the *sicicouet.*[1] The six
women are the last.

When the Chief has directed them to approach, they advance; those who have the calumets, chant and dance with
much agility, now turning around each other, and now presenting themselves in front, but always with violent move-
ments and extraordinary contortions. When they have entered the circle, they dance about the chair on which the chief
is seated, they rub him with their calumets from his feet even
to his head, and after that go back to find those who belong to
their suite. Then they fill one of their calumets with tobacco, and holding the fire in one hand, they advance all together before the Chief and smoke it; they direct the first
puff of smoke toward the Heavens, the second toward the
Earth, and the others around the horizon, after which they
without ceremony present the pipe to the Princes and to the
other Chiefs.

---

[1] *Sicicouet;* evidently the Algonkin word—written also *chichikoue* and *cicikwan*
—used to designate the rattle or small drum used by the Indian medicine-men
in their incantations.—*Ibid.*, lxviii., *note* 16.

The ceremony having been finished, the Ambassadors, as a token of alliance, rub their hands on the stomach of the Chief, and rub themselves over the whole body; they then place their calumets before the Chief on small forks, while the person among the Ambassadors who is particularly charged with the orders of his Nation, delivers a harangue which lasts for an entire hour. When he has finished, they make a sign to the strangers to be seated on the benches ranged near the great Chief, who responds to them by a discourse of equal length. Then the Master of ceremonies lights the great calumet of peace, and makes the strangers smoke, who swallow the tobacco smoke. The great Chief inquires of them whether they arrived safe,—that is, whether they are well, and those who are around them go one after the other to discharge the same office of politeness. After which they conduct them to the cabin which has been prepared for them, and where they are feasted.

That same evening at Sunset, the Ambassadors, with the calumet in their hands, go with singing to find the great Chief, and having raised him on their shoulders, they transport him to the quarter in which their cabin is situated. They spread on the ground a large skin, on which they cause him to sit down. One of them places himself behind him, and putting his hands on the Chief's shoulders he agitates all his body, while the others, seated in the circle on the ground, chant the history of their distinguished deeds. After this ceremony, which is repeated night and morning for four days, the great Chief returns to his cabin. When he pays his last visit to the Ambassadors, these place a stake at his feet, about which they seat themselves: The Warriors of the Nation having arranged themselves in all their finery dance around, striking the stake, and in turn recounting their great exploits, then follows the giving of presents to the Ambassadors, which consist of kettles, hatchets, guns, powder, balls, etc.

The day following this last ceremony, it is permitted to the

Ambassadors to walk through the whole Village, which before they were not able to do. Then every evening they give them spectacles,—that is to say, the men and women in their most beautiful dresses assemble at the public place, and dance until night is far advanced. When they are ready to return home, the Masters of the ceremonies furnish them with the provisions necessary for the journey.

After having thus given you a slight idea of the character and customs of the *Natchez* Savages, I proceed, my Reverend Father, as I have promised you, to enter on a detail of their perfidy and treason. It was on the second of December of the year 1729, that we learned that they had surprised the French, and had massacred almost all of them. This sad news was first brought to us by one of the planters, who had escaped their fury. It was confirmed to us on the following day by other French fugitives and finally, some French women whom they had made slaves, and were forced afterward to restore, brought us all particulars.

At the first rumour of an event so sad, the alarm and consternation was general in New Orleans. Although the massacre had taken place more than a hundred leagues from here, you would have supposed that it had happened under our own eyes. Each one was mourning the loss of a relative, a friend, or some property; all were alarmed for their own lives, for there was reason to fear that the conspiracy of the Savages had been general.

This unlooked for massacre began on Monday, the 28th of October, about 9 o'clock in the morning. Some cause of dissatisfaction which the *Natchez* thought they had with Monsieur the Commandant,[1] and the arrival of a number of richly laden boats for the garrison and the colonists, determined them to hasten their enterprise, and to strike their blow sooner than they had agreed with the other confederate Tribes. And it

---

[1] Vivier states much more forcibly (in his letter dated Nov. 17, 1750) the cause of the revolt of the Natches, as "the tyranny of the French Commandant at their Village," one Chopart.—*Ibid.*, lxviii., *note* 17.

was thus that they carried their plan into execution. First they divided themselves, and sent into the Fort, into the Village, and into the two grants, as many Savages as there were French in each of these places; then they feigned that they were going out for a grand hunt, and undertook to trade with the French for guns, powder and ball, offering to pay them as much, even more than was customary; and in truth, as there was no reason to suspect their fidelity, they made at that time an exchange of their poultry and corn, for some arms and ammunition which they used advantageously against us. It is true that some expressed their distrust, but this was thought to have so little foundation, that they were treated as cowards who were frightened of their own shadows. They had been on their guard against the *Tchactas*, but as for the *Natchez*, they had never distrusted them, and they were so persuaded of their good faith that it increased their hardihood. Having thus posted themselves in different houses, provided with the arms obtained from us, they attacked at the same time each his man, and in less than two hours they massacred more than two hundred of the French. The best known are Monsieur de Chepar, Commandant of the post, Monsieur du Codère, Commandant among the *Yazous*, Monsieur des Ursins, Messieurs de Kolly, father and son, Messieurs de Longrays, des Noyers, Bailly, etc.

Father du Poisson had just performed the funeral rites of his associate, Brother Crucy, who had died very suddenly of Sunstroke. He arrived among the *Natchez* on the 26th of November, that is, two days before the massacre. The next day which was the first Sunday of Advent, he said Mass in the parish and preached in the absence of the Curé. He was to have returned in the afternoon to his mission among the *Akensas*, but he was detained by some sick persons, to whom it was necessary to administer the Sacraments. On Monday he was about to say Mass, and to carry the holy Viaticum to one of those sick persons whom he had confessed the evening before, when the massacre began; a gigantic Chief six feet in height, seized him, and having thrown him to the ground, cut off his head with blows of a hatchet. The Father in falling only uttered these words, "Ah, my God, ah, my God!" Monsieur du Codère drew his sword to defend him, when he was himself killed by a musket-ball from another Savage, whom he did not perceive.

These barbarians spared but two of the French, a Tailor and a Carpenter, who were able to serve their wants. They did not treat badly either the Negro Slaves, or the Savages who were willing to give themselves up; but they ripped up the belly of every pregnant woman, and killed almost all those who were nursing their children, because they were disturbed by their cries and tears. They did not kill the other women, but made them slaves, and treated them with every indignity during the two or three months that they were their masters. The least miserable were those who knew how to sew, because they kept them busy making shirts, dresses, etc. The others were employed in cutting and carrying wood for cooking, and in pounding the corn of which they make their sagamité. But two things, above all, aggravated the grief and hardness of their slavery; it was, in the first place, to have for masters those same persons whom they had seen dipping their cruel hands in the blood of their husbands, and, in the second place, to hear them continually saying that the French had been treated in the same manner at all the other posts, and that the country was now entirely freed from them.

During the massacre, the great Chief of the *Natchez* was seated quietly under the tobacco shed of the Company. His Warriors brought to his feet the head of the Commandant, about which they ranged those of the principal French of the post, leaving their bodies a prey to the dogs, the buzzards, and other carnivorous birds.

When they were assured that not another Frenchman remained at the post, they applied themselves to plunder the houses, the magazine of the Company of the Indies, and all the boats which were still loaded by the bank of the river. They employed the Negroes to transport the merchandise, which they divided among themselves, with the exception of the munitions of war, which they placed for security in a separate cabin. While the brandy lasted, of which they found a good supply, they passed their days and nights in drinking, singing, dancing, and insulting in the most barbarous manner, the dead bodies and the memory of the French.

Some of the French escaped the fury of the Savages by taking refuge in the woods, where they suffered extremely from hunger and the effects of the weather. One of them, on arriving here, relieved us of a little disquietude we felt with regard to the post we occupy among the *Yazous*, which is not more than forty or fifty leagues above the *Natchez* by water, and only 15 or 20 by land. Not being able longer to endure the extreme cold from which he suffered, he left the woods under the cover of night, to go warm himself in the house of a Frenchman. When he was near it he heard the voices of Savages and deliberated whether he should enter. He determined, however, to do so, preferring rather to perish by the hand of these barbarians, than to die of famine and cold. He was agreeably surprised when he found these Savages eager to render him a service, to heap kindnesses upon him, to commiserate him, to console him, to furnish him with provisions, clothes, and a boat to make his escape to New Orleans. These were the *Yazous*, who were returning from chanting the calumet at *Oumas*. The Chief charged him to say to Monsieur Perrier, that he had nothing to fear on the part of the *Yazous*, that "they would not lose their sense," that is, that they would always remain attached to the French, and that he would be constantly on the watch with his tribe to warn the French pirogues that were descending the river to be on their guard against the *Natchez*.

We believed for a long time that the promises of this Chief were very sincere, and feared no more Indian perfidy for our post among the *Yazous*. But learn, my Reverend Father, the disposition of these savages, and how little one is able to trust their words, even when accompanied by the greatest demonstrations of friendship. Scarcely had they returned to their own village, when, loaded with the presents they received from the *Natchez*, they followed their example and imitated their treachery. Uniting with the *Corroys*, they agreed together to exterminate the French. They began with Father Souel, the Missionary of both tribes, who was then living in the midst of them, in their own village. The fidelity of the *Ofogoulas*, who were then absent at the chase, has never been shaken, and they now compose one Village with the *Tonikas*.

On the 11th of December, Father Souel was returning in the evening from visiting the Chief, and while in a ravine, received many musket-balls, and fell dead on the spot. The Savages immediately rushed to his cabin to plunder it. His Negro, who composed all his family and all his defense, armed himself with a wood-cutter's knife, to prevent the pillage, and even wounded one of the Savages. This zealous action cost him his life, but, happily, he had received Baptism less than a month before, and was living in a most Christian manner.

These Savages, who even to that time seemed sensible of the affection which their Missionary bore them, reproached themselves for his death as soon as they were capable of reflection; but returning again to their natural ferocity, they adopted the resolution of putting a finishing stroke to their crime by the destruction of the whole French post. "Since the black Chief is dead," said they, "it is the same as if all the French were dead—let us not spare any."

The next day, they executed their barbarous plan. They repaired early in the morning to the fort, which was not more than a league distant, and whose occupants supposed on their arrival, that the savages wished to chant the calumet to the Chevalier des Roches, who commanded the post in the absence of Monsieur de Codère. He had but seventeen men with him, who had no suspicion of any evil design on the part of the Savages, and were therefore all massacred, not one escaping their fury. They, however, granted their lives to four women and five children, whom they found there, and whom they made slaves.

One of the *Yazous*, having stripped the Missionary, clothed himself in his garments and shortly afterward an-

nounced to the *Natchez,* that his Nation had redeemed their
pledge, and that the French settled among them were all massacred. In this city there was no longer any doubt on that
point, as soon as they learned what came near of being the fate
of Father Doutreleau. This Missionary had availed himself
of the time when the Savages were engaged in their winter
occupations, to come to see us, for the purpose of regulating
some matters relating to his Mission. He set out on the first
day of this year, 1730, and not expecting to arrive at the residence of Father Souel, of whose fate he was ignorant, in time
to say Mass, he determined to say it at the mouth of the little
river of the *Yazous,* where his party had cabined.

As he was preparing for this sacred office, he saw a boat full
of savages landing. They demanded from what Nation they
were. "*Yazous,* comrades of the French," they replied, making a thousand friendly demonstrations to the voyageurs who
accompanied the Missionary, and presenting them with provisions. While the Father was preparing his altar, a flock
of bustards passed, and the voyageurs fired at them the only
two guns they had, without thinking of reloading, as the Mass
had already commenced. The Savages noted this and placed
themselves behind the voyageurs, as if it was their intention
to hear Mass, although they were not Christians.

At the time when the Father was saying the *Kyrie eleison*
the Savages made their discharge. The Missionary perceiving himself wounded in his right arm, and seeing one of the
voyageurs killed at his feet, and the four others fled, threw
himself on his knees to receive the last fatal blow, which he
regarded as inevitable. In this posture he received two or
three discharges. But although the Savages fired while almost
touching him, yet they did not inflict on him any new wounds.
Finding himself then, as it were, miraculously escaped from
so many mortal blows, he took flight, having on still his priestly
garments, and without any other defense than an entire confidence in God, whose particular protection was given him, as
the event proved. He threw himself into the water, and
after advancing some steps, gained the pirogue in which two

of the voyageurs were making their escape. They had supposed him to be killed by some of the many balls which they had fired on him. In climbing up into the pirogue, and turning his head to see whether any one of his pursuers was following him too closely, he received in the mouth a discharge of small shot, the greater part of which were flattened against his teeth, although some of them entered his gums, and remained there for a long time. I have myself seen two of them there. Father Doutreleau, all wounded as he was, undertook the duty of steering the pirogue, while his two companions placed themselves at the paddles. Unfortunately, one of them, at setting out, had his thigh broken by a musket ball, from the effects of which he has since remained a cripple.

The *Tchikachas,* a brave Nation but treacherous, and little known to the French, have endeavored to seduce the Illinois Tribes from their allegiance: they have even sounded some particular persons to see whether they could not draw them over to the party of those Savages who were enemies of our Nation. The Illinois have replied to them that they were almost all "of the prayer" (that is, according to their manner of expression, that they were Christians); and that in other ways they are inviolably attached to the French, by the alliances which many of that nation had contracted with them, in espousing their daughters. At the first news of the war with the *Natchez* and the *Yazous,* they came hither to weep for the black Robes and the French, and to offer the services of their Nation to Monsieur Perrier, to avenge their death. I happened to be at the governor's house when they arrived, and was charmed with the harangues they made. *Chikagou,*[1] whom you saw in Paris, was at the head of the *Mitchigamias,* and *Mamantouensa* at the head of the *Kaskaskias.*

Chikagou spoke first. He spread out in the hall a carpet of

---

[1] *Chikagou,* the Illinois chief here mentioned, was induced by Beaubois· to go, with several other chiefs of Western tribes, in company with him to Paris, in 1725. *The U. S. Cath. Hist. Mag.* reprints (vol. III, pp. 160-66) from the London *Post Man* of Jan. 27, 1726, an account of the visit of these "four savages of Mississippi," reporting speeches made by them, and the gifts made to them by the Company of the Indies.—*Ibid.,* lxviii., *note* 25.

deerskin, bordered with porcupine quills, on which he placed two calumets, with different savage ornaments, accompanying them with a present according to the usual custom. "There," he said in showing the two calumets, "are two messages which we bring you, the one of Religion and the other of peace or war, as you shall determine. We have listened with respect to the Governors, because they bring us the word of the King our Father, and much more to the black Robes, because they bring us the word of God himself, who is the King of Kings. We have come from a great distance to weep with you for the death of the French, and to offer our Warriors to strike those hostile Nations whom you may wish to designate. You have but to speak. When I went over to France, the King promised me his protection for the Prayer, and recommended me never to abandon it. I will always remember it. Grant then your protection to us and to our black Robes." He then gave utterance to the edifying sentiments with which he was impressed with regard to the Faith, as the Interpreter Baillarjon enabled us to half understand them in his miserable French.

Chikagou guards most carefully, in a bag made expressly for the purpose, the magnificent snuff-box which the late Madame, the Duchess d'Orléans, gave him at Versailles. Notwithstanding all the offers made to him, he has never been willing to part with it,—a degree of consideration very remarkable in a Savage, whose characteristic generally is, to be in a short time disgusted with anything he has, and passionately desire what he sees, but does not own.

Everything *Chikagou* has related to his countrymen with regard to France, has appeared to them incredible. "They have bribed you," said some to him, "to make us believe all these beautiful fictions." "We are willing to believe," said his relatives, and those by whom his sincerity was least doubted, "that you have really seen all that you tell us, but there must have been some charm which fascinated your eyes, for it is not possible that France can be such as you have painted it."

When he told them that in France they were accustomed to have five cabins, one on top of the other, and that they were

as high as the tallest trees, that there were as many people in
the streets of Paris, as there were blades of grass on the
Prairies, or mosquitoes in the woods, and that they rode about
there and even made long journeys in moving cabins of leather,
they did not credit it any more than when he added that he
had seen long cabins full of sick people, where skilful Sur-
geons performed the most wonderful cures. "Here," he
would say to them in sport, "you may lose an arm or a leg, an
eye, a tooth, a breast, if you are in France, and they will supply you with others, so that it will not be noticed." What
most embarrassed *Mamantouensa*, when he saw the ships, was
to know how it was possible to launch them into the water
after they had been built on land, where arms enough could
be found for this purpose, and above all to raise the anchors
with their enormous weights. They explained both these
points to him and he admired the genius of the French who
were capable of such beautiful inventions.

You can well believe, my reverend Father, that this war has
retarded the French colony; nevertheless we flatter ourselves
that this misfortune will be productive of benefit, by deter-
mining the Court to send the forces necessary to tranquillize
the Colony and render it flourishing. Although they have
nothing to fear at *New Orleans*, either from the smaller neighboring tribes, whom our Negroes alone could finish in a single
morning, or even from the *Tchactas*, who would not dare to
expose themselves on the Lake in any great numbers, yet a
panic terror has spread itself over almost every spirit, particularly with the women. They will, however, be reassured
by the arrival of the first troops from France, whom we are
now constantly expecting. As far as our Missionaries are concerned, they are very tranquil. The perils to which they see
themselves exposed seem to increase their joy and animate
their zeal.

[*Ibid.*, lxviii., *Doc.* cciii.]

XI

MEMOIR BY FATHER CLAUDE GODEFROI COQUART UPON THE POSTS OF THE KING'S DOMAIN

(1750)

[This is a memoir, privately written for the intendant of Canada by Father Claude Coquart, minutely describing the so-called "King's Posts" of Eastern Canada, and making various practical observations and suggestions regarding their resources and management. It is, for purposes of economic study, one of the most valuable documents in our series.—*Ibid.*, lxix., 14.]

LA MALBAYE

La Malbaye should be regarded as The most valuable farm of the country, on account of the quality of the soil, the facilities for raising Cattle there, and other advantages which I shall mention Hereafter.

The land there is good and abundant. They might have cleared more of it than they have done; but, as they desired only wheat enough to feed the farmer and his engagés, they have left uncleared or in the woods the finest region in the world. Those people have not even made this farm as valuable as they might have done, because they have always preferred to show that it was worth more than it yielded, and that their acquisition [*illegible in MS.*] was only to prevent the savages of the domain from coming there to trade. The lands might be increased by obliging the farmer to clear every year a certain number of arpents, and to take his firewood from the good land; and the season that might be assigned to him for this work would be that which comes between the time for sowing seed and that for cutting the hay. The man who today occupies the farm is intelligent, and well qualified to undertake this enlargement. He has at heart its success; by making it a point of honor with him, and enabling him to hope for some gratuity proportioned to the work that would be done, one would soon see this farm extended, and consequently bringing in a greater revenue, and that without expense. For the strongest of his engagés gets 50 Ecus.[1] There are six of them, but they are paid in merchandise which is sent to him, and which he gives them upon the basis of the invoice that he receives. Suppose that he has 1,500 engagés; I am not afraid to assert that he gives them 1,200 livres'[2] worth from the warehouse. Thus no money, or but little has to be paid out. Hitherto the merchandise has been priced too high, and has yielded no returns; as a result, there has been difficulty in securing men. The merchants must try to send articles of good quality, and set a reasonable price. [*Illegible in MS.*] under the name of "beaufort" is not good for making shirts; Canvas at 54 deniers is too dear at this time. Furthermore, some persons are asking permission to come to make Tar upon the lands of la Malbaye, offering to give as rent the 15th Barrel, and to sell to the farmer what they shall make at the rate of 20 livres a barrel. If this enterprise were continued every year, as they seem to desire to do, the advantage would be considerable, since they would thus so soon exhaust the pine forest; and, as the workmen would need food, it could be sold to them from the farm without inconvenience. Orders upon this point are expected from Monsieur The Intendant, which will prevent this being done at la Malbaye which was done some years Ago at baye St. Paul for Tar. Some soldiers were sent there, and a sergeant to keep them in order. They

---

[1] Several of the old French coins were called écus. They date from the period of Charles VII. The écu of Louis XIV is first given in Dye's *Coin Encyclopedia;* value in United States currency, $1.108. The early écu was equal to three francs; later, to about five. *Ibid.,* i., *note* 34.

[2] The livre was a money of account, in value somewhat less than the modern franc. *Ibid.,* iv., *note* 42.

worked during 5 months, and were given their food and a small gratuity after their labor. A like number of good workmen occupied at la malbaye during the same time would produce 250 Barrels of Tar a year; and, this being at the gates of the farm, they could come to sleep every night in the buildings. This profit is sure, without any expenses; and to those who ask to come to make Tar there could be assigned another pine forest, two leagues up the River.

If it be desired to concede lands along the River of la Malbaye, there are many people who would take them; but it would be necessary to insert in the contract a prohibition against trading,—not only with the savages of the domain, but also with all other savages under the most severe penalties. This concession would soon join La Malbaye with les Eboulemens and Baye st. Paul, through the finest country in the world.[1]

Monsieur Cugnet[2] has prohibited his farmer at la Malbaye from trading with any savage; this prohibition caused a great quantity of Martens to be lost last year, and, since then, 400 Livres of Beavers, which were taken to Baye st. Paul by the Algonquin savages. I believe that it is necessary to continue this prohibition with reference to the savages of the domain, but to give orders to the farmer not only to receive but to attract the savages who live outside of it, and to barter food and Merchandise with them, as permission therefor was given last autumn at my solicitation. The same savages are still in the country, and appeared this winter at baye st. Paul. Those who are accused of trading with them are the men named Jasmin and Jacques Perron; and the Peltries which the savages take to baye st. Paul are produced upon the lands of the domain.

[1] *Malbaie,* now the village of Murray Bay, 90 miles below Quebec; the *cheflieu,* for judicial purposes, of the Saguenay district. The village lies at the mouth of the Malbaie River, where that stream falls into the St. Lawrence. A little above this place is the village of Les Eboulements.—*Ibid.,* lxix., *note* 17.

[2] François Étienne Cugnet came to Canada as early as 1720. He became a member of the supreme council in 1730, and six years later, farmer of the revenue for the post at Michillimackinac; he was afterwards, during many years, farmer for the posts in the "King's domain." . . . It is probable that this report of Coquart's was requested from him by the intendant (Biget), as a private check upon Cugnet's reports as farmer of the revenue.—*Ibid.,* lxix., *note* 18.

There might also be accorded to the farmers of la Malbaye and of la Comporté half the proceeds of their hunting; They hunt at the doors of their dwellings, and that causes them to lose no time. It was formerly forbidden to them on account of the difficulties arising between those who at that time occupied the two farms, difficulties which no longer exist. This permission, which may be made valuable to them, will encourage them to perform their duties faithfully.

The advantages that will be found in clearing the lands of la Comporté are too important not to demand attention. I have already suggested that 8 men during five months, at 20 or 25 livres a month, would do a great deal of work. The farm at la Malbaye will support them; it has this year about 400 minots of wheat,—that is to say, a surplus of almost half the quantity that it needs. As it will be necessary to burn the forest, the first two years will not show any profit. But when that shall have been done, we shall see, in the 2nd or 3rd year, an abundant produce; and animals will be brought to consume it, in case the farm of la malbaye cannot furnish enough animals of its own Breeding.

As formerly it happened that the farmers of la Malbaye and of la Comporté were always quarreling, both having equal authority in their respective farms, it was proposed to make the farmer of la Malbaye sole master of the two farms. He furnishes the one at la Comporté what he needs, and receives from his Hands the commodities and cattle, noting the place whence they come. Since that time, all is at peace; so I believe that it is well to continue this superiority of the farmer of la Malbaye, who alone will answer for what shall be sent him for the two farms, and for what they shall produce. Consequently, it will be the said farmer of la Malbaye to whom will be entrusted the enterprise that is being planned for the lands of la Comporté,—directing him to select its most fertile Cantons, and to constitute the farmer of la Comporté master of the work when he himself cannot be there; forbidding him from using during the hay or harvest time, the men employed to clear The lands of la Comporté,—unless the hay or grain be exposed to loss for lack of people and work. To occupy them elsewhere during these two seasons would retarde the work too much.

The Cattle are beyond a doubt the principal object in these two farms; and, the more of them shall be raised, the more considerable the profit. It is a question then, of seeking prairies and pasture-lands to feed them, which will not be difficult, if the farmers will give themselves the trouble. But there is one thing to be observed, which is, that the various Kinds of animals are degenerating; for Example, one does not see at la Malbaye so fine oxen as at Beaupré and on the South Shore. Could there not be sent cows and bulls of the large Varieties which, multiplying little by little, would furnish the farms with fine animals? 2nd, The pigs are extremely small, and the fattest of them hardly weigh 180 Livres. There are some enormous ones at the little River; one could have some of that breed without great expense; It costs no more to feed them, and there would be more pork. Proper orders given to the farmer would remedy that, and the profit would be considerable. Instead of seven or 8 barrels of pork, which 20 pigs now furnish, they would have twelve or fourteen; and they would not be obliged to buy pork to furnish to the other posts.

The farmer would be obliged to Raise more Sheep than he is raising. He will, perhaps, plead that fodder might be lacking; but, 1st, He always has a large surplus of it remaining in the spring; 2nd, There will always be time enough, at the second voyage of the ship, to send to Quebec such animals as he will foresee cannot pass the winter; 3rd, if this last point received attention, a great number of sheep would leave la Malbaye every year, instead of the 20 that are generally Sent. The sheep do not cause expense, and it is astonishing that there is not at la Malbaye a flock of 2 or 300. There are hardly 50 there during the winter.

I say nothing of the poultry; this is a small matter. Encouragement for Raising them can always be given; but the girls, who are occupied in Raising the calves and lambs, can hardly give their attention to the rest; besides the housekeeping is considerable.   They have to churn the milk two or three times a week; to do them justice, it can be said that they are busy all day, even going beyond their strength.   The two farms every year give from 30 to 40 pairs of chickens, sometimes fewer; that is all that can be Expected of them.

In general, the following is what la Malbaye can produce this year; provisions for The farms; 4 or 6 oxen, 25 sheep, 2 or 3 cows, 1,200 Livres of pork, 14 to 1500 Livres of butter, one barrel of lard.   If the men there did not have to work at la comporté the farm would produce 4 or 500 Livres of pork more than the above, and more than 100 minots of wheat.   As for sheep, it ought to be ordered that only the Males be sold, and that the ewes be kept; the following year an increase would be perceived.

There is one last item which is not to be overlooked; it is the salmon-fishing.   Usually the farmers get from it their supply, and nothing more; but if they were furnished with Nets, It would be easy for them to salt a great quantity, especially in the years when that fishery yields most abundantly.   This would not be an increase of work, since the fishing is done in The River, and upon the shores of the bay.

If the farm of la Malbaye is not today upon the footing on which it ought to be, the cause must be attributed to the frequent change of farmers,—either because they were not such as were desirable for the post, or for other reasons; What is certain is, that those who occupied the farm before the man who now occupies it let everything go to ruin.   The thistles were choking the wheat, the Cattle were not kept in by the fences; all those who saw la Malbaye in those times can certify to the truth of this.

They would also say that they have never seen la Malbaye upon so good a footing as it now is.   One sees there neither thistles nor black wheat, all the fences are in Place, and Joseph Dufour has a special talent for making everything profitable. If he can be induced to continue his services, it will be a benefit to his employer.   Last year, however, He wished to leave;

VIEW OF QUEBEC, IN 1722.

[From La Potherie's "Histoire de l'Amérique Septentrionale."]

Here are his Reasons; Nearly all his wages are used in The Support of his family. He has three grown daughters who help him in carrying on the establishment, and a boy for the stables. If he had not these girls, he would be obliged to hire servants, to whom he would have to give farm wages. His eldest girl is at the head of the farm; for the Housekeeping she gets only 50 livres a year. He asks that the wages of this girl be increased to the amount of 100 livres, and that 20 Ecus be given to the second; with this He will be more comfortable, and he prays Monsieur the Intendant to give Attention to his request. Moreover, He has 8 sheep on the farm which are his own; up to the present, Monsieur Cugnet has always taken their wool, and he has paid for what was absolutely necessary for the use of his family; and he asks that they consent to grant him half of the fleeces of his sheep. The wool is a small matter; as to the wages he asks for his two daughters, I believe he would be satisfied—at least, he ought to be—if 80 livres were given to the elder, and 50 to the younger. He deserves something for his care and attention, and one can say in his praise that la Malbaye has never been in so good a condition as it is now.

Total wages of the farms, 2,060.

TADOUSSAC

The post at Tadoussac does not produce many Peltries; 3 or 4 packages of Beavers, 100 or 120 Martens, some thirty lynxes, some Foxes in ordinary years, a few livres of Beaver pouches,[1]—these are the things usually furnished every year. The principal occupation of that post is hunting the seal, which is carried on from the month of december to the end of March. This hunting is precarious; yet, since françois Dorée has been agent at Tadoussac, the least he has made every year

[1] The "pouches" (prenuptial glands) of the beaver have been used in medicine from the time of Hippocrates; and, in the earliest times, the animal was hunted mainly to secure these pouches. The belief in the medicinal efficacy of castoreum (the substance secreted therein) is, at the present day, more popular than scientific.—*Ibid.*, lxix., *note* 20.

is from 80 to 90 Casks of oil. It would be more abundant
if there were more hunters, for it rarely fails when the savages give themselves up to it with enthusiasm; but this good
will depends somewhat upon the manner in which they are
managed by the agents. The one who at present governs them
does with them whatever he wishes, and one would risk a little
too much in changing him. The Seals killed for 90 Casks of
oil would naturally produce from 900 to 1,000 sealskins; yet
hardly 5 to 600 are obtained, because the savages keep many
of them to make shoes and to clothe their children, without
counting the skins lost by their lack of care. It would be
easy to increase the number of hunters in this post, where there
are a number of very capable young men. The agent of
Chekoutimi might be ordered to send the orphan boys to
Tadoussac. These children live with their relatives, or with
others, and are quite poorly cared for; instead of such a life,
they would, if they were at Tadoussac, aid in managing the
canoes of those young men who are capable of hunting; these
latter, if they are not provided with steersmen, either are themselves obliged to act in that capacity, or they go in pairs to
hunt, which diminishes the number of canoes. Besides, the
last epidemic has greatly afflicted the posts of Tadoussac and
the Jeremie islets; and these orphans, who have to be drudges
on the land, either at Chekoutimi, or on the Jeremie islets,
would little by little repeople the port of Tadoussac; and the
hunting there would be more profitable, since next year There
would be, instead of twelve canoes which hunt today, 17 or 18,
and perhaps more. This plan was proposed last autumn to
Monsieur Cugnet, who in accordance therewith gave his orders
to the agent at Chekoutimi. It would be well to renew those
orders to him, and to induce him to use all his efforts to bring
people to Tadoussac. He could do so without injuring his
post; but it will be necessary to conquer a certain Envy and
jealousy, up to the present almost insurmountable, among the
agents. The Missionary might influence some of them, but
he will always find the agents in his way; they cannot bear to
have him enter in anyway into the arrangements that may be

made—which appeared plainly last autumn, when Monsieur Cugnet told the Agent of Chekoutimi to send some Young men to Tadoussac. "I will do what I can," he replied, "provided that the Father does not meddle in it." It would be, however, very proper that he should sometimes meddle, for the Reason that I have just given,—namely, that the agents being jealous of one another, and seeing only with annoyance the success of others, are not much inclined to give up, in favor of others, young men who are of no use to themselves, but who would be useful to others. In a word, when one considers that the seal is much more abundant at Tadoussac than at the Jeremie Islets, and that it is rare to see the chase fail there, while they hardly make 30 or 40 Casks of oil at the Jeremie islets, I think it will be decided to take the savages away from the islets and from Chekoutimi, in order to place Tadoussac upon a sure footing. There are savages who would not ask for anything better, but they are afraid of the agent at their post; and it will never be except by virtue of suitable orders that these savages can be had at Tadoussac, against the opposition made by the Agents. I will even add that the savages of whom I speak accomplish very little about Chekoutimi, and that they have trouble in paying their debts; whereas in coming to Tadoussac they would be better off and would furnish some profit.

A great amount of food is consumed at the post of Tadoussac. This ought not to cause surprise when one remembers; 1st., that the savages are there in the course of the year. They go into the woods in the autumn, to seek something with which to clothe themselves; and, in the spring, to indemnify themselves for the bad food upon which they have lived during the winter, and to capture a few martens on the way. 2nd, during The summer, they are occupied in making their Canoes for hunting. A great many of these are needed. They make them at the Post or in the environs, and when they lack food they come there to get it. 3rd, The whole winter is occupied in hunting; there is not a day when they do not go to the places where game may be found. It is, therefore, by means of the

warehouse that they live,—that is to say, they are furnished
provisions, their expenditures therefor being noted down.
They get flour, peas, and indian corn, sometimes a piece of
bacon; for, to season their soup, both french and savages use
hardly anything else than seal-oil.   4th, The Post of
Tadoussac is The approach to all the other Posts.   People stop
there in going and coming, and sometimes, when one counts
upon ten persons to be supplied with food, there are twenty.
5th, When the ship arrives, it is the savages who are employed
to unload the provisions and merchandise, or to load oil and
other goods; They do not get for this work any other recompense than their living.   Besides, the captains are obliged to
employ the savages, especially at the place where the ships
winter, for the anchorage there is very poor, and too much
diligence cannot be used to dispatch the ship, for fear of a gust
of wind.   That is what causes so great an amount of food to
be consumed at the Post of Tadoussac, and people will cease to
be surprised at it when they shall have considered all these
reasons.

   I have been told that there was a desire to abandon the forge
at Tadoussac, and that it was intended to send from Quebec
axes, tools for chopping, and other utensils suitable for trading,
while they would send to Quebec the guns which would need
to be repaired, etc., etc.   Half of the project might be carried
into effect, that is to say with regard to the products of the
forge; the post of Tadoussac might be so well furnished with
them that it could supply them to the other posts, according
to their needs; but, as for weapons, I consider the thing almost
Impossible.   The interests of the Posts will suffer from it,
and the savages will leave those places.

   1st, the savage who has only one gun would be obliged, when
its lock is out of order, to give it to the agent to send it to
Quebec; and he will either wait with folded arms until it is
returned, or it will be necessary to lend him another, or else
rent him one.   That would require in every post almost a
double supply of guns, which would be an increase in expenses.   2nd, If the savage is obliged to pay the rent of the

gun that will be loaned him until his own is sent back from Quebec, he will incur a double expense—the mending of his own gun, and the rent of the gun loaned; he will not be satisfied with this. Besides, either they will wait for the ship, to send the guns,—and that will be a great delay,—or these will be Sent in Canoes. That would then multiply the voyages to Quebec, which are not made without expense, and which will occupy Engagés who are absolutely needed in the posts during the summer, especially in those of Chekoutimi and the Jeremie islets. On the other hand, by keeping the gunsmith at Tadoussac, the savages can Send their guns thither; and their going, coming, and remaining there will only make a journey of 3 days. In each man's account is noted the cost of the work that has been done, and he pays for it with the rest; and what the savages pay either for the stock of the gun, or for the mending, greatly exceeds the Wages that are given to the two gunsmiths, —one of whom receives 400 livres and the other 20 livres,— as can be seen by the account of the forge which the agent at Tadoussac sends to Quebec every spring. He would ask nothing better than to be freed from these incumbrances; but I think that The Interests of the posts would suffer therefrom.

It is also said that there is a plan to establish a general warehouse at Tadoussac, and that the agent at that post will be charged with furnishing the other posts according to their demands, keeping an exact account of what he shall send them. This project seems to me to be liable to many Inconveniences. Jealous of each other as the agents are, they will not look at the Tadoussac agent except with eyes of envy; and I predict that there will never be any peace among them. They will not consider that it is an increase of work for him; they will only think, "We depend upon the Tadoussac Agent for our needs." 2nd, let the Agent of Tadoussac do well or not, The Letters of the other agents will always be filled with complaints. 3rd, it may happen that the Tadoussac Agent will not have, at the time, either the quantity or the quality of goods that will be demanded of Him; then the blame will be laid upon him for any deficiency in what will be made at the other posts; whereas, continuing upon the same footing on which affairs now are, each agent will have nothing to say. In the spring he sends his memorandum; it is filled out, and they send him what he asks by the 1st voyage of the ship. He sends a second memorandum by the ship, and, on the second voyage, the articles are supplied. In that way, He has nothing to say; and he can only blame himself if He had failed to get anything, because he is obliged to come twice,—1st, to take away the oil; 2nd, for the Peltries. The agents will receive what they need as usual; and the one at Tadoussac will not have the annoyance of having the other agents saddled upon him. I only make this suggestion because I have already Heard unfavorable comments; and, if they begin to complain at a mere plan, what will it be when it shall be necessary to execute it? They now regard themselves, and Rightly, as Equals; They do not even like to communicate their memoranda to others than to those in whose hands these must be placed, because they do not wish any one to know what they are asking, or how frequent are the returns which they make; these are the mysteries that they keep from one another. But, if the agent of Tadoussac had all the merchandise in his hands, and if he were the distributor of it, he would be regarded (with Envy) as their superior, and this pretended superiority would be for him the source of a thousand vexations, which might be Spared him. Besides the Tadoussac agent is not capable of such important details; he would give a good account of things in his way, but people would perhaps not be satisfied with it. I do not think this ought to be done at present, unless they wish to see the post of Tadoussac irretrievably lost. The savages are so attached to him that they do not conceal their sentiments upon this Point; and, besides he is performing his duties well.

THE JEREMIE ISLETS

The Post of the Jeremie Islets, situated 30 leagues below Tadoussac, produces Seal-oil and Peltries. They hunt the Seal from the first ice until toward Twelfth-day, and resume this pursuit from about the 15th of march, sometimes sooner, until the ice disappears. It is done at point des Betsiamioutes, two leagues from the post. The time between the 15th of january and the 15th of March the savages spend in the woods, hunting; thus this post has Varied resources. The usual yearly production is 35 to 40 Casks of oil. I do not know, however, what it will be this winter, for since many people were lost through sickness last year, It may easily happen that this year there will not be a great production of oil. However that may be, not much time is needed to attend to this post. The agent can detain for the sea some of those who have continued to hunt in the woods, unless his experience shows him that the forest hunting is more profitable than that of the sea.

He receives not only the Peltries from the savages domiciled at the Post, but also those of the savages from the interior, who bring them to him at his post. This indeed is the quarrel that has always been carried on between the agents at Chekoutimi and of the islets; the former reproaches the latter with Taking away his savages, but in reality, each attaches to himself the savages of Manawan and Ounichtagan. They have the dispute, but those who have the posts have only the gain, since both agents work for the same master; the noble Emulation, however, between the two posts, the desire to show good returns, keeps up this petty war. They steal each other's savages; they invent a thousand little ruses to attract them. There is no great harm in all this. Moreover, at the beginning of June the agent of the Islets departs for Manikwagan, and goes up the River to a certain place, where he meets the savages who inhabit these lands: he trades with them, and Brings back their Peltries. Thus the post of the islets may well produce 4 to 500 Beaver-skins, sometimes 800 and more handsome martens, well-dressed skins of the Caribou, and seal-skins. When the Foxes are found along the sea, they are not the least resource.

Besides, this post causes no expense. It has no passages to pay for, except that of a canoe in the spring, which is sent from

Sept isles to Quebec; and the agent gives nothing for Nothing. Also Monsieur Cugnet, therefore, said of this Post of the islets that it caused him the least expense, and brought Him in proportion the greatest profit.

CHEKOUTIMI

The Post of chekoutimi is 30 leagues from Tadoussac, on the upper Saguenai; two leagues higher than this post, the saguenai is no longer navigable, except for canoes. This post is the most valuable of the whole domain, on account of the quantity of Peltries which it produces—3,000 Livres, and often more, of Beaver-skins, and about 2,000 Martens in ordinary years; last year, there were more than 3,000 of the latter, besides skins of bears, Lynxes, and otters. In a word, according to The information of the agent himself, his post has, several times during his residence there, produced more than 40,000 livres' worth of Peltries. Consequently, it pays expenses at a smaller profit than is made at the other posts. On the post of Chekoutimi depend Lake St. John, the Mistassins, and Chomoukchwan.

1st. The savages come but little to the Post, except in the months of May, june and july. There are only a few families who can be regarded as domiciled at the post, and who do not go far away; the others go to a great distance. This is a very good thing, for the environs of Chekoutimi are so Drained of animals that they would Risk dying of hunger. If these lands were abandoned for some time, the Beaver would multiply, and animals would become more abundant; but that would be asking The Impossible from the savages. They would travel ten leagues to kill a beaver a year old, summer or winter, if they could find it. It is not, then, from these settled savages that much profit is expected; however They are not entirely useless. They make canoes for the inland trade; and we have them always at hand for the voyages that we are obliged to make. Among these savages there are some who would willingly go to Tadoussac, and it is of them that I have spoken in referring to the last post, saying they would be better off, and that they would furnish more profit.

2nd. The People of Lake St. John are the sad remnants of an astonishing multitude of savages who inhabited the lands 60 or 70 years Ago. There only remain one large family, who work fairly well for the Interests of the post. They bring their Peltries at the time the ships arrive; and, after having tasted the brandy, they return to the lake, to live there during the summer upon Fish.

3rd. Chomoukchwan was formerly dependent upon Lake St. John. The savages took their Peltries thither, or some one went after them, as is being done today. For some years the winter was passed there; but it has been seen to be a quite useless expense, and that it is sufficient to go there at the melting of the ice. This post is situated back of three Rivers. It would be a question of preventing the savages from going there; and, instead of 8 or 900 Martens that are generally obtained at that place, there would be many more. They are attracted thither by The brandy that they get in trade, and that is given them to take into the interior. That is a road which we have not hitherto been able to close.

The Agent of Chekoutimi sends thither a trader, whom he furnishes with merchandise, also two frenchmen and some savages of his post. At the end of july, all these men have returned. The savages are worthless, and one cannot place too little confidence in them; the journeys to three rivers have completely spoiled Them; and it would be a desirable achievement and a great profit for the post of Chekoutimi if they could be retained at home, and if the people of three Rivers could be prevented from sending the savages or frenchmen into the woods with liquor to trade with them. Desgroseilliers pursued this plan during the space of many years—and successfully, whatever Monsieur Cugnet may say of it. The question now is, to find a man who can make the voyage every year in the capacity of a trader, either wintering at Chekoutimi, or repairing thither early in the spring; and I think that he will be always be there in time, if he will leave Quebec at the end of April.

4th. The Mistassins are the best people in the world. They winter about 200 leagues from chekoutimi, toward hudson's bay, where some of them go to trade. Some bring their Peltries to the Post themselves, and a trader is sent to their country to receive those of the others and supply their needs. During the last three years, it is an Engagé of Tadoussac who makes the voyage; it is as fatiguing as that to Choumoukchwan, but it does not take so much time. As to that of choumoukchwan, there are nothing but Rapids to ascend; on the other side, There are portages. It is from the Mistassins that the handsome marten-skins come—not so fine, indeed, as those of the River Moisy, but in greater numbers. As the agent of chekoutimi keeps an exact Account of what he Receives from every post, and gives a receipt for it to the traders, receiving one from them for the merchandise that he delivers to them, it will be easy to see what each separate district furnishes, and the profit that it returns.

5th. There remains one Place to which the agent began to Send goods last year, and whither I think they ought to be Sent this year also. It is Ounichtagan. If this enterprise can be made to succeed, it will be a great advantage; many savages from the interior will be attracted to that place. The Mistassins themselves will repair thither willingly, according to what I have heard; and thus the Frenchmen will afterward be relieved from making the voyage to the Mistassins, because Ounichtagan will be, so to speak, a Common rendezvous, to which all the savages of these regions will flock. The Agent of the islets may, perhaps, inveigh against this Establishment, saying that his savages will be taken away. What does it matter? We shall be sure to obtain their Peltries, and will not be exposed to deception; for there are some who take their Peltries to the islets, where they go to trade, and come straightway to chekoutimi to get goods on credit,—which is plain knavery on their part. This could be obviated by Establishing a post, and perhaps, afterward, by maintaining it in winter, At Ounichtagan.

It is also found that the consumption of food is great at Chekoutimi. The savages whose lands are in the Environs of the post come to the Warehouse when They fast in the woods, for I have already said that animals are rare there. 2nd, The many savages who Assemble for trade in May, June, and july consume an extraordinary amount. I have with my own eyes seen them eat as much as ten quarts a day, and yet they were very moderately portioned. As the merchandise fails in the spring, on account of the goods that have to be Forwarded to the Mistassins and for chomoukchwan, It has happened often that these savages remain ten or twelve days at the Post to await the ship, and with it the merchandise of which they have need. Meanwhile, they have to be fed, and it happens then that everyone suffers. Both frenchmen and savages fast on account of the Delay of the ship, which ought to be at chekoutimi in the first days of June, at the latest; then the consumption would be less, because in two or three days everyone would be sent away. 3rd. When all these savages return to the interior, they are furnished with food, which is placed upon their account; and, if each family were only given the half of a quart, this would go far, but They carry away more. Thus it is very plain, by what I have just said, that this consumption of food is inevitable. 4th, in order to diminish it, It is necessary to have the ship depart early in the spring, in order that the savages may remain less time at the post. A feast is generally made for them at the arrival of the ship, and, rather than to go without this feast, they would remain at the Post until the end of july; but when it is given, and it is given as soon as possible, each is seen to take his share, and plunge into the woods until the following spring.

I do not speak Here of the Construction of the sawmill in The River Pepawetiche, at half a League this side of chekoutimi; I will merely say that only two saws and two mountings are necessary to keep the mill in constant operation. Those whom I have Questioned upon this point, and who are well informed, have assured me that two saws kept going day and night will produce 140 or 150 planks every 24 hours. They also said that no advantage is to be derived from increasing the number of saws, and that they were returning to the other,— one mounting for each saw, and a saw in reserve. If the sawyers relieved each other by the quarter, The mill would continue going from the 15th or 20th of april until the 15th of November,—that is to say, more than six months. The planks could be carried in a raft to the Creek three leagues below the mill; all the ships can go there without danger, and The warehouse would be at Tadoussac.

SEPT ISLES

There are two wintering-places for hunting the seal at sept iles,—Pointe a la Croix and the seven islands themselves. The success of this hunting depends upon the ice; when it is not in too great quantity, and when the winds are not too violent, the yield is much larger. Last year, there were only from 30 to 35 casks of oil, but it was a poor year; there is generally more. The Peltries are not so numerous as at chekoutimi, but they are of better quality. They have obtained as many as 800 fine Martens, some Beavers, and a great many Caribou-hides. The River Moisy, 5 leagues below sept isles, by which most of the savages come from the interior, has given its name to these beautiful and so highly Valued Martens. The post of Sept isles has seldom failed to be profitable, while Dufresne has managed it; but He is hardly in a condition to continue his winter enterprises; the voyages that he has to make into the interior at the end of june have ruined him,—yet upon this voyage depends the success of the trade. The man who is at the Post today is his Pupil; perhaps he will succeed as did his master.

Mingan is injuring Sept isles; this post is 30 leagues from them, and the Limits of the domain are at Riviere aux huitres ["oyster river"], two leagues farther down than the River Moisy. The savages of Mingan come as far as the Riviere aux huitres to hunt, and sometimes debauch the savages of Sept isles. Protest has often been made against This proximity, but How remedy it?

The Salmon-fishing might be made a business at sept isles, if it were kept up every year. It is done in July; in 15 or 18 days the Fishing is over, and I have been assured that they could easily catch some twenty Caskfuls. If the Agent had Nets, and gave proper orders to the Engagés who remain at the Post during his journey into the interior, this fishing would be done without anyone's noticing it. It is true that the ship from sept isles would arrive at Quebec 15 days later, but what would that matter? It would always get there before The 15th of August, and would have more time than it needed to prepare for its return. The expenses would not be increased, since the Engagés contract for The year; and as, besides, They have nothing very important to do at that season. By making all these little advantages avail, each post would increase profits.

That is all I can say regarding the posts; if my knowledge is limited, it is correct.

2060
2660
1610
1360
2050
———
9740

I will add one word in reference to the Agents.

I think that there would be a great risk in changing them now, and that, on the Contrary, everything possible ought to be done to engage them to remain. 1st. No better farmer for La Malbaye could be found. He is so attached to it that he regards as his very own what is placed in his hands, using all his efforts to make it valuable, so far as that depends upon him. *Joseph Dufour*
2nd. The Tadoussac agent has found the way to attach the savages to him. He does with them as he pleases; and during the 4 years while he has been agent, his post has always succeeded in regard to Seal-oil. He is not very skillful in Writing, but he renders his Accounts faithfully and Monsieur Cugnet has always appeared satisfied with him. Besides the savages would perhaps disperse if anyone whom they did not like were given to them. 3rd. The chekoutimi agent has been managing the post for more than 14 years; He is liked by the savages who are quite difficult to lead in this Canton. He has talent to Encourage them; and, if he were removed, It is to *François Dorée*   *Joseph Dorval*

be feared that the Mistassins, who are attached to him, would have their Peltries taken to hudson's bay, from which they are not as Far as from chekoutimi; and that the savages of chomoukchwan would carry theirs to three Rivers.

4th. The agent of the Jeremie islets has always conducted his post well; and I have, in the proper place, remarked that his careful administration has brought profit to Monsieur Cugnet. 5th. The agent of Sept isles is an old Stager in the trade; it is a pity that he is worn out. If he were exchanged

with The agent at the islets, He would be in very good condition to continue his services, and would willingly Devote himself to it. The point is, to ascertain whether the agent at the islets would like this change.

I pray Monsieur the Intendant to keep this memorandum to himself; and, if he judge it proper to make some extracts from it, not to say from whom It comes to him.

april 5th, 1750.

The manner of trade is uniform in all the posts, except at Sept isles, where they sell at a higher price. Every twenty sols represents a beaver of good size; while for the little ones they get two, and sometimes three. A marten, however fine it is, is taken at the same rate, as well as the common Foxes, Otters, Pecans, bears' cub, etc. The Lynx, when it is fine, is worth [*blank space in Ms.*], beavers, sometimes more, sometimes less; its size and its fur determine its price. A silver fox is worth 6 Beavers; a black fox, 20 or 22. Thus for example, an ell of cloth which is marked upon the invoice " . . . . 8 livres", is sold for 8 martens or 8 beavers, etc. The savages at Tadoussac and of the islets trade their oil for the Beaver; Five pots of oil for one, and A Cask for 22; one large Sealskin for a Beaver; and so on, in the same proportion.

[*Ibid.,* lxix., *Doc.* ccxviii.]

XII

EXTRACTS FROM THE JOURNAL DES JÉSUITES

(1645-1668)

[The *Journal des Jésuites* was, as its title indicates, a brief record, from day to day, of events occurring in the Jesuit residence at Quebec, and written by the superior in charge.

The *Relations* were formal accounts, carefully edited in Quebec and in Paris, and avowedly published for the purpose of attracting money and recruits for the missions of New France; it is to the letters and other informal documents of the period, that we must look for the side lights with which to illumine the heroic picture of the Jesuits in New France. Among the mass of material which will be supplied in the present series, no document will be more serviceable than the *Journal des Jésuites*,[1] which is the more valuable because obviously not intended for the public eye. *Ibid.*, xxvii., 11.]

[1] In publishing the *Journal des Jésuites*, we follow the original manuscript in the library of Laval University, Quebec. It covers the period from September, 1645, to June, 1668, excepting some lacunae between February 5, 1654, and October 25, 1656. This manuscript belonged originally to the archives of the old Jesuit Fathers at their house in Quebec, and was found there after the death of their last survivor, Father Jean Joseph Casot, who died March 16, 1800. Afterwards it disappeared, but was recovered about the year 1815, when Andrew William Cochran, civil attorney to Governor Sir John Cope Sherbrooke, accidentally discovered it in an obscure corner of his office. After Mr. Cochran's death—which occurred on July 11, 1849,—his widow presented it to George Barthélemy Faribault, of Quebec. Mr. Faribault died December 21, 1866, and by his last will and testament bequeathed all of his books, manuscripts, paintings, and engravings, relative to the history of Canada, to the Seminary of Quebec. The original of the *Journal des Jésuites* thus passed to the Seminary, and is now among the matchless treasures of Laval University. *Ibid.*, xxvii., 307.

JOURNAL BEGUN, *1645*

October

Chrestiennaut enters our service

On the 17th, Chrestiennaut was received into our service, at wages of thirty écus a year, and was sent to 3 rivers to serve there as Cook and Clothier,—in a word, for everything. He had come hither from france in Monsieur de repentigny's retinue; and had become discontented there, so that he had resolved to retreat to the woods rather than go back [to France]; there was no written contract with him.

Oven

On the 19th, we began to build an oven at our house, after having asked permission from Messieurs the owners of the house.

Savage garments for the king

On the same day there left the house a little box, in which were 3 or 4 savage garments, all complete, to be presented to the king by Monsieur de repentigny,—because the king had expressed a desire that something from over here should be sent him. The warehouse had borne the main expense thereof.

Building for our Fathers at Montreal

When I arrived at montreal, they had prepared a timber dwelling for our Fathers, and it seemed that there was nothing more to be done than to raise it; but when they were on the point of doing so, the vessels arrived, bringing orders from france to whose who commanded at Montreal, to employ all the workmen for other things,—namely, in erecting a hospital, for which large funds had been received in the preceding years;

Materials used for the Hospital

and yet no beginning had been made. *Monsieur de maison-neuve*, who was then at Montreal, found it hard to tell this news to our Fathers; I took it upon myself to do so, and to persuade them to regard the matter favorably; afterwards they flung the cat at my legs, as if I were the one who had hindered that work.

November, *1645*

Marriage Contract

On the 4th, we were Invited, father Vimon and I, to witness the marriage Contract of Monsieur Giffar's daughter; we were present, but we did not sign it. Monsieur the governor and several others signed.

On the 6th, Monsieur Nicolet again took away an oratory *Oratory lent for a year* completely furnished, to the Isle aux oyes; there was a gilded silver chalice, a chasuble of white damask, etc. We gave him two cakes of candle wax, and 3 large paper Images; and we lent him two books—the life of Jesus Christ, and the abridgment of dupont.

On the 12th, we give Mademoiselle giffar some black stuff *Given to mademoiselle giffar* from an old cassock, for lining sleeves.

On the 21st occurred the marriage and the nuptials of Marie *Marriage* Giffar [1] and the son of Monsieur de Maure, at which father Vimon was present.

On the 27th, Marriage of the daughter of Monsieur Couil- *Marriage of Guyon* lar to The son of Jean Guion; there were two violins, for the 1st time.

December, 1645

On the 3rd the Ursulines sent dinner to the house, a perfect *Ursulines send us dinner* banquet indeed. It was the 1st Sunday in Advent when Father Dendemare began to preach there, and I to the Hospital Nuns.

About this time we began to make bread at the house,—not *Bread made at the house* only because that made for us at the warehouse oven was not good, but because we wished to use the corn of the land, which they did not use at the warehouse.

On the 17th, Began the Jubilee granted by Innocent X. The Ursulines, among others, gave noble alms of Cloth to the french and savage poor; as for us, our chief Alms were 7 loaves, each of the value of 15 sols, for as many persons as we were in this house at Quebek,—however that was exchanged for cloth, shoes and linen, of which things the poor people had more need.

On the 23rd of December, the Ceremonies of baptism were *Ceremonies completed, an 1st Communion of Caterine, wife of Atiron* completed upon Caterine, wife of Atironta, and on her son mathieu, aged two years; this took place in the chapel at Quebek; they sat in Monsieur the governor's pew, at the start, and were thereby introduced to the Church. Monsieur Tron-

---

[1] Marie Françoise, eldest daughter of sieur Giffard, was but eleven years and five months old at the time of her marriage. *Ibid.*, xxvii., *note* 15.

quet, secretary to monsieur the Governor, was godfather to the little one; and Madame de la ferté, the newly married daughter of monsieur Giffar, was godmother to Caterine, who received her 1st Communion at Midnight.

Ceremonies at the feast of Christmas
The 1st stroke of the midnight mass rang at eleven o'clock, the 2nd, a little before the half-hour; and then they began to sing two airs—*Venez, mon Dieu*, etc., and *Chantons noe*, etc. Monsieur de la ferté sang the bass; St. martin Played the violin; there was also a german flute, which proved to be out of tune when they came to the Church. We had finished a little before midnight; they nevertheless sang the *Te Deum*, and a little later a cannon shot was fired as the Signal of midnight, when mass began.

Danger of fire
There were four candles in the Church in small iron candlesticks in the form of a Bracket, and that is enough. There were, besides, two great kettles full of fire, furnished by the warehouse in order to warm the chapel; they were kindled beforehand, on the bridge. Directions had been given to remove them after mass, but that having been neglected, the fire caught in the night on the floor under one of the kettles, in which there were not enough ashes at the bottom. But fortunately, *dirigente Domino*, the fire did not appear till toward 5 o'clock in the morning, above our hall or refectory, and kitchen, in which was pierre gontier, our Cook—who, perceiving this, immediately went up and, without other noise, put out the fire.

Christian savages wintering at Sillery
There were at Sillery, this year, about 167 souls, all Christians or Catechumens—98 Communicants, 47 not qualified for Confession, 14 qualified for Confession alone, the rest were considered Catechumens.

January, 1646

They Saluted Monsieur the Governor,—to wit, the soldiery with their arquebuses; *Item*, the Habitans in a body. He forestalled us, and was here at 7 o'clock to greet all our fathers. I went to greet him after high mass; (another time we must
New-year's gifts anticipate him). Monsieur giffar also came to see us, and the

nuns sent letters early in the morning, to offer their Compliments. The Ursulines also sent many beautiful New-year's gifts, with tapers, rosaries, etc.; and, toward the dinner, two handsome pieces of pastry. I sent them two Images of St. Ignace and St. françois Xavier in enamel. We gave Monsieur Giffar a book of father bonnet's about the life of our Lord; to Monsieur de Chastelets one of the little volumes of Drexellius *de Aeternite;* to Monsieur bourdon a galilean telescope in which there was a compass; and to others, reliquaries, Roasaries etc. We gave a Crucifix to the woman who washes the Church linen, 4 handkerchiefs to the wife of Abraham, and to him a bottle of brandy; two handkerchiefs to robert hache and then two more that he asked for. The Ursulines sent to beg that I would go to see them before the end of the day. I went thither and also greeted Madame de la pelleterie,[1] who sent New-year's gifts; I came near omitting that, and it is not proper to omit it.

On the 3rd or 4th of January, Monsieur the Governor sent 3 capons and 6 pigeons. *Present from monsieur the governor*

At evening on the 5th, Monsieur Giffar gave a bottle of hippocras; the hospital mothers a cake and 6 wax Candles; and the next day they sent a fine dinner. *Entertainment from the hospital Mothers*

From the 15th to the 21st the savages departed to go to the chase; there remained at Sillery about 22 savages, whom the hospital and our Fathers undertook to assist. *Savages go to the chase*

On the Sunday before Septuagesima, Madame Marsolet, having to prepare bread for consecration, desired to present it with the greatest possible display; she had it furnished with a toilet,—a crown of gauze or linen puffs around it. She wished to add candles, and quarter-écus at the Tapers, but seeing that we were not willing to allow her this, she nevertheless had it carried with the toilet and the Crown of puffs. However, before consecrating it, I had all that removed, and blessed it with the same simplicity that I had observed with all the preceding portions, especially with that of Monsieur the Governor, —fearing lest this change might occasion Jealousy and Vanity. *Innovations regarding the consecrated bread*

[1] *See* p. 153, ff.

February, 1646

On the 12th, while returning from the benediction at the hospital, I met two Hurons coming from three rivers, who reported the news *of the death of father Anne de noüe.* He started from 3 rivers to go to richelieu, to spiritually assist the garrison, on the 30th of January, in company with two soldiers and a Huron. They lay down for the night, 6 leagues above 3 rivers; but the Father left them after midnight, in order to send people to meet them and relieve them of their sledge; and he set forth *by the light of the moon.* But the sky became overcast, and it began to snow. His companions follow him by the trail of his snowshoes, and at last they find him, 4 leagues above richelieu,—kneeling in a hollow of the snow, with his arms crossed and his eyes raised to Heaven, his hat and snowshoes near him.

April, 1646

The 1st Day was easter, which was very beautiful.

The Ursuline mothers of the Incarnation employed nearly the whole of Lent in painting two pieces of Architecture to match the Tabernacle of the parish church; Monsieur bourdon painted some steps.

The savages returned from the chase toward the middle of April and came back quite rich and burdened.

On the 26th I held a Consultation with reference to father Jogues's journey to the Annieronons.

On the 17th or 18th of April, the river was free, and planting began a little before that.

The savages vigorously began everywhere to till the soil. At Sillery they freshly prepared more than 15 arpents of land; at 3 rivers, more than 30 savage families began cultivation; *Item,* at Montreal. The french on their side did no less.

July, 1646

On the 4th, two Abnaquiois Captains came to Monsieur the governor, to beg him to make arrangements for a black gown to go to the Abnaquiois, to Instruct them. Monsieur the governor sent them back to me, and I put them off till Autumn, in order to take time to consider the matter. They were given a bag of Indian corn for a Parting Gift, some tobacco, some fish, etc.; and we gave them a feast, and also one to the principal persons of Sillery.

On the 8th, a little savage girl named Charité, aged 5½, died at the Ursulines'; she was interred at the french Cemetary, where her Father was buried. She was borne thither by 4 domestics of the Ursulines, with 4 others bearing torches, and 2 french girls and two savage girls holding the corners of the pall.

Death and burial of Charité

The savages of Sillery kill a cow of monsieur Nicolas, which had been in their corn; she was valued at 75 livres. The savages were summoned by Monsieur the governor, to do Justice in this matter, and he ordered them that they should pay 6 Beavers, which was done,—with the assurance that when they should complain, Justice would be done for them for the damage which the cows might have wrought in their corn.

Savages sentenced to a fin of 6 Beavers for having killed a cow

September, 1646

It was the 20th, when Monsieur de maisonneuve arrived; and on the 23rd arrived Monsieur de repentigny.

Arrival of vessels from franc

With Monsieur de repentigny were *father Quentin* and some men both for the Hurons and for work down here; *Item,* a Young gentleman from the house of Courtené, who had been converted at la rochelle and had subsequently made a vow to go to the Hurons. But it proved that he was *only a swindler,* who had appeared in England as grandson to the house of Sancerre, and nephew to Monsieur desnoyers,—who made a pretense of intending to become a heretic. But learning that news from france was on the way, in consequence of information that had been given about him, he fled; He played a thousand tricks here, and finally avowed, or lied, that he *was a benedictine religious,*—a professed, for several years,—and that he was a subdeacon; and it was affirmed here that he *had entered, at Alençon, a monastery of benedictine nuns,* where

Father Quentin

The sieur de l'aubinière

A Benedictine apostate, a vagabond

he had heard the confession of a dying nun. He affected to wish to remain, and was enraged because they had written about him that he was a bastard; but those who had seen him in England whispered to him to be quiet; and he then went away. He cheated us by more than 200 livres, which we advanced for him.

1646, October

On the 28th, bastien entered our service for 100 livres in wages and a pair of shoes.

On the last Day of october the vessels sailed; father Quentin was the only one of Ours on board. With them returned the sons of Monsieur de repentigny, Monsieur Couillar and monsieur giffar, and the nephews of Monsieur deschastelets,— all *rogues*, for the most part, who had played a thousand tricks on the other voyage; and they all were given high salaries.

They are making a new oven and a brewery at Sillery.

We begin with 6 men to quarry stone and to prepare the site for the clergy-house and the Church.

They caught, this year, forty thousand eels, most of which were sold at half an écu the hundred. They began to fish for them in August, and they finished about the 9th or 10th of November.

In october, father le Jeune exhibited a picture to the Savages at Sillery, which had come from the queen,—containing her

portrait, that of the king, etc. At the same time they were given three Blankets and three arquebuses, at the expense of the warehouse; and we made a feast for them.

1646, November

On the 14th, Madame de la pelleterie sent a present here. It was a package, in which there was an Alter-stone and a small missal; two cloths, of which one was Damask; two dozen napkins, and two sheets,—which were given to our brother liegeois.

A few days later, Sister Charlotte sent four brasses, and more, of blue cloth, and a brasse and a half of red cloth; and several thousand porcelain beads,—all for the savages, as something which had been given her for this purpose.

On the last Day of the year, they gave a performance at the *Comedy* warehouse, Enacting the *sit.*[1] Our Fathers were present,—in deference to Monsieur the governor, who took pleasure therein, as also did the savages,—that is, fathers de Quen, Lalemant, and defretat: all went well, and there was nothing which could not edify. I begged Monsieur the governor to excuse me from attendance.

The Year 1647, January

On the 1st, I went at the 2nd bell for mass to salute Monsieur the governor.

The Hospital nuns sent a letter by Monsieur de St. Sauveur, *New-year's gifts* and two boxes of Lemon-peel by a man.

The Ursulines sent a letter, a keg of prunes, a Rosary and a paper Image.

There were sent us, by Monsieur the governor, 4 Capons, two bustards, and 8 young pigeons; by others, some 10 or 12 pieces of other poultry.

On the 2nd, we gave a dinner to Monsieur de *St. Sauveur*, *We regale three priests Monsieur the prior, and Monsieur Nicolet.*

We sent to Sillery a bustard and four capons.

To the Ursulines, a picture of St. Joseph;

7 or 8 pairs of Savage shoes to our servants.

I went on the 4th of the month to Sillery. On the morning *Renewal of vows at Sillery.* of the 5th occurred the renewal of the vows of father gabriel *2 fathers lalemant and of father defretat.* I made a feast for the Savages and gave them 6 loaves.

On the 7th, the Hospital nuns regaled us magnificently. *Hospital nuns give us a dinne*

On the 27th of february, there was a ballet at the ware- *Ballet* house; it was the wednesday in shrovetide. Not one of our fathers or brethren was present; also none of the sisters of the hospital and the Ursulines.

About this time one of our cows with calf was drowned in *Cow drowned* the St. Charles river; she broke through the ice.

---

[1] *Le sit;* probably *Le Cid* of Corneille, which had been first represented in **Paris** about ten years before. *Ibid.,* xxviii., *note* 35.

Return of the savages

Toward the end of the month, Noel, Jean baptiste, and other savages of Sillery returned from the chase; the fear of the yroquois caused them to hasten.

Wood

This month, all the Timber for our house was brought over the snow by our oxen.

May, 1647, and June

Fishing

On the 10th the 1st fish were taken, and among others a salmon.

On the 22nd, Monsieur the governor departed, and I with him, for 3 rivers.

News of the Death of father Jogues

On the 4th of June, we set out to return from 3 rivers; on the 5th we arrived at Quebek. The same Day, a Shallop arrived from 3 rivers, which informed us that the son of Ignace otouolti had returned from the yroquois,—who announced the death, or rather the murder, of father Jogues and his companion Lalande, for whom the next day we said a high mass for the dead.

Hospital

Incidit in dementiam Mother de Ste. genevieve at the hospital.

1st Horse imported

On the 20th of June, the 1st vessel arrived at Tadousak. That same vessel brought the 1st Horse, of which the habitans made a present to Monsieur the governor.

January, 1649

Execution of justice

On the 19th occurred the first execution by the hand of the hangman, in the case of a Creature of 15 or 16 years, a thief. At the same time they accused Monsieur Abraham of having violated her: he was imprisoned for this, and his trial was postponed till the arrival of the vessels. On the 19th of february, The 2nd execution of Justice took place.

The winter's Work was to pile sand for building, and wood for heating.

May, 1649

Famine

Return of the Shallops from 3 rivers and Montreal, where famine was found on all sides. We succored the people down here, in the matter of seed and food, with 16 casks of wheat sent from 3 rivers, and several puncheons of peas and Indian corn; and furthermore by the grist of the mill,—making in all more than 40 casks of grain.

July, 1649

On the 10th and 17th, the Abnakiois arrived, to the number of 30. They brought letters from the English. There was one from Mademoyselle de repentigny to her husband, dated 31st of July, 1648, with news of the death of Monsieur de chastelets.

Abnaquiois

1st news from france

On the 20th at night, arrived the sad news of the destruction of the Hurons, *and of the martyrdom of 3 fathers. Vide relationem hujus anni.*

and from the Hurons Their destruction

March, 1652

On the second day of March, 12 Hurons, six Algonquins and ten Algonquin women, having left Three Rivers for Montreal, were attacked on the way by the Iroquois. *Desiderati sunt decem Hurones,*—Torotati, burned; Athohonchiwanne, killed; Ora'kwi, Otarawia, burned.

On the 4th of April, Father Buteux left Three Rivers for his Mission to the Atikamegues, with Tsondoutannen, a Huron, and fontarabie.

May, 1652

On the 5th, some one has a glimpse of the Iroquois on the coast of Lauson; *vanus tamen rumor.*

On the 10th day of May, Father Jacques Buteux, in company with a frenchman named fontarabie and a Huron named Thomas Tsondoutannen, was killed by a band of 14 Iroquois. The two frenchmen remained dead on the spot; the Huron was Led away captive. This took place on the Three Rivers, at the third portage. The Huron afterward escaped, and arrived at Three Rivers on the 28th, giving news of the disaster.

Death of Father Buteux and a frenchman

*Defeat of
the Hurons*

On the 13th of the same month of May, the Algonquins, having gone up for trade to the whitefish tribe, fell into the ambushes of that band of 14 who had killed Father Bureux.

15th. Two Huron women, mother and daughter, Annendok and Atondech, with a little son four years old, were seized at Montreal by a band of 50 or 60 Iroquois. They had gone to a secluded place, to get some meat from a Moose, which four frenchmen had killed there.

On the 26th, a troop of 50 Iroquois killed the cowherd at Montreal, named Antonie Róos, near the hill St. Louys.

August, 1652

On the 10th, news arrived from Montreal that, on the 29th of July, two Iroquois, having slipped in under cover of the corn, had attacked Martine, wife of Antoine Primot,—who, by defending herself courageously, gave the soldiers of the fort time to come to her aid, and put the enemy to flight. She received six shots, not one of which was mortal.

*Capture of a
frenchman at
the cape*

On the 18th, 4 frenchmen were attacked by 8 Iroquois canoes, between 3 Rivers and the Cape; Maturin Guillet and La Boujonnier were killed on the spot. Plassez, a surgeon, and Rochereau, were taken away as captives.

*Defeat of the
garrison at
three rivers*

19th. 2 french shallops having been in search of the cattle of 3 Rivers,—killed or scattered by the Iroquois, above 3 Rivers, along the lake,—the following persons were killed or carried away captive:

Monsieur Du Plessis, the
  Governor.
Monsieur Grandmesnil.
Guillaume Isabelle.
francheville, captive
Poisson.
Turcot.
Normanville, captive.
Du Puis.
Matris Belhomme, burned.

Langoulmois, killed.
  captive.
La Palme, captive.
La Gravé.
St. Germain.   ⎫
Chaillon.   ⎬ Soldiers.
Des Lauriers,   ⎭
  died from his
  wounds.

May, 1665

On the 5th, Monsieur de Mesy, the Governor, died. *Death of Monsieur the governor*
On the 14th, father Alloues left for his mission among the *Father Alloues leaves*
Outawats, accompanied by two of our Servants, La tour and
Nicolas.

June, 1665

Father Thiery beschefer arrived on the 19th, in Le Gan- *Arrival of ships father beschefer*
gneur's Ship, with 4 Companies of the Carignan regiment.
And on the 30th, father Claude bardy and Father francois *Father bardy. Monseigneur de Tracy*
duperon arrived, with Monseigneur de Tracy[1] and 4 other
Companies.

July, 1665

On the 16th, Captain poulet arrived, with Monsieur bour- *Arrival of poulet*
don, 12 Horses, 8 girls, and others.
On the 23rd, the first 4 Companies left to commence fort *Departure for the Beginning of the war*
richelieu; father Chaumonot went with them.

September, 1665

The 12th. The *st. sebastien* arrived, having on board Monsieur de Courcelles, the governor, and Monsieur Talon, the
Intendant.
The 14th. The Ship called la Justice arrived, with more
than 100 sick in all. Most of them were placed in the hospital,
some in the sick-ward, and some in the Church. Many of
them died.

October, 1665

The 1st. 4 companies departed, to wait for Monseigneur
de Tracy at three Rivers.
The 2nd. The ship from Normandy arrived, with 82 girls
and women—among others, 50 from a charitable institution
in Paris, where they have been very well taught. *Item*, 130
laboring men, all in good health; an excellent cargo for the

[1] *See* p. 316, *note.*

company, and at good prices; all the communities had on board all that comes to them from france.

November, 1665

The 10th. The earth was white with snow.

Father françois du perron died at fort st. Louis

The 15th. A vessel arrived from Richelieu, bringing us the body of Father Francois du Peron, who died on the 10th at fort st. Louys. In the evening, 5 soldiers brought the body in a coffin of boards that Monsieur sorel, the governor of Richelieu, had ordered to be made for him, after going to receive him at the water's edge with all his soldiers under arms. We also learned that he had had him guarded all the night, with lighted tapers around him. We had the body placed in the room occupied by the congregation. As he had been dead 7 days, we did not open the coffin.

The 16th. We assembled at half past nine in the morning and issued forth in procession. Master Julien garnier bore the cross; two of our little pupils, the candlesticks; two others, the censer and the holy water. We said the office, at which *Monseigneur de Tracy* assisted. He was buried in the vault of the chapel, near the confessional on the side of the street. There remains only enough room for one more body.

[*Ibid.*, xxvii-xlix]

XIII

MISSION OF THE HURONS AT DETROIT, 1733-56

By Father Armand De La Richardie, and Father Pierre Potier

[This interesting document is the account-book of the Jesuit mission farm near Detroit, conducted by La Richardie and Potier for the Hurons settled there. The opening entry is a copy of a contract made (July 16, 1733) by the former with one Jean Cecile, who agrees to work a forge for the mission during six years. The account-book proper begins "on the feast of St. John, 1740." One of the opening entries records the hiring of an engagé for the coming year, at a salary of "160 livres in peltries, a shirt, and a pair of mitasses [leggings]." Various transactions are recorded for which payment is to be made "in peltries, at Detroit prices." The mission farm also includes a trading post, conducted by a lay brother in the mission. Among the commodities are flour, wheat, corn, wine, brandy, tobacco, powder and shot, blankets, shirts, porcelain beads, kettles, and vermilion.

La Richardie lends the Huron elders "four great white branches of porcelain beads, half black, half white." Many entries record payments by habitants for masses, to be said by the priests. (The Paris livre, worth about twenty five cents of our money, was the usual money of account; but the actual currency was most often the "caster" or beaver-skin, worth at that time four livres a pound.)—*Ibid.*, lxix., 24.]

CONTRACT WITH JEAN CECILE, TOOLMAKER

On the 16th of july, 1733, Father La Richardie, Missionary of The Society of jesus, and jean Cecile entered into the following covenant:

1st. The said cecile, Toolmaker and armorer, binds himself to work constantly and assiduously at The forge of the said Reverend father at detroit, in The huron village, for all The needs of the french and of the savages, in all matters connected with his trade.

2nd. The Reverend father will supply The tools and the steel; if any deficiency of tools shall occur; The said cecile shall make Them, and they shall remain in The forge when he leaves it.

3rd. The said Cecile shall not do any work to be sold on his private account under the pretext that he has iron or steel of his own; but if he earn or purchase any at detroit, and The forge lack the same, The Reverend father may buy The steel; as regards the iron, it shall be purchased on joint account for the said Reverend Father and The said Cecile.

4th. The said Reverend Father will give the assistance of his servant, when he has one, to The said Cecile, for chopping wood and building his charcoal furnaces; but when these are once erected, The said cecile shall attend to Them alone.

5th. The said cecile shall perform gratuitously, and in good season, The work that may be needed by The Reverend Father, either for Himself or for his house, church, etc.—such as hatchets, hinges, etc.; and, if The said Cecile shall do Any work for His own personal use, he shall neither sell nor give away the Same.

6th. All the provisions received by The said Cecile in payment, such as fat, tallow, meat, indian corn, etc., shall be divided equally between him and the Reverend father; or else be sold, if necessary, for the benefit of both.

7th. All the profits derived from the work of the said cecile shall be divided between The said reverend father and Him.

8th. When the said cecile shall not be occupied in The forge, he shall assist The Reverend father in all the work that he may have to do, in The present condition of his establishment.

9th. Although The said cecile engages himself for 6 years, he may, for valid reasons, leave before the expiration of that term; and in such case he shall notify The Reverend father in good time, so that the latter may find some one to replace him. In the same manner, should the Reverend father not be satisfied with him, he may dismiss Him after having notified Him some time beforehand.

10th. As The said cecile will not Lodge with The Reverend father, as his predecessors have done, he shall build himself a Suitable house near The forge, and The Reverend father's engagé shall assist Him in Building the Same. And, as regards firewood for the said cecile, the latter shall chop it during The winter, and The said Reverend father consents that The cost of cartage shall be paid for by work which The said cecile shall do for the Teamsters in payment thereof.

Thus agreed, and undertaken by both parties at detroit, on The day and in the year above written.

DE LA RICHARDIE, jesuit Missionary
CUILLERIER, Witness.+.

ACCOUNT-BOOK OF THE HURON MISSION OF DETROIT; BEGUN ON THE FEAST OF ST. JOHN, 1740

All payments for The post of detroit are made. I have paid all:

DELIVERED to charles courtois wheat, wine, etc., for The sum of 294 livres 15 sols, which he is to pay me in the month of may, 1741.

Prisque has reengaged to serve me for one more year,— that is to say, until the convoy of 1741 comes,—for The sum of 160 livres in peltries, a shirt, and a pair of mitasses. During the current year there is paid: paid to the same 7 livres 10 sols; also 7 livres 10 sols; also 20 livres; also 7 livres 10 sols; also 30 livres 5 sols; paid in full.

Paid to the man named Roy 40 livres, for 2 arpents of cleared land. *Item,* to one du chene 40 livres, for 2 arpents of cleared land.

Advanced to Roy for clearing my land, at 20 livres An arpent, 2 minots of grain, One of french wheat, and The other of indian corn; also a minot and a half of indian corn; also 7 livres of tallow, at 10 sols a livre; finally, 50 livres of flour, 18 livres; also half a minot of wheat, 5 livres.

35 minots of wheat sold by sieur jaques Campeau, for which he has received payment at 10 livres a minot. 2 casks of wine sold to the same, 35 Livres A cask.

Madame Campeau paid for me 32 Livres to d'agneaux, 20 livres 5 sols to Navarre, 18 livres to Madame baroy, and 14 livres to madame louison.

Ego Hodie [I myself today]; 2 pots of brandy—one 3 livres, The other 3 livres 10 sols; also 4 minots of indian corn at 18 livres A minot; received, in all, 163 livres 15 sols. The same received for me from one destaillis The sum of 26 livres, which he owes me; also 110 livres which the same sieur Campeau owes me; for value received he owes me 381 livres.

Sold a gun to sieur chauvin.

Lent to the [Huron] elders 4 great branches of porcelain beads, half black, half white.

I have been paid by rencontre; prisque is to pay me for him.

Paid to goyau on my works The sum of 12 livres; also, to the same, 6 livres; also 3 livres; also 3 livres; also 3 livres in tobacco; also 5 drinks of brandy; also a minot of pease, 12 livres.

I have lent to sieur chapoton, surgeon of this fort, The sum of 100 livres in raccoon- and lynx-skins, which he is to repay me in the month of may, 1743, in similar peltries. at detroit, this 13th of june, 1742.

Madame La foret owes me 31 Castors [beaver-skins], the balance of what I sold to her last year.

I owe francois Campeau 500 large nails, at 45 sols A hundred. I owe the same 800 shingle nails, at 10 sols a hundred; also 200 shingle-nails, at 10 sols A hundred; also 4 livres of powder, 6 livres; and 300 large and 100 medium-sized nails.

20 masses said for Reverend Father bon.

I owe meloche, for all The buildings that he has erected and is to erect for me, 3,100 Livres.

I owe janis, for The masonry of the said buildings, The sum of 600 livres; also, to the same, 10 livres, for The farmer's house and The stable; also, to the same, 100 livres for minor repairs, and for what he has done for The blacksmith. The latter item is to be paid only in 1744. Also 30 livres for The partitions, on which I have paid him 48 livres in wheat; also paid to the same, 160 livres; also 100 livres, which he accepts out of what Cecile owes me; also 227 livres. The 635 livres are paid; thus I owe nothing more to janis for The church and The house. I still owe him, for The farmer's house and other works, The sum of 200 livres, less 21 livres 15 sols; The said sum is paid.

On this day, the 2nd of july, 1743, Sieur jean baptiste goyau, a habitant at the post of detroit, agreed to come here with his family in The course of the month of september of the same year, to take charge of The farm belonging to the mission of the Fathers of The society of jesus, on the following conditions.

1st. The said fathers lease The said farm to the said goyau for The term of 6 years; but should he not be satisfied with the Reverend Fathers, or The Reverend Fathers with him, either party shall be Free to terminate the engagement by giving notice to one another, one year in advance.

2nd. The said Reverend Fathers shall supply the said goyau with seed for all The grain that he will sow on Their farm; and they shall share with Him, in equal portions, the produce of such seed; and the said goyau shall not be at Liberty to sow, for Himself or His family, anything on the said farm without sharing The produce with them, except as regards such indian corn as he may wish to plant for his own use. And, in order that the Reverend fathers may not lack corn, he shall every year Plow 2 arpents of land, on which they may plant some for their sole use.

3rd. An inventory shall be made of all the implements and of cart and Plow harness, which the said Reverend Fathers shall Hand over to the said goyau in order that he may return Them in the same state and condition as that in which he took Them.

4th. As regards the animals, he shall be bound to give back at the end of his lease The same number, and in the same condition, as he received, or may Hereafter receive, together with one-half the produce of such animals.

5th. He shall make a suitable enclosure for keeping and pasturing the said animals, and shall carefully keep in order The fences on the land handed over to Him, Which he shall Leave in good condition at The end of his lease.

6th. The said Reverend Fathers consent that The said goyau may use Their animals for carting and Plowing, both for the french and for the savages; The whole on condition that he shall haul 40 Cords of wood for Them Every winter, for Their fuel and for Their share of Their blacksmith's furnaces; and The said goyau shall also be obliged to lend The animals to the said Reverend Fathers for hauling or carting, whenever they need the same.

I Delivered to goyau on his entering upon the farm of ile aux bois blancs: 6 minots and a half of pease, for seed; 5 minots of oats for the same purpose, and 14 minots and a half of wheat for seed,—Which seed he shall return when he leaves The farm. I also Gave him a Plow complete, with its wheels, quite new; a cart, with almost new Wheels; a new sled, 2 illinois oxen, with a cow of the same breed; 2 mares worth 80 livres each,—The whole costing 400 livres. Also 2 cows bred in the country and a yearling heifer.

To replace The 3 cows that died or were killed while in goyau's hands, I Gave him 2 illinois heifers,—one of which cost me 40 livres, and The other 75. I also Gave him an illinois heifer, which I exchanged for a cow that had not calved that year.

Madame goyau began to do the laundry-work and baking for this mission, on St. micheal's day, 1743, for the sum of 100 livres per annum.

Madame Goyau has received a shirt, 3 livres; a Quart of brandy, 3 livres; a Quart of brandy; 3 livres; a pair of mitasses, made of molleton; a pair of mitasses made of molleton; a Quart of brandy; 2 minots of pease, 18 livres; 6 blankets, 54 livres; 3 livres; a pair of mitasses, 3 livres. Madame Goyau is paid in ful for The 1st year.

Lent mallet 3 quarts of brandy; 3 livres of powder; 5 livres of shot; 1 blue blanket; 3 large shirts; 3 small shirts.

Received from Mallet 6 deer; 16 turkeys; 6 bustards; 1 swan; 8 ducks; 1 bear's ham; 5 or 6 partridges; 2 small beavers, etc.

2nd YEAR, FROM ST. MICHAEL'S DAY, 1744, TO ST. MICHAEL'S DAY, 1745

Gave goyau's wife, on The 100 livres: 45 livres in deerskins; 40 livres less 5 sols in castors; 4 livres of powder, 10 livres. Madame goyau is paid in full for The 2nd year.

3rd YEAR, FROM ST. MICHAEL'S DAY, 1745, TO ST. MICHAEL'S DAY, 1746

Meloche supplied and used 300 boards for roofing my house and my church, at 45 livres a hundred, all being used; for these he has reserved 90 livres, this 10th of july, 1744. I lent to the same meloche 400 large and 200 medium-sized nails, which he will return when I require him.

I gave goyau an advance of 45 livres on the washing and baking for The year 1745.

I let charles courtois have 40 livres' worth of Pork and 40 livres' worth of brandy. The same owes me *The money for*

4 livres of hide; also The money for 2 masses, which françois campeau asked me to say; also 500 livres; also 3 livres.

Madame L'oeil eraillé, a cloak, 3; glass beads, 4 cj.; rouge (vermilion) 4 c; slippers, 6 shirts, 4; Le roy, 55.

I paid janis 75 livres for The 2 stone chimneys which he made for me. For The remainder of his payment I gave him orders on Father ben, who owes me 50 livres; and on Monsieur de Longueuil, who owes me 25 livres.

Cecile made me a mattock; Madame St. martin supplied to me the iron for it, which is worth 5 livres.

Goyau owes 80 livres to The mission for a cow belonging to The farm, with which Monsieur the commandant gave a feast to the savages.

End of Father de la Richardie's accounts.

CONTINUATION OF THE BOOK OF ACCOUNTS OF THE HURON MISSION ON THE ILE AUX BOIS BLANCS FROM THE 30TH OF JULY, 1746, THE DATE OF FATHER DE LA RICHARDIE'S DEPARTUE

I owe 24 livres 10 sols to thomas courtois for a saw and 2 axes.

I owe 40 sols to jacques godet for 200 tacks.

I owe 30 sols to chène for 100 shingle nails.

I owe 12 livres to dubois for a pair of shoes.

I owe 12 livres to mallet for a pair of shoes.

I owe 60 nails to Father bon.

INSTRUCTIONS OF FATHER LA RICHARDIE

The brother proclaims everywhere that he is to be The master. Church of stone, of The same width as The old one but 10 feet longer; a frame Sacristy, 15 feet square. *100 pistoles to Meloche,* to lengthen the barn 20 feet. New refectory, and domestics' room beside the old refectory. Enlarge The kitchen, by taking a portion of the former refectory. The lumber from The church will be used for enlarging The barn, refectory, etc. 12 francs to janis per toise (the toise is 6 feet square) on condition that The mortar shall be well made. A belfry like that of the fort.

The farm. 1st. Everything that grows on our farm is shared equally with The farmer. The produce of the animals is also shared equally. When the present farmer came he was given 5 cows and one Heifer, a pair of ilinois oxen, with 2 mares. He is to give back everything complete when he leaves. Of 45 hens given Him, he is to give back 45 fowl good to eat and 45 dozen of eggs. Of the 1st 6 cows given him, one was eaten by takiet's dogs, which cost 60 livres, paid for in raccoon-skins, of which 45 livres were paid in Deer-skins. A heifer perished on The island, by falling from the rocks; the 3rd died of sickness; a 4th was sold, and exchanged for the ilinois cow La blanche. The other young ilinois cows were bought and paid for by the mission—One cost 75 livres, and The other 40.

1747

Goio received a note for 90 livres, payable at Montreal, for La Commandante.

Major and dos blanc ["white back"] belong to us altogether. La noire also belongs to us. He had La blanche at two years; she had not calved that year. La deruisseau and La niagera were given as original stock, at the age of 5 weeks. 2 calves to be shared; Maurice and taupin, draught-oxen, to be shared; 2 head of young cattle to be shared. Souris ["Mouse"] the mare, belongs to us.

With gaudet and gervais: 20 fowl. 3 kettles,—2 large and one of medium size; 6 earthen plates, 3 cups, a sugar-bowl, 8 or 10 bottles, 5 preserve jars, and 2 pewter jugs. 2 large pewter basins, 1 pewter salt-cellar, and a coffee-Mill.

At Monsieur de Longueuil's: a clock, a bell, panes of glass, a war-club, and a paddle.

I owe:

74 livres and a half of flour, lent by cuillerier.
80 roofing nails, to father bon.

2 livres 2 sols to caron's wife, for 62 brasses of deerskin thongs.

2 small flasks of brandy, borrowed from Captain Campeau, about The 6th of july.

2 small flasks of brandy, borrowed from campeau on The 17th of july.

10 livres, or one pistole, to goyau, for washing and baking.

3 flasks of brandy, borrowed from Monsieur The commandant.

bolting of 2 minots.

12 francs to dubois, for a pair of shoes.

83 Livres of flour, borrowed from Father bon for the feast of Mary.

There is due to me:

Caron's wife, 100 pistoles for The purchase of a farm, etc.

Caron's wife, 30 sols for porcelain beads sold.

Caron's wife, 500 nails—400 large, 100 small.

4 minots of wheat, given to St. Martin's wife for 2 pairs of stockings, etc.

100 small nails, lent to Monsieur de longueuil.

480 large nails, lent to father bon.

5 boards, lent to father bon.

1747.

The 24th of september; 10 minots of Indian corn, delivered to Monsieur de la Perade; no price fixed; it was selling at one pistole—which makes 100 francs.

The 30th of september; sold to sieur Bart, armorer; 1st, three packets of Files at 6 francs A packet; 2nd, thirteen Files, at 10 sols on the average; 1 knife-file; 5 square files; 7 rattail files.

I owe st. andré 20 sols, for one hundred tacks.

[*Ibid.*, lxix., *Doc.* ccxxiv. Of this Document, continued in vol. lxx, of *The Jesuit Relations and Allied Documents*, only a brief extract is here given.]

PART V
THE BANISHMENT OF THE JESUITS FROM THE KING'S DOMAIN
(1763)

I

BANISHMENT OF THE JESUITS FROM LOUISIANA

[François Philibert Watrin]

[At the time referred to in the text, a keen hostility to the Jesuit order had arisen in most of the European states, and repressive measures against them had been begun by several governments. In France the order had many enemies. Their controversies with the Jansenists had aroused violent partisanship on both sides; their great ecclesiastical and political influence had excited the jealousy of other religious orders: Jeanne Poisson, Marquise de Pompadour, Louis XV's favorite, was bitterly hostile to them; and it was she who had raised to power the Duke de Choiseul, who was minister of foreign affairs from 1759 to 1780. Choiseul was, moreover, opposed to clerical ascendancy—an attitude in which he was supported by the large party of free thinkers, then so numerous and influential. An incident occurred early in his ministry, which led to the expulsion of the Jesuits in France. . . . On April 1, 1762, The Parliament of Paris closed all the Jesuit colleges in its jurisdiction, and defied Louis XV in his efforts to annul its decrees; and, on August 6 following, decreed the suppression of the order and the confiscation of its estates. Other provincial parliaments (except at Besançon and Douay, and in Alsace and Lorraine) quickly followed this example; and finally a royal decree (Dec. 1, 1764) ordered the dissolution of the order throughout the king's dominions—per-

475

mitting the Jesuits, however, to reside therein as private citizens. It is said that at this time the Jesuits of France numbered four thousand.—*Ibid.*, lxx., *note* 36.]

You write me, Monsieur, that you were surprised to learn of the arrival at Paris of Jesuits banished from Louisiana by a decree pronounced against them in that colony.[1] You wish to know the reasons for this decree, and what followed its execution. I am familiar with the affair that interests you, and likewise with all that can in any way relate thereto. I lived for almost thirty years in Louisiana, and only departed thence at the beginning of this year.

In the month of June, 1763, the Jesuits of New Orleans, the capital of Louisiana, were still between hope and fear as to their future fate. As early as the preceding year, they had seen their enemies distribute with a triumphant air, manuscript copies of the decree given by the Parliament of Paris, August 6, 1761. But people worthy of respect had calmed their fears. They were expecting a great deal from the information given in their favor, and, above all, from the petition addressed to the King by the bishops of France. They finally learned what they were to expect, at the arrival of the ship, which brought, with the news of peace, orders for their destruction.

Proceedings were begun. It was decreed that the Institute of the Jesuits should be brought to the council, to be examined. It was a great undertaking for this tribunal. All the judges who composed it ought at least to have studied theology, and civil and ecclesiastical law. But, above all, they ought to have understood the language in which the institute is written. Now, this is not the kind of knowledge that is required from judges of colonies. In selecting them, search is not made

---

[1] The suppression in France of the Jesuit order (1761-62) led to similar proceedings elsewhere; and the superior council of Louisiana, by a decree dated July 9, 1763, expelled the Jesuits from that colony. The present document relates the circumstances of that event, and its consequences; it is written by one of the Fathers thus exiled from Louisiana, evidently Francis Philibert Watrin.—*Ibid.*, lxx., 13.

for pupils of universities, but those among the inhabitants who show some capacity for business are chosen. Accordingly, one finds in these councils elderly shopkeepers, physicians, and officers of troops.

For these reasons we are justified in saying that it was a great undertaking for the council of New Orleans to pronounce upon the Institute of the Jesuits.

The decree was declared on the 9th of July. It was said that the Institute of the Jesuits was hostile to the royal authority, the rights of the bishops, and the public peace and safety; and that the vows uttered according to this institute were null. It was prohibited to these Jesuits, hitherto thus styled, to take that name hereafter, or to wear their customary garb, orders being given them to assume that of secular ecclesiastics. Excepting their books and some wearing apparel which was allowed to them, all their property, real and personal, was to be seized and sold at auction. It was ordained that the chapel ornaments and the sacred vessels of New Orleans should be delivered up to the Reverend Capuchin Fathers; that the chapel ornaments and sacred vessels of the Jesuits living in the country of the Illinois should be delivered up to the Royal procurator for that country, and that the chapels should then be demolished; and that, finally, the aforesaid Jesuits, so-called, should return to France, embarking upon the first ships ready to depart,—prohibiting them, meanwhile, from remaining together. A sum of six hundred livres was assigned to pay each one's passage, and another, of 1,500 francs, for their sustenance and support for six months. They were enjoined to present themselves, after that term, to Monsieur the duke de Choiseul, secretary of State in the department of marine, to ask him for the pensions which would be assigned from the proceeds of the sale of their property. . . .

It is time to speak of the execution of the decree; it was to be carried out first at New Orleans, and afterward in the Illinois country, at a distance of four or five hundred leagues. There was in that country, as has been said above, a mission of the Jesuits, established at four different posts.

They were not forgotten, and a courier was sent to carry the decree of destruction.

Meanwhile it was executed promptly against those of New Orleans. Their establishment was quite near this town, and proportioned to the needs of twelve missionaries; there was quite a large gang of slaves for cultivating the land, and for plying other trades, as is the custom in the colonies; there were also various buildings, with herds of cattle and suitable works. Everything was seized, inventoried, and sold at auction, and this execution lasted a long time; those who were employed therein took their meals in the house. These were the higher officers of justice, with the lesser agents; it is right to suppose that the former kept themselves within the decent behavior that beseemed them, but the others did not consider themselves obliged to assume any disguise. They found themselves well feasted and they were sure that their employment was a lucrative one; so they did not dissemble their feelings. The superior of the Jesuits was obliged to be present at the great feasts which were given at his house during the depredation, and he saw the joy that was shown there.

After the sale of the real and personal property, there remained the chapel, with its ornaments and sacred vessels; it was stated in the decree that these effects should be taken to the Reverend Capuchin Fathers; this was done, and it was the least objectionable use that could be made of them. After that, the chapel was razed to the ground; and the sepulchres of the bodies buried for thirty years in this place, and in the neighboring cemetery, remained exposed to profanation. The Jesuits who came back from Louisiana to France have often been asked the reason for this proceeding; they have been told what astonishment and horror was felt at this event; it has been said to them that this was only to be expected from open enemies of the Catholic religion; the Jesuits could only answer these sayings by silence.

The execution of the decree lacked nothing, save to send back the condemned to France; those who were at New Orleans did not wait to be notified of the order to depart. Father

Carette embarked to cross over to San Domingo; Father Roy took refuge at Pensacola, at the very time when the English entered this port to take possession of it, and the Spaniards evacuated it by virtue of the treaty of peace; he entered the ship which was to bear the Governor of that place to Vera Cruz. The Father was welcomed there, by the Spanish Fathers of the college, with the greatest kindness; a little while afterward he was made an associate in the province that the Jesuits have in Mexico, by Father François Zeballos, superior of that province. His letter written upon this subject expressed most generous and most Christian sentiments, and all the Jesuits banished from the lands under French domination were invited thither to the same refuge.

Father Le Predour was among the Alibamons, at a distance of about two hundred leagues, and much time was necessary for transmitting a copy of the decree to him. Then, after he had received it, he was obliged to await an opportunity to reach the fort of Mobile, and from that place, New Orleans; we have recently learned that he has returned to France. There were no more to send away, then, but Father Baudoin, superior of all missions; but he was seventy-two years old, and infirm,—as one may expect of a man who had passed thirty-five years in Louisiana, and of those thirty-five years about twenty in the midst of the forests, with the Chactas; he had no relatives in France, nor was he accustomed to this country; as he was born in Canada, he was permitted to remain. He was assigned a pension of nine hundred livres, which would be equivalent in France to the sum of three or four hundred francs. Monsieur Boré, an old resident of the country, offered him an asylum with himself, upon his estate, and thus proved the sincerity of the friendship which he had always shown toward the Jesuits.

Meanwhile the courier despatched to Illinois to bear the decree, arrived on the night of September 23, at fort Chartres, distant six leagues from the residence of the Jesuits. He delivered to the procurator of the King the commission which charged him to execute the decree; and on the next day, about eight or nine o'clock in the morning, that officer of justice repaired to the house of the Jesuits, accompanied by the registrar and the bailiff of that jurisdiction. Some days afterward, he tried to turn to account the moderation that he used in not arriving during the night, "as his orders directed," said he; with that exception, they ought to have been satisfied with his exactness.

He read to Father Watrin, the superior, the decree of condemnation, and, having given him a copy of it, he made him at once leave his room to put the seal upon it; the same thing was done with the other missionaries who happened to be in the house. There remained one hall where they could remain together, although with great inconvenience; but this favor was refused them, because the guards placed in custody of the property seized opposed this; they were unwilling that the Jesuits should be able to watch their conduct so closely. The procurator of the King feared to displease these guardians, and would not even permit the Jesuits to remain at the house of one of their confrères,—who, being curé of the place, had his private lodging near the parish church; they did not put the seal thereon, because they knew there was nothing there to seize. The missionaries, driven from their own house, found quarters as best they could. The superior, sixty-seven years old, departed on foot to find a lodging, a long league away, with a confrère of his, a missionary to the savages; and the French who met him on this journey groaned to see persecution begin with him.

As soon as the savages learned that he had arrived among them, they came to show to him and to Father Meurin, and his associate, the share which they took in the distress of their Fathers; the news of their condemnation had already caused many tears to be shed in the village. They were asked why they were thus treated, especially in a country where so many disorders had been so long allowed. The old missionary, after several repeated interrogations, finally replied: *Arechi Kié-couègane tchichi ki canta manghi,—It is because we sternly condemn their follies.* They comprehended the meaning of this answer,—indeed they knew that the Jesuits, in whatever place they may be established, consider themselves bound by their profession to combat vice; and that, in fighting it, they make enemies for themselves.

The Christian savages proposed to send their chief men to Monsieur Neyon, commandant, and to Monsieur Bobé, sub-deputy-commissary of the country, to ask that at least Father Meurin, their missionary, be kept in his mission. The two Jesuits told them plainly to do nothing of the kind, because this proceeding would be scoffed at and ineffectual, as having been suggested. They wished, then, to ask that at least the chapel and the house of the missionary be preserved, in order that the best instructed person among them might assemble the children and repeat prayers to them; and that every Sunday and feast-day he might summon those who prayed, that is to say, the Christians,—by the ringing of the bell, to fulfill as well as possible the duties of religion. They did, in fact, make such a request, and obtained what they asked.

Meanwhile, the Procurator of the King relaxed a little in his severity. About the same time he received in a single day four letters from Monsieur Bobé, the commissary, who begged him to moderate his zeal, and allowed the Jesuits to live together with their brethren, the curés of the French. They were closely crowded there, in a house that was built for only one man. Their rooms had been opened, in order that each might be able to take out his mattress and blankets, which they spread upon the floor in the house of the curé. This way of taking their rest, which lasted nearly a month, prepared them for the voyage which they were soon to make upon the Missisipi, for upon the banks of that river one encamps in hardly other fashion. The Jesuits were also permitted to take their clothes and their books, which the decree had left to them. At last, the support of these Fathers was provided for until the time when they should embark to go down to New Orleans. The greater part of the food that was found in their house, was given up to them, and this provision was, in fact, sufficient for the rest of the time that they passed in Illinois.

Finally, it came to making the inventory; time was necessary to collect and put in order the furniture of a large house, the chattels of an important estate, and the cattle scattered in the fields and woods. Besides, there was reason for not hurrying too much; the longer the delays the better they paid those who were employed in that task.

The auction was finished; the house, the furniture, the cattle, the lands had been sold; the slaves were to be taken to New Orleans, to be sold there for the benefit of the king; and the chapel was to be razed by the man to whom the house had been adjudged: The Jesuits were then permitted to re-enter their former home, the use of which was, by a clause inserted in the bill of sale, reserved to them until their embarkation. They found it well cleared; nothing was left except the bedsteads and the straw mattresses; and, in order to lodge there they were obliged to borrow from their friends each a chair and a little table. They found their chapel in a still more melancholy condition; after the sacred vessels and the pictures had been taken away, the shelves of the altar had been thrown down; the linings of the ornaments had been given to negresses decried for their evil lives; and a large crucifix, which had stood above the altar, and the chandeliers, were found placed above a cupboard in a house whose reputation was not good. To see the marks of spoliation in the chapel, one might have thought that it was the enemies of the Catholic religion who had caused it.

Finally the day set for the embarkation came; it was the 24th of November. The baggage of the Jesuits did not greatly embarrass the vessel in which they had taken their passage; they had only their beds and their clothes in small quantities, with some provisions which they had saved for the voyage; this food served not only for them, but for forty-eight negroes embarked with them. These slaves no longer belonged to the Jesuits, having been confiscated for the benefit of the King. But their former masters always preserved the same care in regard to them, and shared quite willingly with these wretches the provisions which they had saved.

The voyage, which might have been very long, lasted only twenty-seven days. Finally, they found themselves in great perplexity. They saw that they were about to enter New Orleans, and they did not know where they could lodge; they were unable to enter their old house, knowing well that it was sold and occupied by other masters. Meanwhile the Reverend Capuchin Fathers, hearing of the arrival of the Jesuits, had come to the landing place to manifest their intention of rendering them all the kind offices they could, and during the six weeks which elapsed before they embarked, there were no marks of friendship which they did not receive from these Reverend Fathers.

However, the Jesuits perceived that their departure was desired. The season was disagreeable, it being still the month of January, the time of rough seas. But an entirely new and well-built ship presented itself; it was the La Minerve, of Bayonne, commanded by Monsieur Balanquet, a famous shipowner in the last war, and very much esteemed for his integrity. These reasons determined the Jesuits to embark upon this ship.

There were two, however, out of their band of six, who parted from them. Father de la Morinie, remembering how he had suffered upon the sea every evil that can be felt there, postponed his departure until spring; and Father Meurin[1] asked the Gentlemen of the Council for permission to return to the Illinois. This was a brave resolution, after the sale of all the property of the Jesuits; he could not count upon any fund for his subsistence, the French were under no obligations to him, and the savages have more need of receiving than means for giving. His request was granted, and a promise was given him that a pension of six hundred livres would be asked for him at the court. . . .

[The remainder of Father Watrin's letter concerns itself with the ocean voyage and landing of the banished Fathers.

---

[1] *See* Father Meurin's letter to the Bishop of Quebec, p. 485.

Returning to Europe, the Jesuits first land at the Spanish port of San Sebastian, where there is a college of the order, in which they are gladly welcomed. To their surprise, they meet here and at Bayonne many of their brethren from France, also exiled by decrees of the parliaments there.]

[*Ibid.,* lxx., *Doc.* ccxxviii.]

II

LETTER OF FATHER SÉBASTIEN LOUIS MEURIN TO MONSEIGNEUR BRIAND, BISHOP OF QUEBEC [1]

(1768)

[Sébastien Louis Meurin, a native of Champagne, was born in 1707, and entered the Jesuit novitiate in 1729. He came to Canada in 1741, and was sent in the following year to the Illinois mission, where he labored among the savages, mainly at Kaskaskia, until the expulsion in 1763. He alone of the Jesuits obtained permission to remain in the country; he accordingly returned to Illinois, becoming curé of the French parish at Cahokia. He also officiated occasionally at St. Louis, up to 1768. Meurin was appointed vicar-general in the West, by Bishop Briand; but, as he himself explains, he was for a long time unable to exercise vicarial powers, and was practically restricted to the curacy of the French parishes in that region. He died at Prairie du Rocher (in the present Randolph county, Illinois), Aug. 15, 1777.—*Ibid.*, lxx., *note* 24.]

MONSEIGNEUR:

On the 26th of last august, 1767, I received your first letter by which you did me the honor of appointing me your vicar-general in This part of your diocese. At the same time, I received your mandates regarding the jubilee and the preface of the holy trinity, etc.

[1] In the archives of the archiepiscopal palace at Quebec is a portfolio of correspondence between Bishop Briand and the Jesuit Meurin. It contains thirteen letters besides the one here published by us, ranging in date from March 23, 1767 to April 27, 1777. The authorities of the diocese decline to allow the publication of the others, regarding them as too private and personal in character for that purpose.—*Ibid.*, lxxi., *note* 10.

On the 29th of january, 1768, I received your second letters, confirming the first. I would almost wish that my self-esteem might prevent me from telling you, Monseigneur, that I am as unworthy as any one can be of the honor which you confer on me; and more than ever incapable of such an office, of which I know but the name. I have never been acquainted with any jurisprudence, either notarial, pontifical, or any other. I have been too long left to myself, and I barely know the duties of a simple priest. It is no longer possible for me to learn anything else.

My letters of last spring must have omitted to inform you of my age, and of my weakness of body and mind. I retain only a small portion of weak judgment, have no memory, and possess still less firmness. I Need a guide both for the soul and for the body; for my eyes, my ears, and my legs are likewise very feeble. I am no longer good for anything but to be laid in the ground. I trust, Monseigneur, that you will be good enough to forgive me for having neither carried nor sent your graces and favors to new orleans, according to your letters and instructions,—of which I have thought proper to let even our dear ursulines remain ignorant, lest they might have occasion for sorrow, which they do not deserve.

How would I have been received there after having stated over my own signature (in order to obtain permission to return to the Illinois) that I would always act as vicar of the Reverend Capuchin Fathers,—subject to their visits, their reprimands and corrections, and to their jurisdiction, etc., which was to be the only one throughout the missisipi country? Although I might have subscribed to all that before Monsieur the pro-curator-general of the King, solely for such time as the future jurisdiction should be real and established,—compelling them to admit before the magistrate that as yet they possessed it not, and could not convey any portion of it to me,—I would not have been better received. Here is the proof. As soon as they heard, through the voyageurs, that you had honored me with the appointment of vicar-general, a warrant of proscription was issued against me; and it would have been executed had I not, on being warned thereof by a friend in authority, escaped from it by withdrawing to english territory. There, on at once taking the oath of allegiance as a former resident, I secured myself against the spanish prosecutions,—which declare that I am a criminal because I have received jurisdiction from quebec, which is opposed to the intentions and interests of spain, etc.

There is another instance of opposition to your letters, Monseigneur, of which I must not allow you to remain in ignorance,—all the more that I have been assured that a complaint would be made to his excellency, Monsieur de gages, governor-general for his Brittanic majesty. About a month ago, having learned that Sieur jautard (second purchaser of the property of the mission of ste. famille among the Kaskias, sold to sieur Lagrange by monsieur forget, vicar-general of your predecessor, and a missionary curate in said parish, etc.,) was bargaining to resell it to an englishman, I went to oppose the sale on behalf of the gentlemen of your Seminary, who claim this property as still belonging to them, through its having been sold, without their power of attorney, and without their knowledge, by the person who was but the steward thereof. I also undertook to support by the use of your name, Monseigneur, my contention for the preservation of all property belonging to the Churches for their maintenance and that of the missionaries who You deign to employ. Mr. forbes, the commandant (there is no civil government here as yet), asked me for the letters containing my commission; I showed him your letters, and those of Monsieur the superior. As regards the letters conferring the appointment of Vicar-general, he replied that, inasmuch as Monsieur de gages had given no instructions respecting the episcopacy and the office of vicar-general, he could not take cognizance of them; and that this seemed purely a scheme on your part and mine. He therefore expressly forbade me to use the letters or to assume the title of vicar-general in any letter, or deed, or in public, until he should receive an answer from his general regarding both your jurisdiction in the country, and the Kaskias property. He promised me however, that the latter should not be offered for sale until then. Sieur jautard goes to Canada, and thence to new york or london, to obtain release from the possession of the said estate. The land at fort chartres is also, for the same reason, in danger of being carried away by the river. I have caused to be removed, and conveyed to la prairie du rocher, the [*illegible word in Ms.*] of Monsieur gagnon and reverend Father luc, a recollet, worthy missionaries. This is all I could do.

There is also, in this village of the Kaskias, the property of the jesuits which was unjustly seized, confiscated, and sold by the french government after the cession of the country to england, If your lordship or Your missionaries in Canada wish to revindicate it. As for myself, I ask nothing; I am too old. But I would always be grieved to see the chapel and Cemetery profaned, being used as a garden and storehouse by the english, who rent them from Sieur Jean Baptiste Bauvais,—who, under the decree of confiscation and the contract of sale and purchase of the property, etc., was obliged to demolish the chapel and leave its site and that of the cemetery uncultivated under the debris. He says that the subdelegate, the executor of the decree, has since sold the property to him. By what Right? The presses used for the vestments and sacred vessels are now used in his apartments, as well as the altar-cruets and the floor, etc.

My continual reproaches to him on that score have kept him away from me and from the sacraments for three years. I beg you to give me a decision on this, and to say whether, in case of his presenting himself to me or to another, he can be granted absolution and be dispensed from handing over the said articles to the parish church. That is my only request; for I believe that he bought the remainder in good faith—but not the chapel and its furniture, which according to the decree, were to be destroyed and burned. I beg you to decide as judge of supreme authority.

During the four years while I have ministered to these english parishes, I have received no tithes therefrom; I have received naught but what was given me out of charity by some, and the fees for masses. I have always exhorted them to pay the Tithes to the fabrique, for the support of the Churches and of the missionary, when one comes. They, I mean the rich ones, have always claimed that they owe nothing when there is no resident pastor. I beg you to decide the Case; otherwise, three missionaries would be unable to live in a suitable manner, or would be compelled to leave some villages abandoned. I shall soon be unable to do anything more. Threatened beforehand, as I am, with being cast out when others come, I wish all the more ardently for them. I have always had the poor on my side. Priests will be at least as charitable as they, and God will assist me through them; or, if he prefer,—and that would be more advantageous for me,—he will cause me to share his abandonment. If you deem advisable, you will assign me a place or a corner in one of the clergy-houses of the country, for which I tender you in advance my most humble thanks,—happy if I can have the consolation of Christians, dying with jesus Christ in the hands of one of his ministers.

This is on the supposition that the government would suffer my presence there; for Father harding, the superior in philadelphia, wrote me last autumn that they were about to be treated in england as in france, spain, portugal, and prussia and he bade me farewell, fearing that he would have no other opportunity of doing so. Why am I not a great enough enemy of the devil to deserve such treatment for the 3rd time? I forgot last year to ask you whether in the public prayers, at the benediction, etc., The orison *pro rege* etc., is said, and the *Te deum*, if occasion arise. The question is asked whether, —this has not hitherto happened,—when oaths are administered, roman catholics can swear on the protestant bible, owing to the falsities in it, etc. The protestants are often present at our holy mysteries, masses, and benedictions, standing during the time of the adoration, Elevation, and Benediction of the blessed sacrament, and also when it is carried to the sick, etc. The first two commandants, Messieurs Sterling and farmar [*illegible word in Ms.*] prayer, had forbidden their people to attend our prayers,—at least, unless they were willing to do as the roman catholics did. You can perhaps obtain the same order from the government. Our last two commandants in no wise resemble the first two. They forbade me to marry anyone without a license, for which Mr. Reed charged 6 piasters,—five being for him, and one for his secretary. The present one charges only for the secretary. Is it the custom in canada not to marry Catholics without the permission of the magistrate, or of the commandant who fills his office?

Since the english have taken possession of this country, there has been as yet no procession of the blessed sacrament [*illegible words in Ms.*] on the other side french Spanish and english. This year at the request of the habitants, I asked messieurs the commandants to allow the militia to turn out under arms, as is the custom among roman catholics, to escort the blessed sacrament. This they refused. The weather was not settled; I was indisposed and fatigued, through having had a procession very early on the other side, at st. gennevieve. Here I had one only in the church, and likewise on the day of the octave. Is it the custom in canada to parade under arms for that feast, and could you obtain this for us? I have on several occasions been puzzled with reference to the quebec calendar, and the transfer of feasts, as I have found no one who could instruct me on this point. The only answer Monsieur forget could give us in our difficulties was, that he knew nothing about it, and that Monseigneur the bishop had often been at fault in the matter. 1st. Do feasts transferred to a sunday retain a double, which is marked therefor? 2nd. Do those which have an octave retain it entire, commencing from the day to which the feast is transferred? Or is The octave transferred with the feast? If the feast of St. john be transferred to the 27th of june, and its octave come concurrently with the octave of the apostles, which is to have the preference? There are several other difficulties, which I cannot recollect at the moment, but which, as they have been experienced in canada more than here, have already given you an opportunity to decide them. I beg you to communicate your decision to us. I am also ignorant in what Consists the solemnity of the feast whereof the office cannot be celebrated owing to another solemn feast. On a passion sunday can the White vestments be worn for st. Joseph? etc. In what does the solemnity of st. Thomas consist, on the sunday before christmas? etc. Monsieur forget assured us that the solemnity consisted not only in abstaining from work, but perhaps also in the vestments, lights, sermons, and other things which he did not know. I beg you to decide for us these matters explicitly; for I am very Obtuse and shortsighted, to say the least, and am quite overcome by the too heavy burden that you have placed on my shoulders. I assure you that I am and will ever be, with the most profound Respect and devotedness, most dutifully of your lordship,

Monseigneur,

The most humble and

obedient servant,

S. L. Meurin,

of the society of Jesus.

At Kaskias, June 11, 1768.

[*Ibid.*, lxxi., *Doc.* ccxxxii.]

III

LETTER OF FATHER *AUGUSTIN* L. *DE* GLAPION TO MR. HUGH FINLAY, OF THE LEGISLATIVE COUNCIL

(1788)

[Father Augustin de Glapion, Jesuit superior at Quebec, writes (September 10, 1788) to Hugh Finlay, a member of the Legislative Council, which body has cited the superior to appear before it, *in re* the vexed question of the disposal of the estates belonging to his order. He reminds his correspondent of the fidelity and dutiful behavior of the Canadian Jesuits to the English government, and that their property has been given them by the kings of France and by private persons, or has been purchased by their own funds, for the specific purpose of maintaining the education of the savages and Canadians—a work to which every one of the Fathers has devoted his life. He also cites the capitulation of September 8, 1760, which recognized the right of the Jesuits to their property, and to the proceeds of its sale. These considerations lead him to expect from the English government recognition of the Jesuits' rights.—*Ibid.*, lxxi., 15.]

Monsieur The President:

I beg you to excuse me for having so long delayed my answer to the letter which you were pleased to write to me on the 26th of August last.

If you consider it indispensable that we should appear before The honorable Committee, we shall do so on the 15th of the present month, at The hour prescribed. But we shall not be able to say there what I have The honor to write you hereunder:

1st. Since we have been under the English Domination, we have been, we are still, and we will always be submissive and faithful subjects of his Britannic Majesty. We venture to flatter ourselves that the English Governors who have commanded in this province would not refuse us Their Certificates of our fidelity and obedience.

2nd. It seems, therefore, that in this instance it is not so much our persons as our temporal properties that are in question. Our properties or real estate have come to us from three different sources: 1st. The Kings of france have given us a portion of them. 2nd. Some individuals have given us another portion. These gifts were made with the view of providing for the subsistence of the jesuit Missionaries employed in instructing the savages and Canadians. The majority of the Fathers ceased to devote themselves to these charitable works only when they ceased to live; and those who survive them are engaged in the same work, and intend to continue the same until their deaths—which in The course of nature, cannot be very far distant. 3rd. Finally, our predecessors have, with Their own Money, purchased The third part of our property.

3rd. All our Title deeds, which are properly and duly recorded in the Record-office of The province, show that all these properties or real estate have always belonged to us in full ownership, and we have always managed and administered Them as our own, without opposition or hindrance.

4th. Our property was fully recognized in The Capitulation of Canada, signed in the camp before Montreal on the 8th of september, 1760,—inasmuch as, by article 35, Lord Amhurst permitted us to sell our real estate and effects, in whole or in part, and to send The proceeds to france.

In any case, Monsieur, we are in his Majesty's hands, and he will decide according to his good pleasure. But subjects and children without reproach can look forward to nothing but a favorable *treatment*—[*crossed out in Ms.*] decision from so benevolent a Monarch and so kind a father as his Majesty George III.

I have the honor to be, with profound respect,
Monsieur,
Your very humble and very obedient Servant,
Augustin L. De Glapion,
Superior of the jesuits in Canada.
Quebec, September 10, 1788.

[*Ibid.*, lxxxi., *Doc.* ccxxxvi.]

IV

LETTER OF REVEREND FATHER DE GLAPION TO MONSIEUR LOUIS GERMAIN (LANGLOIS), fils.

(1789)

[In this document Glapion offers (December 31, 1789) to the citizens of Canada all the possessions of the Jesuits in that country, to be applied to the same use as hitherto, the instruction of Indian and Canadian youth. Certain conditions are stipulated in the transfer, which relate to the maintenance and comfort of the four Jesuits still living in Canada; These include the free use of all their churches, residences, and personal property, and an annual pension of 3,000 livres each for the four Fathers, for the remainder of their lives.—*Ibid.*, lxxi., 16.]

The greater part of the property, estates and possessions which have been and still are, held by the Jesuits living in Canada, whether in fief and seigniory or *en rôture,* were given to them in full proprietorship by the King of France, the Duke de Vantadour, the Trading Company of Canada, and by generous individuals, for the maintenance of the said Jesuits, on the condition that they should be employed for the instruction of the Savages and of the young Canadian French. The Jesuits so well acquitted themselves of both these obligations that, in acknowledgment of their merits, Louis XIV., of glorious memory, renewed and ratified in their favor, by his great charter of [*blank space in MS.*] all those concessions and gifts which had been made to them. Some other pieces of property had been bought by the early Jesuits, with their own funds, and those purchases were ap-

proved by the charter aforesaid; but in October, 1789, the
number of Jesuits living in Canada was reduced to four, all
of them advanced in years. Consequently, they were no longer
able to fulfill the stipulated obligations to instruct the Savages
and the young Canadians. For this reason, they renounce,
unconditionally, voluntarily, and in good faith, all ownership and possession of the said gifts and concessions granted
them up to this time, and yield and transfer the ownership
and possession of these to the Canadian Citizens, in whose
behalf those grants had been made—in order that under the
direction and authority and with the approbation of Monseigneur Jean Francois Xavier Hubert, Most Illustrious and
Reverend Bishop of Quebec, and of the Bishops his successors, provision may be made for the instruction of the Savages of Canada, and of the young Canadians.

This surrender, renunciation, and transfer of ownership for
the benefit of Canadian citizens, and of the Province of Canada, is made with the following provisos and conditions:

1.   That the Jesuits resident at Quebec shall possess, until
the death of the last of their number, the building which
they occupy, which affords a view over their upper garden, and
which faces the south; that they shall possess the said upper
garden, and the grove or thicket which is at the northwest
end of said garden; that they shall retain possession of their
cart-house, stables, ice-house, poultry-yard, laundry, well, and
wood-house. They shall also enjoy the use of their library,
and of the articles of furniture which are in their own rooms
and in the entire building, which they reserve for themselves.
They shall retain possession of their Church and Sacristy; of
their entrance-hall, and of the hall of the Congregation, where
the citizens who are members of that body hold assemblies at
least once a week to the edification of the public. . . . And the
said Jesuits resident at Quebec shall continue to receive, every
year, a certain quantity of hay which is their due by virtue
of a contract entered into between them and Sieur Jean Baptiste Normand, who lives near the ferry over the River St.
Charles.

Second condition. That Father Etienne Thomas de Villeneuve Girault, Missionary to the Hurons of New Lorette, shall during his entire life retain possession of his Church and Sacristy, and of all the furniture and ornaments which are therein; that he shall enjoy the use of all the buildings, of all the furniture and utensils, of the garden and court, and of all the meadows, of which he has hitherto had the use; and that the said Father Girnault shall during all his life be entitled to receive, without payment, at the mill of New Lorette, whatever grain he shall need for his own maintenance and that of his servants.

Third condition: That Father Bernard Well shall continue, during his entire life, to enjoy possession of the Chapel and Sacristy, of the ornaments and furniture which are therein, and of the buildings, gardens, and courts of which he has had possession up to the present time in the town of Montreal.

Fourth condition. That Messieurs the Canadian Citizens shall pay annually, to each of the four Jesuits who are still living, a life-pension of three thousand livres, at the rates current in the Province. This pension shall be paid in two installments; that is, the Citizens shall pay to each of the four Jesuits fifteen hundred livres every six months; and the said pension shall cease to be paid for each of them at the decease of each.

Quebec, December, 31 1789.

MONSIEUR:

I had forgotten to notify Messieurs the Canadian Citizens that our Montreal residence is charged with a constituted rent on 20,000 livres of capital, in consequence of which Fathers Floquet and Well have, for several years past, made to Monsieur Panet, Judge at Quebec, an annual payment of 1,000 livres. I request that you will inform them of this, and oblige your servant,

GLAPION, Jesuit.

[*Ibid.*, lxxi., *Doc.* ccxxxvii.]

INDEX

499

504

I N D E X

CHAUMONOT, Pierre Joseph Marie, Jesuit, xli, 217, 260, 264-279, 286, 287-289, 290, 461; sketch, 263, note 1.
Chauvin, ——, fur trader, xxi.
Chauvin, Charles, Detroit blacksmith, dealings with Detroit mission, 466.
Chegoutimy. *See* Chicoutimi.
Cherokees, Maskoki tribe, xxvii.
Cherries, 62.
Chesne (Chêne), Pierre, *dit* La Butte, dealings with Detroit mission, 470.
Chicago. *See* Portages *and* Rivers.
Chicasas (Chickasaws, Tchikachas), Maskoki tribe, xxvii, 421, 426.
Chicoutimi (Chigutimini, Chikoutimy, Chegoutimi), xv, 5, 10, 391; Coquart's report on, 436, 439, 442-446, 448.
Chihwatenhwa (Chiohoarehra), Joseph, Huron convert, 183, note 1.
Chikagou (Chicagou), Illinois chief, visits Paris, 426-428.
Chimneys, of stone, cost, at Detroit, 470.
China, western route to, 301, 307.
Chippewas, xxvi, xliii, xliv, 130, note 1.
Choctaws. *See* Cha'htas.
Choiseul, Étienne François, duc de, 477.
Cholenec, Pierre, Jesuit, 292.
Chomoukchwan (Chaumoukwan), Coquart's report on, 442, 443, 444, 445, 448.
Chopart (Chepar), ——, de, French commandant at Natches, 420, note 1, 421, 422.
Chrestiennot, serves Jesuits, 450.
Churches: heated by kettles, 452; at Quebec, 38, note 1, 456, 462; building of, at Detroit, 467, 470-471; at Lorette, 291-292. *See also* Chapels *and* Jesuits: Missions.
Cinnemon, hospital nuns ask for, 169.
Clergy-houses: Jesuit, at Quebec, 456.
Cloaks, in Jesuit invoice, 393.
Clock, 471; Indians believe to be a demon, 109-110.
Cloth, 140, 346, 361, 451, 456; hospital nuns ask for, 169; of gold, 146; "for lining sleeves," 451; in Jesuit invoice, 394, 395; price, 448.
Cloves, 265; hospital nuns ask for, 169; in Jesuit invoice, 394.
Clubs, 352, 353, 361.
Coadjutors, Jesuits, xxiii, xxv, xlv, 212.
Coal, exported from England, 199; used by Siouan tribe, 313.
Cochran, Andrew William, discovers

MS. of *Journal des Jesuites*, 449, note 1.
Cod, 17.
Coffee, mill at Detroit mission, 471.
Coins: écu, 156, 435; value of, 430, note 1; livre, value of, 430, note 2, 463, 472; pistole, value of, 472; sol (sou), value of, 448. *See also* Prices.
Collet, Luc, Récollet, body reinterred at Prairie du Rocher, 488.
Colonies: Dutch, xliii, 180, note 1; *see* Dutch; English, xliii; *see* English; French, xx-xxiii, xxix, 24, note 1, 30, note 2, 30-31, 33, 40, note 1, 42, 87, 96-97, 260, 406-407; *see also* French.
Columbus, Christopher, xix.
Combalet, Marie Madeleine de, founds hospital at Quebec, 152, note 1.
Combs, hospital nuns ask for, 169; in Jesuit invoice, 393.
Comets, 60.
Commandants: English, 487; French, 397, 407, 420-422.
COMPANIES, commercial:
Company of New France, 13, note 1, 42, note 1, 45, note 1, 93, note 2, 95-96, 144, 145, 152, note 1, 156, 176, 178, 404, 494.
Company of the Indies, 422, 426, note 1.
Hudson Bay Company, 312, note 1.
Compass, 85, 311, 453.
Conscience, cases of, 297.
Contracts, for operation of Detroit farm, 467-468, 471; for that of forge, 464-465; for supply of hay, 496.
CONVERTS, xxiv, xxxviii, 47-48, 128, 142-143, 166, 213, 247-248, 250, 256, 257, 267-268, 293-297, 301, 305, 451-452; fund for, 389.
Convicts, sent to colonies, xxi.
Copper, 97, 319; on Lake Superior, xlv, 306, 319-320, note 1, 322, 327, 334, note 2.
Coquart, Claude Godefroy, Jesuit, 429, 431, note 2; *Mémoire sur les Postes*, 429-448.
CORN, Indian (Indian wheat, maise), 194, 290, 292, 336, 363, 459, 463, 466, 467; cultivated by Indians, xxxv, 22, 51, 62, 139, 412; by Jesuits, 24, 41; gifts of, 140, 372, 373; methods of cooking, 140, 248, 364, 451; price of, at Detroit, 472. *See also* Cornmeal *and* Sagamité.
Cornmeal, 194, 239; porridge of, 141; caches of, 86, 102. *See* Corn *and* Sagamité.

Divorces. *See* Indians: marriage and marriage customs.
Dogs, xvi, 76, 77; as food, 127, 349, 363; as sacrifice, 321; kill a cow, 471.
Dolbeau. *See* Olbeau, Jean d'.
"Domain, King's": Coquart's report on posts of, 429-448; Jesuits' banishment from, 476-484.
Dongé, Pierre, Jesuit, xlvii.
Dongon, Thomas, governor of New York, sends English Jesuits to Iroquois, xliii.
Donnés. *See* Jesuits: organization.
Dorei, François, agent at Tadoussac, 435, 447.
Dorval, Joseph, agent at Chicoutimi, 443-446, 447.
Dos blanc, name of cow at Detroit mission farm, 471.
Douay, Anastase, Récollet, xlvii.
Doutreleau. *See* Outreleau, d'.
Dowries: given to marriageable Indian girls, 156; of nuns, 168.
Dragons, in Ottawa mythology, 321.
Drama, at Quebec, 457.
Dreams: Indians' belief in, xxxi, 53, 104, 113, 141, 353; the language of the soul, 142, note 1.
Drugs, 134; list of, needed at Quebec hospital, 169-170.
DRUILLETTES, Gabriel, Jesuit, xxix-xxx, xxxi, xliv, 179, 263, note 2, 301, 305, note 1.
Drums, 59, 354, 418, note 1.
Du Bois, ——, habitant, dealings with Detroit mission, 470, 472.
Dubuque, Iowa, lead mine at, xlv.
Du Chene, ——, sells land to Jesuits, 466.
Ducks, 61, 311, 339, 366, 374, 469.
Du Codère, ——, commandant among the Yazoos, 421, 422, 424.
Dufour, Joseph, farmer at Malbaye, 434-435, 447.
Dufresne, ——, agent at Sept Isles, 446, 448.
Du Marché, Charles, Jesuit, 87, 130, note 1.
Du Maure, Jean. *See* Juchereau, Jean.
Du Peron, François, Jesuit, 461, 462; writings, 137-143.
Du Peron, Joseph Imbert, Jesuit, xli.
Du Plessis, Pacifique, Récollet brother, xxiv.
Duplessis-Bochart, Guillaume Guillemot, French naval officer, 24, note 1, 29, 30, 40, note 1, 42, note 1, 46, 73, 87, 99-101, 124, 460.

Duplessis-Kerbodot, ——, governor of Three Rivers, slain by Iroquois, 460.
Du Poisson, Paul, Jesuit, slain by Natches, xlvii, 421-422.
Du Pont, ——, nephew of Richelieu, 16.
Du Rue, Paul, Jesuit, xlvii.
Dutch, 275, 290; colonies, xliii, 180, note 1; trade with Iroquois, 180-181, 193, 282, 288, 304; assist Jogues to escape, xxxviii, 130, note 1, 138, note 1, 183, 185, 198-199; assist Bressani to escape, 175, note 1.
Du Thet, Gilbert, Jesuit brother, xxiii, xxix, 8.
Du Verger, Forget, abbé, missionary in Illinois, 487, 490, 491.

Eagles, 18; wooden, on Natches temple, 407.
Earth, in Indian mythology, 53, 54, 84-85; gods in depths of, 322. *See* Indians: mythology, folk-lore and religion.
Earthenware, 364, note 1.
Eataentsic, Huron divinity, creates the world, 112; *see Indians:* mythology, folk-lore and religion.
Echon, appellation given to Brebeuf, by Hurons, 105, 106, 220.
Eclipses, in Indian mythology, 60.
Eçu, value of, 430, note 1; *see* Coins.
Eels, 61, 64, 68-69, 161, 246; skin, eaten during famine, 78; used as ribbon, 296; price, 456.
Eggs, 213; for the sick, 131, 165; at Detroit mission farm, 471.
Elders, Indian: *See* Indians: government.
Elks, 61, 344, note 2, 366; hunting of, 64-65, 78; in mythology, 53, 55; for food, 63.
Elms, 108; along Mississippi, 361.
Engagés, 395, 429-430, 439, 444, 447, 463, 465. *See* Jesuits: organization.
England, xix, xxiii, xxv; relations with France, xxvii, xxxii, xxxiv, xxxvii, 8-10; Jesuits in, 199.
English, xliii, 23-24, 334, note 1.
Epictetus, cited, 74.
Epidemics, xxxi, xxxviii, 100, 104, 123, 130-132, 152, 157, 289-290.
Erborie, ——, Sulpitian missionary, xlvii.
ERIES, Huron-Iroquois tribe, xl; *see* Cat nation.
Eudemare (Dendemare), Georges d', Jesuit, 481.
Executions, 458.
Exploration, xix-xx, xliv-xlvi, xlviii-li,

508

INDEX

Frémin, Jacques, Jesuit, xxix, xlii, 285, 292.
Frémont, Claude, Jesuit lay brother, 34.
FRENCH: number in New France (1626), 12; character of colonists, xx-xxi, 24, 31, 32-33, 46, 142, 174; character of women sent, 461; children educated—by Ursalines, 155; by Jesuits, 116; daily life of—at Quebec, 449-462; at Detroit, 463-472; life of, at the King's posts, 429-448; farmer's occupations at La Malbaye, 429-435; Iroquois and, xl, xli, 6, 42, note 1, 131, note 1, 182, 185, 186, 191, 264, 285, 303-304, 334, note 1, 314, 384, 458-460. See also New France.
Fretat, Amable de (Defretat), Jesuit, 457.
Frontenac, Louis de Buade, comte de, li, 334, note 2, 336, 348, 349; sketch, 334, note 1.
Fruits, cultivated in Canada, 41; native, 62; as gifts, 268, 286.
FUR TRADE: xlv, xlix, 6, note 4, 30, note 2, 176, note 1, 312, 369, 371, 375; monopoly in Acadia given to De Monts, xxii; intemperance and, xxxi, xxxiii, 399-404; Iroquois's interference with, 303, 304, 309; regulation of, 400, note 1; centres of, 6, note 4, 18, note 1, 30, note 2; Coquart's memoir on the King's posts and, 429-448; at Detroit, 465, 466, 469. See also Beaver and other animals, and Prices.

Gage (de Gages), Gen. Thomas, 487.
Gagnon, ——, secular priest, body reinterred at Prairie du Rocher, 486.
Galena, Ill., lead mined at, xlv.
Gambling, 399.
Game, 61, 116, 311, 343, 351, 374, 469.
Gand, François Derré, sieur de, 148.
Gandeaktena, Catherine, Erie convert, xlii.
Gannentaa, site of mission of Ste. Marie, 271, note 1, 286, 289.
Garemand (Garmant), Charles, captured by Iroquois, 274-275.
GARNIER, Charles, Jesuit, xxxvii, 124, 124, 127, 130, note 1, 132, 248, 255; life and death, 227-237; writings, 234, 236-237.
Garnier, Henri, Carmelite monk, brother of Charles, 236-237.
Garnier, Julian, Jesuit, xlii, xliii.
Garreau, Léonard, Jesuit, xxxviii, xli, 179.

Garrisons, 397-405; 454.
Gaspé, district on Gulf of St. Lawrence, xxiv, xxix, 18.
Gaulin, ——, Louisiana, priest, xlvii.
Gauntlet, Indian torture, 193-194.
Geese, 61, 311, 374.
Genii (Khichikouai), spirits believed in by Indians, 54-55, 322.
George III, of England, 492, 493, 494.
Gervais, Louis, Detroit habitant, dealings with mission, 471.
Giffard, Marie Françoise, daughter of Robert, marriage, 451, note 1, 452.
Giffard (Giffar), Robert, sieur de Beauport, physician, 24, note 1, 92, 450, 451, 452, 453, 456; sketch, 40, note 1.
Ginger, hospital nuns ask for, 169.
Girault, Étienne Thomas-de-Villeneuve, Jesuit, 496; writings, 91-92.
Girdles, iron, 233, 293, 294.
Glapion, Augustin Louis de, Jesuit, letters of, 492-497.
Glass: beads; see Beads; panes of—used at Detroit mission, 471.
Gnats, in Canada, 22, 102, 289; on Mississippi, 394.
God, aboriginal idea of, 133, note 1.
Goffestre, Jean, Jesuit lay brother, 14.
Gold, xx, 306, note 2, 334.
Gonaterezon, Onondaga chief, 268.
Gontier, Pierre, Jesuit donné at Quebec, 452.
GOUPIL, René, Jesuit scholastic, a surgeon, xxxviii, 130, note 1, 183, 190, 192-195, 203-210; sketch, 183, note 2.
Gourds, uses of, 364.
Gouyou (Goio, Goyau), Jean Baptiste, Detroit habitant; contract of Detroit mission with, 467-469; dealings with missions, 466, 470, 471, 472.
Gouyou, Marie; works for Detroit mission, 469; wages, 469.
Grandmaison, Eleanore de, 263, note 1.
Grandmesnil, Jean Véron, sieur de; slain by Iroquois, 460.
Grapes, 62, 130, 236, 341.
Gravier, Jacques, Jesuit, xlvi; letter of, 392-395.
Grease, a delicacy with the Indians, xvii, 63, 134; as an offering, 55-56.
Great Lakes, xxvii, 344, note 2.
Greenland (Gröeslande), xix, 308.
Groseilliers, Médard Chouart, sieur de, explorer, 301, 312, note 1, 443.
Guillet, Maturin, colonist on Jesuit lands, slain by Iroquois, 460.
Gulfs: St. Lawrence, called "Square Gulf," xix-xx; California, 358, note

Wolf Nation. *See* Mohegans.
Women, in New France, 24, 450, 451, 452, 453, 456, 458, 460; at La Malbaye, 433-434; wages, 435; at Detroit, 466, 469, 470, 472; girls and women arrive, 461. *See also* Hospital nuns, Ursulines, *and* Indians, women.
Wood, used for utensils, 140, 351, 363; for temple fire, 408.
Woodcock, in Canada, 61.
Wood's Holl, Mass., Champlain at, 46, note 1.
Workmen (laborers), for colonists, 31, 97, 306, 450, 455; for Jesuits, xxxvii, xlv, 13, note 1, 31, note 1, 32-35,

38-43, 50, 140, 161, 286, 456, 461; at La Malbaye, 430-435; treated at hospital, 166.
Writing, superstitious regard of Indians for, 110-111, 251, 273.
Wyandots, xxiv, xxxv.

Yazoos, Maskoki tribe, xlvii, 423-425, 426.
Yroquois. *See* Iroquois.

Zeballos, Francisco, Jesuit, superior of Mexico, 479.

THE END

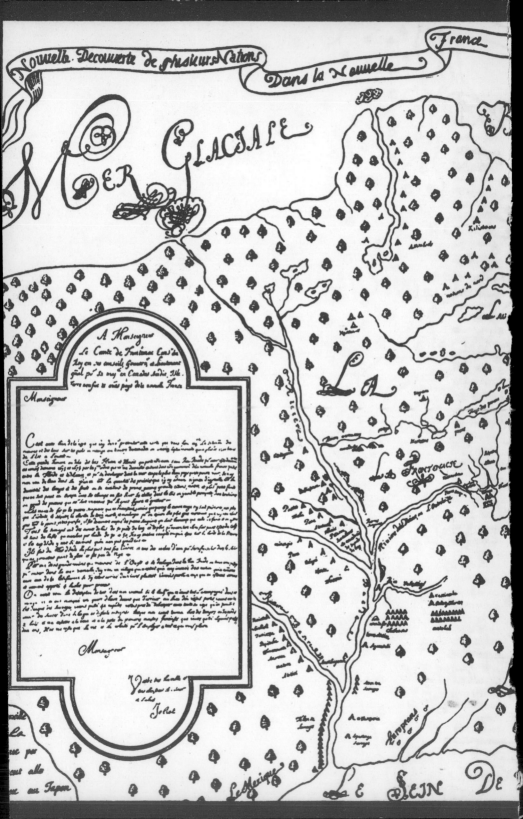